FIRST STEPS IN EGYPTIAN

A BOOK FOR BEGINNERS

By Ernest Alfred Wallis Budge

ISBN: 978-1-63923-623-7

Printed: January 2023

Published and Distributed By:
Lushena Books
607 Country Club Drive, Unit E
Bensenville, IL 60106
www.lushenabks.com

ISBN: 978-1-63923-623-7

I DEDICATE THIS LITTLE BOOK

TO

SIR FRANCIS W. GRENFELL, K. C. B., G. C. M. G.,

SOLDIER AND ARCHAEOLOGIST,

AS A MARK OF SINCERE GRATITUDE

AND ESTEEM.

PREFACE.

THE widespread interest in Egyptology which has sprung up during the last few years has produced an increased demand for books upon every branch of the science; Egyptologists have striven to meet this demand, and the wants of almost every class of student have been adequately supplied. Only the beginner has been somewhat forgotten. One of the chief obstacles to the study of the Egyptian language is the want of suitable material for elementary work, that is to say editions of texts of all periods of Egyptian history, which may be obtained easily and at a reasonable price. The main sources of information on ancient Egypt must always be such works as the *Description de l'Égypte*, the *Denkmäler*, the *Select Papyri in the Hieratic Character in the British Museum*, the editions of texts by Mariette, etc.; but these are only to be found in large libraries, and their great cost puts them out of the reach of all but the few. Moreover, many of the most important texts in them have been republished with corrections and emendations, and they have formed the subjects of special studies by various scholars who have issued the results of their labours either in the form of independent treatises or as contributions to serial archaeological periodicals. Thus there has grown up around the subject a large and scattered literature which the beginner cannot penetrate alone without loss of time.

The following pages have been drawn up with the view of helping the beginner to take his first steps in Egyptian. In brief, they contain a sketch of the commonest and most useful facts connected with the writing and grammar, short lists of the signs and determinatives which occur most frequently, a short vocabulary of about five hundred common words, a series of thirty-one texts and extracts, with interlinear transliteration and word for word translation, which belong to the period that lies between B. C. 4200 and 200, and a few untransliterated and untranslated texts, with glossary, to be worked out independently. The Introduction is intended to enable the beginner to use with advantage and with little loss of time any of the grammars which he will find in English, French and German, and it is hoped that the frequent examples of words in it will make him familiar with the use of the alphabetic and syllabic signs and determinatives. The hieroglyphic texts which follow the Introduction include examples of the chief divisions of Egyptian literature, historical, funeral, religious, moral, mythological, etc., and the aim has been to give passages which are at once interesting and complete in themselves. The translations have been made as literal as possible.

To learn the hieroglyphic characters and words the beginner is recommended to write them out frequently. Nothing will help him so much in this direction as copying inscriptions, and nothing will teach him the values of the signs and the meanings of determinatives and words so well as constant practice in writing and reading texts. He should note, too, that a few new words learnt correctly each day will, in a short time, enable him to read new texts.

E. A. WALLIS BUDGE.

London, August 31, 1895.

CONTENTS.

PART III.

* These texts are taken from the Papyrus of Nebseni, the *Papyrus of Ani* (2nd edition), Lieblein, *Que mon nom fleurisse*, Birch, *Egyptian Antiquities at Alnwick Castle*, etc.

A LIST OF EGYPTIAN GRAMMARS.

Champollion (le Jeune), *Grammaire Égyptienne ou principes généraux de l'écriture sacrée Égyptienne appliquée à la représentation de la langue parlée, publiée sur le manuscrit autographe,* Paris, fol. MDCCCXXXVI.

Birch, S. *Hieroglyphic Grammar* (Published in Bunsen, *Egypt's Place in Universal History,* Vol. V, pp. 590—716, London, 1867).

Rougé, Emmanuel de, *Chrestomathie Égyptienne ou Choix de Textes Égyptiens transcrits, ... et précédés d'un abrégé grammatical.* Fasc. 1, Paris, 1867; fasc. 2, Paris, 1868; fasc. 3 and 4, Paris, 1875, 1876.

Brugsch, H. *Hieroglyphische Grammatik,* Leipzig, 1872.

Renouf, P. le Page, *An Elementary Grammar of the ancient Egyptian language in the hieroglyphic type,* London, 1875.

Rossi, Francesco, *Grammatica Copto-Geroglifica con un' appendice dei principali segni sillabici e del loro significato,* Roma-Torino-Firenze, 1877.

Erman, A. *Neuägyptische Grammatik,* Leipzig, 1880.

Coemans, E. M. *Manuel de la langue Égyptienne,* Gand et Paris, 1887.

Loret, V. *Manuel de la langue Égyptienne,* Paris, 1889.

Erman, E. *Egyptian Grammar with table of signs, bibliography, exercises for reading and glossary,* London, 1894. Published in German and in English. The English translation is by J. H. Breasted.

DICTIONARIES.

Birch, S. *Dictionary of Hieroglyphics* (Published in Bunsen's *Egypt's Place in Universal History*, vol. V, pp. 337—586, London, 1867.

Brugsch, H. *Hieroglyphisch-Demotisches Wörterbuch enthaltend in wissenschaftlicher Anordnung die gebräuchlichsten Wörter und Gruppen der heiligen und der Volkssprache und Schrift der alten Aegypter*, Bdd. I—IV, Leipzig, 1867, 68.

Do. Do. Do. Do., Bd. V—7, Leipzig, 1880.

Pierret, P. *Vocabulaire Hiéroglyphique*, Paris, 1875.

Levi, S. *Vocabolario geroglifico copto-ebraico*, tomm. I—VII. Torino, 1887—1889.

INTRODUCTION.

THE first decipherer who succeeded in assigning correct values to any of the Egyptian picture signs or hieroglyphics was Dr. Thomas Young, who already in 1818 had given to six[1] characters values which are accepted at the present time; the values of three others[2] were correctly stated as far as the consonants are concerned. Four years later M. Jean François Champollion published a complete system of decipherment, and was the first European in modern times who was able to translate Egyptian inscriptions and to understand them. He recovered the long lost alphabet, and deduced the values of many of the syllabic signs from a careful and exhaustive examination of all the names and titles of Greek and Roman kings of Egypt which are found written in hieroglyphic characters, and from the bilingual inscriptions in Greek and Egyptian which are found on an obelisk that stood originally[3] on the island of Philae, and on the famous Rosetta Stone now preserved in the British Museum.[4]

Egyptian decipherment.

[1] *Viz.*, 𓇋𓇋 *i*, 𓐝 *m*, 𓈖 *n*, 𓊪 *p*, 𓆑 *f*, 𓏏 *t*.

[2] *Viz.*, 𓎛, 𓃭 and 𓋴 which he read *bir*, *ole*, and *osh* or *os*, instead of *ba*, *r* or *l*, and *s*; if we accept the value of *qeb* for 𓅬 as some would do, we must not forget that Young assigned the value of *ke* to this sign.

[3] It was discovered by Mr. J. W. Bankes in 1815, and was removed at his expense by G. Belzoni to be set up at Kingston Hall in Dorsetshire. Both obelisk and pedestal are of red granite; the former is inscribed with one column of hieroglyphics on each side, and the latter with 24 lines of Greek.

[4] Southern Egyptian Gallery, No. 24.

Great antiquity of picture writing.

The inventors of the Egyptian system of picture writing are unknown and it is impossible either to assign a date to the period when it was introduced into Egypt, or to say what people first made use of it; that it belongs to a remote antiquity is certain. It is a remarkable fact that, whereas the ancient inhabitants of Mesopotamia, who wrote their inscriptions in cuneiform characters which were originally pictures like the Egyptian signs,[1] modified them in such a way that their original forms had disappeared some thousands of years before Christ, the Egyptians preserved the original forms of their picture signs from the time of the first historical king Menȧ to the period of the rule of the Roman Emperors, that is to say for a space of about five thousand years.

Permanence of hieroglyphic characters.

Various kinds of hieroglyphic writing.

Egyptian writing exists in three forms to which the names Hieroglyphic, Hieratic and Demotic have been given. **Hieroglyphic**[2] or picture writing is the earliest form known, and it remained in constant use in all periods of Egyptian history; it was employed chiefly for monumental purposes, *i. e.*, for inscriptions upon tombs of all kinds, temples, stelae, etc. The oldest hieroglyphic inscriptions are probably those which are found in the *maṣṭaba* tomb of Seker-khā-baiu, which MM. Mariette and Maspero believe to belong to the period of the first dynasty or

[1] This fact is proved by the fragment of a baked clay tablet, found on the site of the ancient Nineveh, whereon we have a number of cuneiform characters and the original pictures from which they have been developed arranged in parallel columns. The fragment is exhibited in the Nineveh Gallery, Table-case B. No. K. 8520; for the literature see Bezold, *Catalogue of the Cuneiform Tablets in the Kouyunjik Collection*, vol. II., p. 934.

[2] The first to describe the hieroglyphic characters systematically was the late Dr. Birch. In Bunsen's *Egypt's Place in Universal History*, Vol. I. London, 1867, pp. 505—579 he quoted, with references, some 890 signs, and gave 201 determinatives. Lists of characters have also been given by de Rougé, *Chrestomathie Égyptienne*, Paris, 1867, p. 86 ff.; Brugsch, *Hieroglyphische Grammatik*, Leipzig, 1872, pp. 119—138; Loret, *Manuel de la Langue Égyptienne*, Paris, 1889, pp. 113—135; and Erman, *Aegyptische Grammatik*, Berlin, 1894, pp. 171—193.

earlier. **Hieratic** is a form of writing in which only the most salient features of the hieroglyphics or pictures are preserved.[1] It originated, no doubt, in the hastily written memoranda and drafts of inscriptions with which the scribes supplied the masons or sculptors who cut hieroglyphics in stone, and subsequently it was much used in making copies of literary compositions on papyrus, and for letters, etc. **Demotic**[2] is an abbreviated form of hieratic writing which was much used in legal documents from about B. C. 650 to the Roman period.

Egyptian palaeography:—Hieroglyphic inscriptions.

Hieroglyphics are written in columns or in horizontal lines which are sometimes to be read from left to right, and sometimes from right to left. In the former case the writing follows the direction in which Assyrian and Ethiopic texts are written, and in the latter that of inscriptions in Phoenician, Syriac and Arabic. This being so it is impossible to say which is the proper direction; there seems to be no example of a text written from left to right, and from right to left, alternately (*βουστροφηδόν*) as is found in Himyaritic. To ascertain the direction in which an inscription is to be read we observe in which way men, and birds, and animals face, and then read towards them. When hieroglyphics are written in columns this rule generally enables us to ascertain the correct order of the letters in the words. Allowance must, however, be made at times for the scribe's ideas of symmetry which made him misplace a letter that the balance of the arrangement of the hieroglyphics might be maintained. The following examples explain this paragraph.

[1] For lists of hieratic characters see Pleyte, *Catalogue raisonné de Types Égyptiens Hiératiques*, Leyden, 1865; Levi, *Raccolta dei Segni ieratici Egizi*, Turin, 1880.

[2] For the Demotic characters see Brugsch, *Grammaire Démotique*, Berlin, 1855, p. 18, and plates A. B. C. at the end of the book; Hess, *Der Demotische Roman von Stne Ḫa-m-us*, Leipzig, 1888, pp. 190—205.

Direction in which hieroglyphics are to be read.

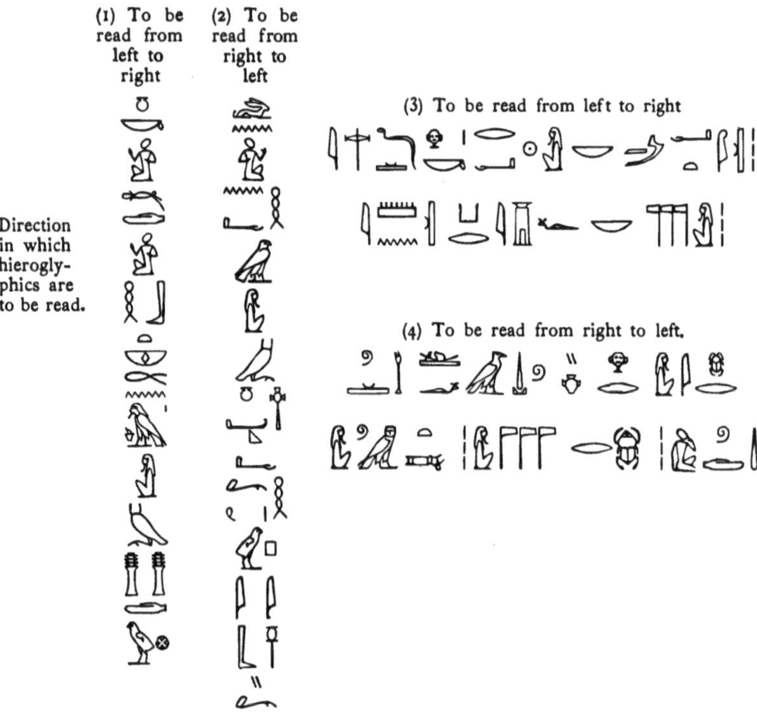

(1) *nuk sešeṭ ḥebet en ba em Ṭeṭṭeṭu*

(2) *un-ȧ ḥenā Ḥeru em neť qāḥ pui ȧbi*

(3) *ȧneť ḥrȧ-k Rā neb maāt ȧmen karȧ-f neb neteru*

(4) *χeperȧ ḥeri-ȧb uťa-f utu meṭu χeper neteru tememu.*

Hieratic and Demotic.

Hieratic is usually written in horizontal lines which are to be read from right to left, but in some papyri of the XIIth dynasty preserved at Berlin and in the British Museum the texts are arranged in short columns. Demotic texts are usually read from right to left.

Hieroglyphics as ideographs and phonetics.

Every hieroglyphic could be used either to express an idea, in which case it is called an ideograph, or as a character which represented a sound, in which case it is called a phonetic; phonetic characters may be either alphabetic or syllabic. Thus , *reθ* (for *remθ*), represents a man, *maa*, an eye, *ḥentasu*, a lizard, *mȧu*, a lion, *māχait*, a pair of scales, *sa*, a goose, and so on; these are examples of ideographs. But is the letter *p*, is the letter *f*, is the letter *r*, is the letter *ṭ*, and so on. The signs , , , and represent a door, a worm or snake of some kind, a mouth, and a hand, and, originally, when used as ideographs, would probably be pronounced *ptaḥ* (?), *fenṭ*, *re* and *ṭeṭ*; at a very early period, however, these, together with about twenty other ideographs, were set apart to represent alphabetic sounds. These sounds seem to have been obtained in the following way: the sound of the first letter in the name of an object was given to the picture or character which represented it, and henceforward the character bore that phonetic value. Thus is the picture of a door made up of a number of boards fastened together by three cross-pieces at the back, and there is no doubt that the word for door was connected with the root *ptḥ* "to open", and that it was pronounced something like *ptaḥ* (compare the Hebrew פְּתַח *pĕthaḥ*); the sound of the first letter of *ptaḥ* is *p*, and henceforward the phonetic value of was *p*. Similarly to the signs , and , the initial sounds of the words for which were *f*, *r*, and *ṭ*, were assigned the alphabetic values of *f*, *r*, and *ṭ*. Signs having alphabetic values are used to form words without any reference to their ideographic meanings. Thus the group of signs *sfnṭ* forms the word for "knife". The first is the picture of the back of a chair, as we have seen is the picture for a snake, is the picture of the wavy surface of water, and as we have seen, of a hand; the last two signs are *determinative* characters which will be discussed presently. Now in the word *sfnṭ* all these signs are used to express sounds only, and their original ideographic meanings of chair-back, snake, water, and hand are not considered. The Egyptians must have found at a very early date that when they needed to write the name of some foreign country or king, they

Origin of alphabetic signs.

Names of ideographs used as phonetics without reference to their meanings.

were obliged to use their ideographic signs to express alphabetic sounds only, or perhaps they found it necessary to preserve words by writing them alphabetically. Be this as it may, the use of alphabetic signs in Egypt is very ancient, for in the oldest inscriptions they appear side by side with signs used ideographically. Why the Egyptians did not go a step farther and abolish all signs which were not used alphabetically cannot be said; we owe them much, however, for our English alphabet is derived from the cursive hieratic forms of certain hieroglyphics through the Phoenician and Greek alphabets.[1] The Egyptian alphabetic characters are as follows:—

gyptian lphabetic igns.

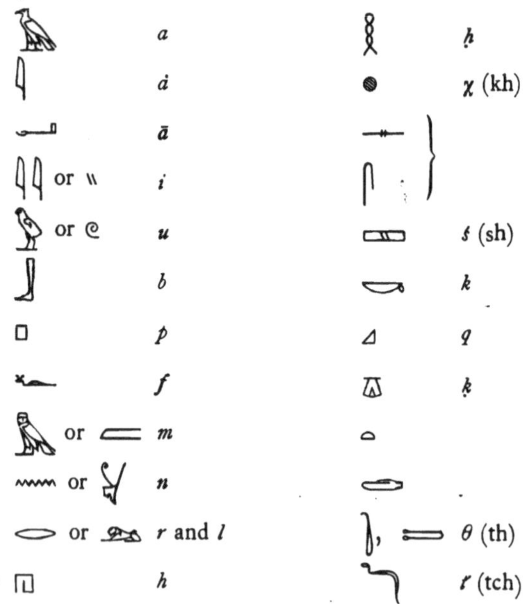

The values given above are those of one of the many systems of transliteration which have been proposed since the decipherment of the Egyptian hieroglyphics, and though it is probable

[1] For proofs of this statement see J. de Rougé, *Mémoire sur l'origine Égyptienne de l'Alphabet Phénicien*, Paris, 1874, 820; Dr. Maunde Thompson, *Handbook to Greek and Latin Palaeography*, London, 1893, plate facing p. 10;

that a few of them will eventually be modified, they are sufficiently simple and accurate to be retained for some time. It is evident from the above signs that we are dealing with an alphabet which resembles that of Phoenician or Hebrew, Syriac, Arabic, and the like, and it is equally clear that only the consonants which constitute the pith and substance of the language were set down as real letters, whilst, of the vowel-sounds, only the fuller ones, and even those not always, were represented by certain consonants. The pronunciation of Egyptian words was, of course, known to the educated in all periods, but curiously enough the Egyptians never invented a system of marks like the "points" in Arabic, Hebrew, and Syriac, whereby the correct vocalisation of every word was preserved. Speaking generally, the three primary vowel sounds A, I, U, were represented by , , and , and these are practically equivalent to the Hebrew letters א, י, and ו; for the other signs may be transcribed in Hebrew by ע *ayin*, by ב, by פ, by מ, by נ, by ר, by ה, by ח (has the sound of *ch* in the Scotch word *loch*, or the German *Rache*), by ס (?), by שׂ, by שׁ, by כ, by ק, by ג (*i. e.*, represents a sound similar to the hard *g* with which the people in Northern Africa pronounce the strongly articulated guttural ק), by ת, and by ת, by ט, and by צ.[1] From what has been said above it will be understood that the vowel sounds with which the Egyptian pronounced many of their words

Affinity of Egyptian and Semitic alphabets.

Consonants used for vowels.

Dr. Maunde Thompson in *Facsimiles of MSS. published by the Palaeographical Society*, Series II. plate 101; the article *Alphabetum* (Daremberg and Saglio, *Dictionnaire des Antiquités Grecques et Romaines*, Paris, 1873, p. 188 f.) by F. Lenormant; Isaac Taylor, *The Alphabet*, 2 vols. London, 1883; and Kirchoff, *Studien zur Geschichte des Griechischen Alphabets*, Berlin, 1877.

[1] Among recent contributions to Egyptian phonology the following should be consulted: Brugsch, *Die Aegyptologie*, Leipzig, 1891, p. 42; Erman, *Das Verhältniss des Aegyptischen zu den semitischen Sprachen* (*Zeitschrift d. Deutsch. Morgenl. Gesellsch.* Bd. XLVI. ss. 93—129); and Steindorff, *Das altägyptische Alphabet und seine Umschreibung* (*ibid.* ss. 709—730).

are unknown, and where this is the case a short *e* is usually inserted to make the transliteration pronounceable; thus *nfr* "good" is usually transcribed *nefer*, *ntr* "God" by *neter*, and so on.

Direct and symbolic meanings of ideographs.

Ideographic signs, *i. e.*, those which express an idea, are sometimes to be interpreted literally, and sometimes symbolically thus *seš* "nest", *sexet* "field", *àneb* "wall", *texen* "obelisk", are examples of ideographs which are to be understood literally; but the musical instrument is symbolic of "happiness", the seal of "treasure", the instrument of "God", the bier of "death", and so on.

Phonetic values of ideographs.

The phonetic values of ideographic signs were employed in the spelling of words without any reference to the original ideographic meaning. Thus , the picture of a digging tool, the phonetic value of which is *mer*, is found in the words *mer* "to love", *meri* "tree", *mer* "eye", simply because it has the syllabic value of *mer*. Again , the picture of a branch of a tree, is found in the words *em χet* "after", and *χet* "to engrave", etc., but only as a syllabic value. In theory every hieroglyphic could be used both as an ideograph and as a syllable. Some ideographs have more than one phonetic value, in which case they are called **polyphones**, and many different ideographs have similar values, in which case they are called **homophones**. The following signs and their values should be learnt by heart:—

List of signs with their phonetic values.

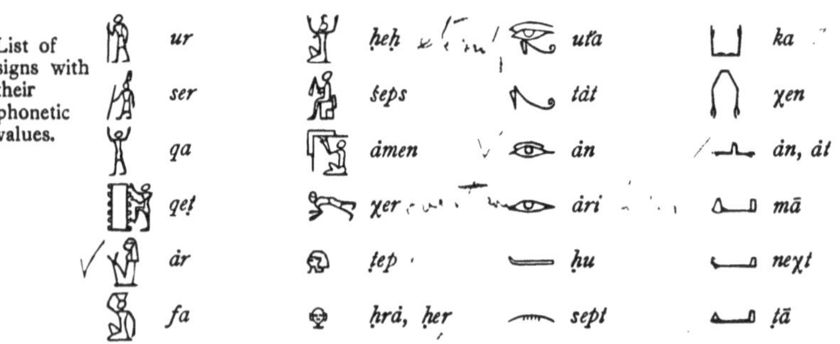

List signs their phone values

χu	ḥā	qem	bener
teser	at	ti	nefem
χen	šef	pa	uaṯ
tebā	usr	ten	χa
ka, met	χen	rexit	meḥ
sem	χent	ta	ḥa
seb	fenṯ hṣ	senṯ	neḥeb
šem	mesṯer āten	meḥ ṯenḥ	enen
àn	seṯem	maāt, šu	su
šes (šems)	àp	àr, sa	res
θet	àau	àn	qemā
ret, uār	āb	χa	renp
āu	χepeš	sebek	trà
ser	peḥ	hefen	ša
sāb	uḥem, nem	serq	seχet
set	ḥeru, baḳ	qem	mes
nefer	ba	net, bàt	ḥeṯ
āu	χu	χeper	sen
ka	āq	àm	šen
àua	šerà	χeṯ	ḥen
àb	ur	ḥen	ut
ba	ba	un	às
màu	sa	uaḥ	ṯer
peḥ	neḥ	sek	pet

List of signs with their phonetic values.

kerḥ	useχt	šet, sešeṭ	uṭa
àat	seḥ	χu	mer
θeḥen	ḥeb	ṭem	nefer
rā	àneb	ḥeq	ḥes
χu, àχu (?)	āa	āu, āam	seχem
ḥem	àn	qem, us	men
χā	ṭeṭ	seχem	maā
àāḥ	àuset	χerp	sa
sba	sṭer	men, àmen	ḥeṭ
ta	ṭeba	āb, mer	net or bàt
ṣet (semṭ)	neter	seṭeb	meḥ
ṭu	ṭes	meṭ	šu
sept	sem	ta	seχeṭ
àṭeb	nemmat	θes, res	atf
àner	seqḥ (?)	qes	kes
mu	ṭep	saḥ	šen
mer	āa	neṭ	reṭ
àa	uā	ḥemt	menχ
āb	peṭ	āba	uṭ, ḥeseb
nu	ṣemer, pet	men χ	sta
per	āba	χa	ua
per χeru	qeṭ	sa	net, seṭaut (?)
ḥet	ma	sam	mer
āḥā	meḥ	setep	nes

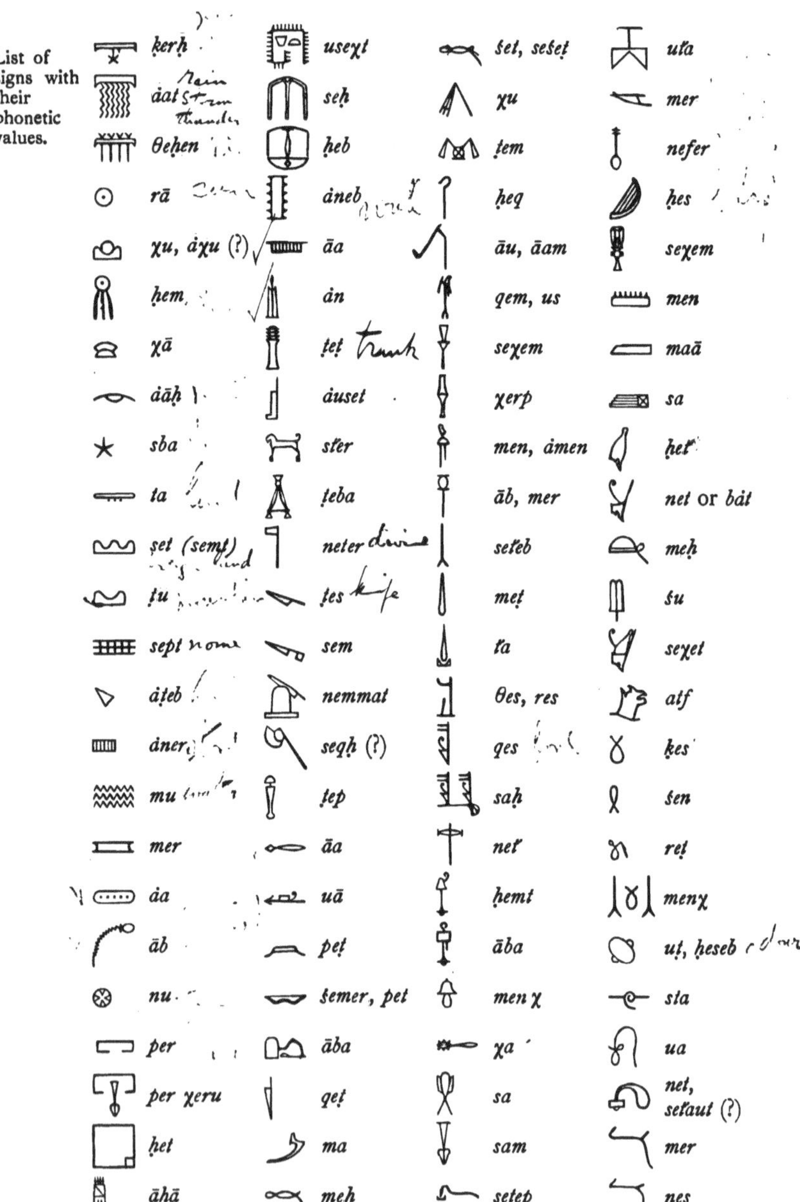

List of signs with their phonetic values.

⋈	*āt*	△	*tā*		*hes*		*χent*
	θes	⩘	*hap*		*χent*		*ām*
	net	×	*uu, ur, šes*		*qebh*		*uā, uḥā*
	sa	⊔⊓	*mer*		*hen*		*χer*
	āper		*rer*		*mā*		*hem*
	nub		*teben*	▽	*āb, useχ*		*nef*
	het		*ren*		*ba*		*āḥā*
	smu, usm	⊃	*tenā, peχ*		*ta*		*χent*
	χaker	⋔	*her*	⊔	*ta*		*sešep*
Ω	*ten*	—┼—	*tet*		*hetep*		*āu*
	ten	┝━┥	*qen, tata*		*āa*		*her, uat, māten*
♀	*ānχ*		*āmsu, min*		*χer*		*tem*
⊗	*sep*		*āp*	⌣	*neb*		*āmaχ*
⊖	*paut*		*nu*		*heb*	┼	*ām*
♡, ◻	*χemt*		*χnem*		*ān*		*χesef*
△	*sept*		*db*		*nem*		*seχet*

DETERMINATIVES.

As long as the Egyptians used picture writing pure and simple their meaning was easily understood, but when they began to spell their words with alphabetic signs and syllabic values of picture signs which had no reference whatever to the original meaning of the signs, it was at once found necessary to indicate in some way the meaning and even sounds of many of the words so written; this they did by adding to them signs which we call **determinatives.** It is impossible to say when the Egyptians first began to add determinatives to their words, but all hiero-

Great antiquity of the use of determinatives.

glyphic inscriptions known contain them, and it would seem that they originated in prehistoric times. It is, however, clear that they occur less frequently in the texts of the earlier than of the later dynasties. The following example will show how determinatives were added, and how ideographs were spelled out in alphabetic signs, and what alterations were made when ancient texts were copied by scribes.

The version given in (1) is from the pyramid of Unȧs, the last king of the Vth dynasty, and that in (2) is from a coffin of the XIth or XIIth dynasty (see Maspero, *Rec. de Trav.*, t. III, p. 201).

Meanings of words indicated by determinatives.

It frequently happened that two or more words of different meanings had the same sound; in such cases the proper determinative is most useful in determining the exact sense of a word. Thus *āḥā* "to stand", and *āḥā* "boat", are two words having the same sound but different meanings; in the one case a pair of legs is the determinative, and in the other a boat. Similarly *men* "to abide", and *men* "to be ill", are distinguished in meaning by the determinative of abstract ideas, and by [hieroglyph] the determinative of evil or discomfort.

Determinatives may be divided into two groups: those which determine a single species, and those which determine a whole class. Examples of the first group are [hieroglyphs] *teχen* "obelisk", [hieroglyphs] *seš* "nest", [hieroglyphs] *āa* "donkey", etc.; strictly speaking this group consists of pictures of objects preceded by the words for them written in alphabetic and syllabic characters. Of general determinatives the following are the most used:—

General and specific determinatives.

Common determinatives.

Character	Determinative of	Character	Determinative of
1. [hieroglyph]	to call	16. [hieroglyph]	to cut, slay
2. [hieroglyph]	man	17. [hieroglyph]	fire, to burn
3. [hieroglyph]	to eat, to think, to speak, and whatever is done with the mouth	18. [hieroglyph]	odour
		19. [hieroglyph]	to overthrow
		20. [hieroglyph]	strength
4. [hieroglyph]	inertness	21. [hieroglyph]	actions performed with the legs
5. [hieroglyph]	woman	22. [hieroglyph]	flesh
6. [hieroglyph] or [hieroglyph]	god, what is divine	23. [hieroglyph]	animal
7. [hieroglyph]	goddess	24. [hieroglyph]	bird
8. [hieroglyph]	tree	25. [hieroglyph]	evil, little
9. [hieroglyph]	plant, flower	26. [hieroglyph]	fish
10. [hieroglyph], [hieroglyph]	earth, land	27. [hieroglyph]	rain, storm-cloud, thunder
11. [hieroglyph]	road, to travel	28. [hieroglyph]	time
12. [hieroglyph]	foreign land	29. [hieroglyph]	town, city, village
13. [hieroglyph]	nome	30. [hieroglyph]	stone
14. [hieroglyph]	water	31. [hieroglyph] or [hieroglyph]	metal
15. [hieroglyph]	house		

Character	Determinative of	Character	Determinative of
32.	wood	35.	liquid, unguent
33.	wind, air	36.	abstract idea.
34.	foreigner		

The following words will show how the above are used

xamples f words ith com- on deter- inatives.

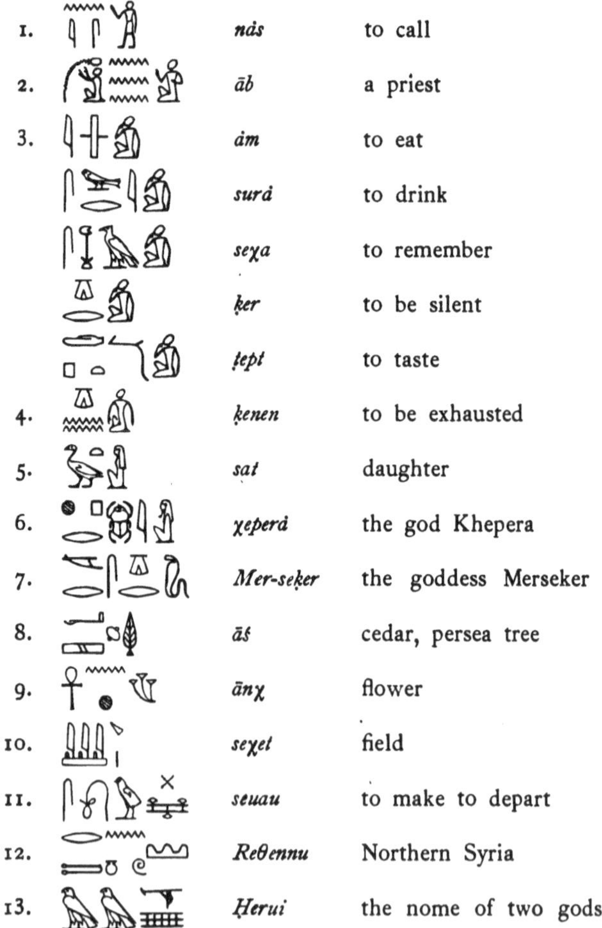

1.	*nȧs*	to call
2.	*āb*	a priest
3.	*ȧm*	to eat
	surȧ	to drink
	seχa	to remember
	ḳer	to be silent
	ṭept	to taste
4.	*ḳenen*	to be exhausted
5.	*sat*	daughter
6.	*χeperȧ*	the god Khepera
7.	*Mer-seḳer*	the goddess Merseker
8.	*āś*	cedar, persea tree
9.	*ānχ*	flower
10.	*seχet*	field
11.	*seuau*	to make to depart
12.	*Reθennu*	Northern Syria
13.	*Ḥerui*	the nome of two gods

14.	*qebḥ*	cold water
15.	*beχennu*	house
16.	*sma*	to slay
17.	*ṭa*	to burn
18.	*šefuṭ*	putrid sore
19.	*seχer*	to throw down
20.	*āṭ'au*	violence
21.	*āḥā*	to stand
	peḥ	to arrive
	hab	to send
	χenṭ	to step
	sper	to come
22.	*ḥāu*	members
23.	*pennu*	mouse
24.	*apṭ*	duck
25.	*àtu*	the destitute
26.	*nāru*	the nāru fish
27.	*šenrā*	tempest
28.	*rek*	time
	hru	day
29.	*Àbṭu*	Abydos
30.	*reṭ*	sandstone

31. *teḥt* lead

32. *ses* bolt

33. *meḥ* air, wind

34. *Āāmu* Asiatics

35. *merḥet* unguent

36. *χet* thing.

lurality f deter- inatives.

Many words have more than one determinative. Thus *beṭeš* "to be exhausted" is determined by "exhaustion", and "evil"; *qebḥ* "cold water" is determined by (the phonetic value of which is *qebḥ*) "water flowing from the top of a vase", and "water", and "a thing which contains water"; *šāṭ* "to slay" is determined by "something which is hacked to pieces", "a knife", and "strength"; *fa māhani* "carrier of milk" is determined by "liquid", "strength", and "man"; *reχit* "rational beings" is determined by, the phonetic value of which is *reχit*, "man", and, "woman", and, the sign of the plural.

ords ıving) deter- inative.

A large number of words are written without any determinative, *e. g.*, *ḥenā* "with", *ȧm* "in", *māk* "verily", etc.; these and similar common words were probably thought to need no determinative.

Many words are spelt wholly with alphabetic characters, *e. g.*, *sešeni* "lily", *ȧner* "stone", *semeḥi* "left side", *ḥeqt* "beer", etc.; but the greater number are written with a mixture of alphabetic and syllabic signs, which, though eventually helpful in showing the correct reading of the words, are at first confusing. Thus *ȧm* "to eat" is written

se of ,llabic ith al- habetic characters.

and *i. e.*, *ȧm* + *m*, which does not mean that we are to read the word *ȧmm*, but only *ȧm*, the was only added to help the reader to give the sound of the word readily; similarly *mesṭem* "eye-paint" is written , *i. e.*, *mesṭem* + *m*; and *merer* "to love" is written *mer* + *r* + *r*, etc. For convenience' sake we may call such alphabetic helps to the reading of words "phonetic complements". Many examples occur of words which are practically written twice, once in alphabetic and once in syllabic signs, *e. g.*, *neterit* "goddesses", wherein to *neter* are added the signs *ter* and the determinative of divinity; *ā̆ba* "courtyard of a temple" wherein we have the signs *ā̆b* + *b* + *ba* + *a*; *Tem* "the god Tmu", where we have *t* + *tem* + *m*; *nefer* "good", where we have *nefer* + *f* + *r*; *neḥeḥ* "eternity", where we have *n* + *neḥ* + *ḥ* + *ḥ*; *sṭa* "to bring", where we have *s* + *t* + *ṭa* + *a* + *sṭa*; *χeper* "to come into being", where we have *χ* + *p* + *χeper* + *r*, etc.

Importance of variant readings.

The values of many characters have been ascertained by means of the variant readings which are found in different copies of the same text; compare the following:—

= *neferu*

= *ȧri*

= *reχit*

= *ua*

= *uṭat*

= *ermenui*

= *hru*

= *āāabet*

= *seba*

= *χepeš*

= *ba*

= *χeperȧ*

We have now seen how ideographs and alphabetic and syllabic phonetic signs, and determinatives may be used in writing words, let us now take a connected passage from a text and observe how the hieroglyphics are arranged therein.

Extract from a text analysed.

In the first place we must break the extract up into words, for whether written horizontally or perpendicularly the words of an inscription are never separated from each other by the Egyptians. Thus we have:—

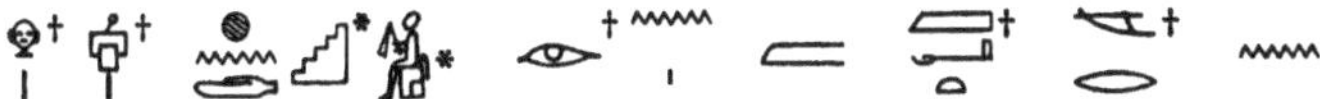

The determinatives are marked by * and the syllabic values by †; the remaining signs are alphabetic. The passage may be transliterated :— *àu àri-nà ḥesesei reθ hereret neteru ḥer-s àu ṭā-nà tau en ḥeqer sesa-à àt àu šes-nà Ḥeru em per-f àn āā re-à em šenit àn peṭ em nemmat-à šem-à ḥer-sa χenṭ àri-nà em maāt mer en suten,* and read :—

"I have done (*àu àri-nà*) what is pleasing (*ḥesesei*) to men (*reθ*), and what is gratifying (*hereret*) unto the gods (*neteru*) ; because of it (*ḥer-s*) I have given (*àu ṭā-nà*) cakes (*tau*) to (*en*) the hungry (*ḥeqer*), I have satisfied (*sesa-à*) the poor and needy (*àt*), I have followed (*àu šes-nà*) Horus (*Ḥeru*) in (*em*) his house (*per-f*), not (*àn*) magnifying (*āā*) my mouth (*re-à*) against (*em*) nobles (*šenit*), not (*àn*) making long (*peṭ*) in (*em*) my stride (*nemmat-à*), I walked (*šem-à*) according (*ḥer-sa*) to the step of measure (*χenṭ*), I wrought (*àri-nà*) according to (*em*) what was right and true (*maāt*), which was beloved (*mer*) by (*en*) the king (*suten*)."

Difficulty of finding the meanings of words.

It has been shown on p. 17 how variant readings supply the correct values of many syllabic signs, and it is self-evident that the probable meaning of many words can be at once known by the determinatives which follow them, but there remains a large number of words the exact meaning of which cannot be exactly stated by the help of the hieroglyphics only. The early decipherers of the cuneiform inscriptions, when once they had obtained the alphabetic and syllabic values of the signs, relied largely on their knowledge of the languages cognate to that which they were studying for help in determining verbal forms, and for a supply of roots which, having made allowances for change in letters, etc., they believed would give them a clue to the meanings which they sought. Thus Sir Henry Rawlinson relied upon Zend and Sanskrit in his immortal work on the Behistun Inscription, and Norris and others succeeded in deciphering Babylonian and Assyrian inscriptions by the help of

Importance of cognate languages in decipherment of cuneiform and hieroglyphic inscriptions.

[illegible]

Egyptian			Coptic	
[illegible]	[illegible]	[illegible]	[illegible]	[illegible]
[illegible]	[illegible]	[illegible]	[illegible]	
[illegible]	[illegible]	[illegible]	[illegible]	
[illegible]	[illegible]	[illegible]	[illegible]	
[illegible]	[illegible]	[illegible]	[illegible]	
[illegible]	[illegible]	[illegible]	[illegible]	
[illegible]	[illegible]	[illegible]	[illegible]	
[illegible]	[illegible]	[illegible]	[illegible]	
[illegible]	[illegible]	[illegible]	[illegible]	
[illegible]	[illegible]	[illegible]	[illegible]	
[illegible]	[illegible]	[illegible]	[illegible]	
[illegible]	*r*	mouth	ⲣⲟ	
[illegible]	*qenā*	bosom	ⲕⲟⲩⲛ	
[illegible]	*ātf*	father	ⲉⲓⲱⲧ	

[1] The Coptic alphabet is as follows:— ⲁ *a*, ⲃ *b*, ⲅ *g*, ⲇ *d*, ⲉ *e*, ⲍ *z*, ⲏ *ē*, ⲑ *th*, ⲓ *i*, ⲕ *k*, ⲗ *l*, ⲙ *m*, ⲛ *n*, ⲝ *x*, ⲟ *o*, ⲡ *p*, ⲣ *r*, ⲥ *s*, ⲧ *t*, ⲩ *y*, ⲫ *ph*, ⲭ *kh*, ⲯ *ps*, ⲱ *ō*, ϣ *sh*, ϥ *f*, ϧ *ḫ*, ϩ *h*, ϫ *dj*, ϭ *tch*, ϯ *ti*.

Hebrew and other Semitic dialects. Now although Egyptian is in many particulars, similar to the great family of Semitic languages, yet among them all there is none which is as valuable in explaining its words and grammar as are Zend and Sanskrit to the Persian cuneiform inscriptions, and as are Hebrew Syriac, and Chaldee to the cuneiform inscriptions which are written in the Semitic dialects of the ancient dwellers in the land which lay between the Tigris and Euphrates. We must then, look elsewhere for help in determining the meaning of Egyptian words, and we find it in the language called Coptic *i. e.*, the Egyptian language of the Graeco-Roman period which is written in Greek letters, and has been preserved for us chiefly by the ecclesiastical literature of the Egyptian Christians. Early in the first quarter of this century Champollion found it of the greatest value in deciphering the hieroglyphic inscriptions, indeed it is most probable that without the great knowledge of Coptic which he possessed his labours would never have been crowned with such brilliant success; the value of the study of this language remains undiminished for the purposes of Egyptian philology, and every student of hieroglyphics should make himself acquainted with as much of it as possible.[1]

Great value of Coptic.

It is not possible to say when the Egyptian language was first written in Greek letters; some believe the Bible to have been translated into Coptic in the second and others in the eighth century of our era. Be that as it may, it is a fact th t Coptic has preserved a large number of the words which are found in ancient hieroglyphic inscriptions, and when an allowance has been made for phonetic decay and for the changes of letters which occur in all dialects of cognate languages, it is found that the meanings of words suggested by their determinatives are confirmed, that new ones are supplied, that many

Ancient Egyptian words preserved in Coptic.

[1] The beginner will find Steindorff's *Koptische Grammatik*, Berlin, 1894, a very useful book; it contains 64 pages of Coptic text and a vocabulary which will carry him on to larger works.

grammatical forms, etc., can be identified, and that the vowels which are added to the words in Coptic indicate the correct vocalization. Where there exists no Coptic equivalent of a word, the meaning of which cannot be decided by its determinative, the sense of that word can only be guessed at. The following examples show the close connection of Egyptian and Coptic words.

Egyptian			Coptic
	ḥrȧ	face	ϩⲣⲁ[1]
	χaṭ	body	ϧⲏⲧ
	ren	name	ⲣⲁⲛ
	pet	heaven	ⲫⲉ
	χatur	ichneumon	ϣⲁⲑⲟⲩⲗ
	nehet	sycamore	ⲛⲟⲩϩⲉ
	bȧa en pet	iron	ⲃⲉⲛⲓⲡⲉ
	χeper	to be	ϣⲱⲡⲓ
	erṭeb	because of	ⲉⲑⲃⲉ
	fa	to carry	ϥⲁⲓ
	remθ	man	ⲣⲱⲙⲓ
	re	mouth	ⲣⲱ
	qenȧ	bosom	ⲕⲟⲩⲛ
	ȧtf	father	ⲉⲓⲱⲧ

Egyptian and Copti words compared.

[1] The Coptic alphabet is as follows:— ⲁ *a*, ⲃ *b*, ⲅ *g*, ⲇ *d*, ⲉ *e*, ⲍ *z*, ⲏ *ē*, ⲑ *th*, ⲓ *i*, ⲕ *k*, ⲗ *l*, ⲙ *m*, ⲛ *n*, ⲝ *x*, ⲟ *o*, ⲡ *p*, ⲣ *r*, ⲥ *s*, ⲧ *t*, ⲩ *y*, ⲫ *ph*, ⲭ *kh*, ⲯ *ps*, ⲱ *ō*, ϣ *sh*, ϥ *f*, ϧ *ḥ*, ϩ *h*, ϫ *dj*, ϭ *tch*, ϯ *ti*.

	mâu	lion	ⲙⲟⲩⲓ
	bener	date palm	ⲃⲉⲛⲛⲉ
	χemt	copper	ϩⲟⲙⲧ
	at	back	ⲱⲧ
	neḥem	to deliver	ⲛⲱϩⲉⲙ
	ḥeqer	to hunger	ϩⲕⲟ
	surâ	to drink	ⲥⲱ
	erper	temple	ⲉⲣⲫⲉⲓ

PRONOUNS.

The **personal** pronominal suffixes are:

Sing. 1.	, , , ,	*â*	Plur. 1.		*n*
„ 2 m.		*k*	„ 2.	,	*ten, θen*
„ 2 f.	, ,	*t, θ*			
„ 3 m.		*f*	„ 3.	,	*sen*
„ 3 f.	or	*s*			

The following examples illustrate their use:—

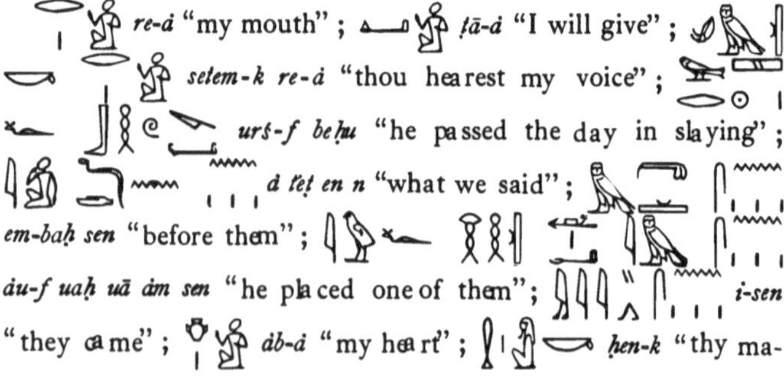

re-â "my mouth"; *ṭā-â* "I will give"; *seṭem-k re-â* "thou hearest my voice"; *urš-f beḥu* "he passed the day in slaying"; *â ṭeṭ en n* "what we said"; *em-baḥ sen* "before them"; *âu-f uaḥ uā âm sen* "he placed one of them"; *i-sen* "they came"; *âb-â* "my heart"; *ḥen-k* "thy majesty"; *ṭet-k* "thy body"; *ṭes-á* "myself"; *ṭes-f* "himself".

The forms of the pronouns are:—

(A) Sing. 1.	*uá*	Plur. 1.	*n*		
" 2 m.	*tu, θu*	" 2.	*ten, θen*		
" 3 m.	*su*				
" 3 f.	*set*	" 3.	*sen*		

(B) Sing. 1.	*nuk, ánuk*
	entek, entuk
	entet, entut
	entef, entuf
	entes, entus
Plur. 1. (wanting)	
" 2.	*ent-ten, entu-ten*
" 3.	*ent-sen, entu-sen*

The **demonstrative** pronouns are:

Sing. m.	*pen*	this
" f.	*ten*	this
" m.	*pef, pefa*	that
" f.	*tef, tefa*	that
" m.	*pa*	this
" f.	*ta*	this

Plur. m.		*ȧpen, pen*	these
" f.		*ȧpten, peten*	these
"		*nefa*	those
		na	these
"		*pau*	these.

Other words for this are or *enen,* and *ennu.*

The **relative** pronouns are :— *ȧ* and *ent,* or *enti,* or *entet.*

Nouns.

ouns the ingular.

Masculine nouns end in *u,* though this characteristic letter is usually omitted by the scribe : *e. g.,* *hru* "day", *ānu* "scribe", *uḥemu* "herald", *ta* "earth", *sen* "brother", etc. Feminine nouns end in *t, e. g.,* *reṭȧat* "side", *ȧnt* "valley", *ȧuset* "place", *ȧmentet* "west", etc. Masc. nouns in the plural end in *u* or *iu*; *e. g.,* *seru* "princes", *utennu* "offerings", *māṭ'aiu* "police", *ȧpiu* "envoys", *trȧiu* "seasons". Fem. nouns in the plural end in *ut,* but often the *t* only is written ; *e. g.,* *ȧustut* "places", etc.

ouns in he Plural.

The oldest way of expressing the plural is by writing the ideograph or picture sign three times :—

	qesu	bones
	ȧat	regions, zones
	seχet	fields

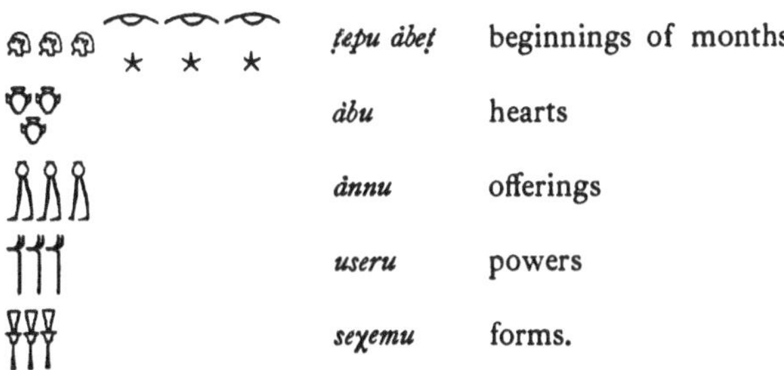

	ṭepu ȧbeṭ	beginnings of months
	ȧbu	hearts
	ȧnnu	offerings
	useru	powers
	seχemu	forms.

These examples are taken from the pyramid texts of the Vth and VIth dynasties; in the same texts we find also *χu* "intelligences", and *uru* "chiefs", *i. e.*, an ideograph written once and also thrice followed by which afterwards, when modified into or III, became the common sign of the plural. Words spelt in full with alphabetic signs are also followed, at times, in these texts by ; *e. g.*, *ȧt* "fathers", *reθ* "men", *ȧt* "wheat", *beṭet* "barley", *ḥuaat* "humours", *ḥunut* "young women", *seχtet* "fields", *urȧu* "great ones", *šerru* "little ones".

The plural is also expressed in the earliest times by writing the word in alphabetic or syllabic signs followed by the determinative written thrice: *e. g.*,

	neterut	goddesses
	unnut	hours
	meru	lakes
	ȧru	divine guardians
	ȧpt	registers
	šesat	darknesses

	ăārui	uraei
	henu	coffins
	tāmu	sceptres
	sept	nomes
	pet	heavens.

Other examples of ways of writing the plural are :— *āat* "stones", *šenut* "granaries", *šāt* "sand", *āḥu* "oxen", *neteru* "gods", *ḥenu* "priests", *ḥent* "priestesses". *ṭuau* "praises", *θenre* "mighty deeds", *āaut em ḥefnu* "animals in hundreds of thousands", etc.

The dual. In the oldest inscriptions the dual is usually expressed by doubling the ideograph ; *e. g.*, *mesṭerui* "two ears", *χuti* "two horizons", *baui neterui* "two souls divine", etc. Frequently the word is spelt alphabetically or syllabically and is determined by the double ideograph ; *e. g.*, *petti* "two heavens", *ḳesui* "two sides", *χui* "two lights", *θebut* "two soles of the feet", etc. Sometimes \\ is the mark of the dual in the early texts, *e. g.*, *āāui-k* "thy two hands", and this sign, which strictly speaking should be written | |, indicated the dual to the latest times ; compare *āāui* "two hands", *reṭui* "two feet", *pa teχenui urui* "the two great obelisks" (also written in the same inscription), etc.

In Egyptian the noun is undeclined.

The Article.

Definite article. The definite article masculine is or *pa*, feminine *ta* ; the plural is *na*.

EXAMPLES.

pa ser	the prince
pa ḥer	the terrifier
pa Rā	the Sun
pa sen	the brother
pa suten	the king
ta reȧat	the side
ta ḥurere	the flower
ta ȧuset	the place
na ābauti	the strivings
na reθ	the men
na ṡauabu	the persea tree
na ȧṭau	the thieves
pa neter	the god
pa sep	the time
pa āā	the great one
pa ki	the other
pa χemti	the coppersmith
ta ȧnt	the valley
ta paut neteru	the company of the gods
ta ḥet	the temple
na ānu	the scribes

[hieroglyphs]	*na mu*	the water
[hieroglyphs]	*na neteru*	the gods.

Indefinite article.

The masc. indefinite article is expressed by [hieroglyphs] *uā en* literally "one of", and the fem. by [hieroglyphs] *uāt en.*

EXAMPLES.

[hieroglyphs]	*uā en ḥennu*	a jar
[hieroglyphs]	*uā en θebu*	a pot
[hieroglyphs]	*uā en šauabu*	a persea tree
[hieroglyphs]	*uā en bȧn*	a bad thing
[hieroglyphs]	*uā en sfenṭ*	a knife
[hieroglyphs]	*uā en beχennu*	a house
[hieroglyphs]	*uā en ka*	a bull
[hieroglyphs]	*uā en nefer*	a good thing.

Definite article and suffixes.

From the union of the definite article with the personal suffixes is formed the following series of words:—

SINGULAR.

[hieroglyphs]	*pai-ȧ*	(masc.)	[hieroglyphs]	*tai-ȧ*	(masc.)
[hieroglyphs]	*pai-ȧ*	(fem.)	[hieroglyphs]	*tai-ȧ*	(fem.)
[hieroglyphs]	*pai-k*	(masc.)	[hieroglyphs]	*tai-k*	(masc.)
[hieroglyphs] / [hieroglyphs]	*pai-t*	(fem.)	[hieroglyphs] (or [hieroglyphs])	*tai-t*	(fem.)
[hieroglyphs]	*pai-f*	(masc.)	[hieroglyphs]	*tai-f*	(masc.)

pai-s } (fem.)	(or) *tai-s* } (fem.)
pai-set	*tai-set*
pai-n	*tai-n*
pai-ten	*tai-ten*
pai-sen	*tai-sen*
pai-u	*tai-u*

PLURAL.

nai-ȧ	(masc.)	*nai-n*
nai-ȧ	(fem.)	
nai-k	(masc.)	*nai-ten*
nai-θ }	(fem.)	
nai-t }		*nai-sen*
nai-f	(masc.)	
nai-s	(fem.)	*nai-u*

These are added to words in the following way:—

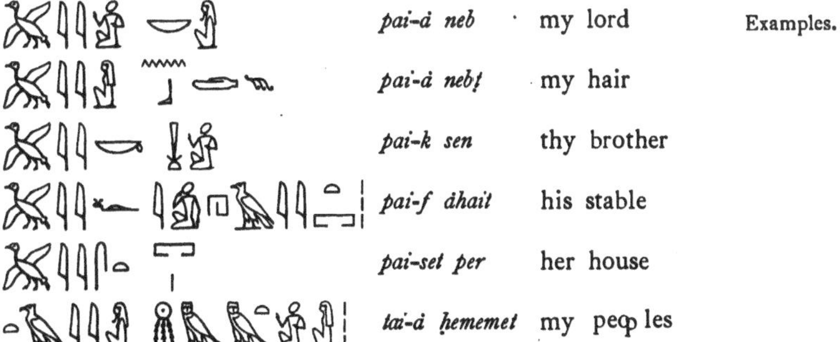

pai-ȧ neb	my lord	Examples.
pai-ȧ nebṭ	my hair	
pai-k sen	thy brother	
pai-f ȧhait	his stable	
pai-set per	her house	
tai-ȧ ḥememet	my peoples	

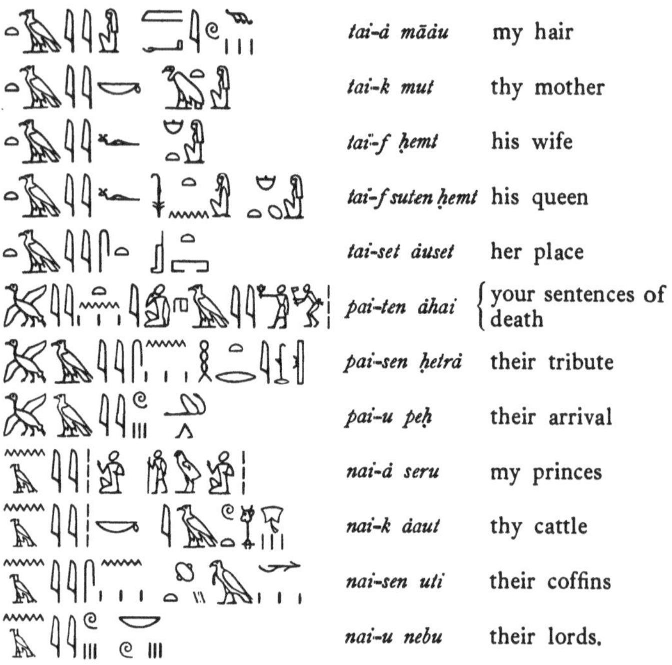

	tai-ȧ māȧu	my hair
	tai-k mut	thy mother
	tai-f ḥemt	his wife
	tai-f suten ḥemt	his queen
	tai-set ȧuset	her place
	pai-ten ȧhai	your sentences of death
	pai-sen ḥetrȧ	their tribute
	pai-u peḥ	their arrival
	nai-ȧ seru	my princes
	nai-k ȧaut	thy cattle
	nai-sen uti	their coffins
	nai-u nebu	their lords.

Adjectives.

The adjective is, in form, often similar to the noun, with which it agrees in gender and number; with a few exceptions it comes after its noun, *e. g.*,

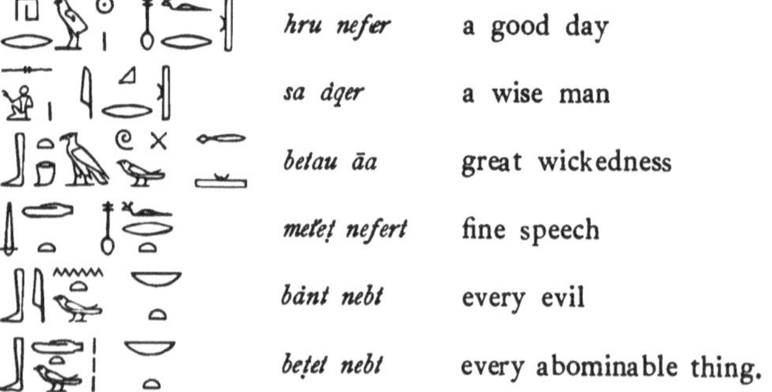

	hru nefer	a good day
	sa ȧqer	a wise man
	betau āa	great wickedness
	meṭeṭ nefert	fine speech
	bȧnt nebt	every evil
	beṭet nebt	every abominable thing.

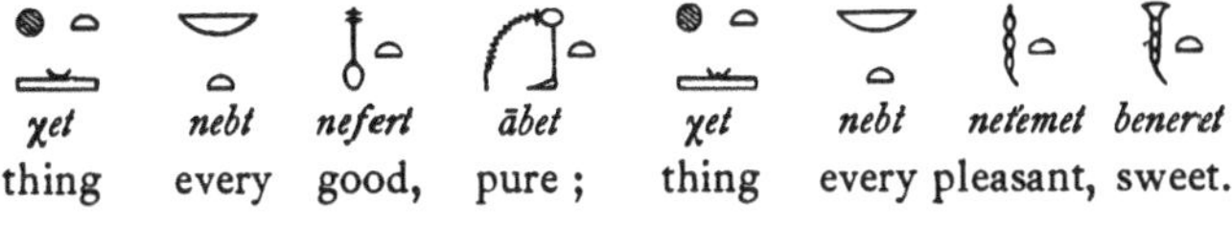

χet nebt nefert ābet χet nebt neťemet beneret
thing every good, pure; thing every pleasant, sweet.

 *ḥebsu neferu*	beautiful clothes
 *seru āāaiu*	great chiefs
 *nefer neferui*	a good thing doubly good
sti neťem	a sweet smell
 *ȧusetut āāaiut*	great abodes.

The adjectives "royal" and "divine" are usually written before the noun: *e. g.*,

suten ān "royal scribe",  *suten mesu* "royal children", 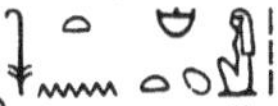 *suten ḥemt* "royal women" (*i. e.*, queens),  *suten mut* "royal mothers", 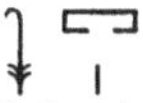 *suten per* "royal house" (*i. e.*, palace),  *neter ḥet* "divine house" (*i. e.*, temple), *neter ḥen* "divine servant", *neter ȧtf* "divine father".

Methods of comparing adjectives.

Adjectives are without degrees of comparison in Egyptian, but the comparative and superlative may be expressed in the following manner:—

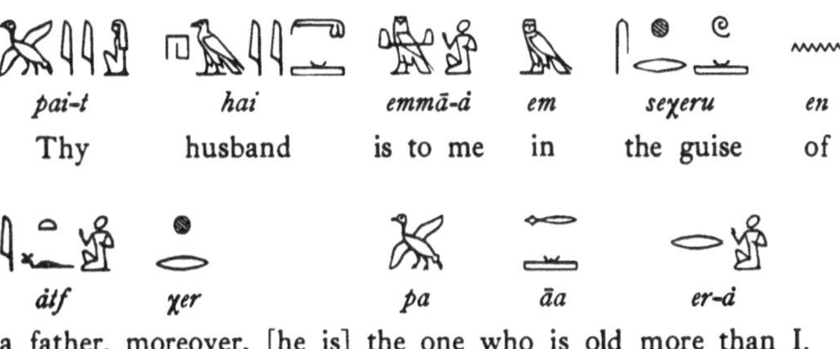

pai-t hai emmā-ȧ em seχeru en
Thy husband is to me in the guise of

ȧtf χer pa āa er-ȧ
a father, moreover, [he is] the one who is old more than I.

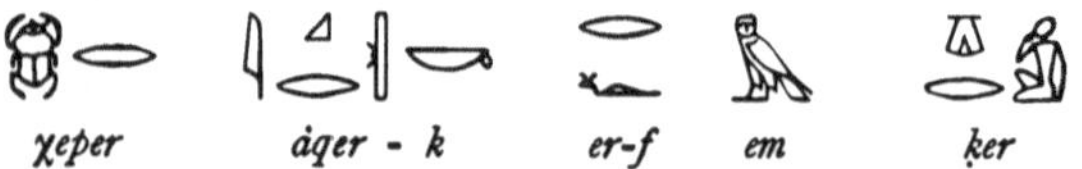

χeper *àqer - k* *er-f* *em* *ker*

Thou wilt be wise more than he in keeping silence.

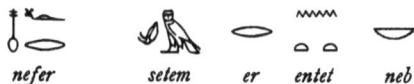

nefer *setem* *er* *entet* *neb*

[It is] good to hearken more than anything, *i. e.*, to listen, or to obey, is better than anything, or best of all.

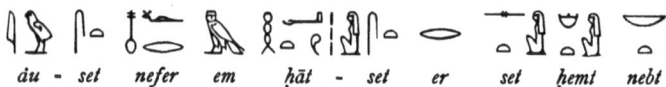

àu - set *nefer* *em* *ḥāt - set* *er* *set* *ḥemt* *nebt*

Was she beautiful in her person more than woman any.

Numbers.

	=		*uā*	=	
II	=	II	*sen*	=	2
III	=	III	*χemet*	=	3
IIII	=		*ftu*	=	4
II III or ★	=	★	*ṭuau*	=	5
III III	=		*sàs*	=	6
III IIII	=		*sefeχ*	=	7
IIII IIII	=	or	*χemennu*	=	8
IIII IIIII	=		*paut* / *pesṭ*	=	9
∩	=		*met*	=	10
∩∩	=		*ṭaut*	=	20

māb	=	30
ḥement	=	40
	=	50
	=	60
sefex	=	70
xemennui	=	80
	=	90
śaā	=	100
śetau	=	200
xa	=	1,000
ťāb	=	10,000
ḥefennu	=	100,000
ḥeḥ	=	1,000,000
śennu	=	10,000,000

Fractions.

(1) = 1/3, = 1/2, = 2/3, = 1/10, = 1/100, = 1/1000, = 1/45, = 17 1/2, = 1/18, = 1/60, = 1/2090.

(2) that is, 1/2 × 400 = 200.

(3) that is, 1/3 × 400 = 133 1/3.

Numbers are expressed in the following manner:—

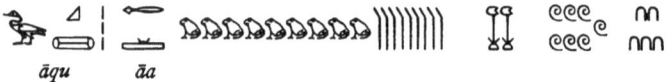

āqu *āa*

loaves large, 900,000 + 90,000 + 2000 + 700 + 50, *i. e.*, "992,750 large loaves of bread".

Ordinal numbers are indicated either by *meḥ* placed before the figure, or by following it; *e. g.*, *meḥ sās* "sixth", "fifteenth", *meḥ met ṭuau*, *sefex* "seventh", etc.

Measures.

(1) Of length:— *meḥ* "cubit"; *suten meḥ* "royal cubit" of 7 palms or 20 fingers; *meḥ neṭes* "little cubit" of 6 palms or 24 fingers; *ermen* "arm" of 20 fingers; *teser*, of 16 fingers; *šа āa* "the great *šа*" of 14 fingers; *šа neṭes* "the little *šа*" of 12 fingers; *šepui*, the "double palm" of 8 fingers; *xefā*, the "fist" of 6 fingers; *ṭeṭ*, the "hand" of 5 fingers; or *šep*, the "palm" of 4 fingers; *ṭebā*, the "finger".

(2) Of superficies:— *sa ta*, the *arura*, *i. e.*, 100 cubits; *ermen*, one half of an *arura*; *ḥesp*, one quarter of an *arura*; *sa*, one eighth of an *arura*; *su*, one sixteenth of an *arura*; *erma*, one thirty-second part of an *arura*.

(3) Dry measure:— = 1/4 *hin*; *hin* = 9/20 of a *litre*; *ṭenāt* = 20 *hin*; *āpt* = 40 *hin*: *ḥetep* = 160 *hin*.

(4) Of weight:— *θen*; *qeṭ* = one tenth of a *θen*; *pek* = 1/128 of a *θen*.

Time.

The principal divisions of time are :—

	ḥat	second		*at*	minute
or	*unnut*	hour		*hru*	day
	ābeṭ	month		*renpit*	year
	seṭ	period of 30 years		*ḥen*	period of 60 years
	ḥenti	period of 120 years		*ḥeḥ*	a long period of time
	ṭetta	eternity		*ḥeḥ*	a million of years.

In an interesting inscription quoted by Brugsch (*Thesaurus*, Abth. II., p. 195) the god Thoth, addressing one of the Ptolemies says that he has ordained the sovereignty of the royal house for a period of time equal to:— that is, "an eternity of periods of 120 years, "and an indefinite number of periods of 30 years, and millions "of years, and ten millions of months, and hundreds of thousands "of days, and tens of thousands of hours, and thousands of mi- "nutes, and hundreds of seconds, and tens of third parts of "seconds."

The year, *renpit*, consisted of twelve months of thirty days each (or thirty-six weeks of ten days each), to which were added five additional days to make up 365 days . Each month was dedicated to a god. The twelve months were divided into three seasons of four months each; *šat* = time of inundation and period of sowing, *pert* = time of "coming forth" or growing, and *šemut* = time of harvest and beginning of inundation. The Copts, or

Egyptian Christians, have preserved, in a corrupt form, the old Egyptian names of the months, which read :—

[hieroglyphs]	=	ⲑⲱⲟⲩⲧ	Thoth
[hieroglyphs]	=	ⲡⲁⲟⲡⲓ	Paopi
[hieroglyphs]	=	ⲁⲑⲱⲣ	Hathor
[hieroglyphs]	=	ⲭⲟⲓⲁⲕ	Khoiak
[hieroglyphs]	=	ⲧⲱⲃⲓ	Tobi
[hieroglyphs]	=	ⲙⲉⲭⲓⲣ	Mekhir
[hieroglyphs]	=	ⲫⲁⲙⲉⲛⲱⲑ	Phamenoth
[hieroglyphs]	=	ⲫⲁⲣⲙⲟⲩⲑⲓ	Pharmuthi
[hieroglyphs]	=	ⲡⲁⲭⲱⲛ	Pakhon
[hieroglyphs]	=	ⲡⲁⲱⲛⲓ	Paoni
[hieroglyphs]	=	ⲉⲡⲏⲡ	Epe p
[hieroglyphs]	=	ⲙⲉⲥⲱⲣⲏ	Mesore

[hieroglyphs] *hru ṭuau ḥeru renpit* "the five days over the year".

Thoth, the first month of the Egyptian year, began on the 29th of August.

The verb.

The consideration of the Egyptian verb, or stem-word, is a difficult subject which can only be properly illustrated by a large number of extracts from texts of all periods. Egyptologists have, moreover, agreed neither as to the manner in which it should be treated, nor as to the classification of the forms which have been distinguished. The older generation of scholars were undecided as to the class of languages under which the Egyptian language should be placed, and contented themselves with pointing out grammatical forms analogous to those in Coptic, and perhaps in some of the Semitic dialects; but the modern German Egyptologists boldly affirm the relationship of Egyptian to the Semitic family of languages, and the most recent exponent of this view applies the nomenclature of the Semitic verb or stem-word to that of Egyptian.

The stem-word.

The Egyptian stem-word may be indifferently a verb or a noun; thus *χeper* means both "to be", and the "thing which hath come into being"; so likewise *nefer* may mean "to be good", and a "thing which is good", and placed after a noun it becomes the adjective "good", as we see from the following:— *nefer set ḥer àb-sen* "good is it for their hearts"; *ren-k nefer em reχ en seru* "thy name is good in the opinion of princes"; *hru nefer* "a good day"; with the addition of the prefix *bu, nefer* means "prosperity", "goodness", "happiness", *e. g.*,

bu - nefer	*χeper*	*em*	*bu - bàn*
prosperity	turneth	into	adversity.

The stem-word with additions.

Returning to the word *χeper*: by the addition of *à* we have "I am", or "I was"; by the addition of the stem-word has a participial meaning like "being" or "becoming"; by the addition of in the masc. and in the fem. *χeper* becomes a noun in the plural meaning "things which exist", "created things", and the like; by the addition of *à* we have *χeperà* "the god to whom it belongeth to make things come into being", etc.

Stem-words in Egyptian, like those in Hebrew and other Semitic dialects, consist of two, three, four and five consonants, as examples of which may be cited *qem* "to find",

Biliteral roots.

χesef "to drive back", *seχseχ* "to flee", *nemesmes* "to heap up". The stem-words with three consonants which are ordinarily regarded as triliteral roots, may be reduced to two consonants, which were pronounced by the help of some vowel between; these we may call primary or biliteral roots. Originally all roots consisted of one syllable. By the addition of feeble consonants in the middle or at the end of the monosyllabic root, or by repeating the second consonant roots of three letters were formed. Roots of four consonants are formed by adding a fourth consonant or by combining two roots of two letters; and so on. Speaking generally, the Egyptian verb has no conjugations or species, like Hebrew and the other Semitic dialects, and no Perfect (Preterite) or Imperfect (Future) tenses, but Dr. Erman believes in the existence of the Infinitive and Imperative Moods and of a Participle. The exact pronunciation of a great many verbs must always remain unknown, because the Egyptians never invented a system of vocalisation like the Massorah of the sages of Tiberias, or like the additions and the modifications in the forms of the letters to express the vowels adopted by the Ethiopians, or even any means of indicating the chief vowel sounds like the Syrians and Arabs; but very good guesses may sometimes be made by the help of the Coptic forms of words which are common to the two languages.

Formation of other roots.

Uncertainty of pronunciation.

The Causative.

There is in Egyptian a derivative formation of the word stem or verb, which is made by the addition of ⟶ or to the simple form of the verb, and which has a causative signification; *e. g.*, *ānχ* "to live", *se-ānχ* "to vivify"; *āb* "to wash", *se-āb* "to purify"; *men* "to abide" *se-men* "to perpetuate"; *ḥetep* "to rest, be at peace", *se-ḥetep* "to pacify"; *χeper* "to be", *se-χeper* "to bring into being", etc. In Coptic the causative is expressed both by a prefixed *s* and *t* (see Stern, *Koptische*

Gram., § 328, p. 157 ; Steindorff, *Koptische Grammatik*, § 230, p. 103 f.).

The verb is usually inflected by the addition of the pronominal personal suffixes ; *e. g.*, Inflection.

Sing. 1 com.	*reχ-à*
„ 2 m.	*neḥem-k*
2 f.	(or)	*ṭeṭ-t*
„ 3 m.	*šāṭ-f*
„ 3 f.	*qem-s*
Plur. 1	*àri-n*
„ 2 com.	*mit-ten*
3 com.	*χeper-sen*

The commonest auxiliary verbs are *āḥā* "to stand", *un* "to be", *àu* "to be", *àri* "to do", *ṭā* "to give" ; examples of their use are :—

(1) *āḥā en se-āḥā ḥen en suten net Seneferu*
Stood up made to arise the majesty of the king of the North and South Seneferu,
i. e., when king Huni was dead Seneferu set himself up as king of all Egypt.

(2) *un pa ta en Qemt χaā em ruti*
Was the land of Egypt left in a state of ruin.

(3) 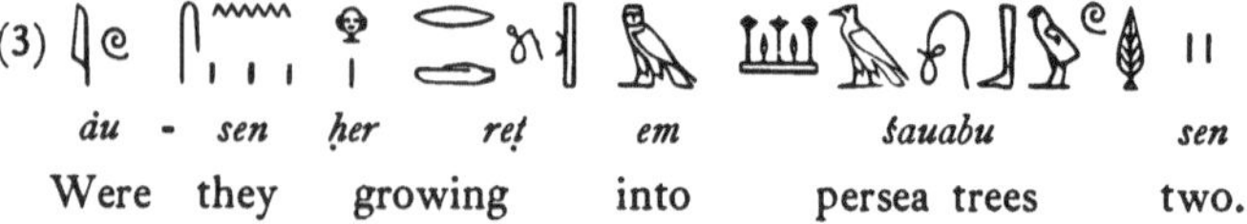

àu - sen ḥer reṭ em šauabu sen

Were they growing into persea trees two.

(4)  *em àri meḥ àb - k aχetu kai*

Do not make to fill thy heart [with] the wealth of another.

(5) 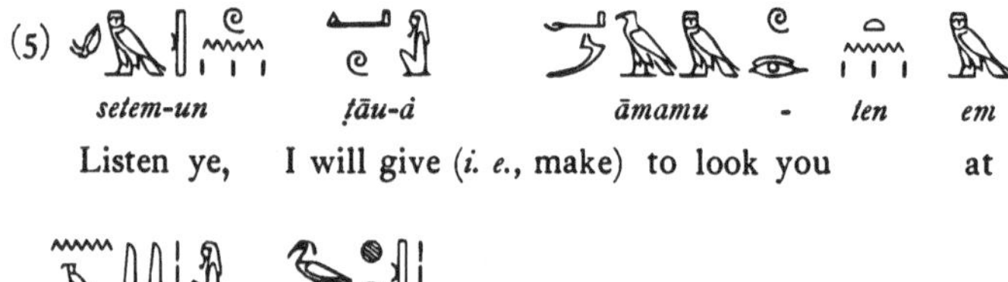

seṭem-un ṭāu-à āmamu - ten em

Listen ye, I will give (*i. e.*, make) to look you at

nai-à χu

my glorious works.

As so many examples occur in the texts at the end of the book the following limited number of extracts must suffice to illustrate the simplest use of the verb :—

1.  *nuk neter āā χeper ṭesef* 2. *Rā pu em*

I am the god great the creator of himself. Rā it is when

uben - f 3. *nuk sef reχ - kuà ṭuau*

he riseth. I am yesterday, I know to-morrow.

4. 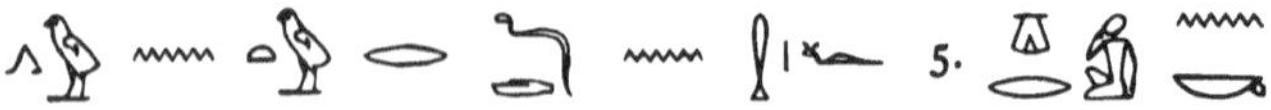 *iu en tu er ṭeṭ en ḥen-f* 5. *ḳer - nek*

Came one to speak to his majesty. Be thou silent.

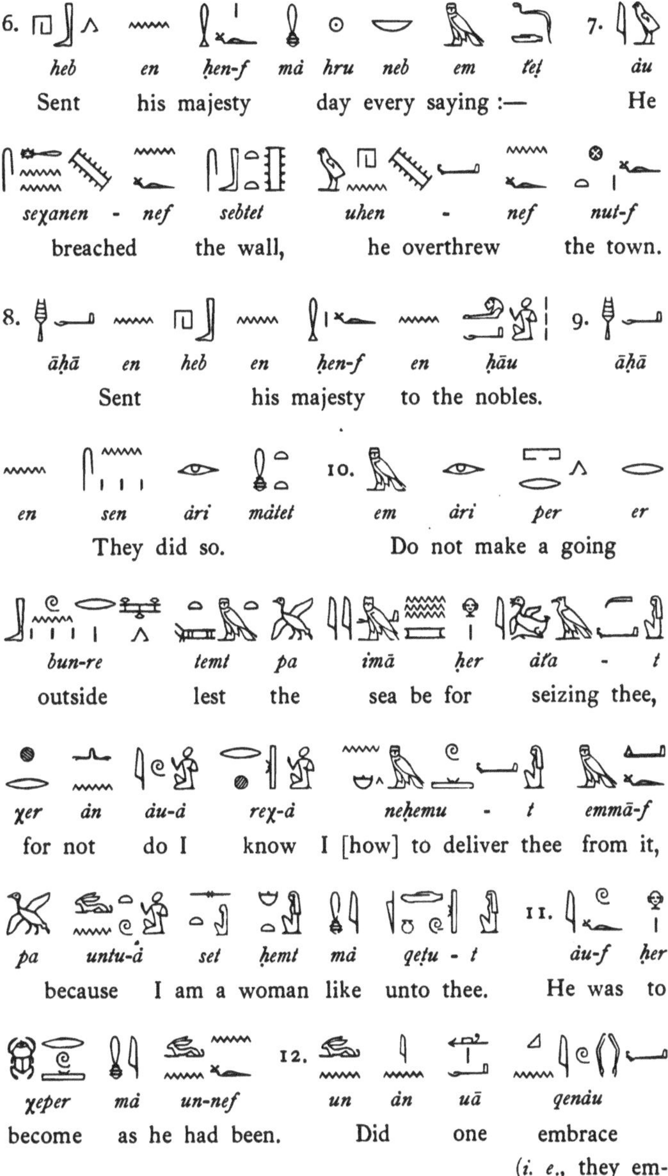

6. *heb en ḥen-f mà hru neb em ṭeṭ* 7. *àu*
Sent his majesty day every saying :— He

seχanen - nef sebtet uhen - nef nut-f
breached the wall, he overthrew the town.

8. *āḥā en heb en ḥen-f en ḥāu* 9. *āḥā*
Sent his majesty to the nobles.

en sen àri màtet 10. *em àri per er*
They did so. Do not make a going

bun-re temt pa imā ḥer àṭa - t
outside lest the sea be for seizing thee,

χer àn àu-à reχ-à neḥemu - t emmā-f
for not do I know I [how] to deliver thee from it,

pa untu-à set ḥemt mà qeṭu - t 11. *àu-f ḥer*
because I am a woman like unto thee. He was to

χeper mà un-nef 12. *un àn uā qenàu*
become as he had been. Did one embrace
(*i. e.*, they em-

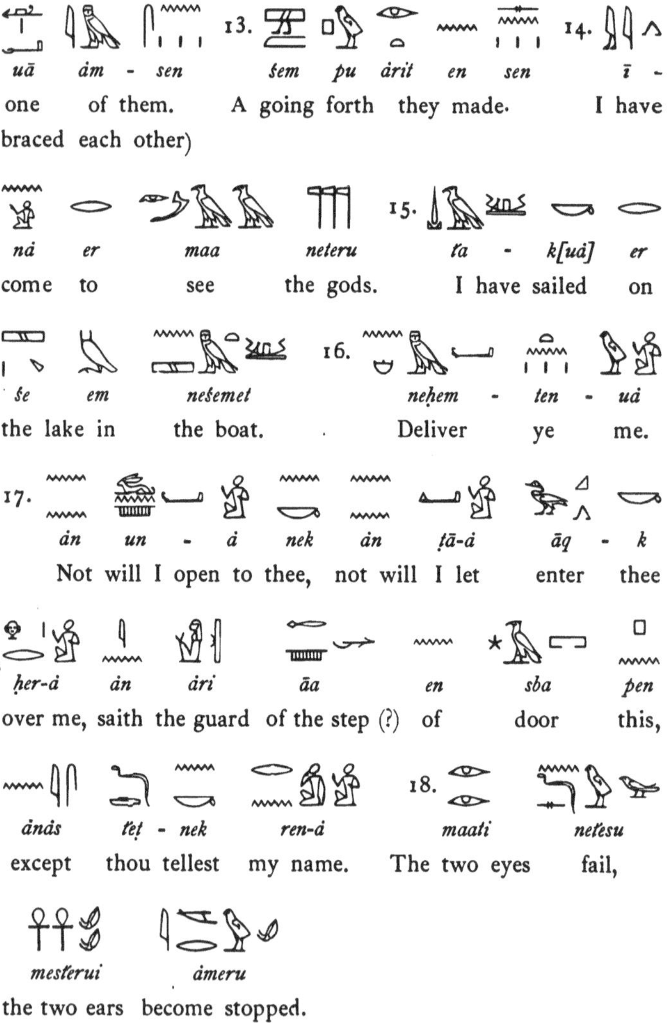

uā ȧm - sen 13. *šem pu ȧrit en sen* 14. *ī -*

one of them. A going forth they made. I have braced each other)

nȧ er maa neteru 15. *ťa - k[uȧ] er*

come to see the gods. I have sailed on

še em nešemet 16. *neḥem - ten - uȧ*

the lake in the boat. Deliver ye me.

17. *ȧn un - ȧ nek ȧn ṭā-ȧ āq - k*

Not will I open to thee, not will I let enter thee

ḥer-ȧ ȧn ȧri āa en sba pen

over me, saith the guard of the step (?) of door this,

ȧnȧs ťeṭ - nek ren-ȧ 18. *maati neťesu*

except thou tellest my name. The two eyes fail,

mesťerui ȧmeru

the two ears become stopped.

Adverbs.

In Egyptian the prepositions and certain substantives and adjectives to which ⊂⊃ *er* is prefixed take the place of adverbs *e. g.*, the preposition *ȧm* "in" becomes the adverb "there". Other examples of adverbs are :— *er bunre* "outside"; *er ȧqer* "very much", "exceedingly", *er āa ur* "very much indeed", "exceedingly".

PREPOSITIONS.

Prepositions, which may also be used adverbially, are simple and compound. The simple prepositions are :— *en* for, to, in, because; *em* from, out of, in, into, on, of, among, as, conformably to, as, with, in the state of, if, when, and *em* sometimes introduces a quotation; *er* to, into, against, by, at, from, every, each, until; or *ḥer* upon, in, besides, from, for, at, by reason of; *ṭep* upon; *χer* under, with; *χer* from, with, under, during; *mā* of, from, by; *ḥenā* with; *χeft* in the face of, before, at the time of; *χent* in front of; *ḥa* behind; *mȧ* like; *ȧmi* among; *ṭer* since; *ȧn* a particle placed between the verb and the subject.

Some compound prepositions are :—

	em ȧsu	in recompense for, in consequence of
	em āqa	in the midst, opposite (?)
	em āb	opposite, against
	em uāu	alone
	em uaḥ ḥer	in addition to
	em baḥ	before, in the presence of (also written)
	emem	in, with, among, together with

emmā	in, with, among, together with
em màtet	likewise
em-rā	in the condition of
em rer	about, around
em ḥau	moreover, besides
em ḥāt	in front, before
em ḥer	opposite, in front of
em ḥer àb	in the middle of
em χem	without
em χennu	within
em χer	with
em χet	after, with
em sa	behind, after, at the back of
em qeb	among, amidst
em qeṭ	around, in the circuit of
em ṭep	upon
em ṭebu	in return for
em ṫer	since
er àmtu	between
er āq	in the middle
er āuṭ	between

er ḳes	at the side of
àire māu	with
er enti	because
er ḥāt	before
er ḥenā	with
er ḥer	in addition to
er ḥer	in the presence of
er χet	after
er tem	so that not
er šaā	as far as, until
er t'er	to the limit of
ḥeru	besides
ḥer ṭep	upon
ḥer àb	in the middle
ḥer ā	at once
ḥer baḥ	before
ḥer χeru	beneath
ḥer sa	behind, at the back
ḥer qeṭ	conformably
χer ā	subordinate to
χer ḥāt	before
χer peḥ	behind

ṭer ā	at once
ṭer baḥ	before, originally
ṭer embaḥ	before, originally
ṭer enti	because
neferit er	up to, as far as
àp ḥer	except

CONJUNCTIONS.

Conjunctions are :— *en* because of, *er* until, *ḥer* because, *χeft* when, *mà* as, *re pu* or, *às*, *àst*, *àsk* when, *χer* now, and the particles *àr*, *àref*, *ref*, now, therefore, etc.

PARTICLES.

Interrogative particles are :— *àn*, which is placed at the beginning of a sentence and is to be rendered by "?" *àχ* "what?", *nimā* "who?", *àšeset* or *àqes* "who?", "what?", *tennu* "where", *petrà* or *peti* (?) "what?", etc. The following passages show their use :—

1. *hau* *ka* *en* *ta* *paut* *neteru* *àn*
O bull of the company of the gods,

àu-k *ṭi* *uā* - *θà*
dost thou remain by thyself?

2. 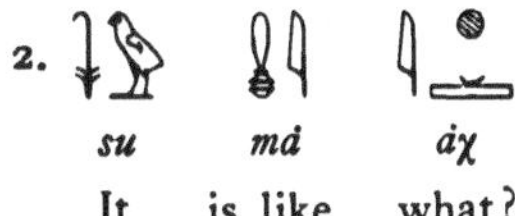

su *mȧ* *ȧχ*

It is like what?

Ȧuθu *mȧ* *ȧχ*

Authu is like what? *I. e.,* "What sort of a place is Authu?"

3. 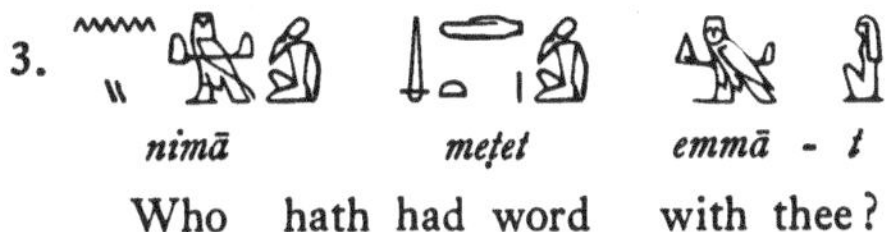

nimā *meṭet* *emmā - t*

Who hath had word with thee?

4. *ȧ* *Tem* *ȧśeset* *pu* *śas* - *ȧ* *er* *set*

Hail Tmu, what is it which I have come into it? *I. e.,* "What manner of place is this into which I have come?"

ȧśeset *pu* *āḥā* *em* *ānχ*

What is [my] duration of life? *I. e.,* "How long shall I live?"

5. *su* *tennu* - *nef*

He, where is he?

6. *petrȧ* *ren* - *k* *petrȧ* *maa* - *nek*

What is thy name? What didst thou see?

Negative particles are :— or *ȧn* "not", *ȧn sep* "at no time", *bu* "not", *ben* "not", *tem* "not", or "so that not",  *ȧm* "not". The following examples show their use :—

1\. 

ȧn qem - f ȧn reχ-tu paif seχeru

Not found he [it]. Not is known his pattern.

2\. 

ȧu bu i na šemi er ta ȧnt

Not came the travellers to the valley.

3\. 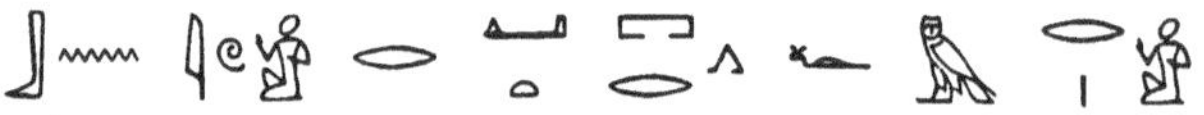

ben ȧu-ȧ er ṭāt per - f em re-ȧ

Not am I for letting come forth it from my mouth.

4\. 

tem - k ṭeṭ tem - k qenṭet

Not do thou speak. Not do thou rage.

5\. 

ȧm - k ḥems du kai āḥā

Not do thou sit being another standing up.

List of Words.

The following common words should be learnt by heart ; this can best be done by writing out a few of them daily.

	*ṭep*	head
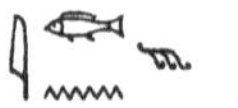	*ȧn*	hair
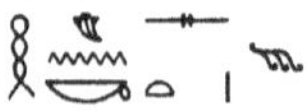	*ḥenkset*	hair
	*šenti*	hair

fenṭ	nose
re	mouth
àbeḥ	tooth
nes	tongue
ānχui	the two ears
t'eru	skull
neḥebet	neck
χ^eχ	neck
θes	vertebrae
erment	arm, shoulder
ā	fore-arm
χ^efā	fist
ṡenbet	body
at	back
menṭ	breast
àb	heart
maāset	liver
χat	belly
mast	thigh
uārt	thigh
reṭ	foot and leg
ànem	skin

	t'et	body
	ḥāu	flesh, members
	āt	limbs
or	*ba*	soul
	χaïbit	shade, shadow
	sāḥu	the spiritual body
	ka	double, genius
	χu	intelligence
	seχem	form, image
	qes	bone
	ren	name
	ḥrȧ	face
	ṭehen	forehead
	ȧnḥu	eyebrow
	maat	eye
	šerȧti	the two nostrils
	septi	the two lips
	ārti	the two jaws
	ȧnā	chin
	mest'er	ear
	ḥenkek	throat
	mākḥa	back of the head

qāḥu	shoulder
qeb	elbow
ṭet	hand
ṭebā	finger
χat	corpse
pesṭ	backbone
ḥāt	heart
ḥetet	lungs
besek	intestines
peḥti	back
sa	back
χepeš	thigh
ment	leg
sebeq	foot and ankle
mesq	skin
àf	flesh
snef	blood
suḥt	egg
χer	voice
pet	heaven, sky
ta	earth
taui	the two lands (*i.e.*, north and south)

taiu	world, universe
ṭuat	underworld
Rā	sun
Åāḥ	moon
χut	horizon
seb	star
χabes	star, luminary
sepṭet	Sothis (Sirius)
saḥ	Orion
χepeš	Great Bear
hru	day
ḳerḥ	night
ṭuat	daybreak
māšer	evening
ḥet' ta	dawn
ḥet'et	light
satut	rays of light
ḥet'ut	light, sunshine
maāu	rays of light
sešep	brilliance
kekiu	darkness
ḥai	rain

ḳep	rain flood
šenār	tempest
mu	water
nebȧt	fire
rekḥu	fire, heat
χet	fire
ṭu	mountain
ȧntet	valley
ìmā	sea
ȧtur	river
ȧaṭet	dew
šā	sand
ȧner	stone
mat	granite
reṭ	sandstone
šes	alabaster
beχan	porphyry
māfek	turquoise
χesbeṭ	lapis-lazuli
uaṭ'et	mother-of-emerald
sehert	cornelian
nub	gold

ḥet'	silver
uasm, smu	electrum (?)
χemt	copper
bȧa	iron
ṭeḥt	lead
χet	wood, stick
χet	tree
šennu	hard wood tree
nehat	sycamore
āš	cedar
baq	olive tree
ṭebaȧa	fig tree
ȧarer	vine
aḥet	field
benrȧ	date palm
beti	barley
peru	wheat, grain
neprȧ	grain
s[ti]mu	vegetables, herbs
ȧrp	wine
ȧarer	grapes
benrȧ	dates

ṭeb	figs
ȧrt	milk
net (*bȧt*)	honey
renp	young plant, flower
ḥeqt	beer
beq	oil
urḥu	unguent
merḥu	unguent
ānta	perfume
ta	bread
pesen	cake
sennu	cake
per āa	Pharaoh
suten	king
sutenit	queen
suteni	royalty
suten ḥemt	royal wife
suten mut	royal mother
suten sa	royal son (prince)
suten sat	royal daughter (princess)
suten mesu	royal child
suten ān	royal scribe

áθi	prince
suten net (*bát*)	King of the South and North
. . . .	lord of crowns
ur	prefect, nobleman
er pā	hereditary prince
ḥā	a title of very high rank
ṭat	general
smer uāti	a title of high rank
suten reχ	royal kinsman
suten reχ maā	real royal kinsman
ḥer ṭep	chief
ḥer ṭep āa	great chief
mer	governor
šennu	royal attendant
sāḥ	noble
ḥen	majesty
χerp	prefect
ḥen	servant
ḥent	servant (female)
neter ḥen	minister, prophet
neter átf	divine father
āb	libationer

χer ḥeb	he that hath the book (*i. e.*, the reader)
χer ḥeb ṭep	the chief reader
sem	name of a priest
setem	name of a priest
ur χerp ḥem	title of the high priest of Memphis
ān	scribe
ān neter ḥet	scribe of the temple
ān neter šāt	scribe of holy books
ḥer	chief, president
menfit (*māša*)	soldiers (rank and file)
qen	soldiers picked for bravery
rem[θ]	men and women
re[*m*]θ	men and women
tememu	mortals
reχit	men and women
pāt	ancestor, noble
ḥememu	mankind
ḥrâu nebu	all faces (*i. e.*, mankind)
sa	person
sat	person (fem.)
sat ḥemt	woman
ḥemt	woman

mut	mother
menāt	nurse
sa	son
sat	daughter
sen	brother
sent	sister
semsu	firstborn
āu	heir
mesu	child
neb	lord
nebt	lady
θesemu	greyhound
maau	cat
uher	dog, jackal
āu	dog
unš	wolf
sȧbi	jackal
pennu	mouse *or* rat
ka	bull
ȧua	ox
ȧḥ	cow, ox
beḥes	calf

rerȧ	pig
ser	ram, sheep
āa	ass
ḥetrȧ	horse
sesemut	horses
maḥeṭ'	antelope
maḥes	lion
ȧbi	panther
ṭebt	hippopotamus
ābu	elephant
bȧḥes	wild animals
āut	quadrupeds
emsuḥ	crocodile
ḥentasu	lizard
ṭ'art	scorpion
χeper	beetle
ārā	uraeus
fenṭ	worm
ḥeft	snake
ṭ'eṭfet	creeping things
pi	flea
aāāni	ape

habu	ibis
bȧk	hawk
šent	heron
šeta	vulture
apṭ	duck, goose
ment	pigeon
bennu	phoenix (?)
smen	goose
pai	birds
remu	fish
χepanen	fish
še	pool
mer	lake, pool
sešet	nest
babat	hole of an animal
ur	great, exceedingly
neťeset	little
neb	all, every
āšt	many
āāa	great
trȧ	season
rek	period, time

	unnet	hour, season
	ḥat	second
	at	minute
	àbeṭ	month
	renpit	year
	seṭ	period of 30 years
	ḥen	period of 60 years
	ḥeḥ	millions of years
	ṫetta	everlastingness
	hru ṭuau ḥeru renpit	the 5 epagomenal days
	ṡat	period of sowing
	pert	period of growing (*i. e.*, winter)
	ṡemut	period of inundation (*i. e.*, summer)
	χer	cemetery
	mer	pyramid tomb
	àsit	tomb
	māḥāit	sepulchre
	useχt	hall, part of a tomb
	uti	coffin
	ṭebu	sarcophagus
	perχeru	funeral offerings

statet	passage in the tomb
àmḫet	hall of the tomb
tut	statue, image
uṭḥu	altar, table
ḥesmen	natron
χet	things, furniture, wealth
urś	pillow
ḥetepu	funeral offerings
utu	tablet, stele
sāḥ	mummy
ḥes	singer, mourner
maāχeru	triumphant, victorious
bent	harp
seśeś	sistrum
ureret	name of a crown
śuti	plumes
ḥeṭ'et	white crown
ṭeśert	red crown
atfu	the *atef* crown
seχti	the double crown
nemmes	the *nemmes* crown
neχeχu	whip

θes	a captain
qem	black
ḥet'et	white
ṭešer	red
χesbeṭ	blue (of lapis-lazuli)
unemi	right hand
semeḥi	left hand
šeps	venerable, sacred
ȧmaχ	revered
mert	beloved, friend
nefer	good, happy
neṭ'em	pleasant, happy
benrȧ	sweet
maā	what is right and true
menu	monuments
peru ḥet'	treasury
šenti	granary
ḥet	temple
per	house
ḥet āat	palace, great house
ȧuset	place, seat
sba	door, doorway

āāui	folding door
sebχet	large doors, pylons
nemmat	block of punishment
χet	staircase
teχennu	obelisk
nest	throne
karȧ	shrine
ṭemȧt	village
nut	city
ťerȧu	bounds, limits
enti	things which do exist
unenet	things which shall exist
uā	one, only
uāu	alone
uat	way
māṭennu	road, way
mesťemut	eye paint
maa-ḥrȧ	seer of the face (*i. e.*, mirror
sešen	lily
šeta	secret, hidden
šāt	book
ťamā	roll of papyrus

mesθà	writing palette
pes	ink-jar
qeš	writing reed
ānχ	life
mit	death
χeft	enemy
χakàb	rebel, coward
àm	camp
pet	bow
šemert	bow
ābau	arrow, bolt
urer	chariot
sebàu	fiend
senb	health
uṭa	strength
uàa	boat
sektet	morning boat of the sun
āṭeṭ	evening boat of the sun
ḥemi	rudder
ḥeqer	hunger
àb	thirst
sam ta	union with the earth, *i. e.*, funeral

ȧnet' ḥrȧ-k hail to thee!

ȧau adoration

peḥti strength

šefit might, terror

āu joy, gladness

sen ta adoration

ȧn not

ben not

ȧt destitute

sebtet wall

feqa reward, wages

seqer prisoner

ḥeb festival

uṭen offering

ȧp messenger, envoy

ȧnnu offerings, tribute

ses bolt of a door

meṭu a word, thing

betau bad, wickedness

ȧsfet faults, sins

ṭenḥ wing

uteb furrow, water-course

neχt	might, victory
usr	to be strong
sfenṭ	knife
nemmat	footsteps
χāu	crowns
χeru	terrestrial beings
ḥeru	celestial beings
seχeru	plans, schemes
t'efau	funeral meals
χert	things, provisions
ṭemṭ	all
χai	defeat
neh	few
χesef	to meet, to repulse
utu	to command
sa	to know
ṭer	to destroy
χāā	to rise, be crowned
senṭ	to fear
uaś	to adore
ḥeḥi	to seek
χaā	to leave

	seb	to pass
	ṭep	to taste
	àmen	to hide, be hidden
	qet	to build
	seś	to open
	ānχ	to live
	mit	to die
	maa	to see
	setem	to hear
	rerem	to weep
	t'eṭ	to say, speak
	mer	to love
	mest'eṭ	to hate
	āḥā	to stand
	ḥems	to sit
	st'er	to lie down
	χeper	to become
	àru	to make
	qemam	to create
	àm	to eat
	surà	to drink
	θetet	to carry off

āq	to go in
per	to come out
sper	to set out
	to come
atep	to load oneself
fa	to bear, to carry
urš	to pass the day
seχem	to gain the mastery
ābau	to fight
sma	to slay, kill
χeṭbu	to slay
uben	to rise (of the sun)
ḥetep	to set
pesṭ	to shine
seḥeṭ'	to illumine
bāḥ	to overflow, to flood
θes	to lift up
qa	to be high
χeṭ	to float down stream
χent	to sail up stream
ušebt	to answer
beṭeš	to be weak, feeble

ḥāā	to rejoice
ṭuau	to praise
smȧ	to announce
ṭā	to give
ṭebḥ	to pray, entreat
ȧpṭ	to announce
men	to stablish, to abide
sam	to unite
sepṭ	to provide, prepare
āper	to be provided with
peṭ	to stretch
pai	to fly
peḥrer	to run
šes	to follow
seχseχ	to flee
hab	to send
šem (*māšem*)	to walk, to travel
ťa	to set out
sen	to pass
seš	to go, to pass by, to go in
peḥ	to attain, to arrive
sau	to watch, to guard

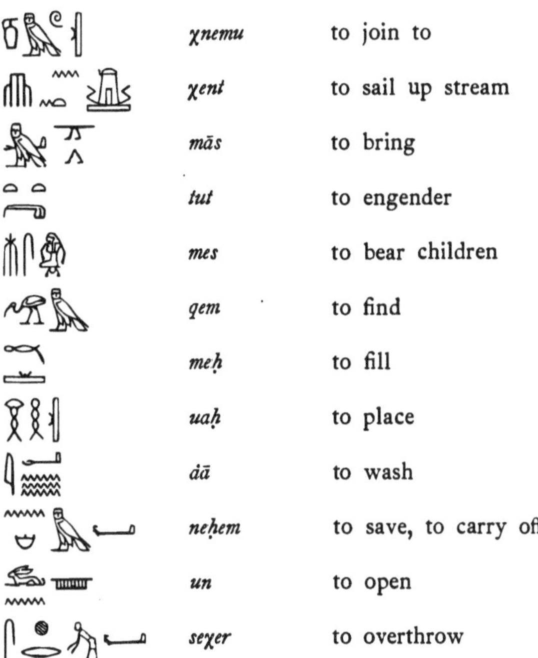

	χnemu	to join to
	χent	to sail up stream
	mās	to bring
	tut	to engender
	mes	to bear children
	qem	to find
	meḥ	to fill
	uaḥ	to place
	āā	to wash
	neḥem	to save, to carry off
	un	to open
	seχer	to overthrow

Gods and Goddesses.

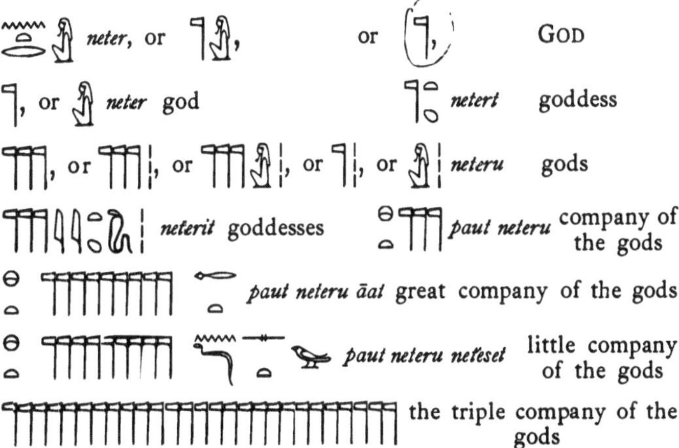

neter, or , or , God

, or *neter* god — *netert* goddess

, or , or , or , or *neteru* gods

neterit goddesses — *paut neteru* company of the gods

paut neteru āat great company of the gods

paut neteru neṭeset little company of the gods

the triple company of the gods

Ȧusȧr	Osiris
Ȧuset	Isis
Ȧp-uat	Ȧp-uat
Ȧmen	Ȧmen (Ammon)
Ȧmen-Rā	Ȧmen-Rā
Ȧmsu or *Min*	Ȧmsu, Min, Khem
Ȧmsu-Ȧmen	Ȧmsu-Ȧmen
Ȧmset	Ȧmset
Ȧni	Ȧni
Ānθȧt	Anata
Ȧnpu	Anubis
Ȧn-ḥeru	Ȧn-ḥeru
Ānqet	Ānqet
Ȧtmu	Ȧtmu (Tmu)
Ȧsṭes	Ȧsṭes
Iusāaset	Iusāaset
I-em-ḥetep	Imouthis
Un-nefer	Un-nefer
Uaṭet	Uatchet
Baba	Baba
Bār	Bār (Baal)

Bes	Bes
Ptaḥ	Ptaḥ
Ptaḥ-Seker-Ȧusȧr	Ptah-Socharis-Osiris
Maāt	Maāt
Menθu	Menthu
Meḥ-urt	Meḥurt
Mesχenet	Meskhenet
Mut	Mut
Nu	Nu
Nut	Nut
Neb-er-ṭer	Neb-er-tcher
Nebt-ḥet	Nephthys
Nefer-Tmu	Nefer-Tmu
Nit	Neith
Rā	Rā
Renenet	Renenet
Rešpu	Reshpu
Ḥu	Ḥu
Ḥāpi	The Nile
Ḥāpi	Ḥāpi
Ḥāpi	Apis

Ḥeruur	Horus the elder (Aroeris)
Ḥeru-sa-Ȧuset	Horus, son of Isis (Harsiesi)
Ḥeru-pa-χarṭ	Horus the child (Harpocrates)
Ḥeru-maati	Horus of the two eyes
Ḥeru-χenti-ȧn-maa	Horus dwelling in darkness
Ḥeru-χenti-Seχem	Horus of Sekhem
Ḥet-ḥert	Hathor
Χnemu	Khnemu
Χensu	Khensu
Χensu-nefer-ḥetep	Khensu-nefer-ḥetep
Sa	Sa
Seb	Seb
Sebek	Sebek
Sept	Sept
Sefeχet	Sefekhet
Serqet	Serqet
Seχetet	Sekhet
Seker	Socharis
Set	Set or Sut
Sati	Sati
Suteχ	Sutekh
Śu	Shu

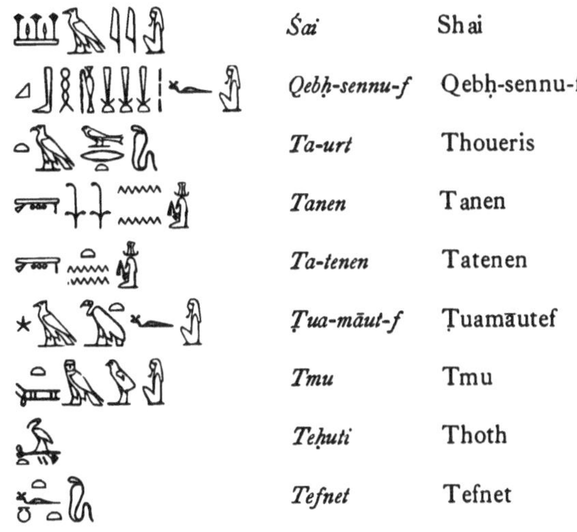

Śai	Shai
Qebḥ-sennu-f	Qebḥ-sennu-f
Ta-urt	Thoueris
Tanen	Tanen
Ta-tenen	Tatenen
Ṭua-māut-f	Ṭuamāutef
Tmu	Tmu
Teḥuti	Thoth
Tefnet	Tefnet

TEXTS

WITH INTERLINEAR TRANSLITERATION
AND WORD FOR WORD TRANSLATION

EXTRACTS FROM THE PRISSE PAPYRUS.

Maxims of Kaqemna and Ptaḥ-ḥetep.

[IIIrd and Vth dynasties.]

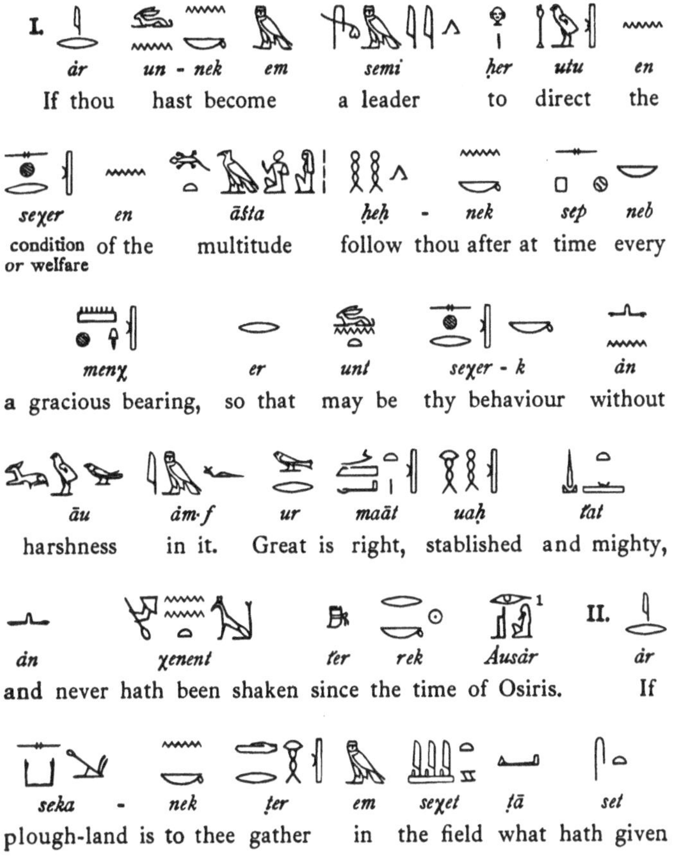

I.
år un - nek em semi ḥer utu en
If thou hast become a leader to direct the
seχer en āšta ḥeḥ - nek sep neb
condition or welfare of the multitude follow thou after at time every
menχ er unt seχer - k ån
a gracious bearing, so that may be thy behaviour without
āu åm·f ur maāt uaḥ ťat
harshness in it. Great is right, stablished and mighty,
ån χenent ťer rek Ausår[1]
and never hath been shaken since the time of Osiris.
II.
år
If
seka - nek ṭer em seχet ṭā set
plough-land is to thee gather in the field what hath given

[1] Plate VI., ll. 3—5.

III.

neter — *ȧr* *un - nek* *em* *sa* *ȧqer* *ȧri - k*

God. If thou wouldst be a man perfect make thou

sa *en* *semam* *neter* *ȧr* *met - f*

[thy] son to please God. If he directeth straight

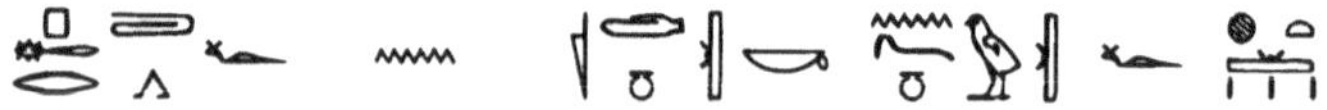

peχar-f *en* *qeṭ - k* *ennu - f* *χet-*

his course according to thy example, and he dealeth in thy

k *er* *ȧuset* *ȧri* *ȧri - nef* *bu* *neb*

affairs in the place belonging thereto, do unto him thing every
or way

nefer *sa - k* *pu* *nesu* *set*

good, for thy son is he belonging unto the seed

ka - k *ȧm-k* *āuṭ* *ȧb-k* *er - f*

of thy person. Do not thou remove thy heart from him,

IV.

ȧu *metu* *ȧri* *senθi* *ȧr*

[for it] is [thy] seed [which] maketh appeal [to thee]. If thou

ȧqer - k *ḳer - k* *per - k* *mer - k* *ḥemt-*

wouldst be perfect possess thou thy house, love thou thy

[1] Plate VII., l. 5. [2] Plate VII., ll. 10—13.

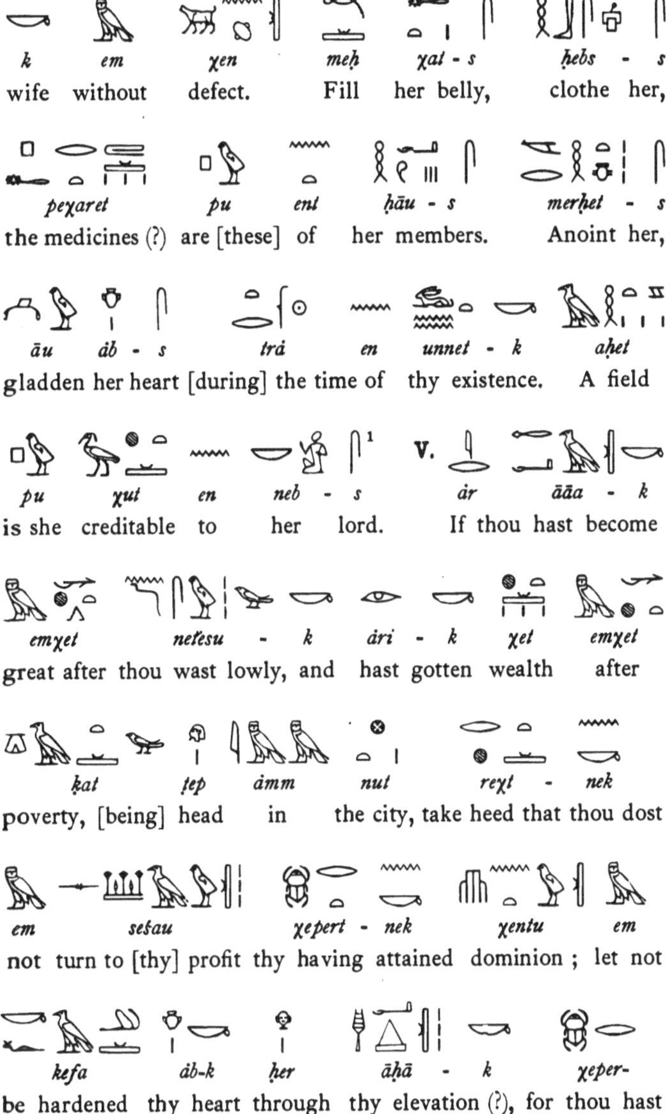

k em χen meḥ χat - s ḥebs - s
wife without defect. Fill her belly, clothe her,

peχaret pu ent ḥāu - s merḥet - s
the medicines (?) are [these] of her members. Anoint her,

āu àb - s ṭrà en unnet - k aḥet
gladden her heart [during] the time of thy existence. A field

pu χut en neb - s[1] V. *àr āāa - k*
is she creditable to her lord. If thou hast become

emχet neṭesu - k àri - k χet emχet
great after thou wast lowly, and hast gotten wealth after

ḳat ṭep àmm nut reχt - nek
poverty, [being] head in the city, take heed that thou dost

em seśau χepert - nek χentu em
not turn to [thy] profit thy having attained dominion ; let not

kefa àb-k ḥer āḥā - k χeper-
be hardened thy heart through thy elevation (?), for thou hast

[1] Plate X., ll. 8—10.

nek mer sepṭ neter[1] VI. *ȧri ṭeṭet*
become [only] the steward of the goods of God. Perform the command

neb - k er-ek nefer-ui sba en
of thy lord to thee. Doubly good is the instruction of

ȧtf - f per - nef ȧm - f χent
his (*i. e.*, a man's) father [for] he hath come forth from him from

ḥāu - f ṭeṭ - nef nef ȧu - f em χat er
his body. [What] he saith to him let it be within [him] to

āu ur ȧrit - nef er ṭeṭet - nef
its fulness greatest, let him do more than his words.

māk sa nefer en ṭāṭā neter rā
Verily a son good [is] of the gifts of God, [he] doeth

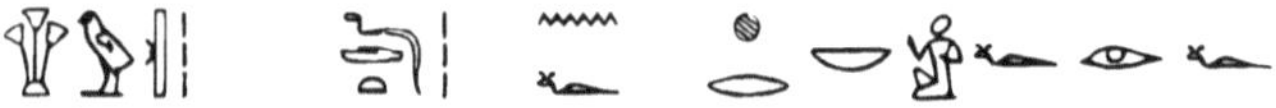

ḥau ṭeṭet - nef χer neb - f ȧri - f
over and above [what] he hath said. Before his lord he doeth right

maā ȧri en ȧb - f er nemtet - f
and truth, and worketh his heart in his steps.

[1] Plate XIII., ll. 6—8.

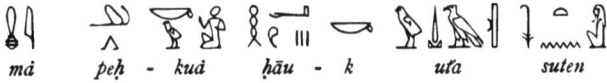

mȧ peḥ - kuȧ ḥāu - k uťa suten
In this manner have I arrived. Thy limbs will be sound, the king

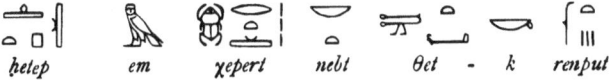

ḥetep em χepert nebt θet - k renput
will be satisfied with [thy] doings all, thou wilt gain years

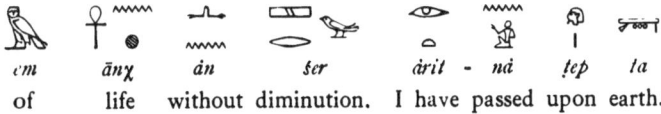

em ānχ ȧn šer ȧrit - nȧ ṭep ta
of life without diminution. I have passed upon earth.

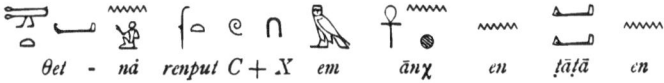

θet - nȧ renput C + X em ānχ en ṭāṭā en
I have gained years 110 of life, for bestowed the

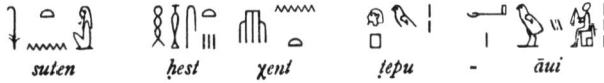

suten ḥest χent ṭepu - āui
king [upon me] favours above those who were before [me],

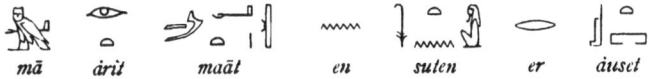

mā ȧrit maāt en suten er ȧuset
for [I was] working right and truth for the king unto the place

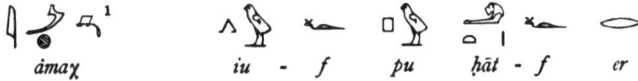

ȧmaχ[1] *iu - f pu ḥāt - f er*
of felicity. It has gone out [from] its beginning to
(*i. e.*, the tomb). (*I. e.*, here endeth the book)

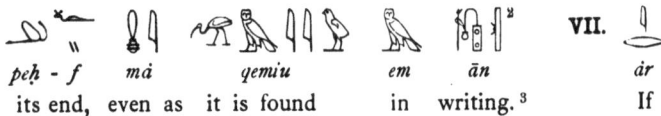

peḥ - f mȧ qemiu em ān[2] **VII.** *ȧr*
its end, even as it is found in writing.[3] If

[1] Plate XIX., ll. 3—8. [2] Plate XIX., l. 9. [3] This is a colo-

enti nebt em ān ḥer pa šeftu

every thing which is in writing upon this book

setem - set mȧ ṫeṭ-ȧ set em sen ḥau

be heard it or obeyed as I have said it, {and the listeners} advance to add

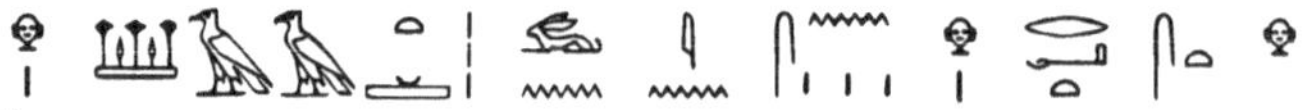

ḥer šaat un ȧn sen ḥer erṭāt set ḥer

unto good counsels, and they are for placing it

χat - sen un ȧn sen ḥer sešeṭet set mȧ

themselves, and they are for reciting it accordin

enti em ān un ȧn nefer set ḥer ȧb - sen

to what is in writing, shall good be it to their hearts

er χet nebt enti em ta pen er ṫer - f

more than thing any which is in earth this to the whole of it

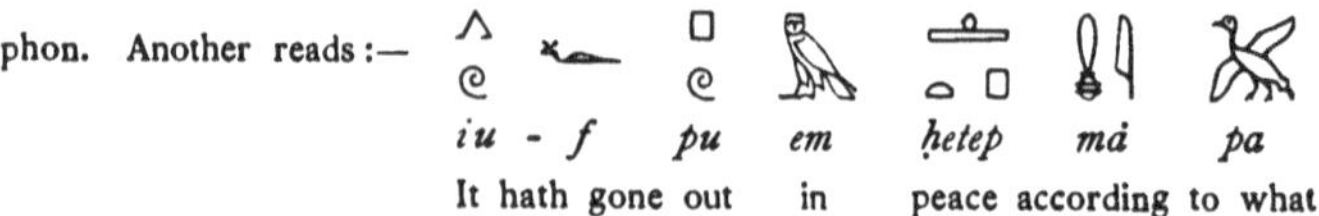

phon. Another reads:— *iu - f pu em ḥetep mȧ pa*

It hath gone out in peace according to what

qemu

was found, *i. e.*, here happily endeth an exact copy.

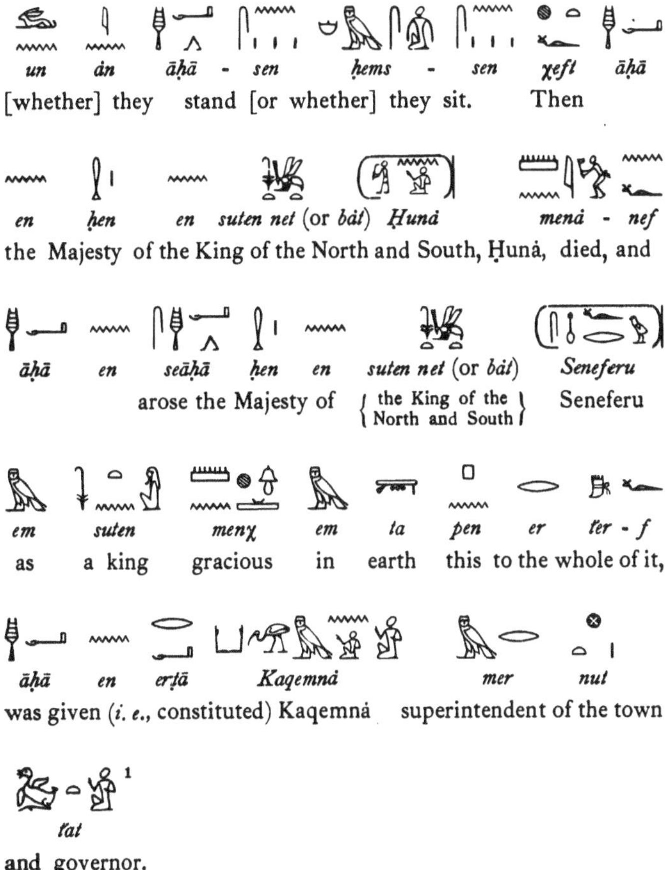

un ȧn āḥā - sen ḥems - sen χeft āḥā
[whether] they stand [or whether] they sit. Then

en ḥen en suten net (or *bȧt*) *Ḥunȧ menȧ - nef*
the Majesty of the King of the North and South, Ḥunȧ, died, and

āḥā en seāḥā ḥen en suten net (or *bȧt*) *Seneferu*
arose the Majesty of {the King of the North and South} Seneferu

em suten menχ em ta pen er ter - f
as a king gracious in earth this to the whole of it,

āḥā en erṭā Kaqemnȧ mer nut
was given (*i. e.*, constituted) Kaqemnȧ superintendent of the town

ṭat[1]
and governor.

[1] Plate II., ll. 4—9.

EXTRACTS FROM THE PYRAMID TEXTS.

Pyramid of Unȧs.

[Vth dynasty.]

I. — II.

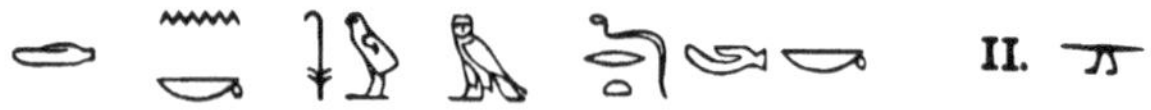

ṭ *nek* *su* *em* *ṭert* - *k* *seb*

Line 3. Place thou it in thy palm. 4. Goeth

III.

Ḥeru *ḥenā* *ka* - *f* *ā* *ka* - *k*

Horus with his *ka* (*i. e.*, double *or* genius). 7. The hand of thy *ka* [is]

IV.

embaḥ - *k* *ā* *ka* - *k* *emχet* - *k* *iu*-

before thee, the hand of thy *ka* [is] behind thee. 11. I have

nȧ *ȧn* - *nȧ* *nek* *maat* *Ḥeru* *qeb* *ȧb* - *k*

come, I have brought to thee the eye of Horus, refresh thy heart

χer - *s* *ȧn* - *nȧ* *nek* *s* *χer* *ṭebti* - *k*

with it; I have brought to thee it beneath thy sandals.

V. — VI.

ȧṭep - *k* *ṭept* - *f* *χent* *neter ḥet* *re* - *k*

14. Taste thou its taste in the divine dwellings. 20. Thy mouth

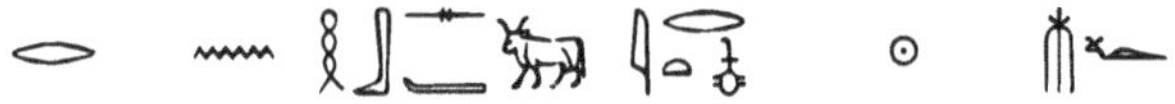

re en ḥebes ȧrt hru mes-f
[is] the mouth of a calf of milk [on] the day of his birth.

VII.  *χerp - nek śȧk Ȧusȧr śȧk*
29. Are presented to thee the nipples of Osiris, the nipples

em ṭep ment' en Ḥeru en ṭet - f [a]m - nek
upon the breast of Horus of his body, thou seizest [them]

ȧr re - k **VIII.** *qebḥ - k ȧpen Ȧusȧr*
with thy mouth. 32. Thy libations [are] these, Osiris,

qebḥ - k ȧpen **IX.** *[a]m maati Ḥeru*
thy libations [are] these. 37. Grasping the two eyes of Horus,

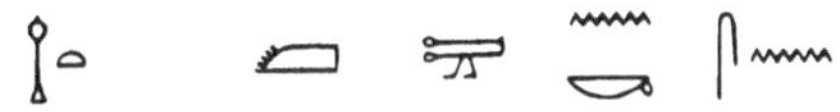

ḥeṭ'et qemt θet - nek - sen **X.** *ḥetep-*
the white and the black thou carriest off them. 39. Make offering

nek . . . . . . **XI.** *χerp - nek ȧbeḥu Ḥeru*
to thee North and South. 41. {Are presented to thee} the teeth of Horus

ḥeṭ'u ḥu re - k **XII.** *pat - k un - nek*
white, they furnish thy mouth. 42. Thou existest, thou art.

XIII. *pat ent uṭen* **XIV.** *seχu - θ su*

42. A cake of offering. 62. Make strong thou him

χer - θ ṭā - θ seχem - f em ṭet - f

with thyself, grant thou that he may gain power over his body

ṭā - θ šāšet - f em maati **XV.** *baqet*

Grant thou that he may be open in his two eyes. 170. The olive tree

àmt Ȧnnu **XVI.** *àn àb àn ḥeqer - f*

in Heliopolis. 172. Not let thirst, not let him hunger,

àn sàr àb en Unàs **XVII.** *χefā - sen*

not let be sad the heart of Unàs. 176. They shall grasp

erṭā - sen - nef am - sen ṭā-

and they shall give to him [what] they have taken, they shall

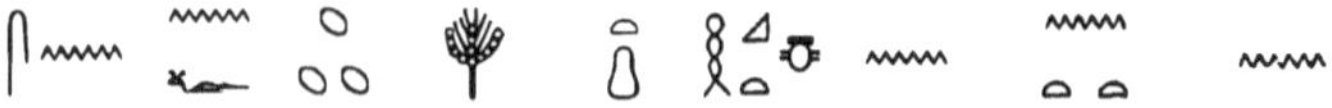

sen nef peru beti ta ḥeqt en entet en

give to him wheat, barley, cakes, ale of that which [is] of

Unàs **XVIII.** *seṭaa ur per em*

Unàs. 187. Trembler mighty coming out of

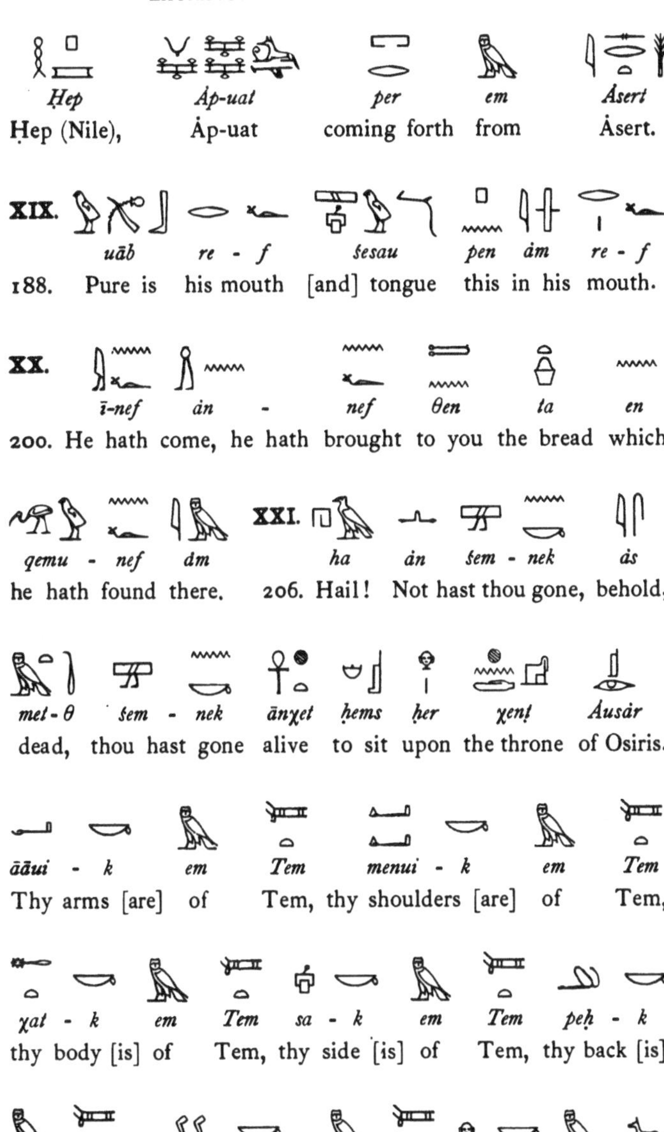

Ḥep *Åp-uat* *per* *em* *Åsert*
Ḥep (Nile), Åp-uat coming forth from Åsert.

XIX. *uāb* *re - f* *śesau* *pen* *ȧm* *re - f*
188. Pure is his mouth [and] tongue this in his mouth.

XX. *ī-nef* *ȧn - nef* *θen* *ta* *en*
200. He hath come, he hath brought to you the bread which

qemu - nef *ȧm* **XXI.** *ha* *ȧn* *śem - nek* *ȧs*
he hath found there. 206. Hail! Not hast thou gone, behold,

met-θ *śem - nek* *ānχet* *ḥems* *ḥer* *χenṭ* *Åusȧr*
dead, thou hast gone alive to sit upon the throne of Osiris.

āāui - k *em* *Tem* *menui - k* *em* *Tem*
Thy arms [are] of Tem, thy shoulders [are] of Tem,

χat - k *em* *Tem* *sa - k* *em* *Tem* *peḥ - k*
thy body [is] of Tem, thy side [is] of Tem, thy back [is]

em *Tem* *reṭ - k* *em* *Tem* *ḥrȧ - k* *em* *Ånpu*
of Tem, thy feet and legs [are] of Tem, thy face [is] of Anpu.

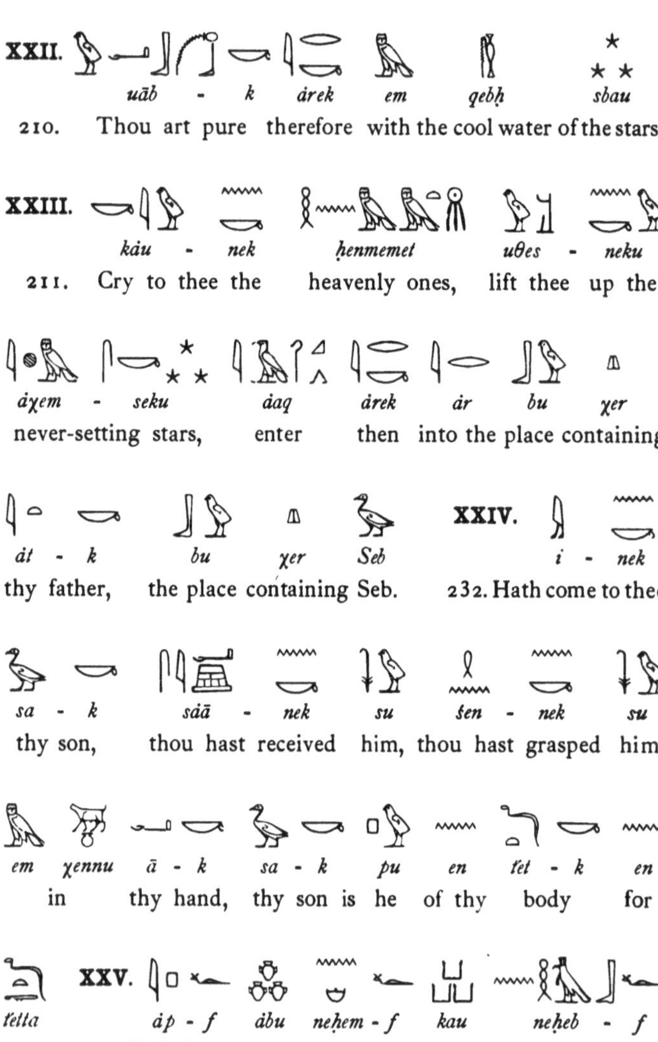

XXII. *uāb - k ȧrek em qebḥ sbau*

210. Thou art pure therefore with the cool water of the stars.

XXIII. *kȧu - nek ḥenmemet uθes - neku*

211. Cry to thee the heavenly ones, lift thee up the

ȧχem - seku ȧaq ȧrek ȧr bu χer

never-setting stars, enter then into the place containing

ȧt - k bu χer Seb **XXIV.** *i - nek*

thy father, the place containing Seb. 232. Hath come to thee

sa - k sȧā - nek su šen - nek su

thy son, thou hast received him, thou hast grasped him

em χennu ā - k sa - k pu en t'et - k en

in thy hand, thy son is he of thy body for

t'etta **XXV.** *ȧp - f ȧbu neḥem - f kau neḥeb - f*

ever. 233. He judgeth hearts, he punisheth *ka*'s, he subdueth

kau **XXVI.** *t-a - f re - f t'eṭ en Seb*

ka's. 234. His bread of his mouth [is] the word of Seb

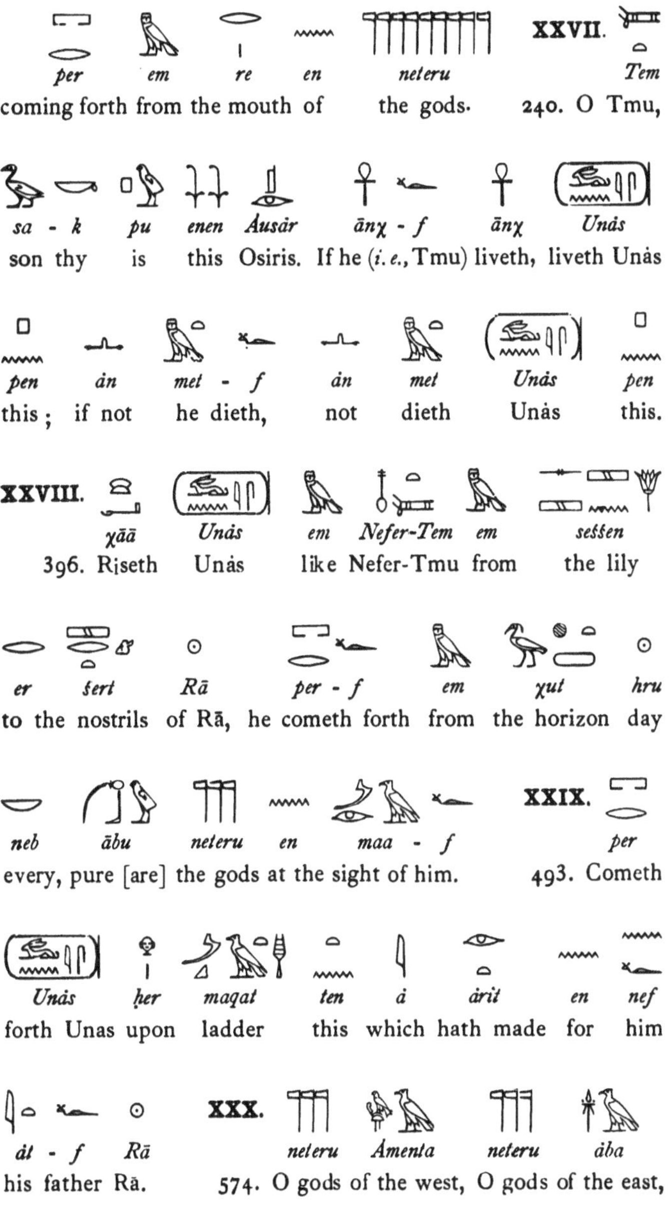

per em re en neteru **XXVII.** *Tem*
coming forth from the mouth of the gods. 240. O Tmu,

sa - k pu enen Ȧusȧr āny - f āny Unȧs
son thy is this Osiris. If he (*i.e.*, Tmu) liveth, liveth Unȧs

pen ȧn met - f ȧn met Unȧs pen
this; if not he dieth, not dieth Unȧs this.

XXVIII. *χāā Unȧs em Nefer-Tem em seššen*
396. Riseth Unȧs like Nefer-Tmu from the lily

er šert Rā per - f em χut hru
to the nostrils of Rā, he cometh forth from the horizon day

neb ābu neteru en maa - f **XXIX.** *per*
every, pure [are] the gods at the sight of him. 493. Cometh

Unȧs ḥer maqat ten ȧ ȧrit en nef
forth Unas upon ladder this which hath made for him

ȧt - f Rā **XXX.** *neteru Ȧmenta neteru ȧba*
his father Rā. 574. O gods of the west, O gods of the east,

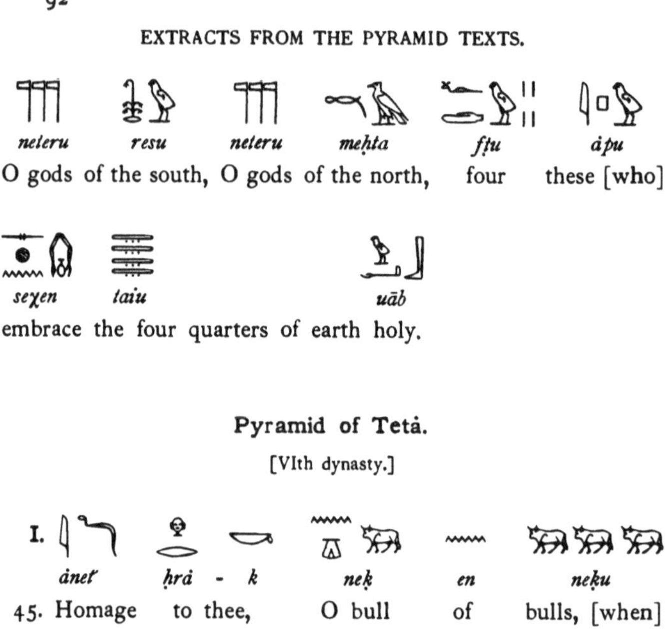

neteru resu neteru meḥta ftu ȧpu

O gods of the south, O gods of the north, four these [who]

seχen taiu uāb

embrace the four quarters of earth holy.

Pyramid of Tetȧ.

[VIth dynasty.]

I. *ȧnet' ḥrȧ - k nek en neku*

45. Homage to thee, O bull of bulls, [when]

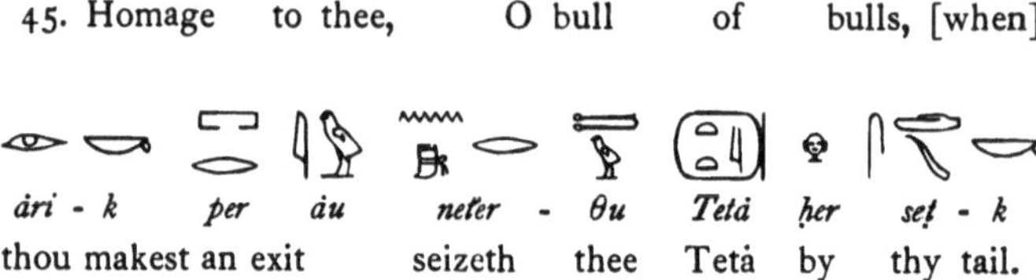

ȧri - k per ȧu neter - θu Tetȧ ḥer set - k

thou makest an exit seizeth thee Tetȧ by thy tail.

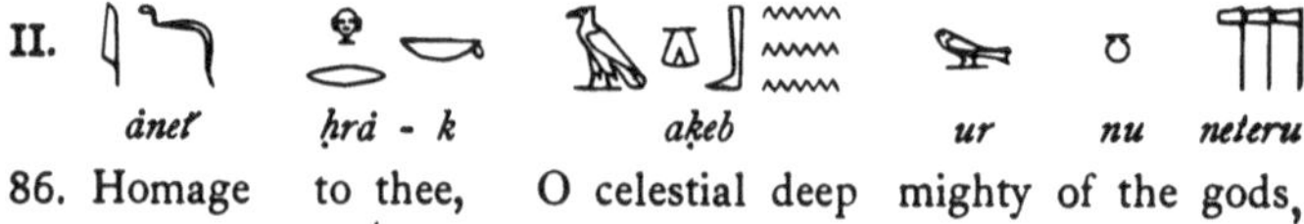

II. *ȧnet' ḥrȧ - k akeb ur nu neteru*

86. Homage to thee, O celestial deep mighty of the gods,

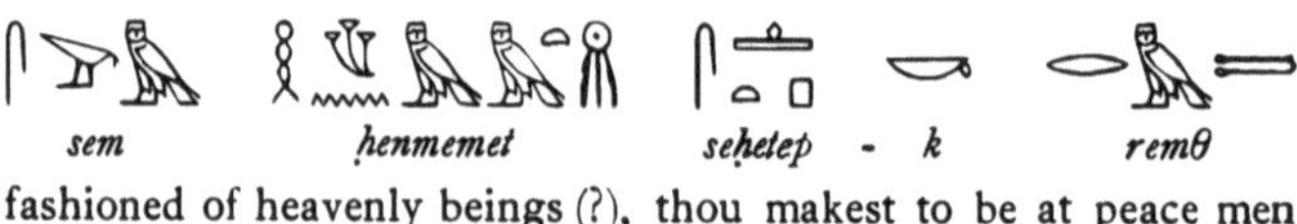

sem ḥenmemet seḥetep - k remθ

fashioned of heavenly beings (?), thou makest to be at peace men

neteru en Tetȧ tā - sen nef χet neb

and gods with Tetȧ, they give to him things (*i. e.*, offerings) of all [kinds].

III. 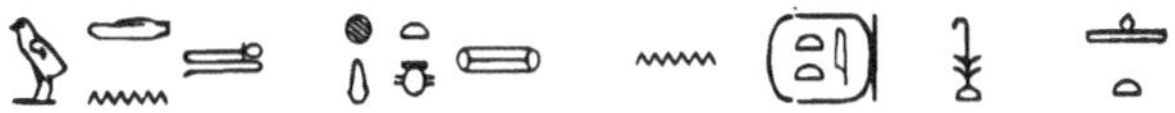 *uṭen* *χet* . *en* *Tetȧ* *suten* *ḥetep*
149. An offering of sepulchral meals to Tetȧ! Royal oblation

ṭā *Seb* *ḥetep* *ṭā* *en* *Tetȧ* *pen* *ṭā* - *nek*
give, O Seb, an oblation give to Tetȧ this. Grant thou

māt *nebt* *uaḥt* *ta* *ḥeqt* *nebt*
gifts all [and] the placing of cakes and ale [of] all [kinds]

mert - *k* *nefert* - *nek* *ȧm* *χer* *neter*
[which] thou lovest, {with / which} thou art pleased there before the god

en *ṭet* *ṭetta* VI. *un* - *nek* *āā* *pet*
for ever and ever. 160. Thou hast opened the doors of heaven,

seneχebχeb - *nek* *qau* *uru* *seθa* - *nek*
thou hast drawn back the bolts mighty, thou hast lifted

ṭebet *meḥat* *āat* *ḥrȧ* - *k* *em* *sab*
the seal of the door great. Thy face is like a jackal,

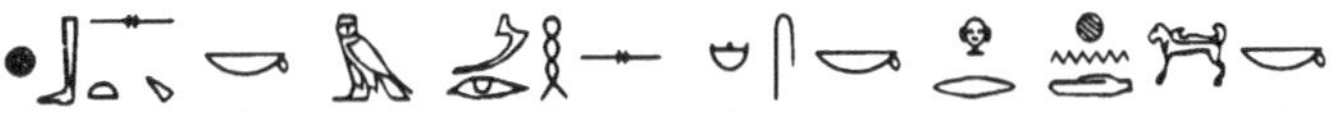

χebset - *k* *em* *maḥes* *ḥems* - *k* *ḥer* *χenṭ* - *k*
thy hind part is like a lion, thou sittest upon thy throne

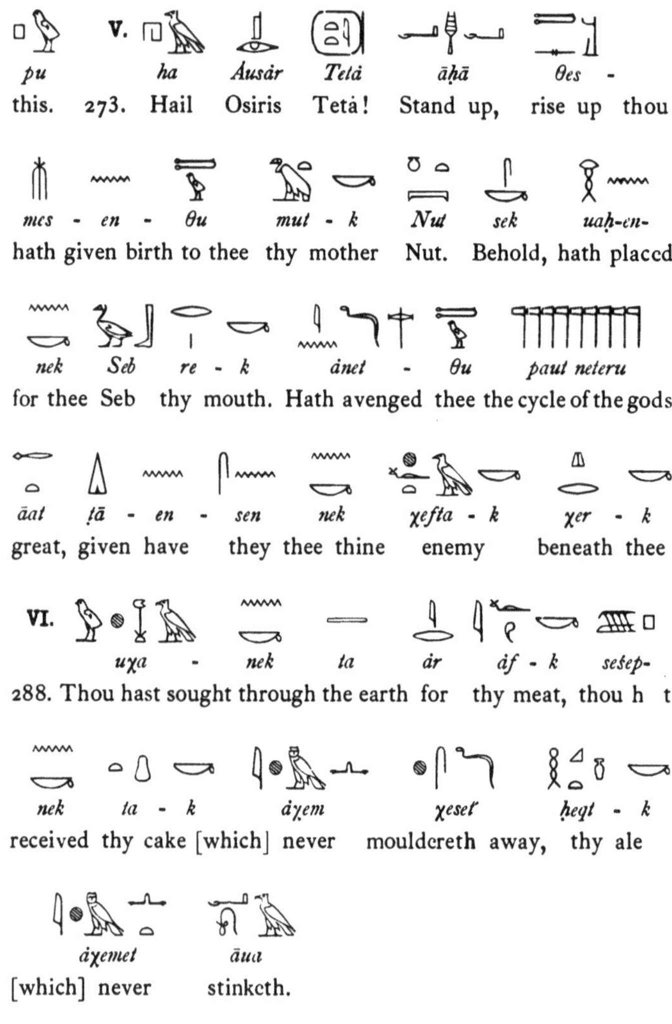

V.

pu *ha* *Ȧusȧr* *Tetȧ* *āḥā* *θes* -

this. 273. Hail Osiris Tetȧ! Stand up, rise up thou

mes - *en* - *θu* *mut* - *k* *Nut* *sek* *uaḥ-en-*

hath given birth to thee thy mother Nut. Behold, hath placed

nek *Seb* *re* - *k* *ȧnet* - *θu* *paut neteru*

for thee Seb thy mouth. Hath avenged thee the cycle of the gods

āat *ṭā* - *en* - *sen* *nek* *χefta* - *k* *χer* - *k*

great, given have they thee thine enemy beneath thee

VI.

uχa - *nek* *ta* *ȧr* *ȧf* - *k* *sešep-*

288. Thou hast sought through the earth for thy meat, thou h t

nek *ta* - *k* *ȧχem* *χeseṭ* *ḥeqt* - *k*

received thy cake [which] never mouldereth away, thy ale

ȧχemet *āua*

[which] never stinketh.

FROM THE TOMB OF ḤER-KHUF AT ASWÂN.

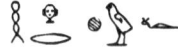

[VIth dynasty.]

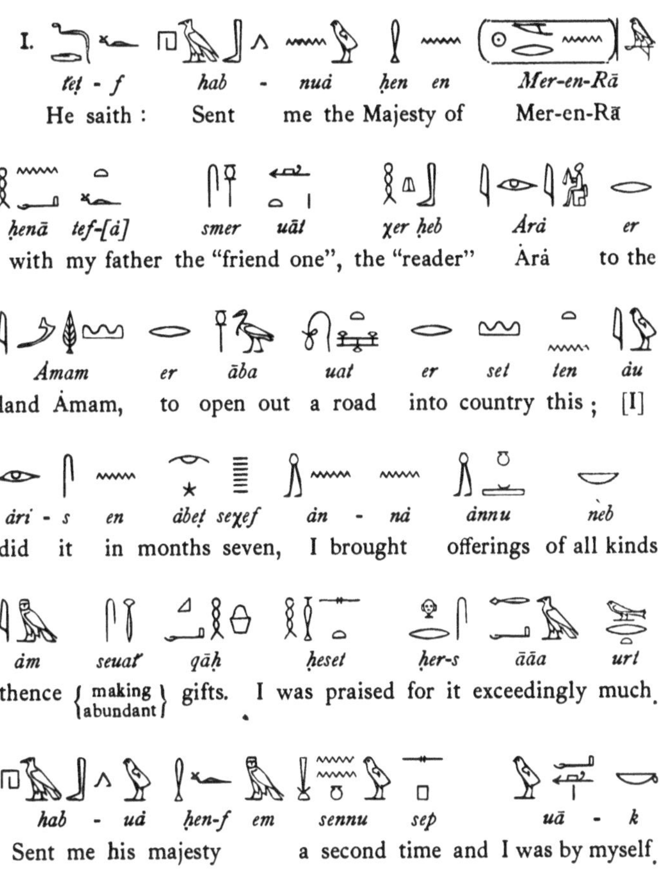

I. *ṭeṭ - f* *hab - nuȧ* *ḥen en* *Mer-en-Rā*
He saith : Sent me the Majesty of Mer-en-Rā

ḥenā tef-[ȧ] *smer uāt* *χer ḥeb* *Ȧrȧ* *er*
with my father the "friend one", the "reader" Ȧrȧ to the

Ȧmam *er* *āba* *uat* *er* *set* *ten* *ȧu*
land Ȧmam, to open out a road into country this; [I]

ȧri - s *en* *ȧbeṭ* *seχef* *ȧn - nȧ* *ȧnnu* *neb*
did it in months seven, I brought offerings of all kinds

ȧm *seuaṭ* *qāḥ* *ḥeset* *ḥer-s* *āāa* *urt*
thence {making abundant} gifts. I was praised for it exceedingly much.

hab - uȧ *ḥen-f* *em* *sennu* *sep* *uā - k*
Sent me his majesty a second time and I was by myself.

per - nȧ ḥer uat Ābu ha - nȧ em

I set out by way of Elephantine, I returned through

Ȧrθet Mesχer Terres Ȧrθeθ em

Ȧrθet, Meskher, Terres [and] Ȧrθeθ in

. . . . . . *ȧbeṭ χemennu ha ȧn - nȧ ȧnnu em*

. . . . . . months eight; returning I brought offerings from

set ten er āāat urt ȧtu sep

country this exceedingly many. [At] no time (*i. e.*, never)

ȧnt mȧtet er ta pen ṭer baḥ ha - nȧ

was brought the like to country this in times of old. I returned

em χerau per . . . . . Set Ȧrθet

through the conquered districts of . . . . . Set and Ȧrθet,

āba - nȧ setu peten ȧn sep qemi ȧri

I penetrated countries these; [at] no time was it found to have been

en smer mer . . . . . neb per

made by a "friend" and superintendent of . . . . . any an advance

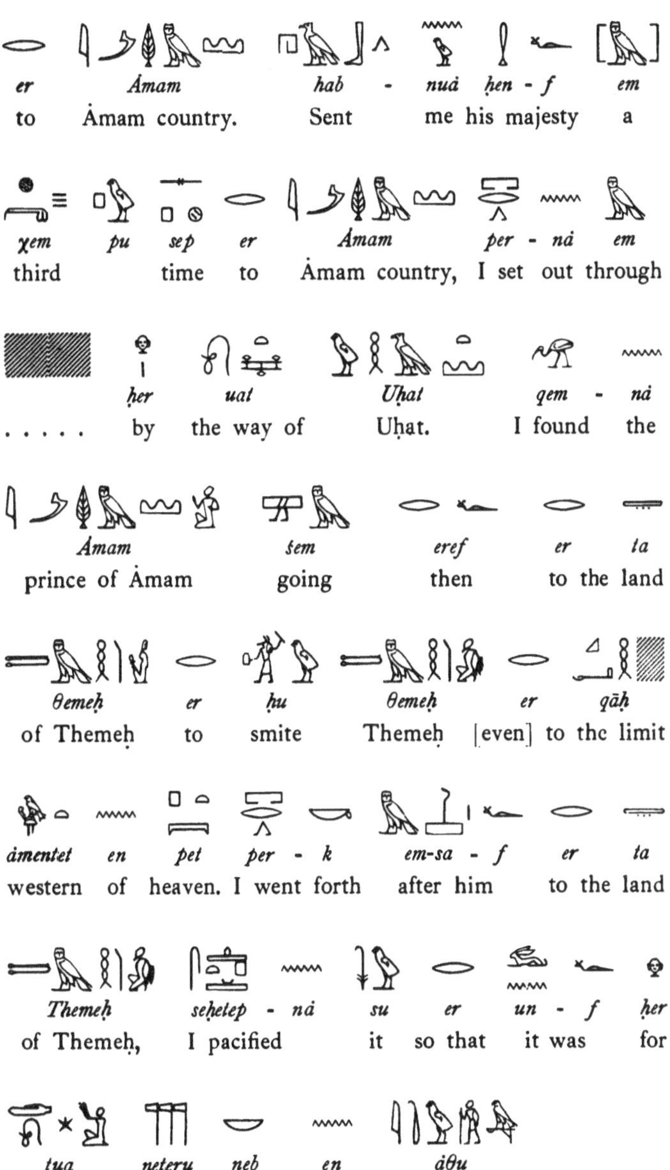

er *Ȧmam* *hab - nuȧ ḥen - f em*
to Ȧmam country. Sent me his majesty a

χem pu sep er Ȧmam per - nȧ em
third time to Ȧmam country, I set out through

ḥer uat Uḥat qem - nȧ
. . . . . by the way of Uḥat. I found the

Ȧmam šem eref er ta
prince of Ȧmam going then to the land

θemeḥ er ḥu θemeḥ er qāḥ
of Themeḥ to smite Themeḥ [even] to the limit

ȧmentet en pet per - k em-sa - f er ta
western of heaven. I went forth after him to the land

Themeḥ seḥetep - nȧ su er un - f ḥer
of Themeḥ, I pacified it so that it was for

ṭua neteru neb en ȧθu
adoring gods all of the Prince.

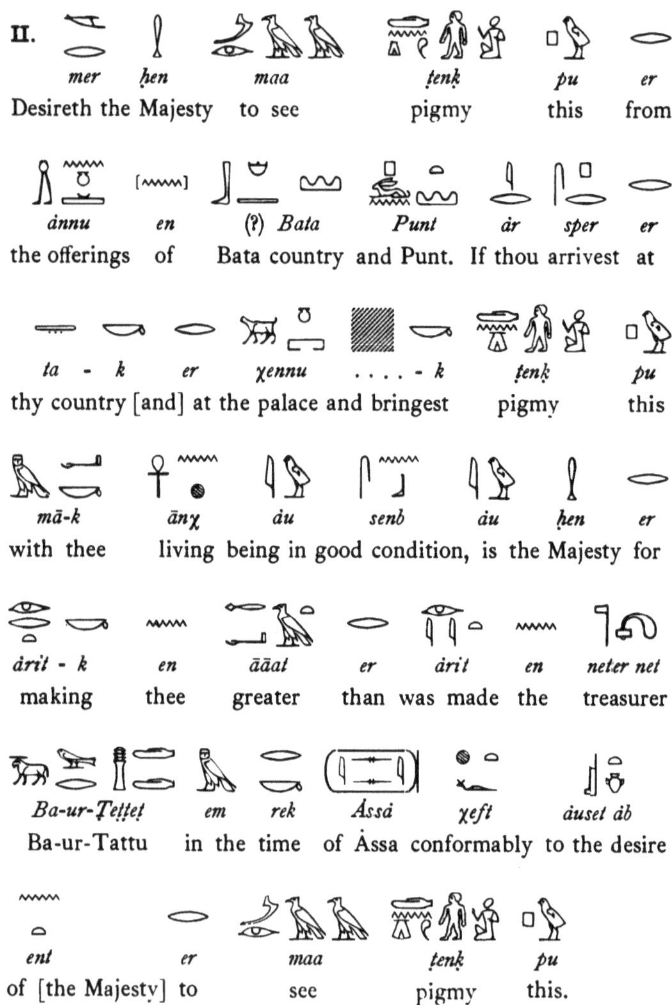

II. 

mer ḥen maa ṭenḳ pu er

Desireth the Majesty to see pigmy this from

ȧnnu en (?) *Bata Punt ȧr sper er*

the offerings of Bata country and Punt. If thou arrivest at

ta - k er χennu . . . . - k ṭenḳ pu

thy country [and] at the palace and bringest pigmy this

mā-k ānχ ȧu senb ȧu ḥen er

with thee living being in good condition, is the Majesty for

ȧrit - k en āāat er ȧrit en neter net

making thee greater than was made the treasurer

Ba-ur-Ṭeṭṭeṭ em rek Ȧssȧ χeft ȧuset ȧb

Ba-ur-Tattu in the time of Ȧssa conformably to the desire

ent er maa ṭenḳ pu

of [the Majesty] to see pigmy this.

FROM THE STELE OF ABU.

[XIth dynasty.]

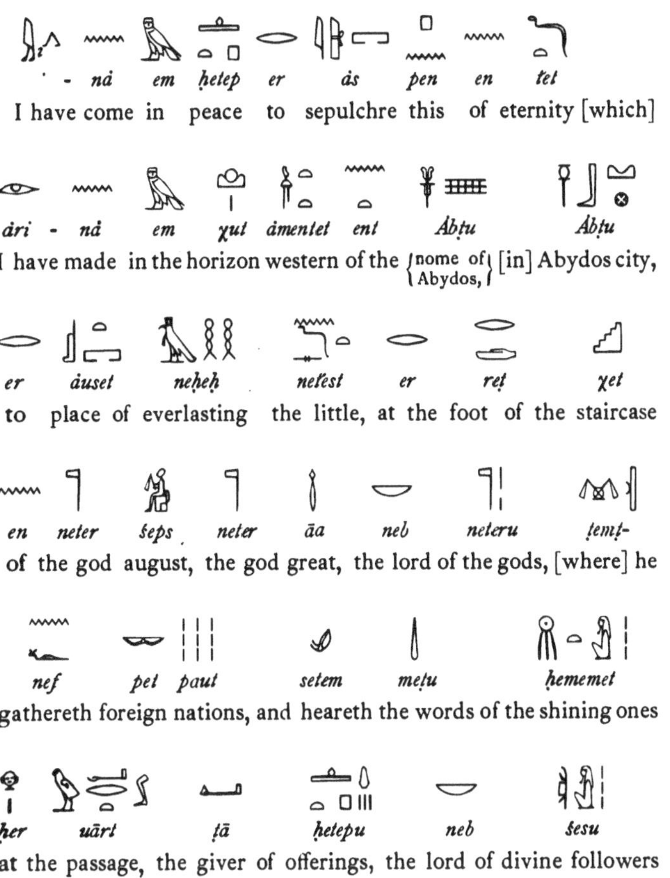

' - nȧ em ḥetep er ȧs pen en ṭet
I have come in peace to sepulchre this of eternity [which]

ȧri - nȧ em χut ȧmentet ent Ȧbṭu Ȧbṭu
I have made in the horizon western of the {nome of Abydos,} [in] Abydos city,

er ȧuset neḥeḥ netʼest er reṭ χet
to place of everlasting the little, at the foot of the staircase

en neter šeps neter āa neb neteru ṭemṭ-
of the god august, the god great, the lord of the gods, [where] he

nef pet paut setem meṭu ḥememet
gathereth foreign nations, and heareth the words of the shining ones

ḥer uārt ṭā ḥetepu neb šesu
at the passage, the giver of offerings, the lord of divine followers

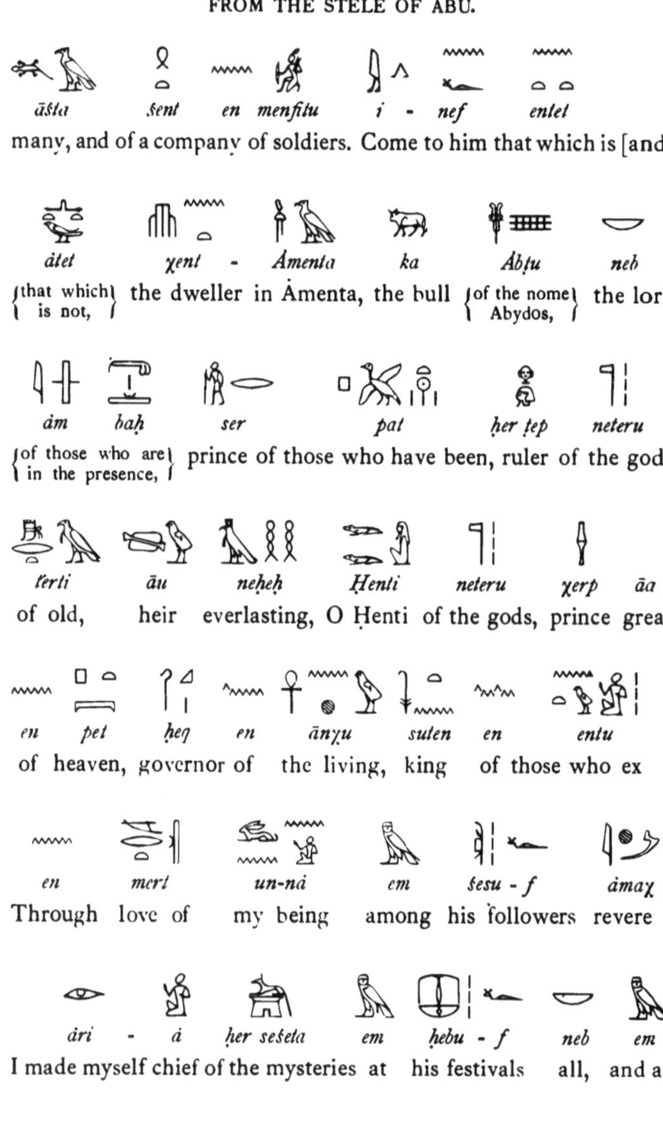

āšta šent en menfitu i - nef entet

many, and of a company of soldiers. Come to him that which is [and]

ȧtet χent - Ȧmenta ka Ȧbṭu neb

{that which is not,} the dweller in Ȧmenta, the bull {of the nome Abydos,} the lord

ȧm baḥ ser pat ḥer ṭep neteru

{of those who are in the presence,} prince of those who have been, ruler of the gods

ṭerti āu neḥeḥ Ḥenti neteru χerp āa

of old, heir everlasting, O Ḥenti of the gods, prince great

en pet ḥeq en ānχu suten en entu

of heaven, governor of the living, king of those who ex

en mert un-nȧ em šesu - f ȧmaχ

Through love of my being among his followers revere

ȧri - ȧ ḥer sešeta em ḥebu - f neb em

I made myself chief of the mysteries at his festivals all, and at

neṭemtet-f neb ṭeṭ en Ȧmentet nefert iu em

processions his all, [and] saith the Amenta beautiful : Come in

FROM THE STELE OF ABU.

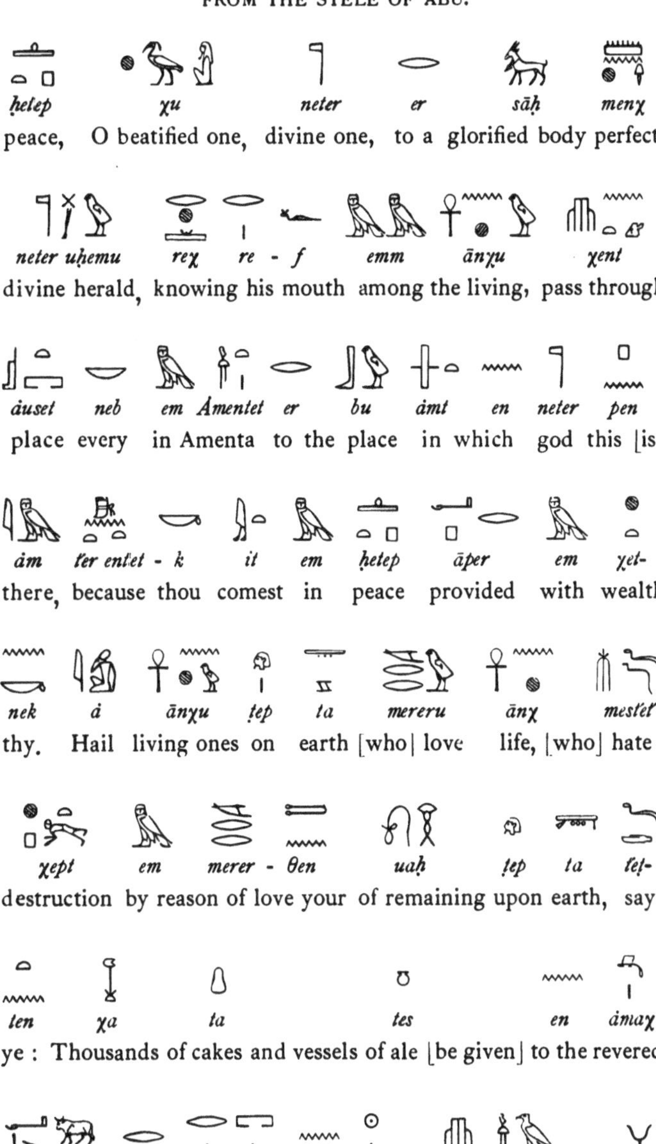

ḥetep χu neter er sāḥ menχ
peace, O beatified one, divine one, to a glorified body perfect,

neter uḥemu reχ re - f emm ānχu χent
divine herald, knowing his mouth among the living, pass through

àuset neb em Àmentet er bu àmt en neter pen
place every in Amenta to the place in which god this [is]

àm ťer entet - k it em ḥetep āper em χet-
there, because thou comest in peace provided with wealth

nek à ānχu ṭep ta mereru ānχ mesťeť
thy. Hail living ones on earth [who] love life, [who] hate

χept em merer - θen uaḥ ṭep ta ťeṭ-
destruction by reason of love your of remaining upon earth, say

ten χa ta tes en àmaχ
ye: Thousands of cakes and vessels of ale [be given] to the revered

Ābu er erper en Rā χent - Àmenta Àp-
Ābu in the temple of Rā, of Khent-Amenta, of Ap

FROM THE STELE OF ABU.

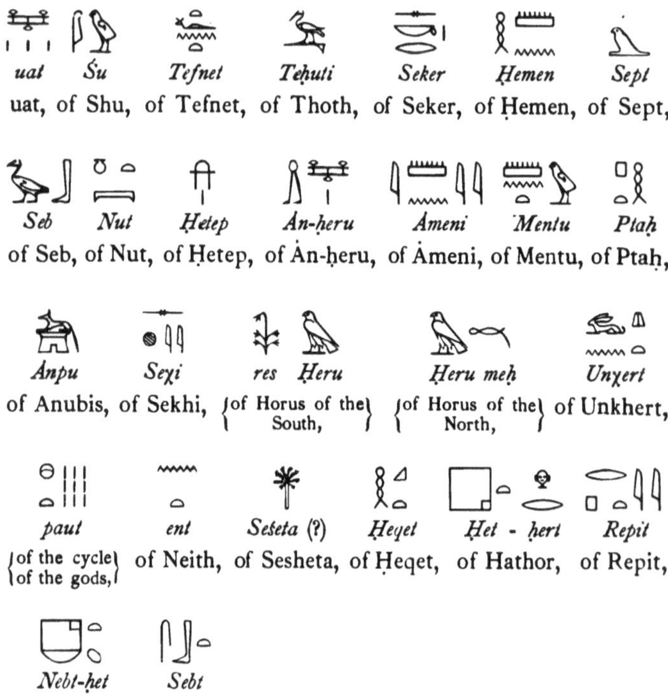

uat Śu Tefnet Teḥuti Seker Ḥemen Sept

uat, of Shu, of Tefnet, of Thoth, of Seker, of Ḥemen, of Sept,

Seb Nut Ḥetep Ȧn-ḥeru Ȧmeni Mentu Ptaḥ

of Seb, of Nut, of Ḥetep, of Ȧn-ḥeru, of Ȧmeni, of Mentu, of Ptaḥ,

Ȧnpu Seχi res Ḥeru Ḥeru meḥ Unχert

of Anubis, of Sekhi, {of Horus of the South,} {of Horus of the North,} of Unkhert,

paut ent Seśeta (?) Ḥeqet Ḥet - ḥert Repit

{of the cycle of the gods,} of Neith, of Sesheta, of Ḥeqet, of Hathor, of Repit,

Nebt-ḥet Sebt

of Nephthys, of Sebt.

INSCRIPTION OF ȦṬA.

[XIIth dynasty.]

renpit ȧbeṭ χemt Śemu hru χemt iut smer uāt

Year .... month three of summer, day three, came the "friend one",

mer ȧḥ Ȧṭȧ er sehat ȧner en

the overseer of cattle Ata to bring down a stone for

neter meri erpā ḥā χer-ḥeb smer

the god-beloved, {the hereditary prince,} the duke, {the chief reader,} the "friend

uāt mer res mer neter ḥen

one", the governor of the south, the overseer of the priests

Ȧmsu ṭatu - ȧqer ȧu seha - ni nef ȧner

of Amsu (or Min), Tchaut - ȧqer. I brought down to him a stone

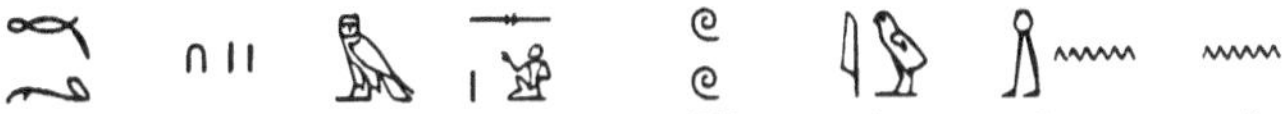

meḥ XII em sa CC ȧu ȧn - nȧ

of cubits twelve with men two hundred, I brought

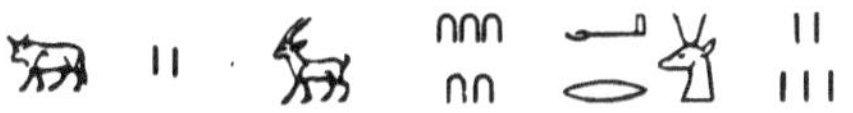

ȧḥ sen maḥeṭ L ār ṭua

oxen two, gazelles fifty, stags five.

ADDRESS TO THE LIVING BY KHNEMU-ḤETEP.

From his tomb at Beni-hasan.

[XIIth dynasty.]

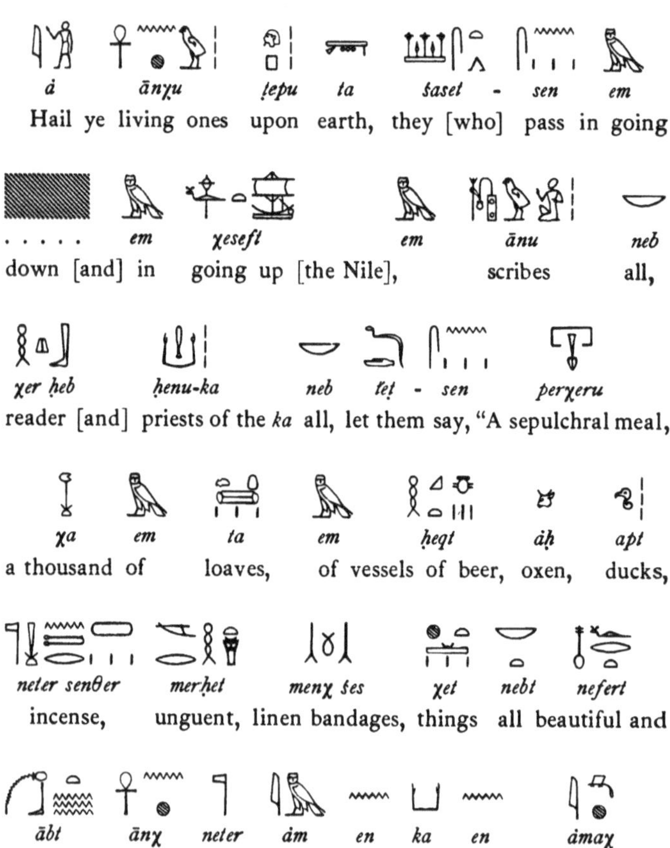

ȧ ānχu ṭepu ta šaset - sen em
Hail ye living ones upon earth, they [who] pass in going
. . . . . em χeseft em ānu neb
down [and] in going up [the Nile], scribes all,
χer ḥeb ḥenu-ka neb ṭeṭ - sen perχeru
reader [and] priests of the *ka* all, let them say, "A sepulchral meal,
χa em ta em ḥeqt āḥ apt
a thousand of loaves, of vessels of beer, oxen, ducks,
neter senθer merḥet menχ šes χet nebt nefert
incense, unguent, linen bandages, things all beautiful and
ābt ānχ neter ȧm en ka en ȧmaχ
pure liveth god on them to the *ka* of the revered one,

meti en sa seḥet neter ḥet χerp

arranger of the *sa* order of priests, inspector of the temple, chief of

neter ḥetep em eru-peru neteru nut ten

the divine offerings in the temples of the gods of city this,

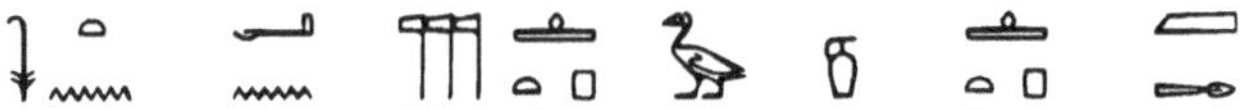

suten ān Neteru-ḥetep sa χnemu - ḥetep maāχeru

the royal scribe, Neteru-ḥetep's son Khnemu-ḥetep, triumphant."

FROM THE TOMB OF ȦMENI-EM-ḤĀT AT BENI-HASAN.

[XIIth dynasty.]

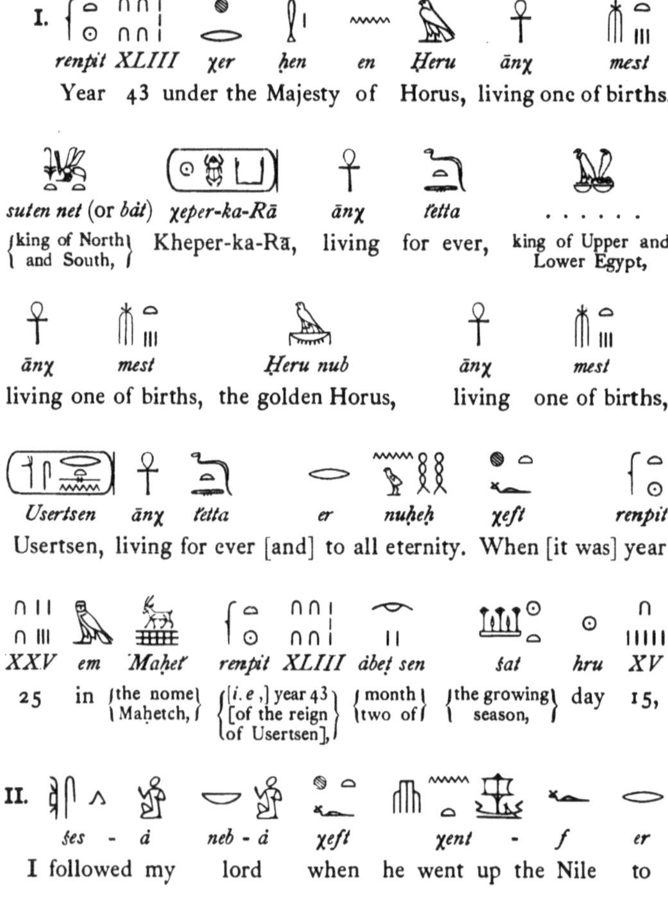

I.
renpit XLIII χer ḥen en Ḥeru ānχ mest
Year 43 under the Majesty of Horus, living one of births,
suten net (or bȧt) χeper-ka-Rā ānχ t'etta . . . . . .
king of North and South, Kheper-ka-Rā, living for ever, king of Upper and Lower Egypt,
ānχ mest Ḥeru nub ānχ mest
living one of births, the golden Horus, living one of births,
Usertsen ānχ t'etta er nuḥeḥ χeft renpit
Usertsen, living for ever [and] to all eternity. When [it was] year
XXV em Maḥet' renpit XLIII ȧbeṭ sen šat hru XV
25 in the nome Maḥetch, [i.e.,] year 43 [of the reign of Usertsen], month two of the growing season, day 15,
II.
šes - ȧ neb - ȧ χeft χent - f er
I followed my lord when he went up the Nile to

FROM THE TOMB OF ȦMENI-EM-ḤĀT AT BENI-HASAN.

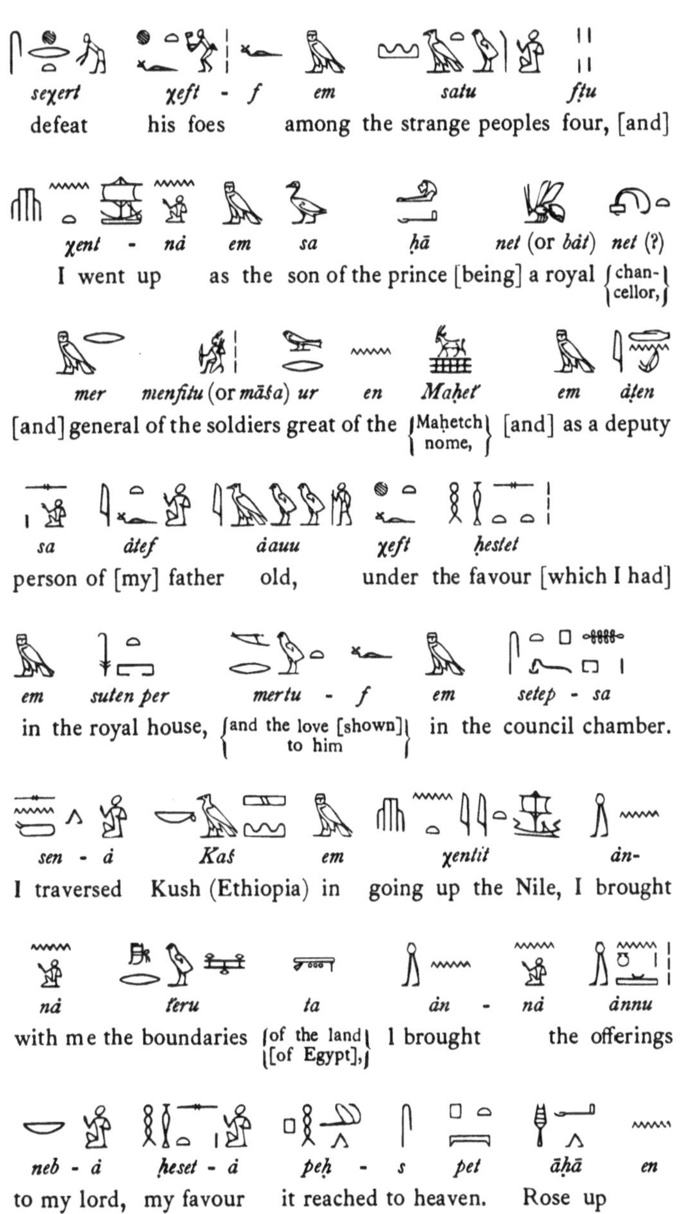

seχert *χeft - f* *em* *satu* *ftu*
defeat his foes among the strange peoples four, [and]

χent - nȧ *em* *sa* *ḥā* *net* (or *bȧt*) *net* (?)
I went up as the son of the prince [being] a royal {chancellor,}

mer *menfitu* (or *māša*) *ur* *en* *Maḥetʼ* *em* *ȧṭen*
[and] general of the soldiers great of the {Maḥetch nome,} [and] as a deputy

sa *ȧtef* *ȧauu* *χeft* *ḥestet*
person of [my] father old, under the favour [which I had]

em *suten per* *mertu - f* *em* *setep - sa*
in the royal house, {and the love [shown] to him} in the council chamber.

sen - ȧ *Kaš* *em* *χentit* *ȧn-*
I traversed Kush (Ethiopia) in going up the Nile, I brought

nȧ *ṭeru* *ta* *ȧn - nȧ* *ȧnnu*
with me the boundaries {of the land [of Egypt],} I brought the offerings

neb - ȧ *ḥeset - ȧ* *peḥ - s* *pet* *āḥā* *en*
to my lord, my favour it reached to heaven. Rose up

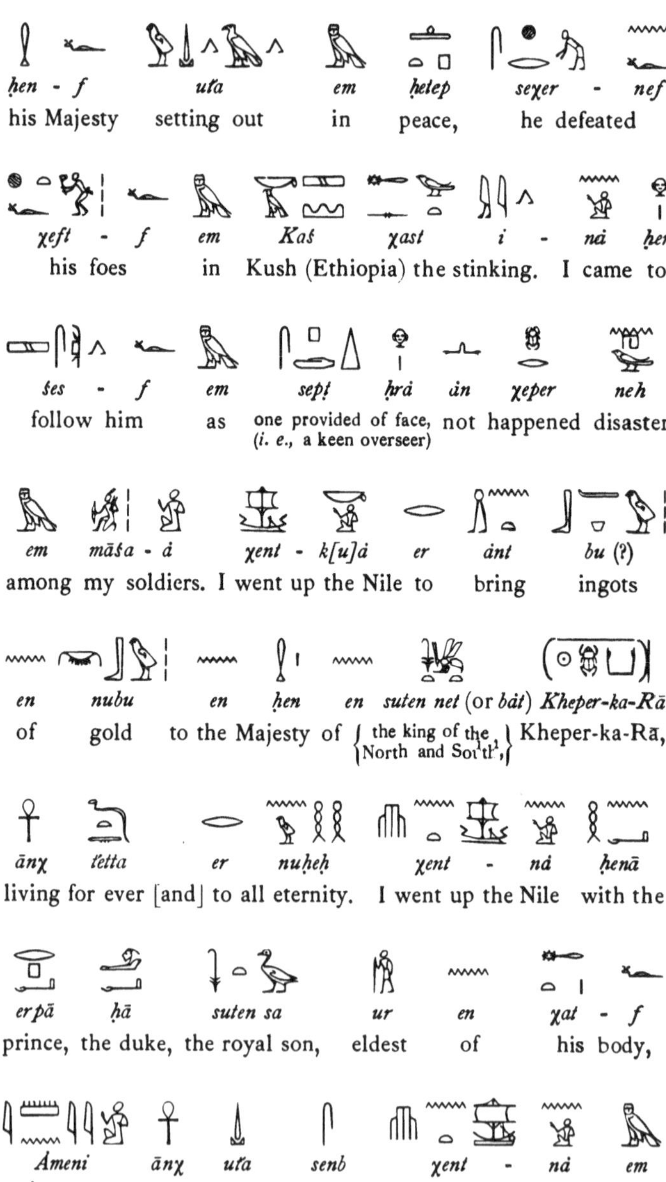

ḥen - f uṭa em ḥetep seχer - nef
his Majesty setting out in peace, he defeated

χeft - f em Kaš χast i - nȧ ḥer
his foes in Kush (Ethiopia) the stinking. I came to

šes - f em sepṭ ḥrȧ ȧn χeper neh
follow him as one provided of face, (*i. e.*, a keen overseer) not happened disaster

em māša - ȧ χent - k[u]ȧ er ȧnt bu (?)
among my soldiers. I went up the Nile to bring ingots

en nubu en ḥen en suten net (or *bȧt*) *Kheper-ka-Rā*
of gold to the Majesty of {the king of the North and South,} Kheper-ka-Rā,

ānχ ṫetta er nuḥeḥ χent - nȧ ḥenā
living for ever [and] to all eternity. I went up the Nile with the

erpā ḥā suten sa ur en χat - f
prince, the duke, the royal son, eldest of his body,

Ȧmeni ānχ uṭa senb χent - nȧ em
Ȧmeni, life, strength, health! I went up the Nile with

FROM THE TOMB OF ȦMENI-EM-ḤĀT AT BENI-HASAN.

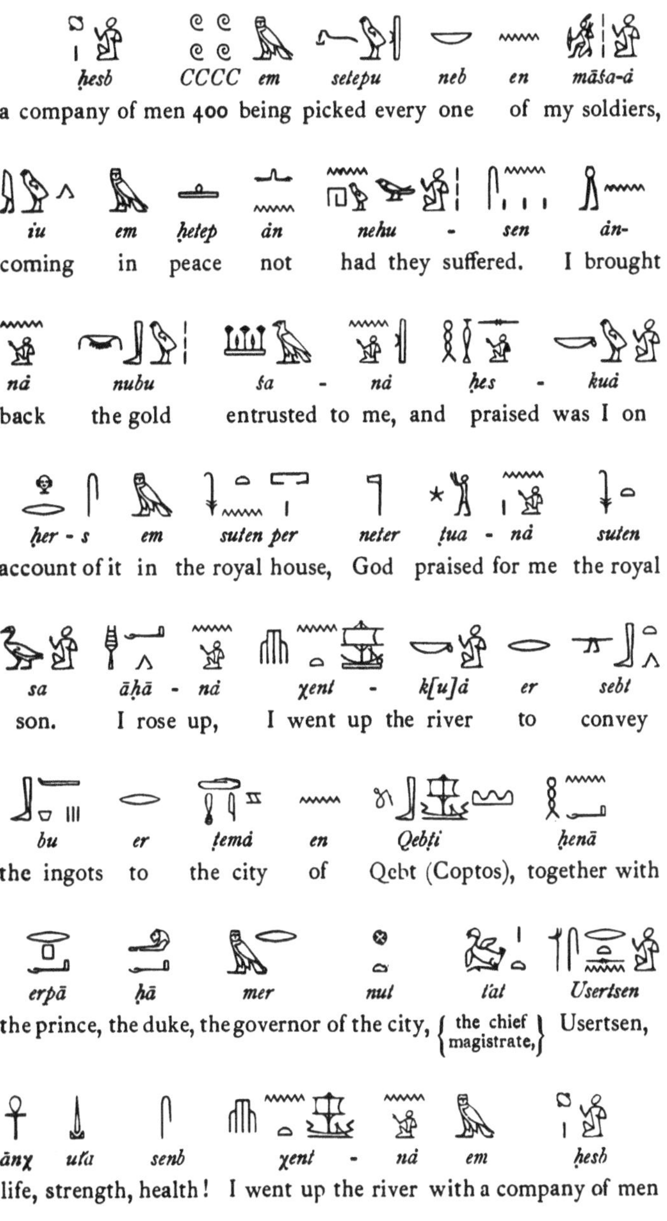

ḥesb CCCC em setepu neb en māša-ȧ
a company of men 400 being picked every one of my soldiers,

iu em ḥetep ȧn nehu - sen ȧn-
coming in peace not had they suffered. I brought

nȧ nubu ša - nȧ ḥes - kuȧ
back the gold entrusted to me, and praised was I on

ḥer - s em suten per neter ṭua - nȧ suten
account of it in the royal house, God praised for me the royal

sa āḥā - nȧ χent - k[u]ȧ er sebt
son. I rose up, I went up the river to convey

bu er ṭemȧ en Qebṭi ḥenā
the ingots to the city of Qebt (Coptos), together with

erpā ḥā mer nut ṭ'at Usertsen
the prince, the duke, the governor of the city, {the chief magistrate,} Usertsen,

ānχ uṭa senb χent - nȧ em ḥesb
life, strength, health! I went up the river with a company of men

FROM THE TOMB OF ÀMENI-EM-ḤĀT AT BENI-HASAN.

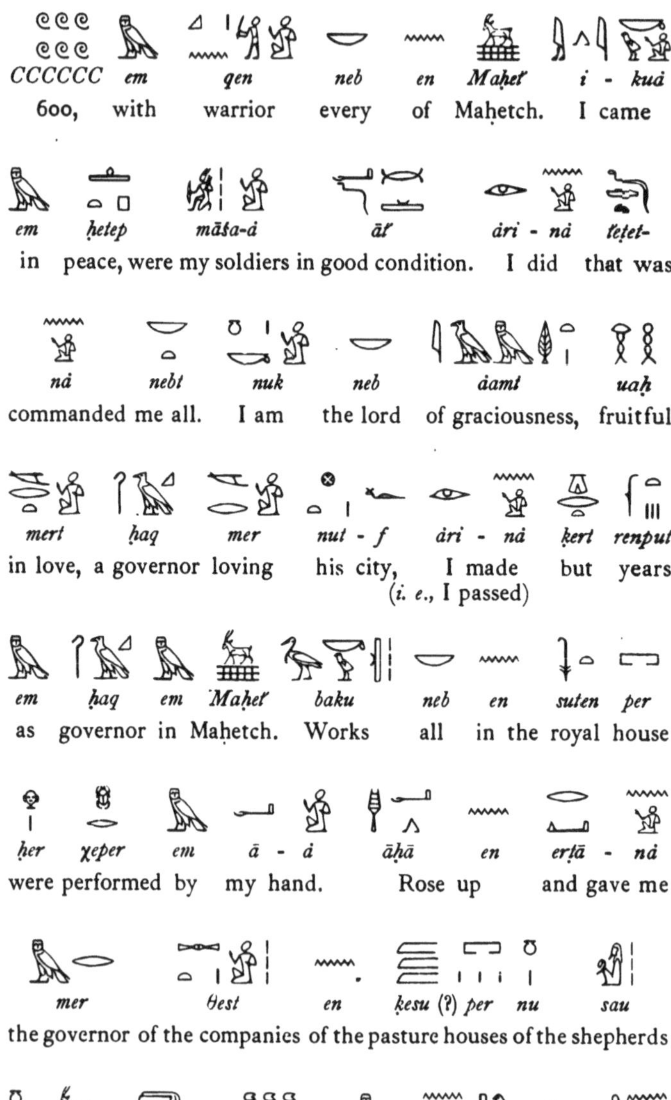

CCCCCC em qen neb en Maḥeṭ i - kuȧ
600, with warrior every of Maḥetch. I came

em ḥetep māša-ȧ āṭ ȧri - nȧ ṭeṭeṭ-
in peace, were my soldiers in good condition. I did that was

nȧ nebt nuk neb ȧamt uaḥ
commanded me all. I am the lord of graciousness, fruitful

mert ḥaq mer nut - f ȧri - nȧ ḳert renput
in love, a governor loving his city, I made (*i. e.*, I passed) but years

em ḥaq em Maḥeṭ baku neb en suten per
as governor in Maḥetch. Works all in the royal house

ḥer χeper em ā - ȧ āḥā en erṭā - nȧ
were performed by my hand. Rose up and gave me

mer θest en ḳesu (?) per nu sau
the governor of the companies of the pasture houses of the shepherds

nu Maḥeṭ ka MMM em nuḥbu - sen
of Maḥetch bulls three thousand of their yoke animals,

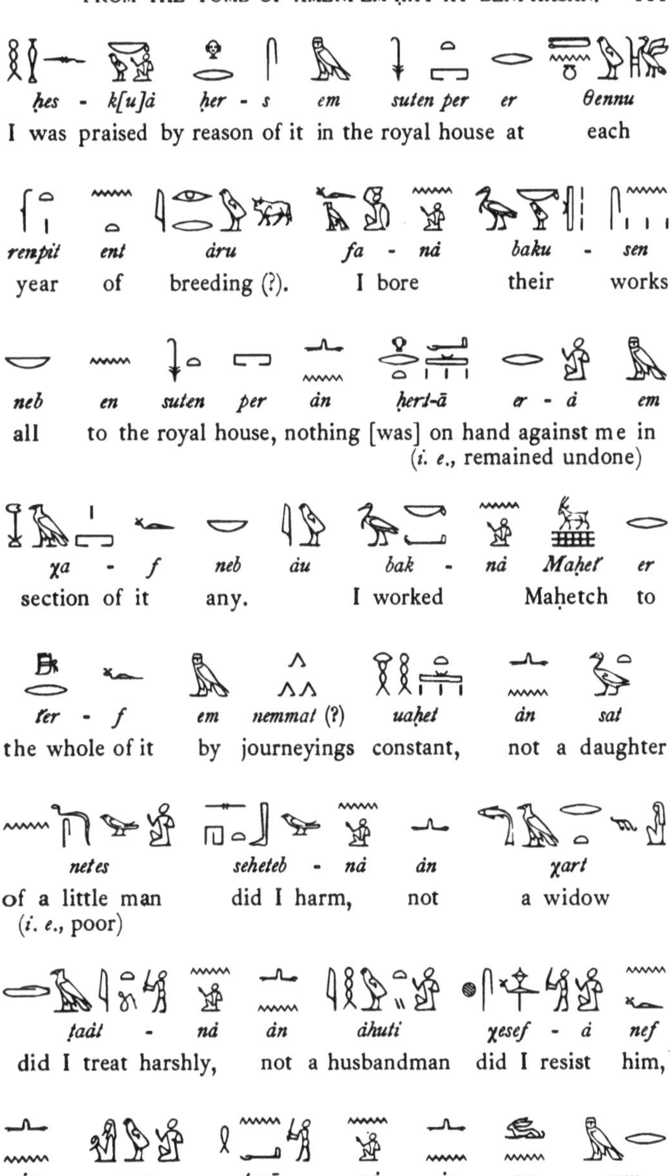

ḥes - k[u]ȧ ḥer - s em suten per er θennu
I was praised by reason of it in the royal house at each

renpit ent ȧru fa - nȧ baku - sen
year of breeding (?). I bore their works

neb en suten per ȧn ḥert-ā er - ȧ em
all to the royal house, nothing [was] on hand against me in
(*i. e.*, remained undone)

χa - f neb ȧu bak - nȧ Maḥet' er
section of it any. I worked Maḥetch to

t'er - f em nemmat (?) uaḥet ȧn sat
the whole of it by journeyings constant, not a daughter

netes seheteb - nȧ ȧn χart
of a little man did I harm, not a widow
(*i. e.*, poor)

ṭaȧt - nȧ ȧn ȧhuti χesef - ȧ nef
did I treat harshly, not a husbandman did I resist him,

ȧn sau šenā - nȧ ȧn un mer
not a shepherd did I turn back, not existed overseer

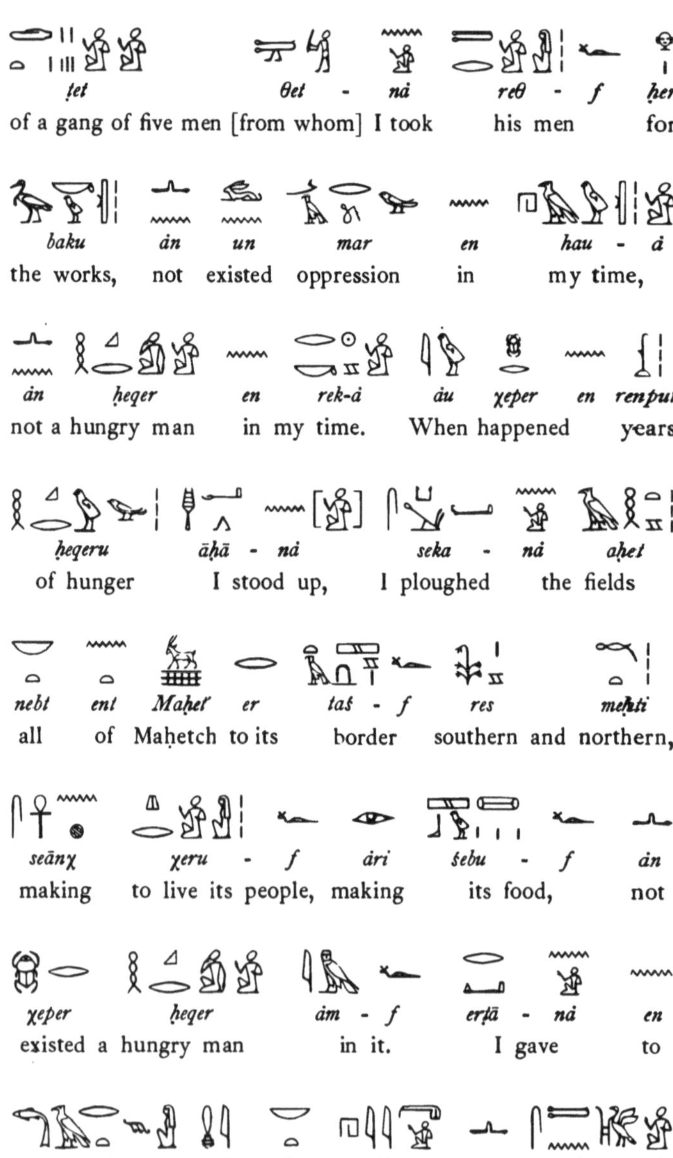

ṭet θet - nà reθ - f ḥer
of a gang of five men [from whom] I took his men for

baku àn un mar en hau - à
the works, not existed oppression in my time,

àn ḥeqer en rek-à àu χeper en renput
not a hungry man in my time. When happened years

ḥeqeru āḥā - nà seka - nà aḥet
of hunger I stood up, I ploughed the fields

nebt ent Maḥeṭ er taš - f res meḥti
all of Maḥetch to its border southern and northern,

seānχ χeru - f àri šebu - f àn
making to live its people, making its food, not

χeper ḥeqer àm - f erṭā - nà en
existed a hungry man in it. I gave to

χart mà nebt hi àn seθen - à
the widow as to the possessor of a husband, not did I magnify

FROM THE TOMB OF ȦMENI-EM-ḤĀT AT BENI-HASAN.

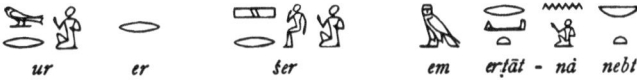

ur er šer em erṭāt - nȧ nebt

the firstborn at the expense of the young child in [what] I gave all.

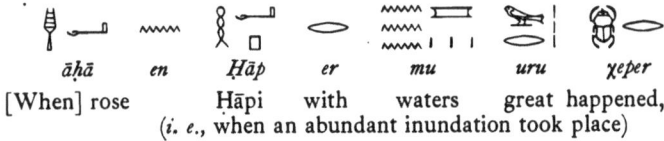

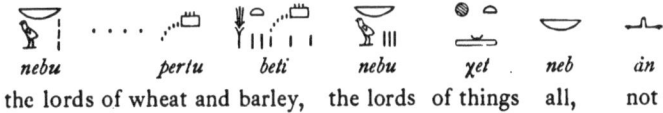

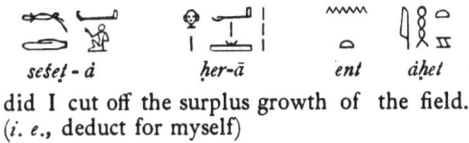

āḥā en Ḥāp er mu uru χeper

[When] rose Ḥāpi with waters great happened,
(*i. e.*, when an abundant inundation took place)

nebu pertu beti nebu χet neb ȧn

the lords of wheat and barley, the lords of things all, not

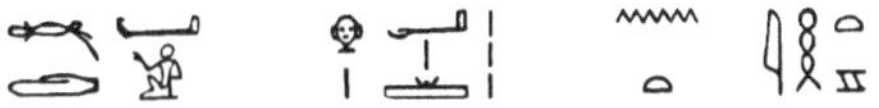

sešeṭ - ȧ ḥer-ā ent ȧḥet

did I cut off the surplus growth of the field.
(*i. e.*, deduct for myself)

STORIES OF THE REIGNS OF SENEFERU AND KHUFU (CHEOPS).

[Early XVIIIth dynasty.]

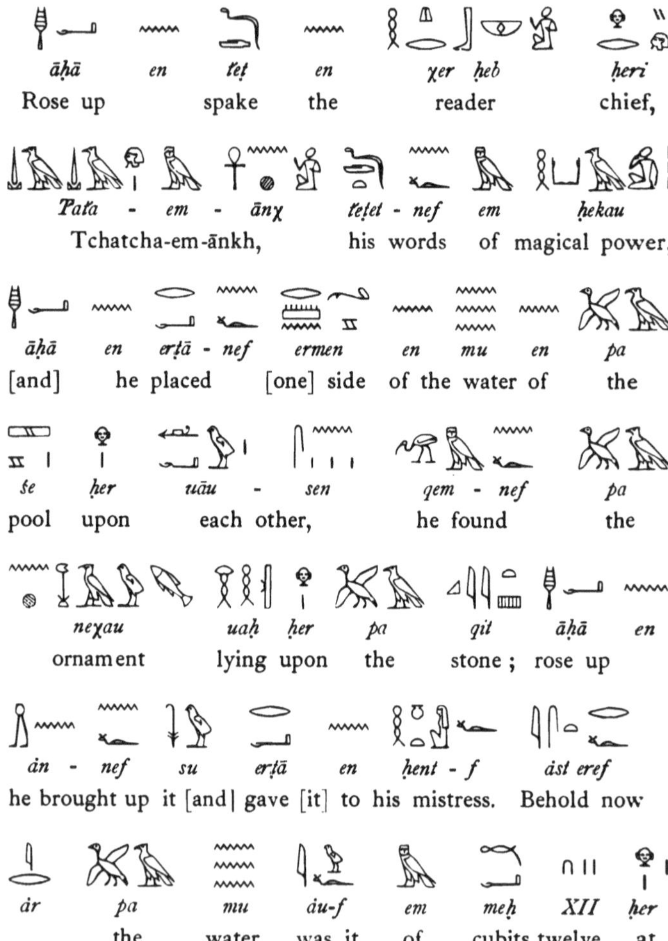

ȧat - f ṭerȧ - nef meḥ XXIV er sa

its back, [but] reached it cubits twenty-four after
(*i. e.*, in its deepest place)

uṭeb - f āḥā en ṭeṭ - nef ṭeṭet - nef

it had been doubled. Rose up he spake his words

em ḥekau āḥā en ȧn - nef na en

of magical power. Rose up he brought back the

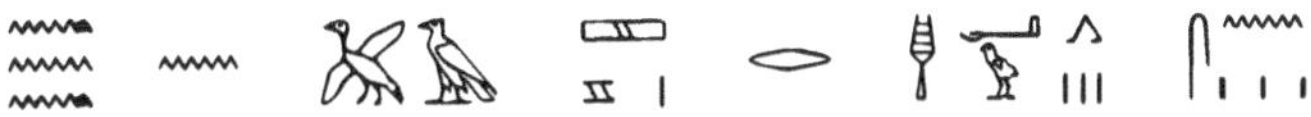

mu en pa še er āḥāu - sen

waters of the pool to their [former] state.

urš en ḥen - f ḥer hru nefer ḥenā

Passed the day his Majesty in [making] a day good with

suten per ānχ uṭa senb mȧ qȧ - f per

[his] royal house, life, strength, health, as was his form. Coming
(*i. e.*, his wont)

en feqa - nef χer ḥeb ḥeri

forth rewarded he the reader chief,

Ṭaṭa - em - ānχ em bu neb nefer

Tchatcha-em-ānkh, with thing every good.

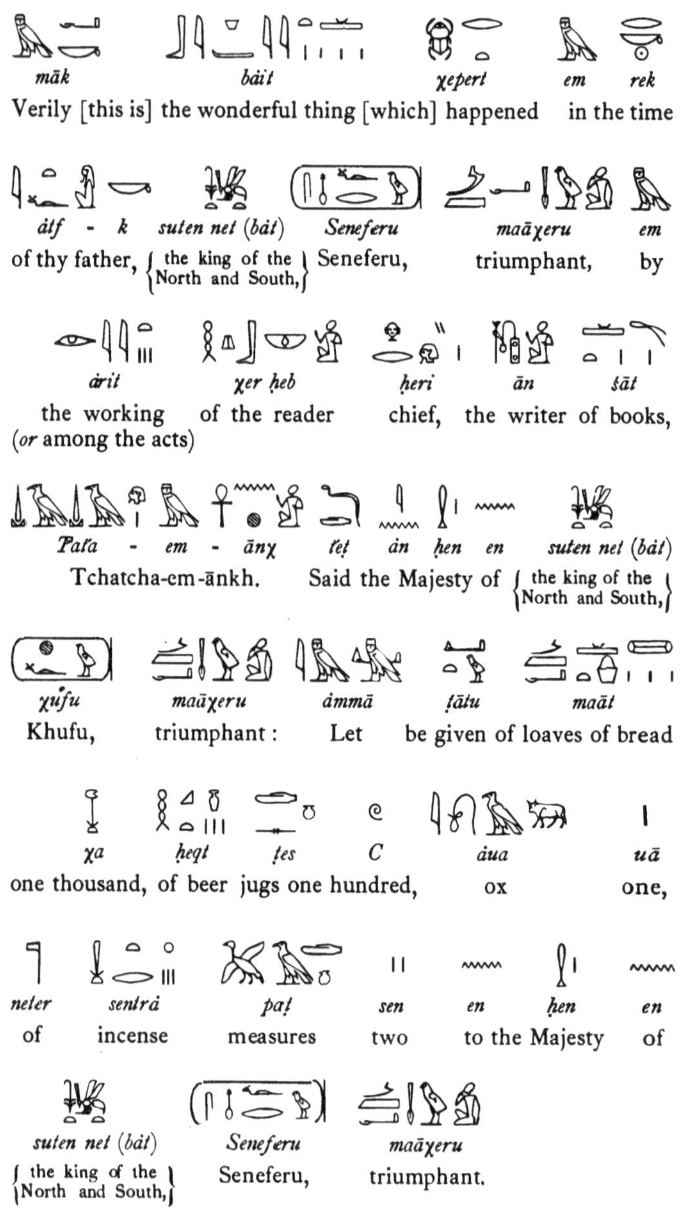

māk *bȧit* *χepert* *em* *rek*
Verily [this is] the wonderful thing [which] happened in the time

ȧtf - *k* *suten net* (*bȧt*) *Seneferu* *maāχeru* *em*
of thy father, {the king of the North and South,} Seneferu, triumphant, by

ȧrit *χer ḥeb* *ḥeri* *ān* *šāt*
the working (*or* among the acts) of the reader chief, the writer of books,

Ṫaṫa - *em* - *ānχ* *ṫeṭ* *ȧn* *ḥen* *en* *suten net* (*bȧt*)
Tchatcha-em-ānkh. Said the Majesty of {the king of the North and South,}

χufu *maāχeru* *ȧmmā* *ṭātu* *maāt*
Khufu, triumphant: Let be given of loaves of bread

χa *ḥeqt* *ṭes* *C* *ȧua* *uā*
one thousand, of beer jugs one hundred, ox one,

neter *sentrȧ* *paṭ* *sen* *en* *ḥen* *en*
of incense measures two to the Majesty of

suten net (*bȧt*) *Seneferu* *maāχeru*
{the king of the North and South,} Seneferu, triumphant.

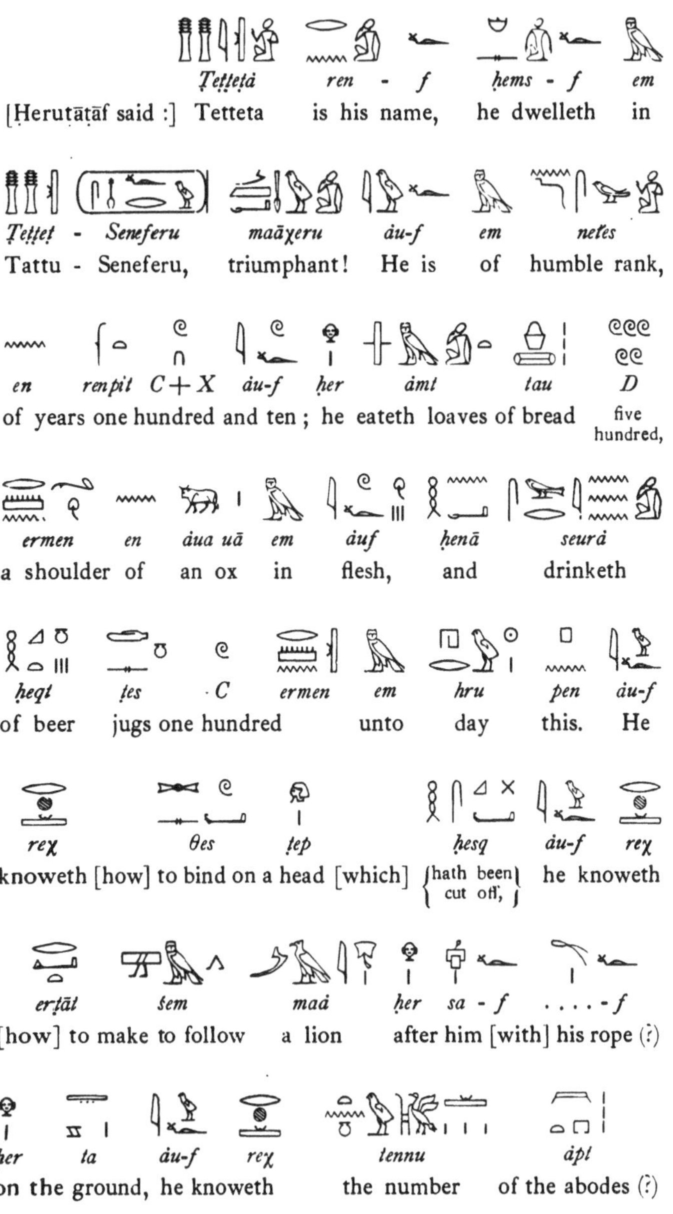

Ṭeṭṭeṭȧ ren - f ḥems - f em

[Ḥeruṭāṭāf said :] Tetteta is his name, he dwelleth in

Ṭeṭṭeṭ - Seneferu maāχeru ȧu-f em neṭes

Tattu - Seneferu, triumphant! He is of humble rank,

en renpit C + X ȧu-f ḥer ȧmt tau D

of years one hundred and ten ; he eateth loaves of bread five hundred,

ermen en ȧua uā em ȧuf ḥenā seurȧ

a shoulder of an ox in flesh, and drinketh

ḥeqt ṭes C ermen em hru pen ȧu-f

of beer jugs one hundred unto day this. He

reχ θes ṭep ḥesq ȧu-f reχ

knoweth [how] to bind on a head [which] {hath been cut off,} he knoweth

erṭāt šem maȧ ḥer sa - f . . . . - f

[how] to make to follow a lion after him [with] his rope (?)

ḥer ta ȧu-f reχ tennu ȧpt

on the ground, he knoweth the number of the abodes (?)

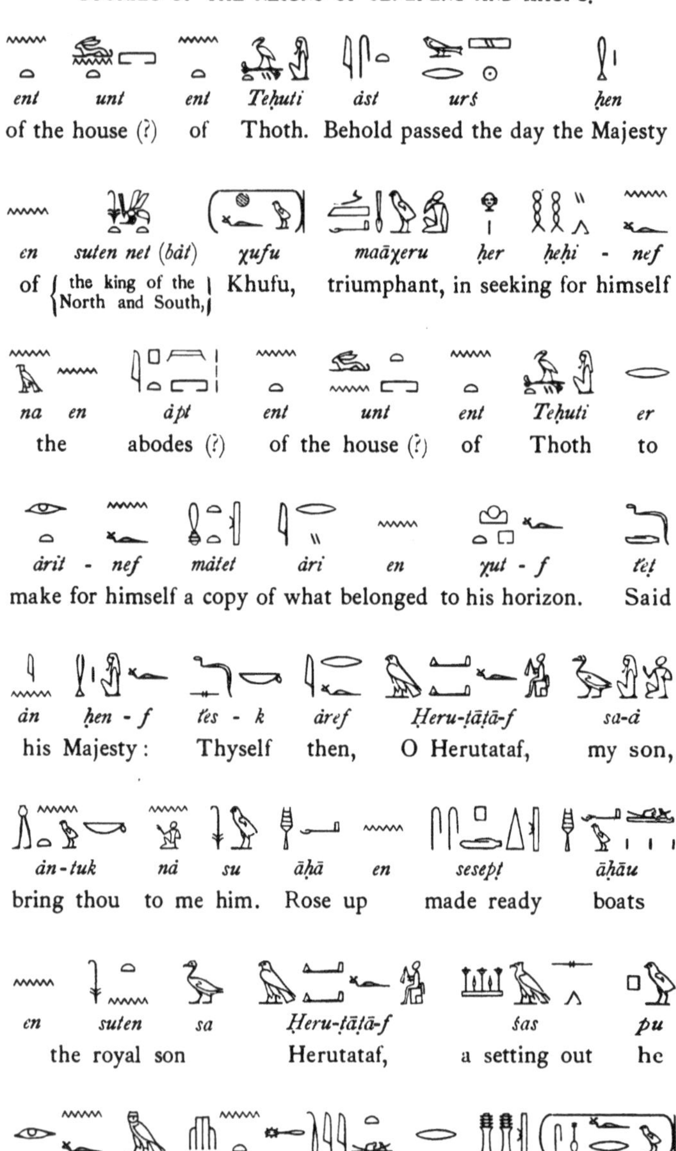

ent unt ent Teḥuti ȧst urš ḥen
of the house (?) of Thoth. Behold passed the day the Majesty

en suten net (bȧt) χufu maāχeru ḥer ḥeḥi - nef
of {the king of the North and South,} Khufu, triumphant, in seeking for himself

na en ȧpt ent unt ent Teḥuti er
the abodes (?) of the house (?) of Thoth to

ȧrit - nef mȧtet ȧri en χut - f ṭeṭ
make for himself a copy of what belonged to his horizon. Said

ȧn ḥen - f ṭes - k ȧref Ḥeru-ṭāṭā-f sa-ȧ
his Majesty: Thyself then, O Herutataf, my son,

ȧn - tuk nȧ su āḥā en sesept āḥāu
bring thou to me him. Rose up made ready boats

en suten sa Ḥeru-ṭāṭā-f šas pu
the royal son Herutataf, a setting out he

ȧri - nef em χentχaθit er Ṭeṭṭeṭ - Seneferu
made in sailing up the river to Tattu - Seneferu,

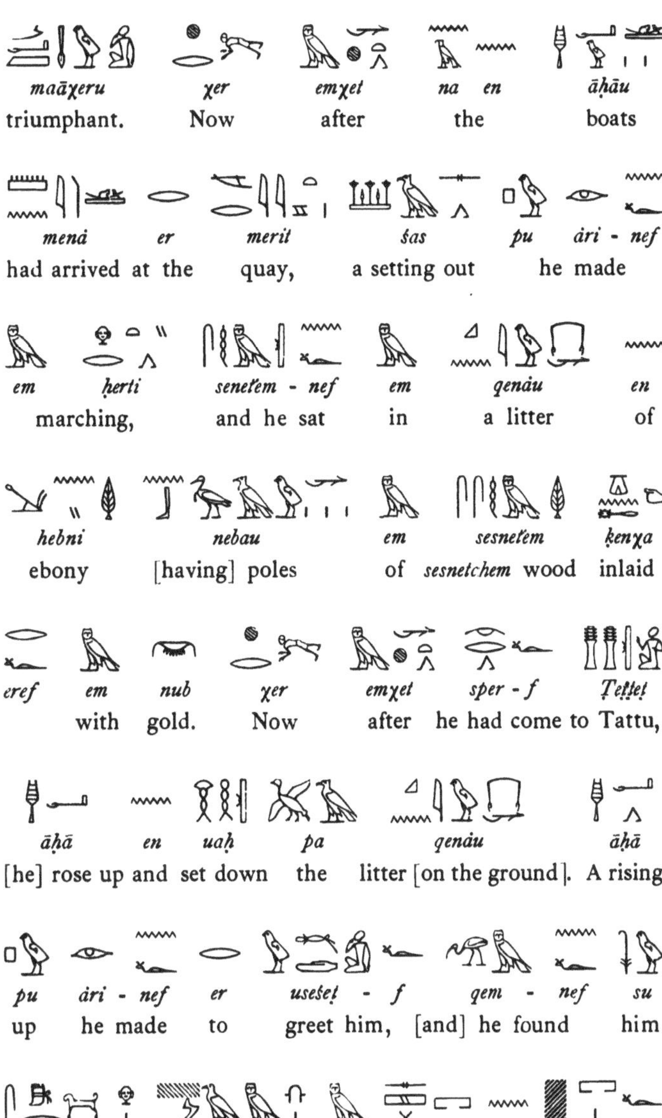

maāχeru χer emχet na en āḥāu
triumphant. Now after the boats

menȧ er merit šas pu ȧri - nef
had arrived at the quay, a setting out he made

em ḥerti seneťem - nef em qenȧu en
marching, and he sat in a litter of

hebni nebau em sesneťem ḳenχa
ebony [having] poles of *sesnetchem* wood inlaid

eref em nub χer emχet sper - f Ṭeṭṭeṭ
with gold. Now after he had come to Tattu,

āḥā en uaḥ pa qenȧu āḥā
[he] rose up and set down the litter [on the ground]. A rising

pu ȧri - nef er usešeṭ - f qem - nef su
up he made to greet him, [and] he found him

sťer ḥer . . . . maam em seš en per - f
lying upon a mattress (?) (or wicker couch [?]) at the door of his house,

ḥenu *χer* *ṭep - f* *ḥer* *āmām-*

[with] one servant at his head that he might rub (?)

nef *ki* *ḥer* *sȧnu* *reṭui-f*

it, [and] another to chafe his feet. . . . . . .

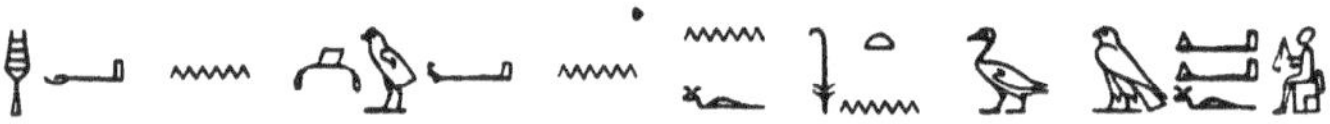

āḥā *en* *āu* *en* *nef* *suten* *sa* *Ḥeru-ṭāṭā-f*

Rose up stretched out to him the royal son Herutataf

āāui-f *āḥā* *en* *seāḥā - nef* *su* *uťa*

his hands, rising he made to stand up him, a going

pu *ȧri - nef* *ḥenā - f* *er* *merit* *ḥer* *erṭāt - nef*

forth he made with him to the quay to give him

ā - f *āḥā* *en* *ťeṭ* *en* *Ṭeṭṭeṭȧ* *ȧmmā*

his arm. Rose up said Tetteta : Prithee

ṭātu - nȧ *uāu* *en* *qaqau* *ȧn-tu-f*

be given to me a *qaqau* boat, let one bring

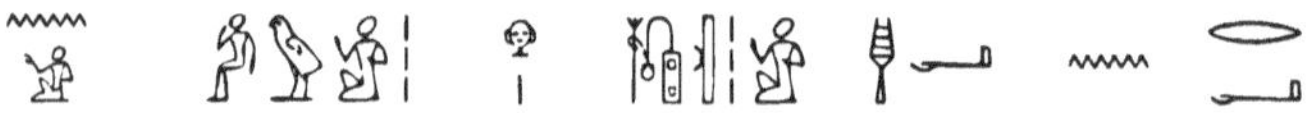

nȧ *χerṭu-ȧ* *ḥer* *ānu-ȧ* *āḥā* *en* *erṭā*

to me my children with my books. Rose up was made

āḥā - nef uàa sen ḥenā qet - sen iut

to stand for him boats two with their sailors. A going

pu àri en Ṭeṭṭeṭà em χeṭ em useχ

made Tetteta sailing down the Nile in the boat

enti suten sa Ḥeru-ṭāṭā-f àm - f χer

which the royal son Herutataf was in it. Now

emχet sper - f er χennu āq pu àri

after he had arrived at the palace an entrance made

en suten sa Ḥeru-ṭāṭā-f er semàit en

the royal son Herutataf to inform the

ḥen en suten net χufu maāχeru ṭeṭ àn

Majesty of {the king of the North and South,} Khufu, triumphant. Said the

suten sa Ḥeru-ṭāṭā-f àθi ānχ uṭa senb

royal son Herutataf: O Prince, life, strength, health,

neb - à 'u àn-nà Ṭeṭṭeṭà ṭeṭ àn ḥen - f

my lord, I have brought Tetteta. Said his Majesty:

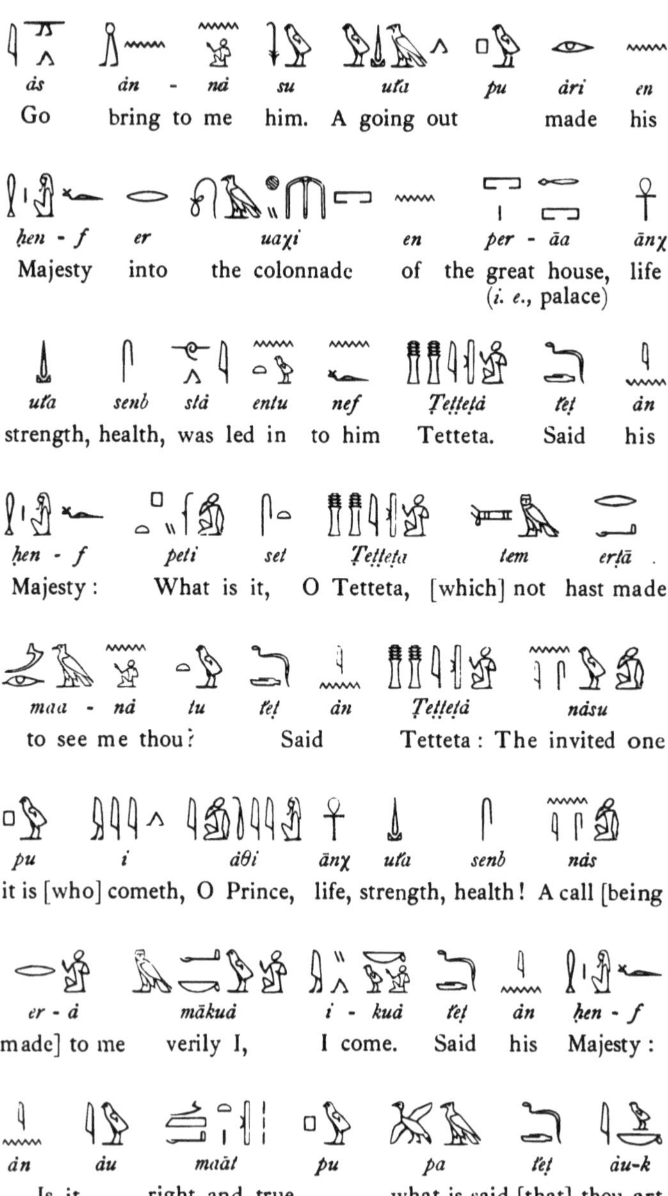

ȧs ȧn - nȧ su uťa pu ȧri en

Go bring to me him. A going out made his

ḥen - f er uaχi en per - āa ānχ

Majesty into the colonnade of the great house, life
(*i. e.*, palace)

uťa senb stȧ entu nef Ṭeṭṭeṭȧ ťeṭ ȧn

strength, health, was led in to him Tetteta. Said his

ḥen - f peti set Ṭeṭṭeṭa tem erṭā

Majesty: What is it, O Tetteta, [which] not hast made

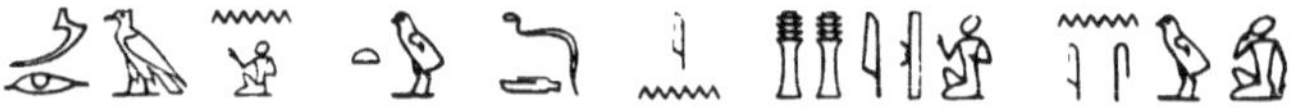

maa - nȧ tu ťeṭ ȧn Ṭeṭṭeṭȧ nȧsu

to see me thou? Said Tetteta: The invited one

pu i ȧθi ānχ uťa senb nȧs

it is [who] cometh, O Prince, life, strength, health! A call [being

er - ȧ mākuȧ i - kuȧ ťeṭ ȧn ḥen - f

made] to me verily I, I come. Said his Majesty:

ȧn ȧu maāt pu pa ťeṭ ȧu-k

Is it right and true what is said [that] thou art

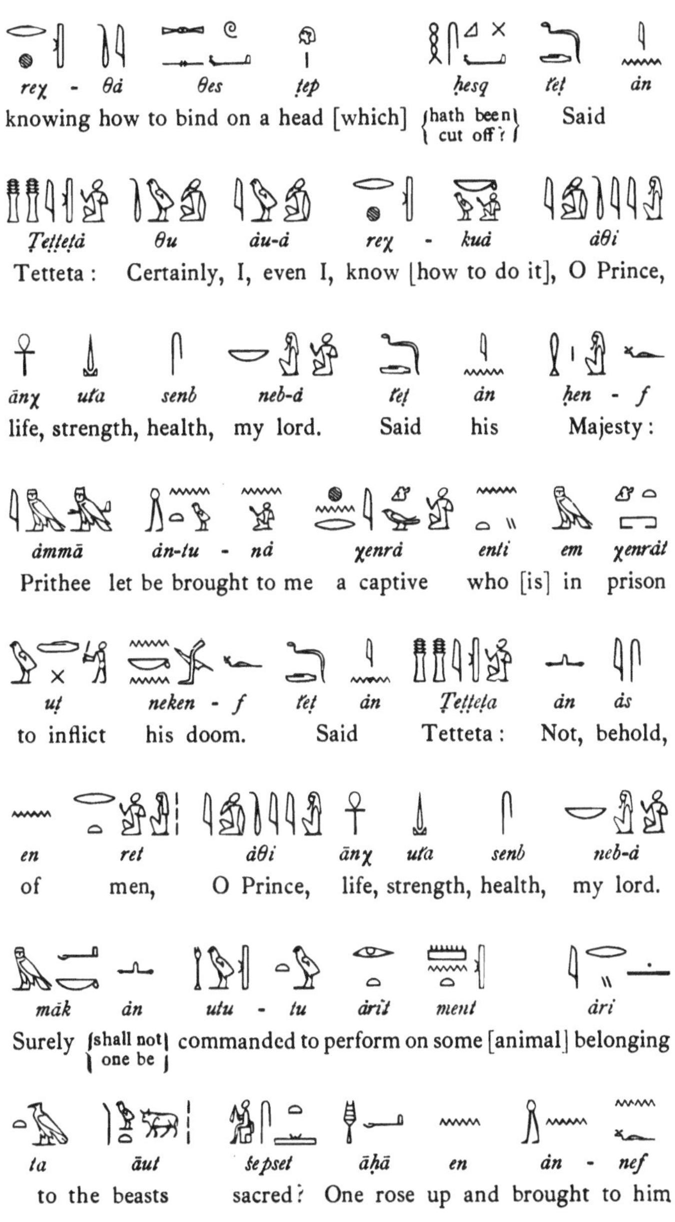

rex - θà θes tep ḥesq ṭeṭ àn

knowing how to bind on a head [which] {hath been cut off?} Said

Ṭeṭṭeṭà θu àu-à rex - kuà àθi

Tetteta : Certainly, I, even I, know [how to do it], O Prince,

ānx uṭa senb neb-à ṭeṭ àn ḥen - f

life, strength, health, my lord. Said his Majesty :

àmmā àn-tu - nà xenrà enti em xenràt

Prithee let be brought to me a captive who [is] in prison

uṭ neken - f ṭeṭ àn Ṭeṭṭeṭa àn às

to inflict his doom. Said Tetteta : Not, behold,

en ret àθi ānx uṭa senb neb-à

of men, O Prince, life, strength, health, my lord.

māk àn utu - tu àrit ment àri

Surely {shall not one be} commanded to perform on some [animal] belonging

ta āut šepset āḥā en àn - nef

to the beasts sacred? One rose up and brought to him

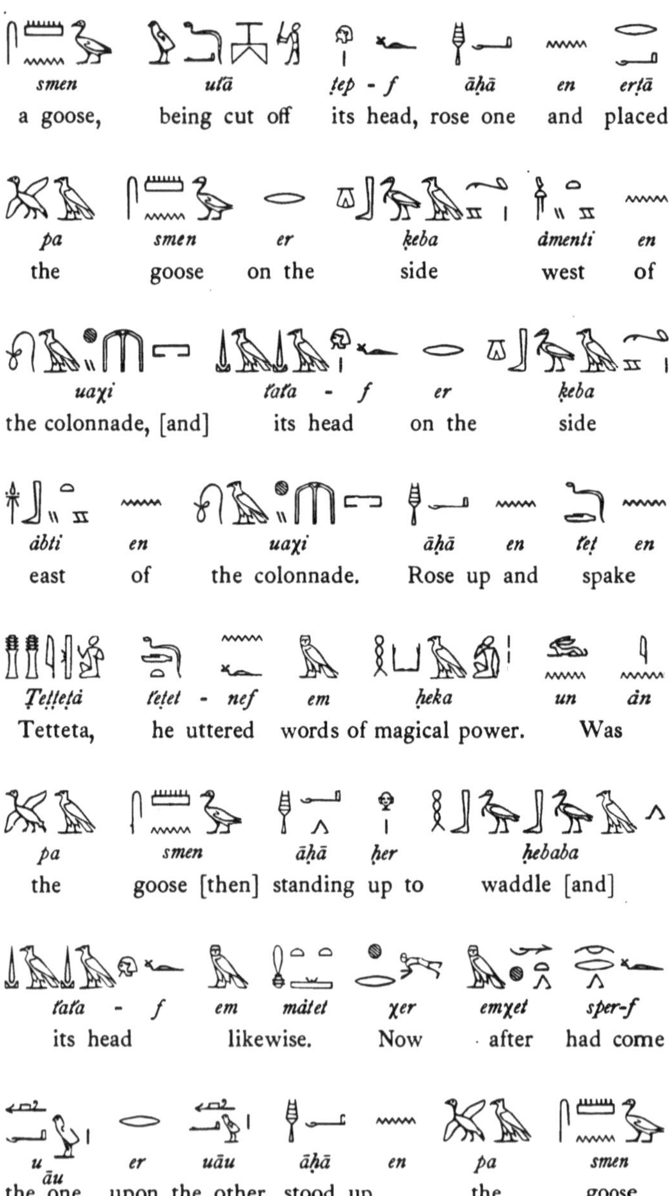

smen *ut'ā* *ṭep - f* *āḥā* *en* *erṭā*
a goose, being cut off its head, rose one and placed

pa *smen* *er* *ḳeba* *ȧmenti* *en*
the goose on the side west of

uaχi *t'at'a - f* *er* *ḳeba*
the colonnade, [and] its head on the side

ȧbti *en* *uaχi* *āḥā* *en* *t'eṭ* *en*
east of the colonnade. Rose up and spake

Ṭeṭṭeṭȧ *t'eṭet - nef* *em* *ḥeka* *un* *ȧn*
Tetteta, he uttered words of magical power. Was

pa *smen* *āḥā* *ḥer* *ḥebaba*
the goose [then] standing up to waddle [and]

t'at'a - f *em* *mȧtet* *χer* *emχet* *sper-f*
its head likewise. Now after had come

u *āu* *er* *uāu* *āḥā* *en* *pa* *smen*
the one upon the other, stood up the goose

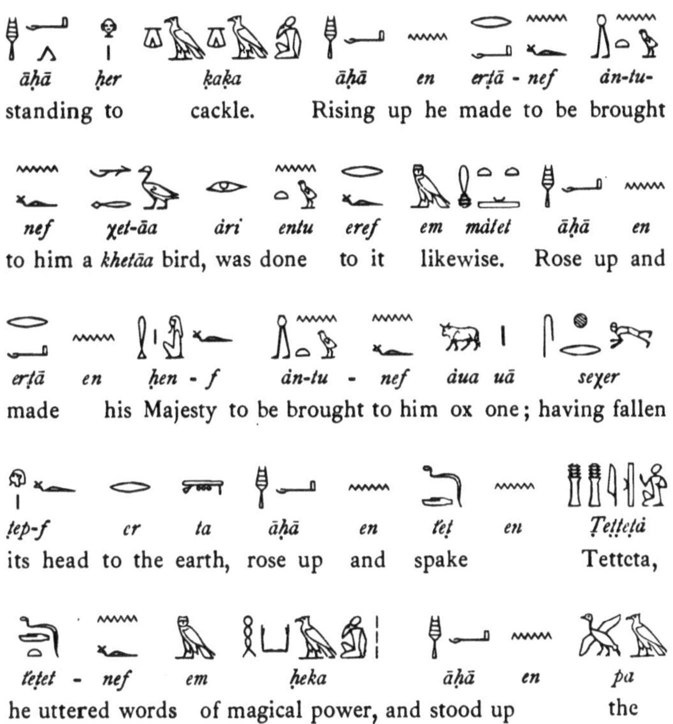

āḥā ḥer ḳaḳa āḥā en erṭā - nef ȧn-tu-
standing to cackle. Rising up he made to be brought

nef χet-āa ȧri entu eref em mȧtet āḥā en
to him a *khetāa* bird, was done to it likewise. Rose up and

erṭā en ḥen - f ȧn-tu - nef ȧua uā seχer
made his Majesty to be brought to him ox one; having fallen

ṭep-f er ta āḥā en ṫeṭ en Ṭeṭṭeṭȧ
its head to the earth, rose up and spake Tetteta,

ṫeṭet - nef em ḥeka āḥā en pa
he uttered words of magical power, and stood up the

ȧua uā
ox.

THE LIFE OF ȦĀḤMES, THE NAVAL OFFICER, AS TOLD BY HIMSELF.

[XVIIIth dynasty.]

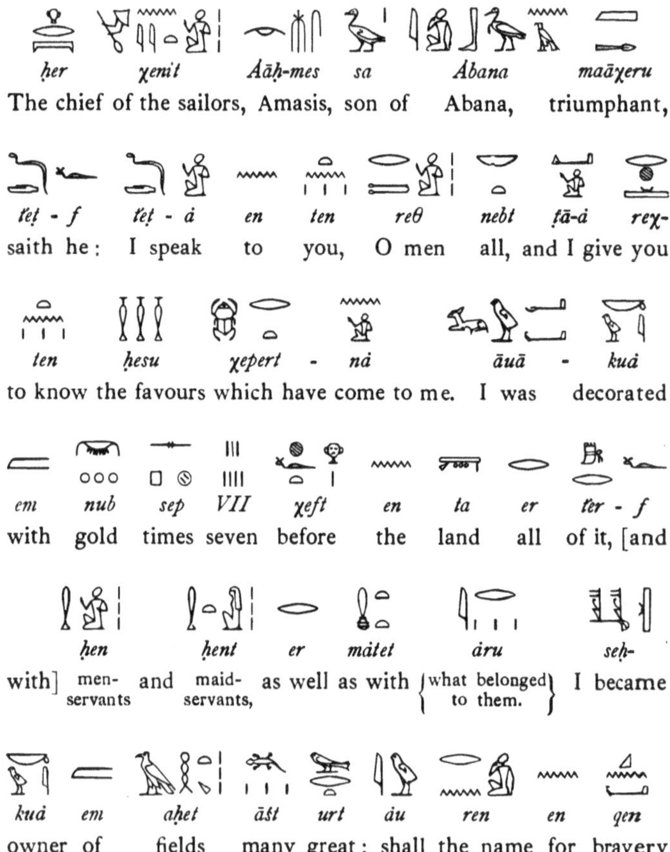

ḥer *χenit* *Ȧāḥ-mes* *sa* *Ȧbana* *maāχeru*
The chief of the sailors, Amasis, son of Abana, triumphant,

t'eṭ - f *t'eṭ - ȧ* *en* *ten* *reθ* *nebt* *ṭā-ȧ* *reχ-*
saith he: I speak to you, O men all, and I give you

ten *ḥesu* *χepert - nȧ* *āuā - kuȧ*
to know the favours which have come to me. I was decorated

em *nub* *sep* *VII* *χeft* *en* *ta* *er* *t'er - f*
with gold times seven before the land all of it, [and

ḥen *ḥent* *er* *mȧtet* *ȧru* *seḥ-*
with] men-servants and maid-servants, as well as with {what belonged to them.} I became

kuȧ *em* *aḥet* *āšt* *urt* *ȧu* *ren* *en* *qen*
owner of fields many great; shall the name for bravery

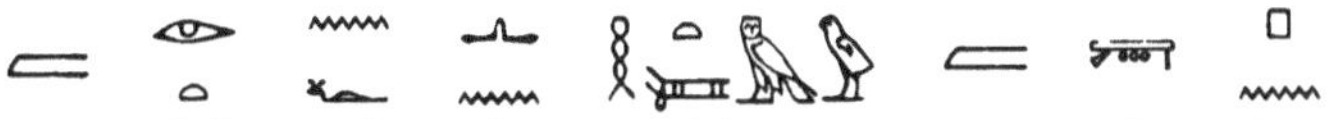

em ârit - nef ân ḥetemu em ta pen

in what he wrought not cease in land this

tetta tet - f erentet âri - nâ χeperu - â em

for ever. He saith : Now I made my coming into being in
(*i. e.*, I was born)

temâ en Neχeb âu âtef-â em uāu

the city of Nekheb. Was my father of the captain[s]

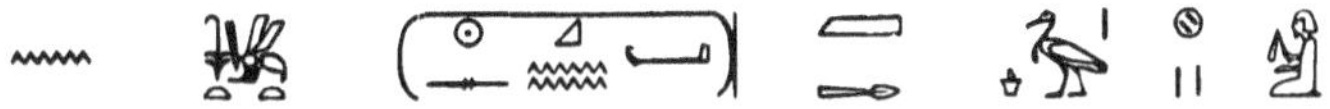

en suten net Se-qenen-Rā maāχeru Ba sep sen

of {the king of the North and South,} Seqenen-Rā, triumphant : Ba twice
(*i. e.*, Baba)

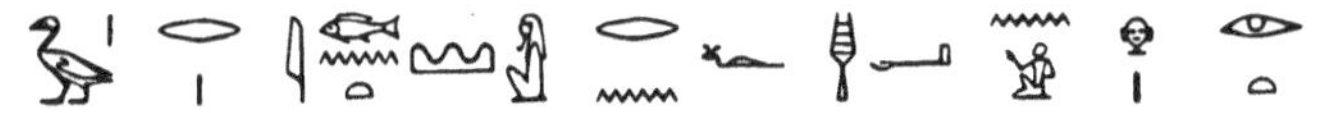

sa Re - ânt ren - f āḥā - nâ ḥer ârit

the son of Reânt [was] his name. I rose up to perform

uāu er teb - f em pa uâa en pa

the captainship as his deputy in the ship of the

Mas em hau neb taui

Mas (*i. e.*, the Bull) in the time of the lord of the two lands

Neb-peḥtet-Rā maāχeru âu-â em šerâ ân

Neb-peḥtet-Rā, triumphant. Was I at the age of a child, not
(Âāḥmes I)

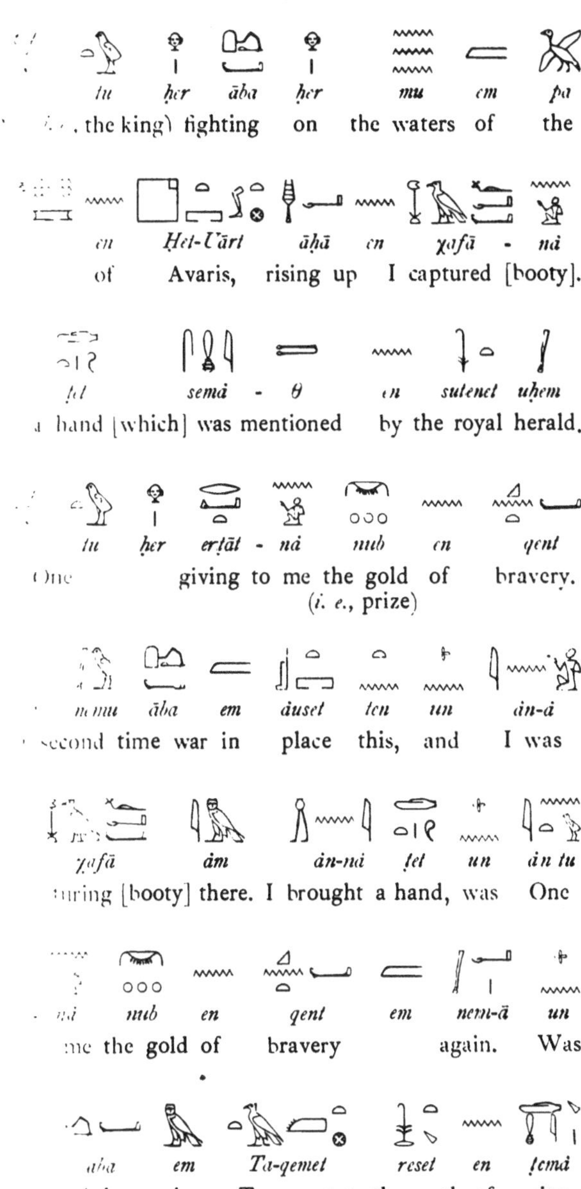

tu ḥer āba ḥer mu em pa
. . . the king) fighting on the waters of the

en Ḥet-Uārt āḥā en χafā - nȧ
of Avaris, rising up I captured [booty].

ṭet semȧ - θ en sutenet uḥem
a hand [which] was mentioned by the royal herald.

tu ḥer erṭāt - nȧ nub en qent
One giving to me the gold of bravery.
(*i. e.*, prize)

nemu āba em ȧuset ten un ȧn-ȧ
second time war in place this, and I was

χafā ȧm ȧn-nȧ ṭet un ȧn tu
turing [booty] there. I brought a hand, was One

nȧ nub en qent em nem-ā un
me the gold of bravery again. Was

āba em Ta-qemet reset en ṭemȧ
ghting in Ta-qemet to the south of city

ȧrị - ȧ ḥemt ȧu sṭer - ȧ em semt

had I married a wife, was I sleeping in the garments

šennu χer emχet ḳer - nȧ per āḥā - nȧ

of netted work. But afterwards I possessed a house, I rose up,

θetet - kuȧ er pa uȧa Meḥti ḥer qenen - ȧ

I betook myself to the ship Meḥti that I might fight
(*i. e.*, the North)

un χer-ȧ ḥer šes ȧθi ānχ uṭa senb

[it] being upon me to follow the Prince, life, strength, health

ḥer reṭ-ȧ emχet sutut - f ḥer ureret - f

upon my feet after his journeyings in his chariot.

ȧu ḥems - tu ḥer ṭemȧ en Ḥet - Uārt

Being encamped One against the city of Avaris
(*i. e.*, the king)

un χer-ȧ ḥer qent ḥer reṭ - ȧ embaḥ ḥen - f

was [it] upon me to fight upon my feet before his Majesty

āḥā - nȧ ṭehen - kuȧ er χāā-em-Men-nefer

I rose up, I was advanced to Khāā-em-Men-nefer.
(*i. e.*, to a ship of this name)

un àn tu ḥer āba ḥer mu em pa

Being One (*i. e.*, the king) fighting on the waters of the

ṭeṭ - ku en Ḥet-Uārt āḥā en χafā - nà

canal of Avaris, rising up I captured [booty].

àn-nà ṭet semà - θ en sutenet uḥem

I brought a hand [which] was mentioned by the royal herald.

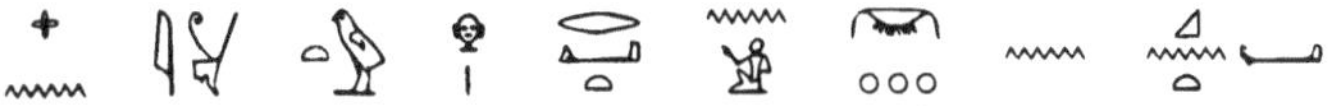

un àn tu ḥer erṭāt - nà nub en qent

Was One giving to me the gold of bravery.
(*i. e.*, prize)

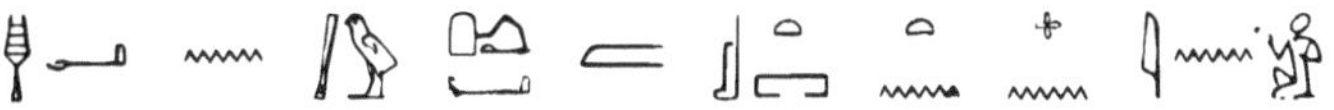

āḥā en nemu āba em àuset ten un àn-à

Was a second time war in place this, and I was

ḥer nem χafā àm àn-nà ṭet un àn tu

again capturing [booty] there. I brought a hand, was One

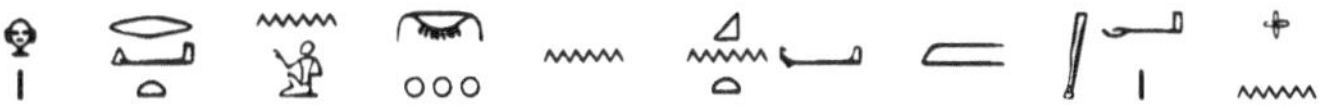

ḥer erṭāt - nà nub en qent em nem-ā un

giving to me the gold of bravery again. Was

àn tu ḥer āba em Ta-qemet reset en ṭemà

One fighting in Ta-qemet to the south of city

pen āḥā en ȧn - nȧ seqerȧ ānχ sa

this, rising up brought I captive a living person.

ha - nȧ er pa mu māk ȧn - tu - f

I went down into the water verily bringing him

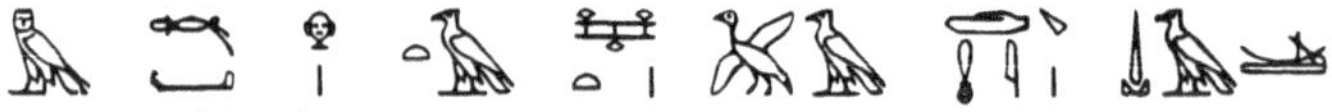

em seśeṭ ḥer ta uat pa ṭemȧ ṭa-

by force along the road of the town, I set out

nȧ χer - f ḥer mu semȧu en sutenet uḥem

with him on the water. Reported it the royal herald,

āḥā en tu māk āuā - ȧ em nub ḥer - s sen

rose up One, verily I was rewarded with gold for it a second time.

un ȧn tu ḥer ḥaq Ḥet-uārt un ȧn-ȧ

Was One capturing Avaris, was I

ḥer ȧnt ḥaqet ȧm sa uā set ḥemt χemt ṭemṭ

bringing in captives there, man one, women three, in all

ṭepu fṭu un ȧn ḥen-f ḥer erṭāt - set nȧ er

heads four, was his Majesty giving them to me for

ḥenu un ȧn tu ḥer ḥemset ḥer Śareḥan
servants. Was One sitting before Sharehan
(*i. e.*, besieging)

em renpit ṭua un ȧn ḥen-f ḥer ḥaq - s
in year five, was his Majesty capturing it.

āḥā en ȧn - nȧ ḥaqet ȧm set ḥemt sen
Rose up brought in I captives there, women two,

ṭet uā un ȧn tu ḥer erṭāt - nȧ nub en qent
hand one. Was One giving to me the gold of bravery,

māk erṭāt - nȧ ḥaqet er ḥenu χer emχet
verily [were] given to me the captives for servants. Now after

sma en ḥen-f mena Satet un
had slaughtered his Majesty the doomed foes of Asia was

ȧn f ḥer χenθit Χent-ḥen-nefer er
he sailing up the Nile to Khent-ḥen-nefer to

seksek ȧnti Kenseta un ȧn ḥen-f ḥer ȧrit
chastise the Anti of Nubia. Was his Majesty making

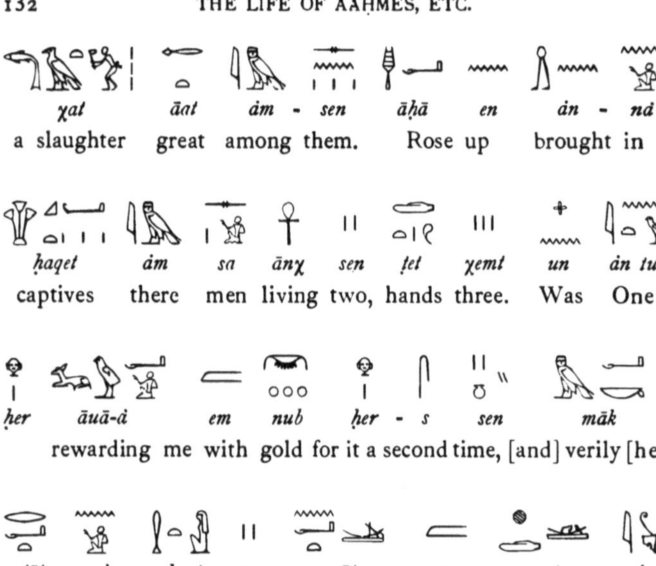

χat *āat* *ȧm - sen* *āḥā* *en* *ȧn - nȧ*
a slaughter great among them. Rose up brought in I

ḥaqet *ȧm* *sa* *ānχ* *sen* *ṭet* *χemt* *un* *ȧn tu*
captives there men living two, hands three. Was One

ḥer *āuā-ȧ* *em* *nub* *ḥer - s* *sen* *māk*
rewarding me with gold for it a second time, [and] verily [he]

erṭāt - nȧ *ḥent* *sen* *nāt* *em* *χeṭ* *ȧn*
gave me female slaves two. Came back sailing down the river

ḥen-f , *ȧb - f* *āu* *em* *qent* *neχt*
his Majesty [having] his heart expanded with might and conquest,

θetet - nef *resu* *meḥta*
[for] he had vanquished those of the south and those of the north.

āḥā *en* *aata* *iu* *en* *res*
Rose up the "Scourge" coming to the south,

seteken *śau - f* *utu - f* *neteru* *qemāu*
making to enter his disease (?), defiled he the gods of the south

ḥer am - f qemt - f ȧn ḥen-f em θent-

by his grip. Found him his Majesty in Thent-

ta - ā un ȧn ḥen-f ḥer ȧntu - f em

ta ā. Was his Majesty bringing him in

seqer ānχ reθ - f nebu mȧs ḥaq

captive alive [and] his men all were led in captive.

āḥā en ȧn - nȧ māḳa sen em

Rising up I brought in enemies two by

sešeṭ em pa uȧa en aata un

force in the boat of the "Scourge". Was

ȧn tu ḥer erṭāt - nȧ ṭep ṭua ḥer ṭenȧu aḥt

One giving to me heads five for [my] share [and] of land

statet ṭua em nut - ȧ ȧru en ta χenit

measures five in my city. Was done [this] to the sailors,

er āu - sen em mȧtet āḥā en χer pef

all of them, likewise. Rose up degraded one that and

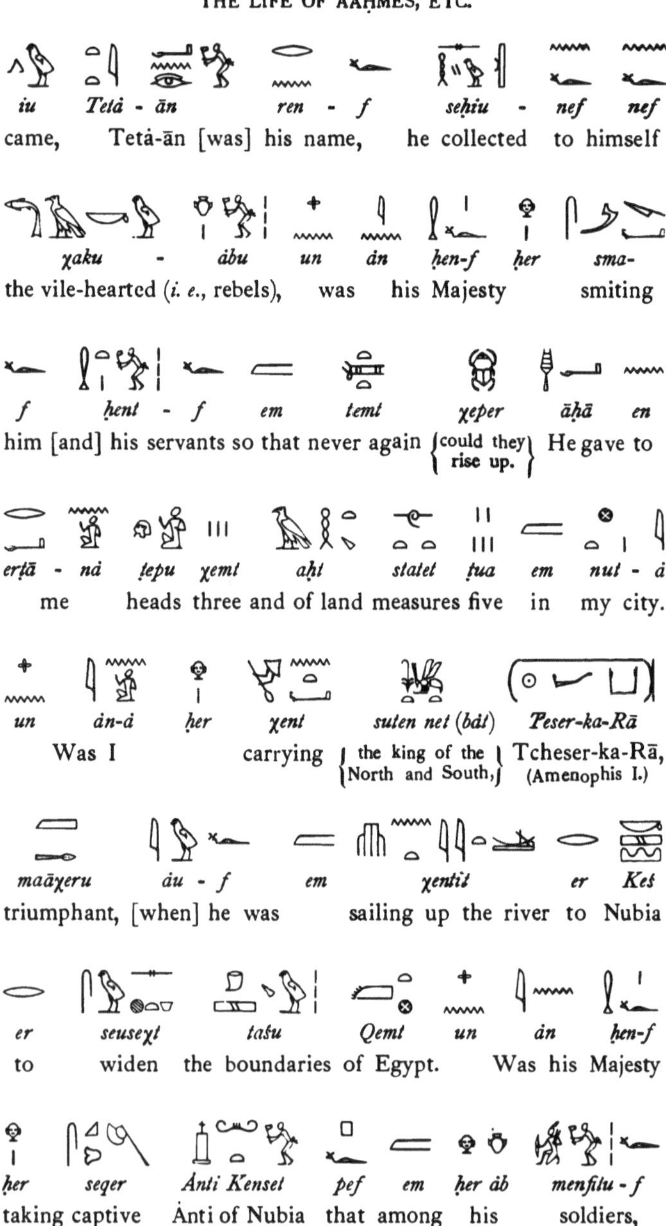

iu Tetȧ - ān ren - f seḥiu - nef nef
came, Tetȧ-ān [was] his name, he collected to himself

χaku - ȧbu un ȧn ḥen-f ḥer sma-
the vile-hearted (*i. e.*, rebels), was his Majesty smiting

f ḥent - f em temt χeper āḥā en
him [and] his servants so that never again {could they rise up.} He gave to

erṭā - nȧ ṭepu χemt aḥt statet ṭua em nut - ȧ
me heads three and of land measures five in my city.

un ȧn-ȧ ḥer χent suten net (bȧt) Ṭeser-ka-Rā
Was I carrying {the king of the North and South,} Tcheser-ka-Rā, (Amenophis I.)

maāχeru ȧu - f em χentit er Keš
triumphant, [when] he was sailing up the river to Nubia

er seuseχt tašu Qemt un ȧn ḥen-f
to widen the boundaries of Egypt. Was his Majesty

ḥer seqer Ȧnti Kenset pef em ḥer ȧb menfitu - f
taking captive Ȧnti of Nubia that among his soldiers,

àntu em ḳua àn nehup - sen
being led into an ambush not could escape they,

uteχu em ṭāi ḥer ḳes mà entu àn
being scattered and yielding on [their] ground so that never again

χeper àst - uà em ṭep en menfitu - n àu
{could they rise up.} Behold I was at the head of our soldiers,

āba - nà er un maā maa en ḥen-f qent - à
I fought in very truth, saw his Majesty my valour.
(*i. e.*, to the utmost of my power)

àn-nà ṭet sen mās en ḥen-f un
I brought in hands two, carrying [them] to his Majesty. Was

àn tu ḥer ḥeḥi reθ - f menment - f
One seeking out his people and his cattle,

āḥā en àn-nà seqer ānχ mās en
rose up brought in I a captive living bringing [him] to

ḥen-f àn-nà ḥen-f hru sen er Qemt
his Majesty. I brought his Majesty in days two to Egypt

em χnemet ḥeru āḥā en tu ḥer āuā-à
from the pool upper, rose up One rewarding me

em nub āḥā en àn-nà ḥent sen em
with gold. Rose up I brought in female slaves two in

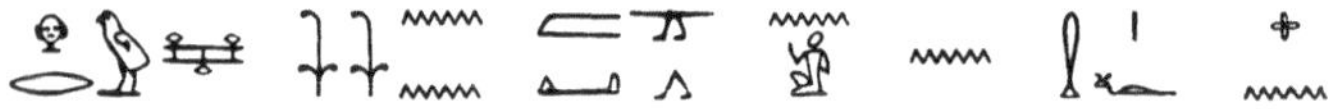

ḥeru enen mās - nà en ḥen-f un
addition to those which I carried to his Majesty. Was

àn tu ḥer erṭāt-à er ābatiu en ḥeq un-
One making me the "Warrior of the Prince". Was
(*i. e.*, "Crown-warrior")

nà ḥer χent suten net (bàt) Āa-χeper-ka-Rā
I conveying up the river {the king of the North and South,} Āa-kheper-ka-Rā, (Thothmes I.)

maāχeru àu-f em χenti er Χent-ḥen-nefer
triumphant, was he sailing up to Khent-ḥen-nefer

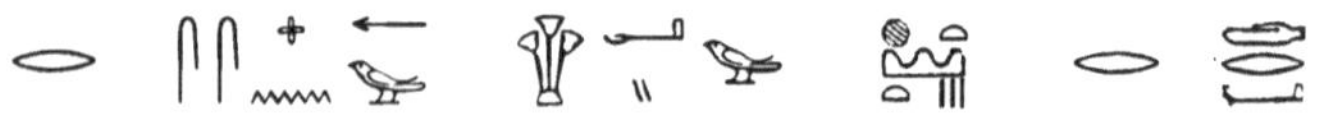

er sesun ḥāi Χetet er ṭer
to punish the disaffected ones of Khetet, and to destroy

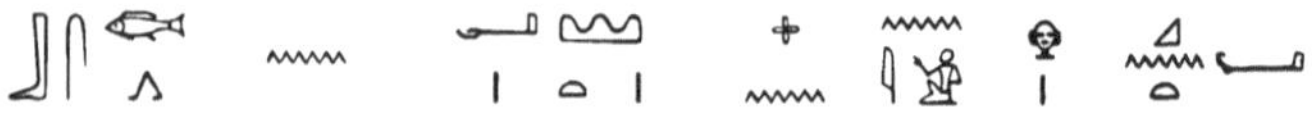

bes en Ā (?) un - àn à ḥer qent
the roads (?) of the district of Ā (?). Was I fighting

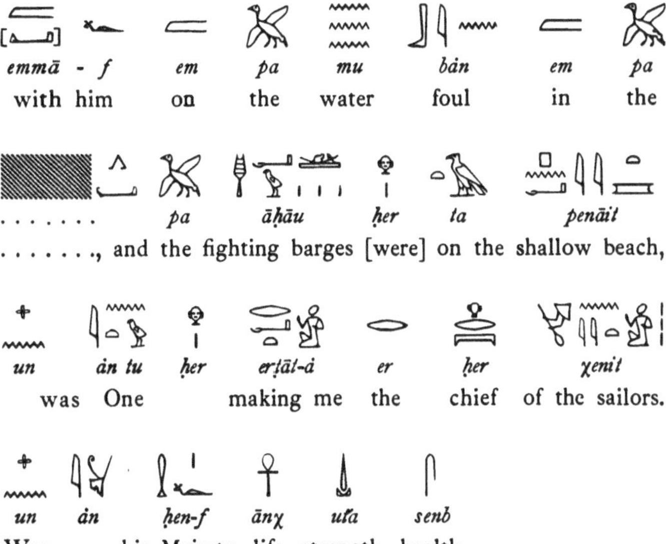

emmā - f *em* *pa* *mu* *bȧn* *em* *pa*

with him on the water foul in the

. . . . *pa* *āḥāu* *ḥer* *ṭa* *penāit*

. . . ., and the fighting barges [were] on the shallow beach,

un *ȧn tu* *ḥer* *erṭāt-ȧ* *er* *ḥer* *χenit*

was One making me the chief of the sailors.

un *ȧn* *ḥen-f* *ānχ* *uṭa* *senb*

Was his Majesty, life, strength, health . . .

THE HARPER'S LAMENT.

From the tomb of Nefer-ḥetep.

[XVIIIth dynasty.]

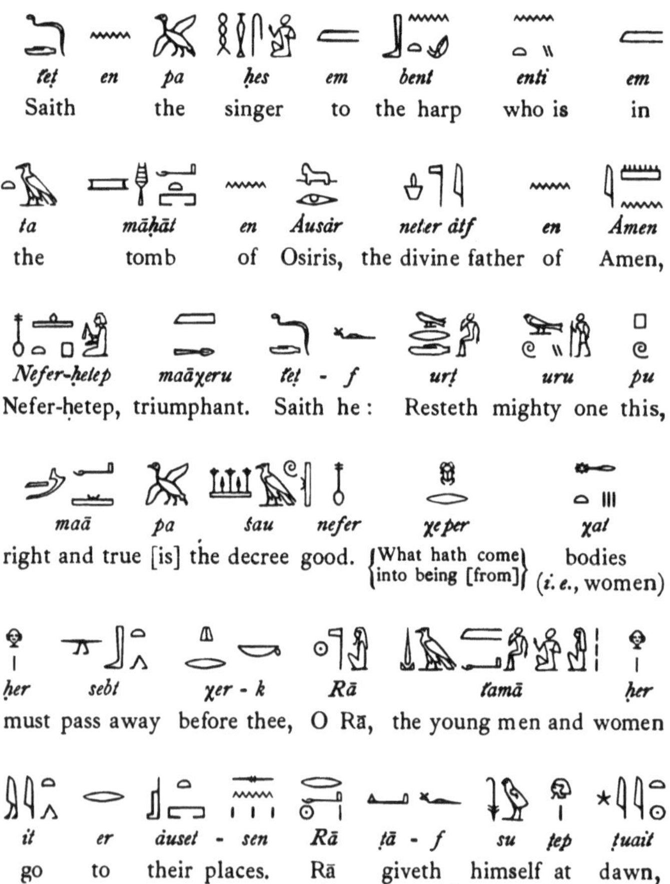

ṭeṭ en pa ḥes em bent enti em
Saith the singer to the harp who is in
ta māḥāt en Ȧusȧr neter ȧtf en Ȧmen
the tomb of Osiris, the divine father of Amen,
Nefer-ḥetep maāχeru ṭeṭ - f urṭ uru pu
Nefer-ḥetep, triumphant. Saith he: Resteth mighty one this,
maā pa šau nefer χeper χat
right and true [is] the decree good. {What hath come into being [from]} bodies (*i. e.*, women)
ḥer sebt χer - k Rā ṭamā ḥer
must pass away before thee, O Rā, the young men and women
it er ȧuset - sen Rā ṭā - f su tep ṭuait
go to their places. Rā giveth himself at dawn,
(*i. e.*, sheweth)

Tem ḥetep em Manu t'ai ḥer utet kant ḥer
Tmu setteth in Manu. Men beget and women

seśep fenṭ neb ḥer tepȧ nefu ḥet' - ta meses
receive, nose every smelling the breath of dawn, and children

ressi iu - sen er ȧuset - ȧru ȧri hru
all alike they come to the place {which belongeth to them.} Make a day

nefer pa neter ȧtef ȧmmā qemȧi ṭept tut
happy, O divine father! Come, unguents and perfumes are set

er χer - k maḥuu seśennu er ermentu
before thee, *maḥu* flowers and lilies for the arms [and]

er śenbet sent - k ȧmt ȧb - k seneṭ'em-θ
for the neck of thy sister dwelling in thy heart, sitting

er-ḳes - k ȧmmā ḥes qemā er χeft - k
near thee. Come then, song [and] music are before thee.

mā ḥa ṭutu nebt seχa - nek reśtu
Set behind [thee] evil things all, think thou upon gladness [only]

er it hru pefi en menȧ ȧm-f er

until cometh day that arriveth [a man] in it at

pa ta mer - s ḳer

the land [which] loveth it silence.

THE BATTLE OF MEGIDDO.

From the Annals of Thothmes III.

[XVIIIth dynasty.]

renpit XXIII ṭep šemu hru XVI er ṭemȧ

Year twenty-three, first month of summer, day sixteen, at the town

en Iḥem utu en ḥen-f neṭu - re ḥenā

of Ihem. Ordered his Majesty a council of war with

menfitu-f en neχt er ṭeṭ erentet χeru

his soldiers of valour, saying: Inasmuch as wretch

pef en Qeṭešu iu āq er

that of Kadesh hath come [and] gone into

Mākθȧ su ȧm em ta at seḥui-

Megiddo, [and] he is there at this moment, and hath

nef nef seru nu set nebt enti ḥer

gathered to him the princes of countries all who are on

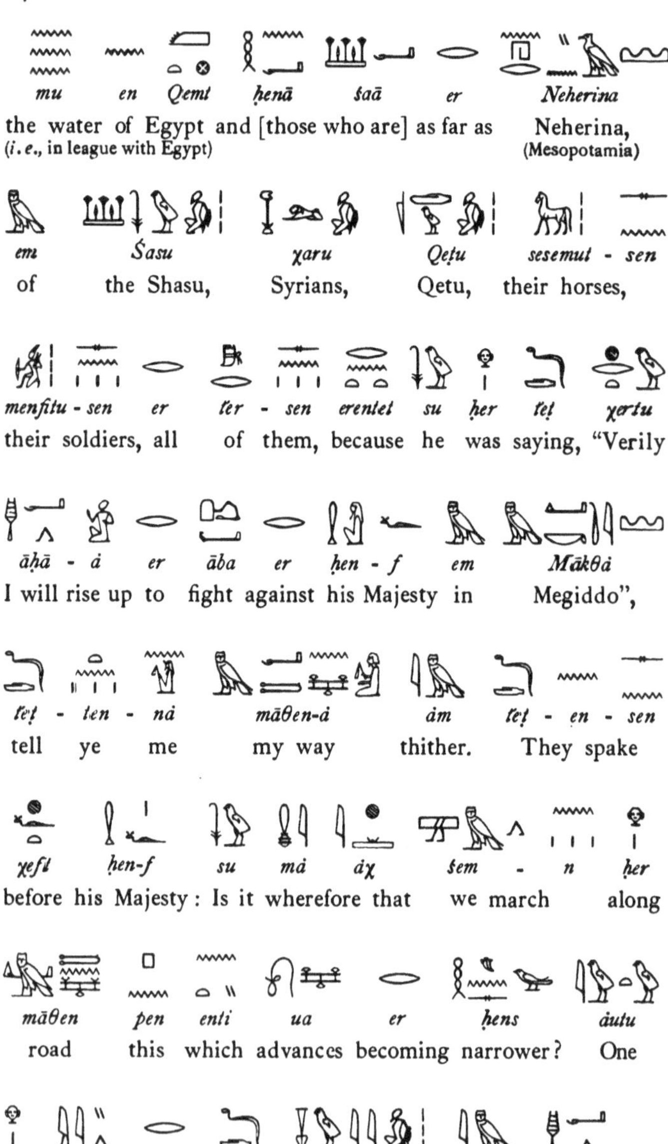

mu en Qemt ḥenā śaā er Neherina

the water of Egypt and [those who are] as far as Neherina,
(*i.e.*, in league with Egypt) (Mesopotamia)

em Śasu χaru Qeṭu sesemut - sen

of the Shasu, Syrians, Qetu, their horses,

menfitu - sen er ťer - sen erentet su ḥer teṭ χertu

their soldiers, all of them, because he was saying, "Verily

āḥā - ȧ er āba er ḥen - f em Mākθȧ

I will rise up to fight against his Majesty in Megiddo",

ťeṭ - ten - nȧ māθen-ȧ ȧm ťeṭ - en - sen

tell ye me my way thither. They spake

χeft ḥen-f su mȧ ȧχ śem - n ḥer

before his Majesty: Is it wherefore that we march along

māθen pen enti ua er ḥens ȧutu

road this which advances becoming narrower? One

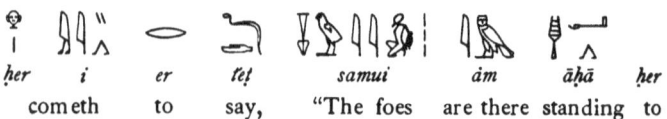

ḥer i er ťeṭ samui ȧm āḥā ḥer

cometh to say, "The foes are there standing to

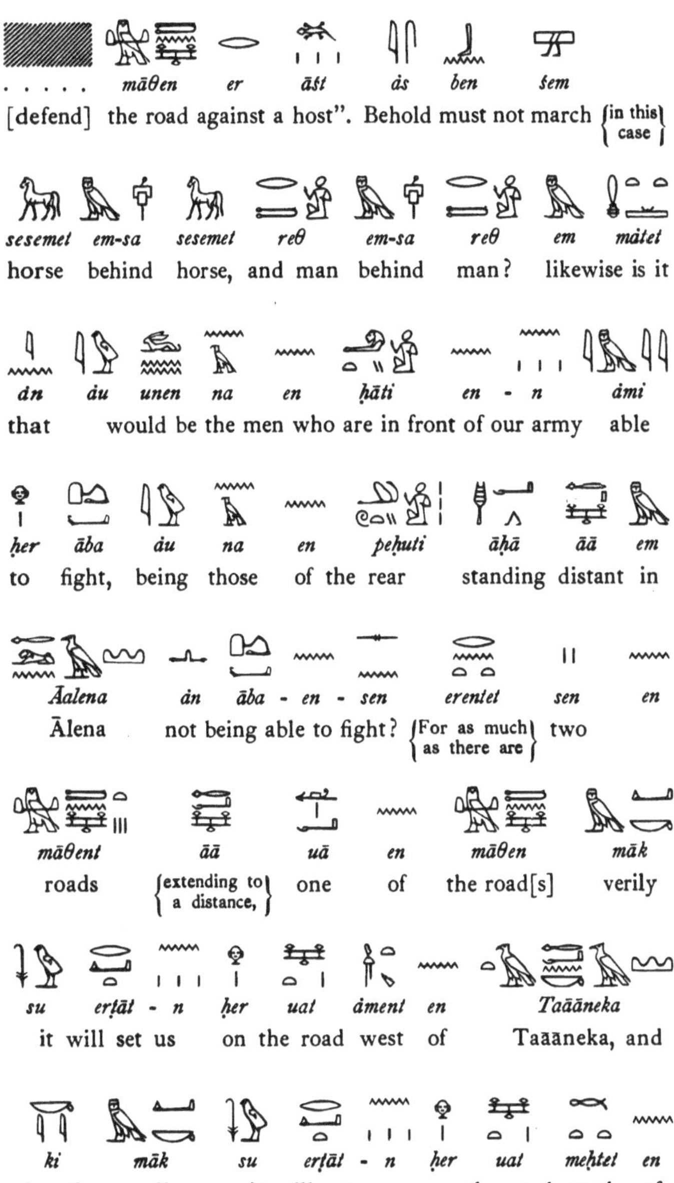

. . . . . *māθen er āšt ȧs ben šem*

[defend] the road against a host". Behold must not march {in this case}

sesemet em-sa sesemet reθ em-sa reθ em mȧtet

horse behind horse, and man behind man? likewise is it

ȧn ȧu unen na en ḥāti en - n ȧmi

that would be the men who are in front of our army able

ḥer āba ȧu na en peḥuti āḥā āā em

to fight, being those of the rear standing distant in

Āalena ȧn āba - en - sen erentet sen en

Ālena not being able to fight? {For as much as there are} two

māθent āā uā en māθen māk

roads {extending to a distance,} one of the road[s] verily

su erṭāt - n ḥer uat ȧment en Taāāneka

it will set us on the road west of Taāāneka, and

ki māk su erṭāt - n ḥer uat meḥtet en

the other verily it will set us on the road north of

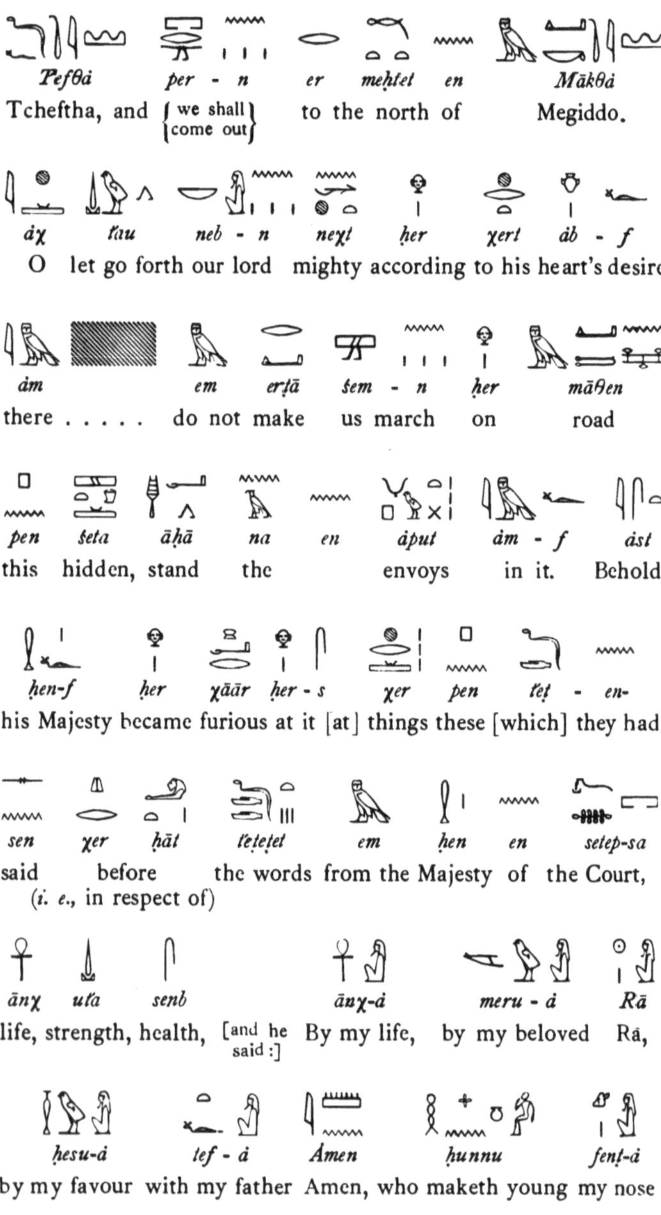

Tefθȧ *per - n* *er* *meḥtet* *en* *Mākθȧ*
Tcheftha, and {we shall come out} to the north of Megiddo.

ȧχ *ťau* *neb - n* *neχt* *ḥer* *χert* *ȧb - f*
O let go forth our lord mighty according to his heart's desire

ȧm *em* *erṭā* *šem - n* *ḥer* *māθen*
there . . . . . do not make us march on road

pen *šeta* *āḥā* *na* *en* *ȧput* *ȧm - f* *ȧst*
this hidden, stand the envoys in it. Behold

ḥen-f *ḥer* *χāār* *ḥer - s* *χer* *pen* *ťeṭ - en-*
his Majesty became furious at it [at] things these [which] they had

sen *χer* *ḥāt* *ťeṭeṭet* *em* *ḥen* *en* *setep-sa*
said before (*i. e.*, in respect of) the words from the Majesty of the Court,

ānχ *uťa* *senb* *ānχ-ȧ* *meru - ȧ* *Rā*
life, strength, health, [and he said:] By my life, by my beloved Rā,

ḥesu-ȧ *tef - ȧ* *Ȧmen* *ḥunnu* *fenṭ-ȧ*
by my favour with my father Amen, who maketh young my nose

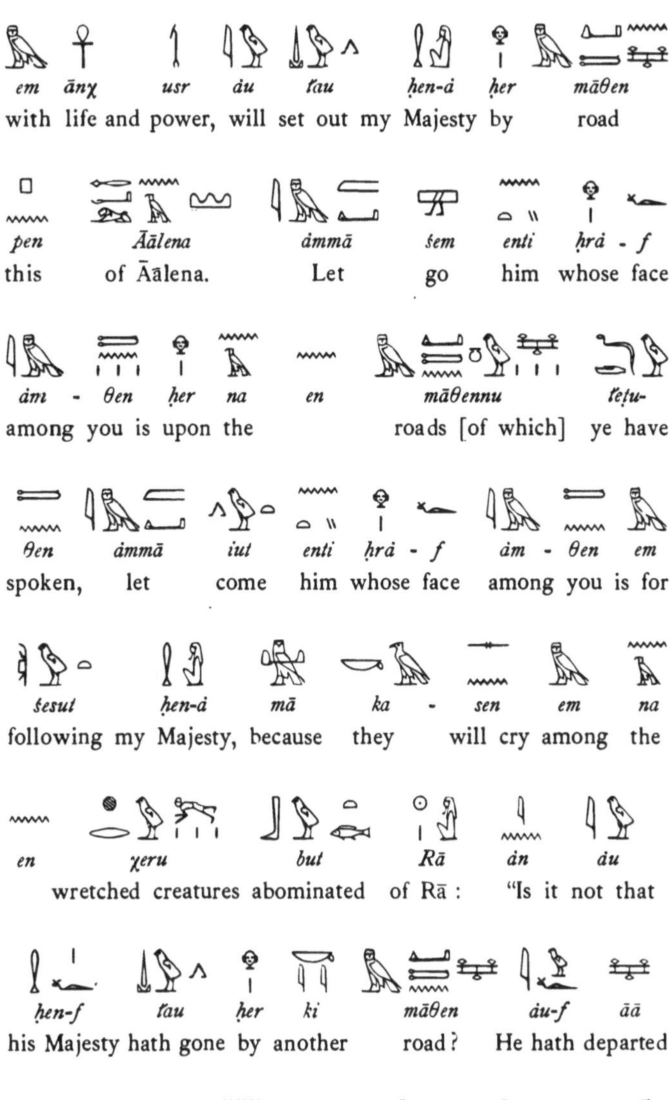

em ānχ usr ȧu ťau ḥen-ȧ ḥer māθen
with life and power, will set out my Majesty by road

pen Āālena ȧmmā šem enti ḥrȧ - f
this of Āālena. Let go him whose face

ȧm - θen ḥer na en māθennu ťeṭu-
among you is upon the roads [of which] ye have

θen ȧmmā iut enti ḥrȧ - f ȧm - θen em
spoken, let come him whose face among you is for

šesut ḥen-ȧ mā ka - sen em na
following my Majesty, because they will cry among the

en χeru but Rā ȧn ȧu
wretched creatures abominated of Rā : "Is it not that

ḥen-f ťau ḥer ki māθen ȧu-f āā
his Majesty hath gone by another road? He hath departed

er senṭ - en - n ka - sen ťeṭ - en - sen
through fear of us;" [this] will they cry. They spake

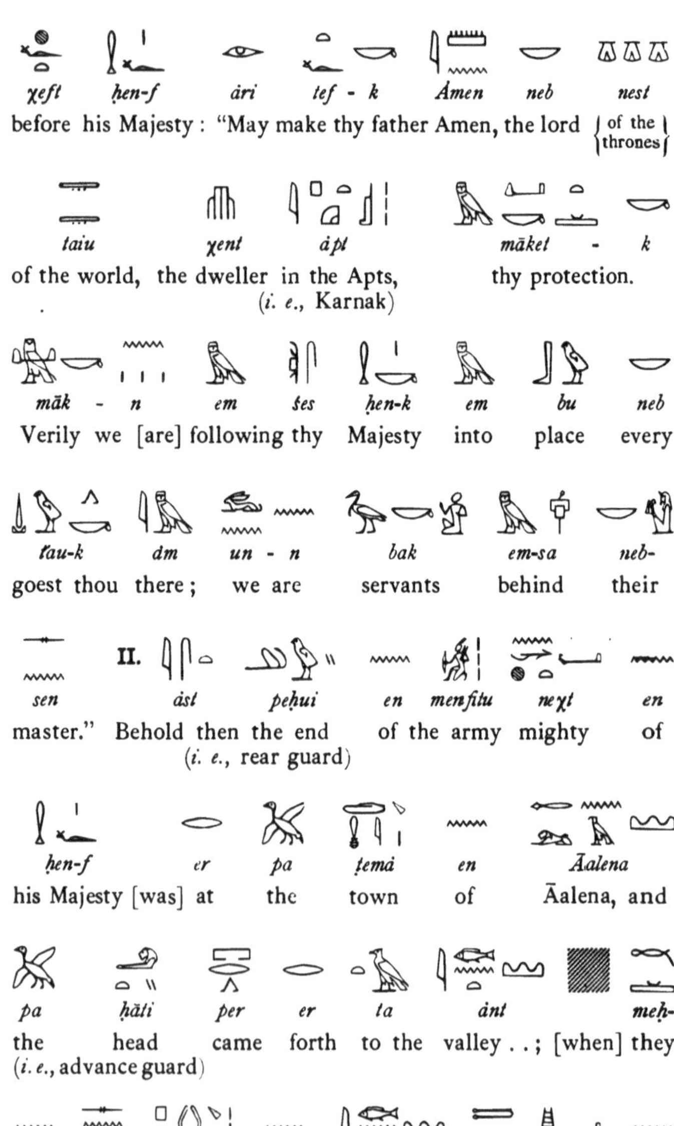

χeft *ḥen-f* *àri* *tef - k* *Àmen* *neb* *nest*
before his Majesty: "May make thy father Amen, the lord {of the thrones}

taiu *χent* *àpt* *māket - k*
of the world, the dweller in the Apts, (*i. e.*, Karnak) thy protection.

māk - n *em* *šes* *ḥen-k* *em* *bu* *neb*
Verily we [are] following thy Majesty into place every

ťau-k *àm* *un - n* *bak* *em-sa* *neb-*
goest thou there; we are servants behind their

sen II. *àst* *peḥui* *en* *menfitu* *neχt* *en*
master." Behold then the end (*i. e.*, rear guard) of the army mighty of

ḥen-f *er* *pa* *temà* *en* *Āalena*
his Majesty [was] at the town of Āalena, and

pa *ḥāti* *per* *er* *ta* *ànt* *meḥ-*
the head (*i. e.*, advance guard) came forth to the valley . . ; [when] they

en - sen *peḳ* *en* *ànt* *θen* *āḥā* *en*
had filled the ravines of valley this, rose and

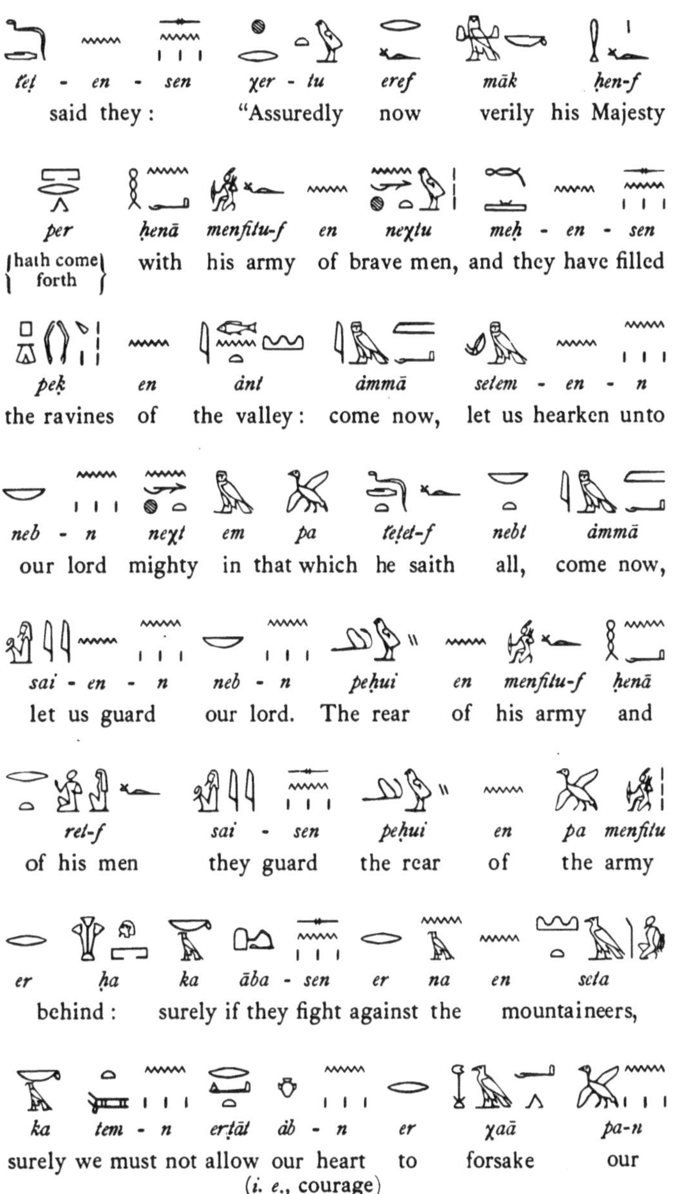
ṭeṭ - en - sen χer - tu eref māk ḥen-f
said they: "Assuredly now verily his Majesty
per ḥenā menfitu-f en neχtu meḥ - en - sen
{hath come forth} with his army of brave men, and they have filled
peḳ en ȧnt ȧmmā setem - en - n
the ravines of the valley: come now, let us hearken unto
neb - n neχt em pa ṭeṭet-f nebt ȧmmā
our lord mighty in that which he saith all, come now,
sai - en - n neb - n peḥui en menfitu-f ḥenā
let us guard our lord. The rear of his army and
ret-f sai - sen peḥui en pa menfitu
of his men they guard the rear of the army
er ḥa ka āba - sen er na en seta
behind: surely if they fight against the mountaineers,
ka tem - n erṭāt ȧb - n er χaā pa-n
surely we must not allow our heart (*i. e.*, courage) to forsake our

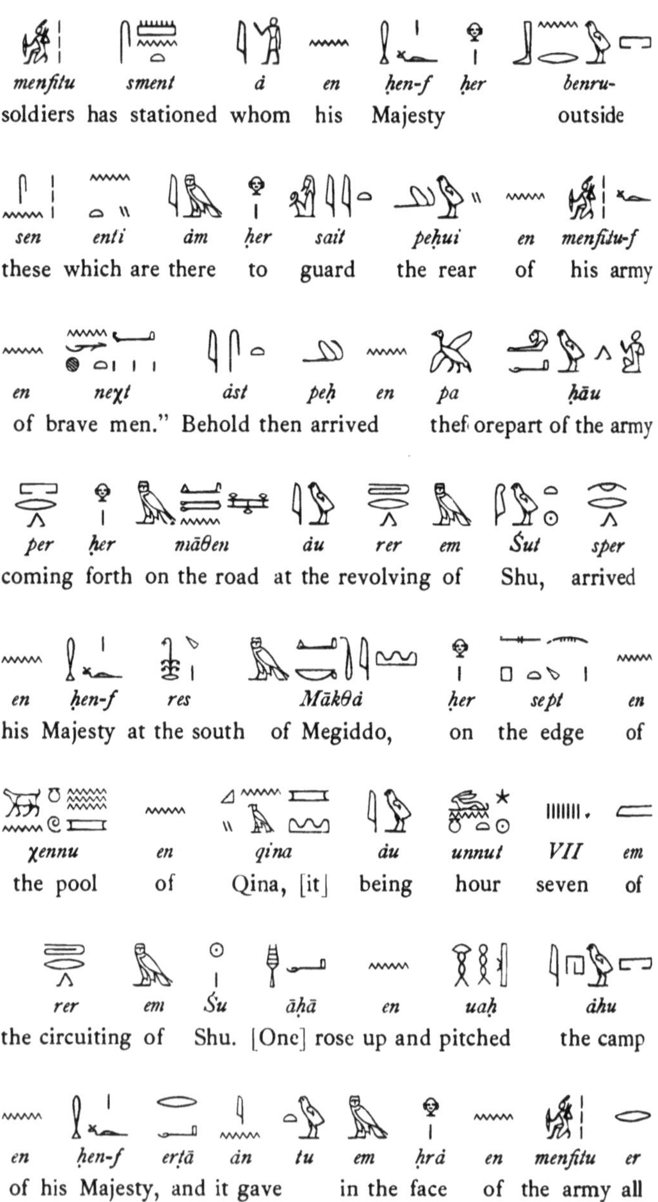
menfitu sment ȧ en ḥen-f ḥer benru-
soldiers has stationed whom his Majesty outside
sen enti ȧm ḥer saït peḥui en menfitu-f
these which are there to guard the rear of his army
en neχt ȧst peḥ en pa ḥāu
of brave men." Behold then arrived thef orepart of the army
per ḥer māθen ȧu rer em Śut sper
coming forth on the road at the revolving of Shu, arrived
en ḥen-f res Mākθȧ ḥer sept en
his Majesty at the south of Megiddo, on the edge of
χennu en qina ȧu unnut VII em
the pool of Qina, [it] being hour seven of
rer em Śu āḥā en uaḥ ȧhu
the circuiting of Shu. [One] rose up and pitched the camp
en ḥen-f erṭā ȧn tu em ḥrȧ en menfitu er
of his Majesty, and it gave in the face of the army all

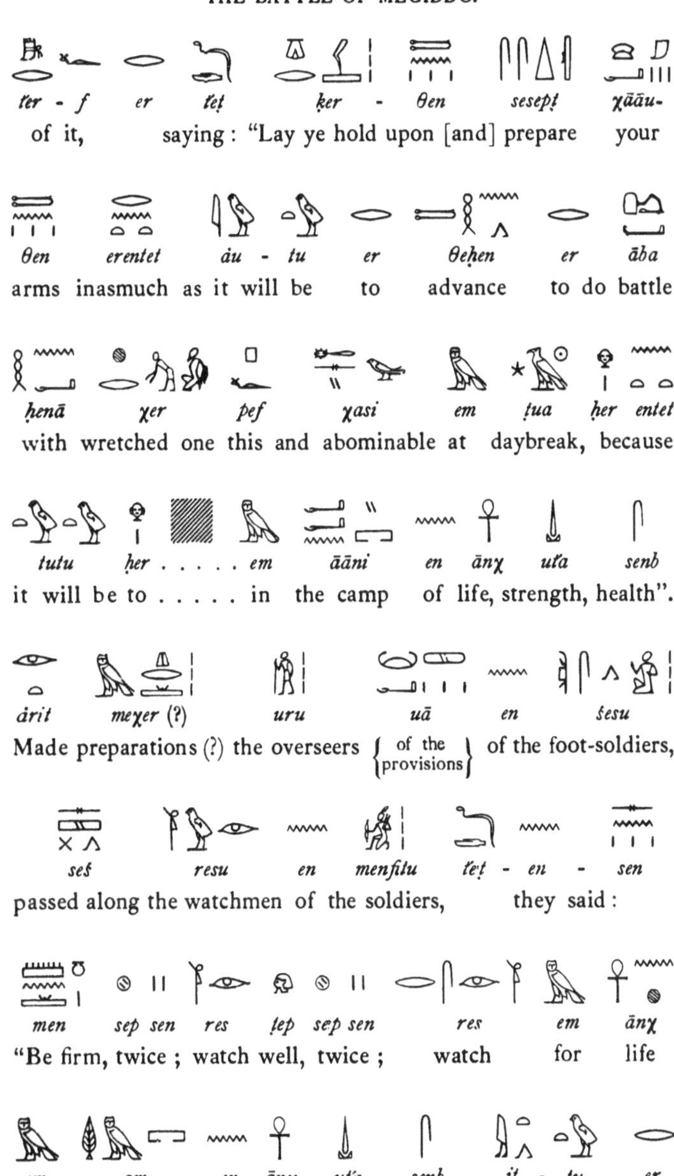

ṭer - f er ṭeṭ ḳer - θen sesepṭ χāāu-
of it, saying: "Lay ye hold upon [and] prepare your

θen erentet àu - tu er θeḥen er āba
arms inasmuch as it will be to advance to do battle

ḥenā χer pef χasi em ṭua ḥer entet
with wretched one this and abominable at daybreak, because

tutu ḥer . . . . . em āāni en ānχ uṭa senb
it will be to . . . . . in the camp of life, strength, health".

àrit meχer (?) uru uā en šesu
Made preparations (?) the overseers {of the provisions} of the foot-soldiers,

seš resu en menfitu ṭeṭ - en - sen
passed along the watchmen of the soldiers, they said:

men sep sen res ṭep sep sen res em ānχ
"Be firm, twice; watch well, twice; watch for life

em am en ānχ uṭa senb it - tu er
in the camp of life, strength, health." Came one to

ṭeṭ *en* *ḥen-f* *meru* *senb* *āuāit*

say to his Majesty: "The mountain {land is in a good state,} {and the bondsmen}

rest *meḥt* *er* *mȧtet* *renpit* *XXIII* *ṭep*

south and north likewise." Year twenty-three, first month

šemu *hru* *XXI* *hru* *en* *ḥeb* *en* *paut* (?) *n*

of the season, day twenty-one, the day of the festival of *paut* (?) *n*
of summer

er *meti* *sutenet* *χāt* *ṭep* *ṭuat*

which corresponds {with that of} the royal coronation, at {the earliest dawn,}

ȧst *erṭā* *em* *ḥrȧ* *en* *menfitu* *er* *ṭer - f* *er*

then was given in the face of the army all of it to

seš *er* *χeft* *ṭau* *ḥen-f* *ḥer* *urerit*

advance against the enemy. Set out his Majesty in a chariot [made]

ent *uasm* (*smu*) *sābu* *em* *χakeru - f* *nu*

of shining bronze decorated with its accoutrements of

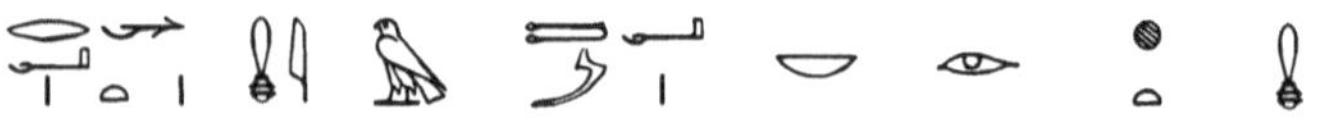

rāt *mȧ* *Ḥeru* *θema* *neb* *ȧri* *χet* *mȧ*

battle, like Horus, the crusher, the lord, maker of things, like

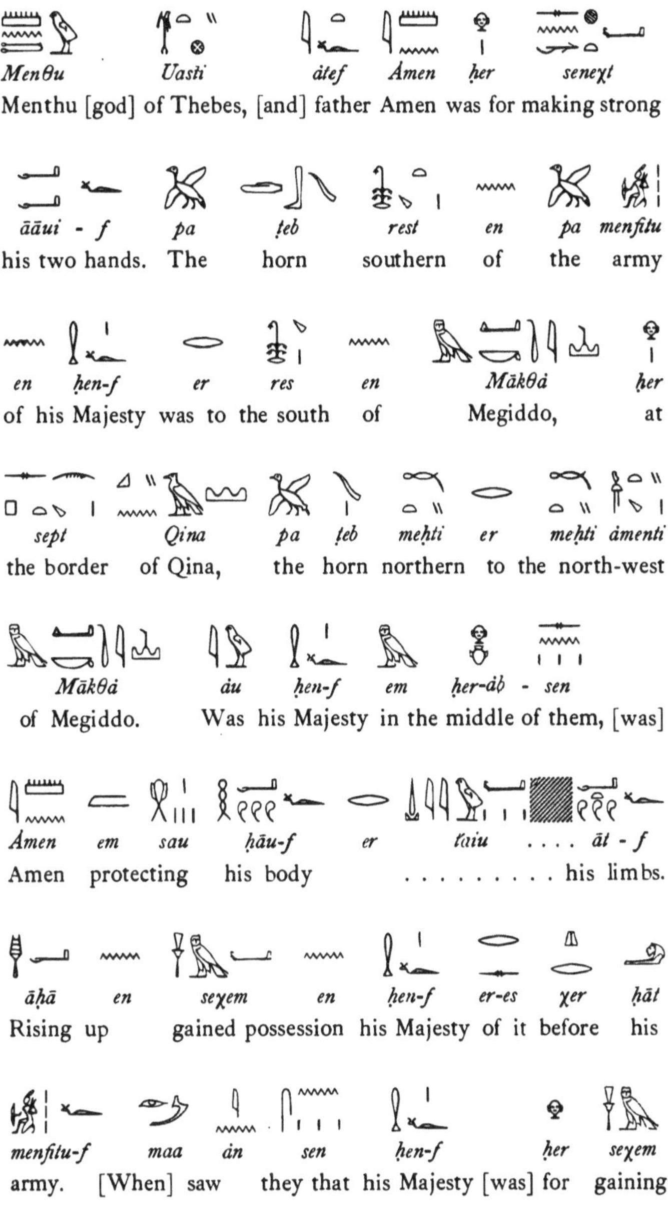

Menθu Uasti atef Ȧmen ḥer seneχt
Menthu [god] of Thebes, [and] father Amen was for making strong

āāui - f pa ṭeb rest en pa menfitu
his two hands. The horn southern of the army

en ḥen-f er res en Mākθȧ ḥer
of his Majesty was to the south of Megiddo, at

sept Qina pa ṭeb meḥti er meḥti ȧmenti
the border of Qina, the horn northern to the north-west

Mākθȧ ȧu ḥen-f em ḥer-ȧb - sen
of Megiddo. Was his Majesty in the middle of them, [was]

Ȧmen em sau ḥāu-f er ṭaiu . . . . āt - f
Amen protecting his body . . . . his limbs.

āḥā en seχem en ḥen-f er-es χer ḥāt
Rising up gained possession his Majesty of it before his

menfitu-f maa ȧn sen ḥen-f ḥer seχem
army. [When] saw they that his Majesty [was] for gaining

er-es *àu - sen* *ḥer* *àf ṭ* *em* *ḳebḳebi*
possession of it, were they for fleeing headlong

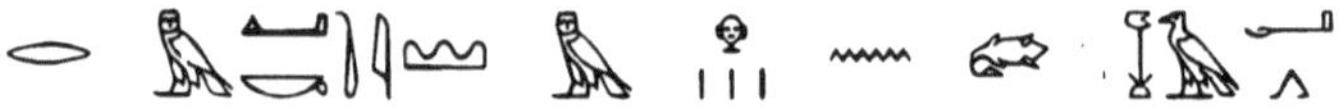

er *Māk θ à* *em* *ḥràu* *en* *sen ṭ* *χaā-*
into Megiddo with faces of fear, they forsook

en - sen *sesemut - sen* *ureret - sen* *nu* *nub* *ḥer*
their horses [and] their chariots of gold upon

ḥet *àt ḥu - tu* *set* *em* *tebteb*
silver, drawn up were they by the strings

ḥebs - sen *er* *ṭemà* *pen* *àst* *χetem*
of their garments into town this, for behold {had shut the gates}

en *na* *en* *re θ* *ṭemà* *pen* *ḥer* *àt ḥu-*
certain of the people of town this, [and] they drew

sen *em* *ḥebs* *er* *θeb θeb - se θ*
up [them] by [their] garments to hoist them

er *ḥer* *er* *ṭemà* *pen* *àst* *ḥa*
over [the walls] into town this. And behold in truth

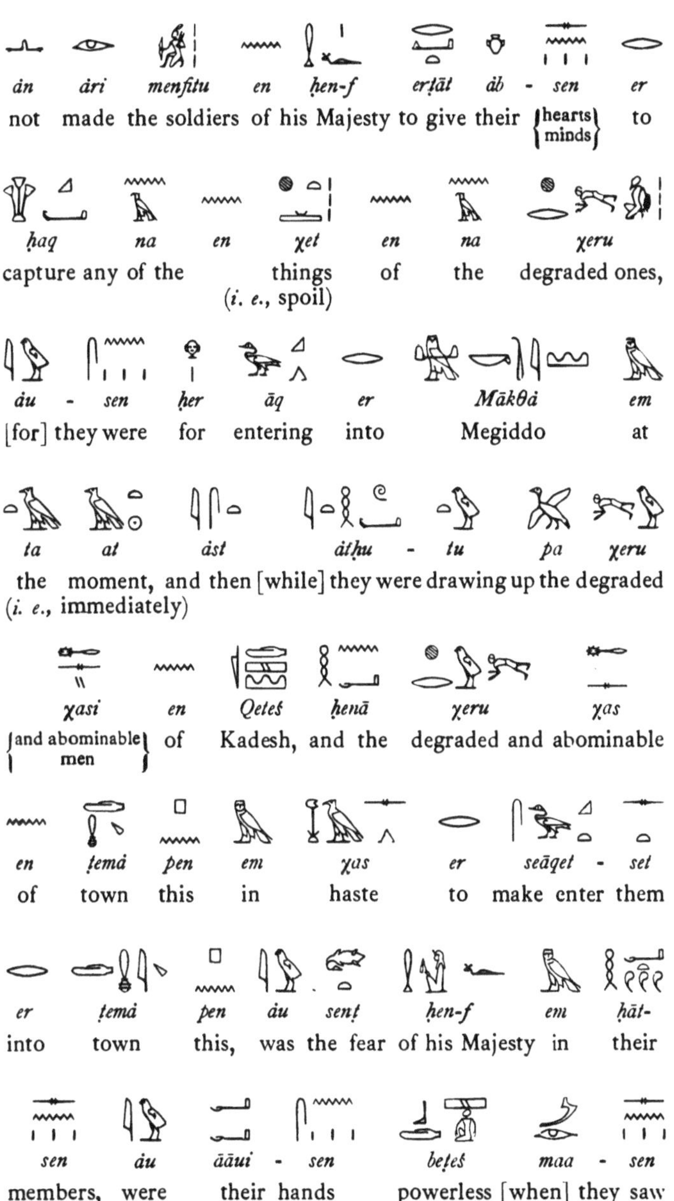

ȧn ȧri menfitu en ḥen-f erṭāt ȧb - sen er
not made the soldiers of his Majesty to give their {hearts / minds} to

ḥaq na en χet en na χeru
capture any of the things (*i. e.*, spoil) of the degraded ones,

ȧu - sen her āq er Mākθȧ em
[for] they were for entering into Megiddo at

ta at ȧst ȧtḥu - tu pa χeru
the moment, (*i. e.*, immediately) and then [while] they were drawing up the degraded

χasi en Qeteš ḥenā χeru χas
{and abominable men} of Kadesh, and the degraded and abominable

en ṭemȧ pen em χas er seāqet - set
of town this in haste to make enter them

er ṭemȧ pen ȧu senṭ ḥen-f em ḥāt-
into town this, was the fear of his Majesty in their

sen ȧu āāui - sen beṭeš maa - sen
members, were their hands powerless [when] they saw

seku en χu - f ȧm - sen

the destruction [wrought] by his uraeus crown among them. [They]

āḥā en ḥaq sesemut - sen ur er et - sen nu

rose up and captured their horses, their chariots of

nub ḥer ḥet' ȧri mȧsi māhut - sen

gold upon silver, and made to pass into captivity their peoples,

qennu - sen st'er em seθesi mȧ

and their mighty men lay prostrate upon their backs dead like

remu em qāḥ šen neχt en

fishes on the river bank, {and the warriors} mighty of

ḥen-f ḥer ȧp χet ȧru . . . . .

his Majesty [were] for counting the spoil belonging to them.

seqer ānχ CCCCXLI ţet LXXXIII sesemut

Captives living 441; hands 83; horses

MM XLI mesit ent sesemut CXCI

2041; the young of horses 191;

åbare VI renpet ureret bak-θ

stallions 6; horses . . . . .; a chariot worked

em nub t'ebu em nub ureret nefert

with gold, and a seat of gold; a chariot beautiful

bak-θ em nub en ser en Mākθ ureret

worked with gold of the prince of Megiddo; chariots

nefert bak-θ em nub en mesu χer pef

beautiful worked with gold of the sons {of wretched creature} that

XXX ureret en menfitu-f χas DCCCXCII ṭemṭ

30; chariots of his soldiers vile 892; in all

DCCCCXXIV χemt meses nefer en āba en

924; of bronze a coat of mail fine of battle of

χer pef pet DII unṭu CCXCVII

{wretched creature} that; . . . . bows 502; . . . . calves 297;

āut net'eset MM āut ḥet'et

beasts small 2000; beasts white 20500.

SPEECH OF ȦMEN-RĀ TO THOTHMES III.

[XVIIIth dynasty.]

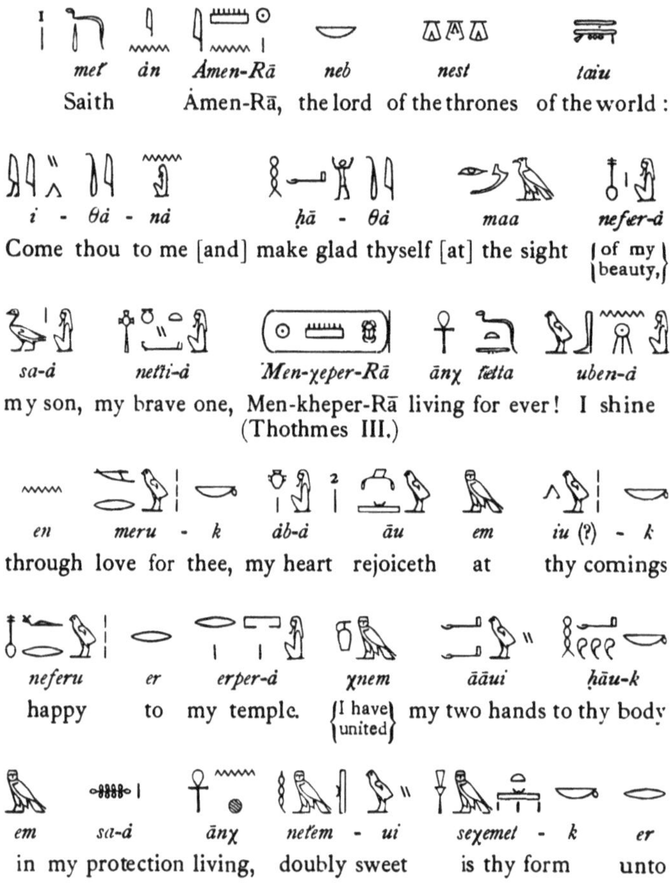

meṭ ȧn Ȧmen-Rā neb nest taiu
Saith Ȧmen-Rā, the lord of the thrones of the world:

i - θȧ - nȧ ḥā - θȧ maa nefer-ȧ
Come thou to me [and] make glad thyself [at] the sight {of my beauty,}

sa-ȧ neṭṭi-ȧ Men-χeper-Rā ānχ ṭetta uben-ȧ
my son, my brave one, Men-kheper-Rā (Thothmes III.) living for ever! I shine

en meru - k ȧb-ȧ āu em iu (?) - k
through love for thee, my heart rejoiceth at thy comings

neferu er erper-ȧ χnem āāui ḥāu-k
happy to my temple. {I have united} my two hands to thy body

em sa-ȧ ānχ neṭem - ui seχemet - k er
in my protection living, doubly sweet is thy form unto

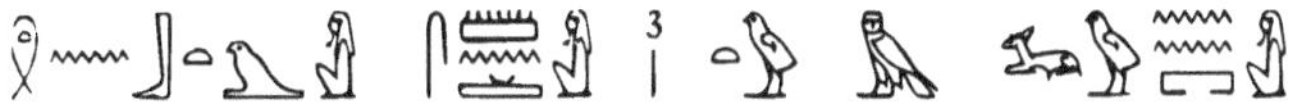

šenbet-à smen-à tu em āunn-à

my divine body. I have stablished thee in my dwellingplace,

bi - à - nek ṭā-à - nek qent neχt

I have made thee a wonder. I have given to thee power and victory

er set nebt ṭā-à baiu-k senṭu - k

over foreign lands all. I have given thy will and the fear of thee

em taiu nebu ḥerit - k er ṭeru

in lands all, they fear thee to the limits

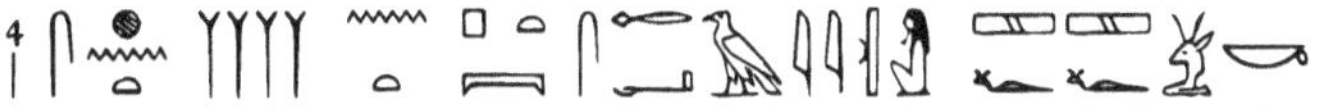

seχent ent pet seāāai - à šefšef - k

of the four pillars of heaven. I have magnified the terror of thee

em χat nebt ṭā-à hemhemet ḥen - k χet

in bodies all, I have given the report of thy majesty among

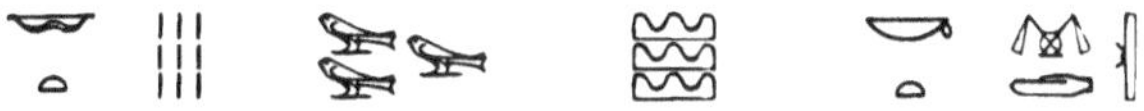

pet paut uru set nebt ṭemṭ

{the nine foreign peoples.} The nobles off oreign nations all in totality [are]

em χefā - k āui - à āāui - à ṭes - à

in thy fist. I have stretched out my hands, mine own,

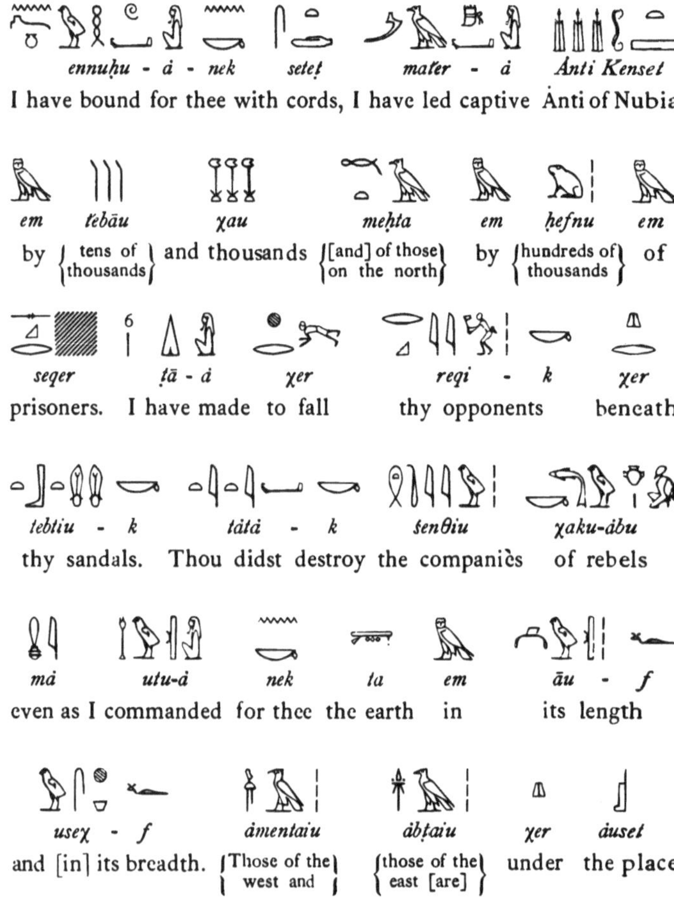

ennuḥu - à - nek setet mater - à Ànti Kenset
I have bound for thee with cords, I have led captive Ànti of Nubia

em tebāu χau meḥta em ḥefnu em
by {tens of thousands} and thousands {[and] of those on the north} by {hundreds of thousands} of

seqer 6 *tā - à χer reqi - k χer*
prisoners. I have made to fall thy opponents beneath

tebtiu - k tàtà - k šenθiu χaku-àbu
thy sandals. Thou didst destroy the companies of rebels

mà utu-à nek ta em āu - f
even as I commanded for thee the earth in its length

useχ - f àmentaiu àbṭaiu χer àuset
and [in] its breadth. {Those of the west and} {those of the east [are]} under the place

ḥrà - k 7 *χent - k set nebt àb - k*
of thy face. Thou hast trodden under foot lands all, thy heart is

āu àn un ḥesi su em hau
glad, not were penetrated they [until] in the time

ḥen - k θ-à em semi sper - k

of thy Majesty. I made myself [thy] guide [when] thou wentest forth

er sen t̔a - nek mu-ur Nehern

to them. Thou hast traversed the great waters of Nehren (Mesopotamia)

em neχt em user utu - nà - nek

in victory [and] in might. I have commanded for thee [that]

setem - sen hemhemet - k āq em

they may hear the noise of thee entering into [their]

baba ḳaq - nà fenṭ - sen em nef en

huts (*or* holes), I have removed their noses from the breath of

ānχ ṭā - à neru nu ḥen - k χet àbu-

life. I have made the terror of thy majesty enter into their

sen χut - à àmt ṭep - k sesun - s

hearts. My uraeus crown is on thy head, it burneth with fire

set àri - s àseb ḥaq em

them, it maketh [thee] to lead away captives from among

SPEECH OF ÀMEN-RĀ TO THOTHMES III.

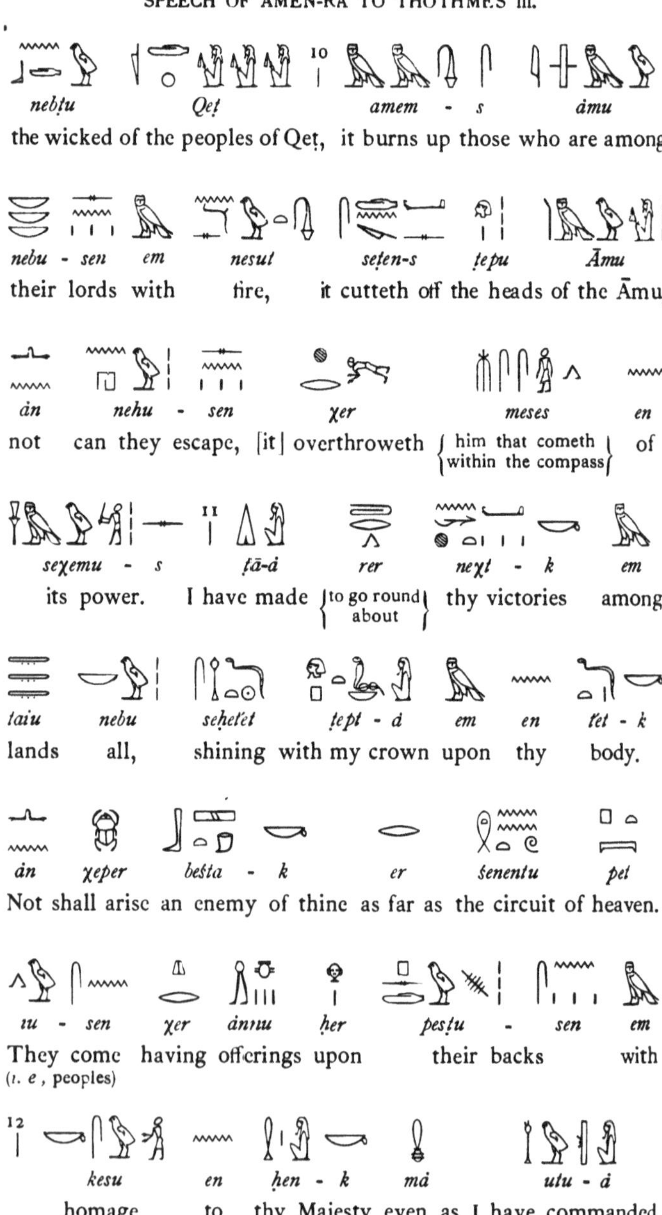

nebṭu *Qeṭ* *amem - s* *àmu*
the wicked of the peoples of Qeṭ, it burns up those who are among

nebu - sen *em* *nesut* *seṭen-s* *ṭepu* *Āmu*
their lords with fire, it cutteth off the heads of the Āmu,

àn *nehu - sen* *χer* *meses* *en*
not can they escape, [it] overthroweth {him that cometh within the compass} of

seχemu - s *ṭā-à* *rer* *neχt - k* *em*
its power. I have made {to go round about} thy victories among

taiu *nebu* *seḥeṭet* *ṭept - à* *em* *en* *ṭet - k*
lands all, shining with my crown upon thy body.

àn *χeper* *beśta - k* *er* *śenentu* *pet*
Not shall arise an enemy of thine as far as the circuit of heaven.

iu - sen *χer* *ànnu* *ḥer* *pesṭu - sen* *em*
They come (i. e., peoples) having offerings upon their backs with

kesu *en* *ḥen - k* *mà* *utu - à*
homage to thy Majesty even as I have commanded

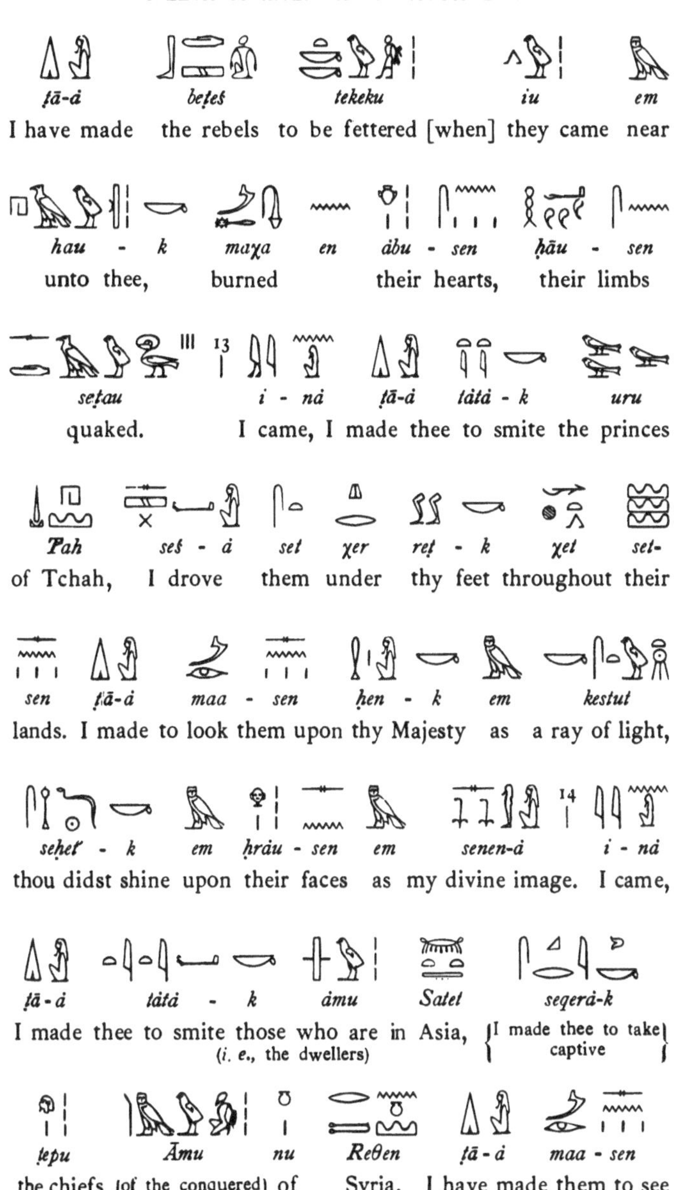
ṭā-à beṭeš tekeku iu em
I have made the rebels to be fettered [when] they came near
hau - k maχa en àbu - sen ḥāu - sen
unto thee, burned their hearts, their limbs
seṭau i - nà ṭā-à tàtà - k uru
quaked. I came, I made thee to smite the princes
Ṭah seš - à set χer reṭ - k χet set-
of Tchah, I drove them under thy feet throughout their
sen ṭā-à maa - sen ḥen - k em kestut
lands. I made to look them upon thy Majesty as a ray of light,
sehet' - k em ḥràu - sen em senen-à i - nà
thou didst shine upon their faces as my divine image. I came,
ṭā - à tàtà - k àmu Satet seqerà-k
I made thee to smite those who are in Asia, I made thee to take captive
(i. e., the dwellers)
ṭepu Āmu nu Reθen ṭā - à maa - sen
the chiefs of the conquered nomads of Syria, I have made them to see

SPEECH OF ȦMEN-RĀ TO THOTHMES III.

ḥen - k āper em χaχer - k seśep-k χāā
thy Majesty provided with thy panoply, {thou didst grasp} [thy] weapons

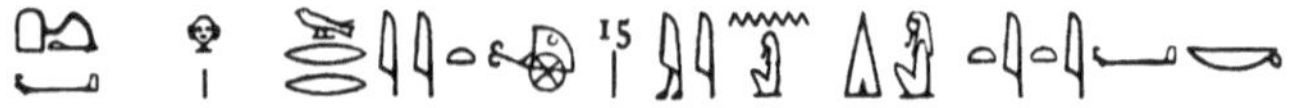

āba ḥer urerit 15 *i - nȧ ṭā-ȧ ṭȧṭȧ - k*
[and] fight upon [thy] chariot. I came, I made thee to smite

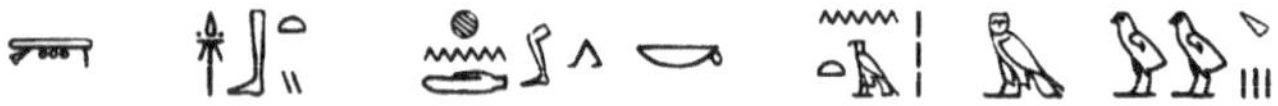

ta ȧbtet χenṭ - k entau em uu
the land of the east, thou didst trample down those in the regions

nu Ta-neter ṭā - ȧ maa - sen ḥen - k mȧ
of Ta-neter. I made them to look upon thy Majesty as one

seśeṭ sba set bes - f em seśet
circling [like] a star and pouring out his radiance in fire,

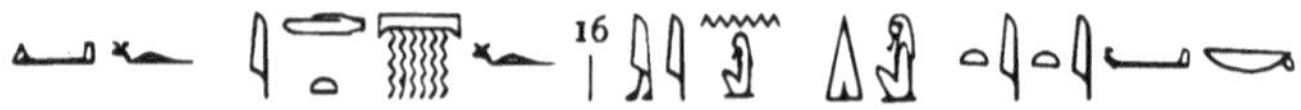

ṭā - f ȧṭet - f 16 *i - nȧ ṭā-ȧ ṭȧṭȧ - k*
he giveth forth his dew. I came, I made thee to smite

ta Ȧmentet Kefa Ȧsebi χer
the land of the west, Phoenicia and Cyprus hold [thee]

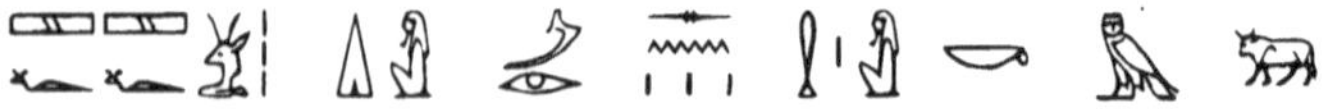

śefśef ṭā - ȧ maa - sen ḥen - k em ka
in fear. I made them to look upon thy Majesty like a bull

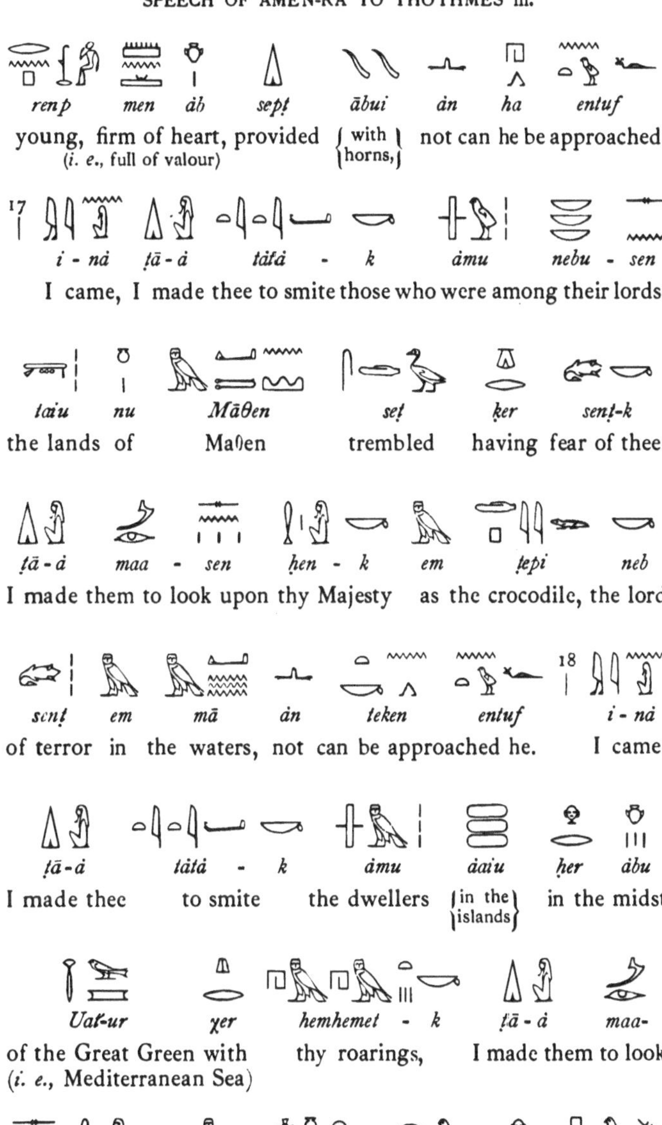

renp men ȧb sepṭ ābui ȧn ha entuf

young, firm of heart, (*i. e.*, full of valour) provided {with horns,} not can he be approached.

17 *i - nȧ ṭā - ȧ tȧṭȧ - k ȧmu nebu - sen*

I came, I made thee to smite those who were among their lords,

taȧu nu Māθen seṭ ḳer senṭ-k

the lands of Maθen trembled having fear of thee.

ṭā - ȧ maa - sen ḥen - k em ṭepi neb

I made them to look upon thy Majesty as the crocodile, the lord

senṭ em mā ȧn teken entuf 18 *i - nȧ*

of terror in the waters, not can be approached he. I came,

ṭā-ȧ tȧṭȧ - k ȧmu ȧaȧu ḥer ȧbu

I made thee to smite the dwellers {in the islands} in the midst

Uaṭ-ur χer hemhemet - k ṭā - ȧ maa-

of the Great Green (*i. e.*, Mediterranean Sea) with thy roarings, I made them to look

sen ḥen - k em neṭeti χāāu ḥer pesṭu

upon thy Majesty as the avenger [who] stands upon the back

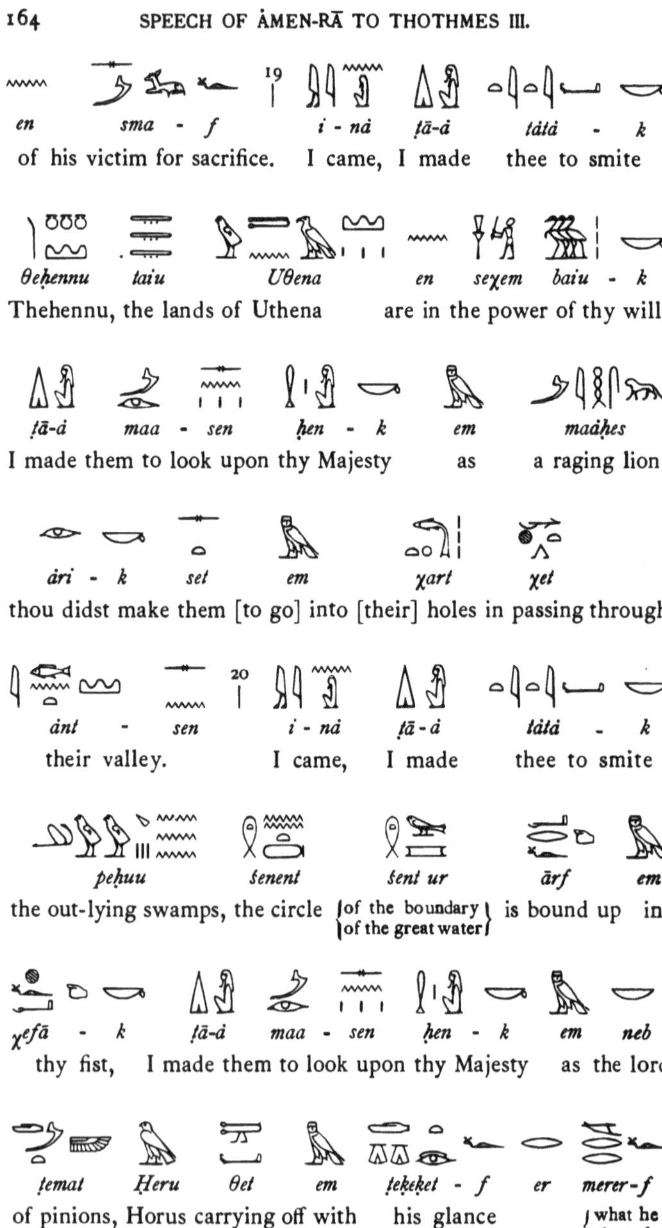

en sma - f 19 *i - nà ṭā-à tàtà - k*
of his victim for sacrifice. I came, I made thee to smite

Θeḥennu taiu UΘena en seχem baiu - k
Thehennu, the lands of Uthena are in the power of thy will.

ṭā-à maa - sen ḥen - k em maàḥes
I made them to look upon thy Majesty as a raging lion,

àri - k set em χart χet
thou didst make them [to go] into [their] holes in passing through

ànt - sen 20 *i - nà ṭā - à tàtà - k*
their valley. I came, I made thee to smite

peḥuu šenent šent ur ārf em
the out-lying swamps, the circle {of the boundary / of the great water} is bound up in

χefā - k ṭā-à maa - sen ḥen - k em neb
thy fist, I made them to look upon thy Majesty as the lord

ṭemat Ḥeru Θet em ṭekeket - f er merer-f
of pinions, Horus carrying off with his glance {what he pleaseth.}

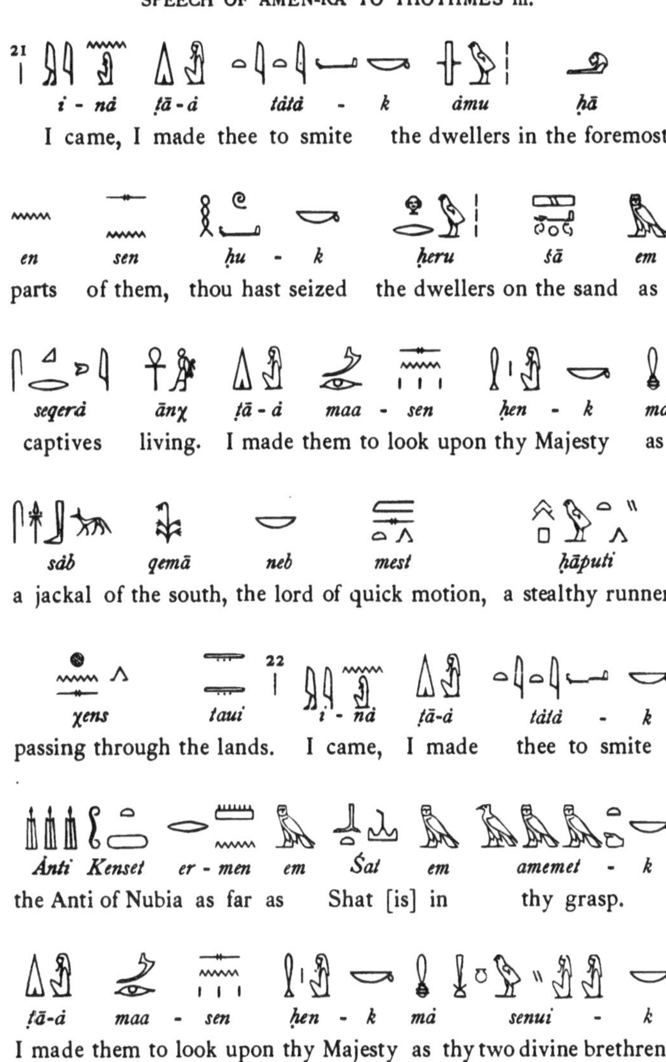

21 *i - nȧ ṭā - ȧ tȧtȧ - k ȧmu ḥā*

I came, I made thee to smite the dwellers in the foremost

en sen ḥu - k ḥeru śā em

parts of them, thou hast seized the dwellers on the sand as

seqerȧ ānχ ṭā - ȧ maa - sen ḥen - k mȧ

captives living. I made them to look upon thy Majesty as

sȧb qemā neb mest ḥāputi

a jackal of the south, the lord of quick motion, a stealthy runner

χens taui 22 *i - nȧ ṭā-ȧ tȧtȧ - k*

passing through the lands. I came, I made thee to smite

Ȧnti Kenset er - men em Śat em amemet - k

the Anti of Nubia as far as Shat [is] in thy grasp.

ṭā-ȧ maa - sen ḥen - k mȧ senui - k

I made them to look upon thy Majesty as thy two divine brethren,

ṭemṭ - nȧ āāui - sen nek em n . . . 23 *sent - k*

I have united their two hands unto thee in . . . . . ., {thy two divine sisters}

tā - nȧ *sen* *em* *sa* *ḥa - k* *āāui* *ḥen-ȧ*

I have given them as a protection {behind thee.} The hands {of my Majesty}

ḥer *ḥert* *ḥer* *seḥer* *ṭut* *tā-ȧ* *χut - k*

are in heaven above to drive away evil. {I have given} {thy glorious strength,}

sa - ȧ *merer-ȧ* *ka* *neχt* *χā* *em* *Uast*

my son, my beloved one, O bull mighty diademed in Thebes,

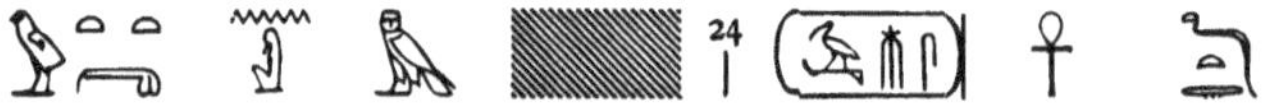

utet - nȧ *em* . . . . . 24 *Teḥuti-mes* *ānχ* *ṫetta*

I have engendered with [my body] Thothmes, living for ever,

ȧri - nȧ *merert* *nebt* *ka-ȧ* *seāḥā - nek*

who did for me wish every of myself. Thou hast raised up

āunen - ȧ *em* *kat* *neḥeḥ* *seāuu* *seusex*

my dwelling in work everlasting, {making it longer} and broader

(*i. e.*, work which shall last for ever)

er *pat* *χeper* *seb* *ur* 25 *seḥeb*

than [it was] before; there came into being {a door great.} {[Thou hast] celebrated by festival}

neferu *en* *Åmen-Rā* *ur* *menu - k* *er*

the beauties of Åmen-Rā, great are thy monuments more

suten - k neb χeper utu - nȧ - nek

than [those of] king any that hath existed. I commanded thee

ȧrit - set ḥetep - ku ḥer - s smen-ȧ

to make them, and thou hast been content thereat. I have established

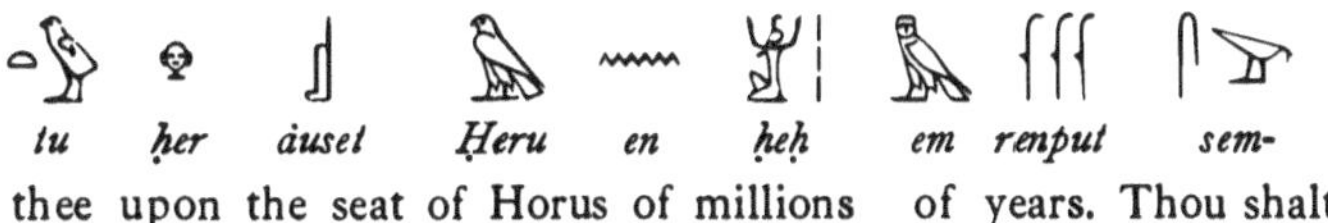

tu ḥer ȧuset Ḥeru en ḥeḥ em renput sem-

thee upon the seat of Horus of millions of years. Thou shalt

k ānχ

guide living .

EXTRACT FROM THE 154TH CHAPTER OF THE BOOK OF THE DEAD.

[XVIIIth dynasty.]

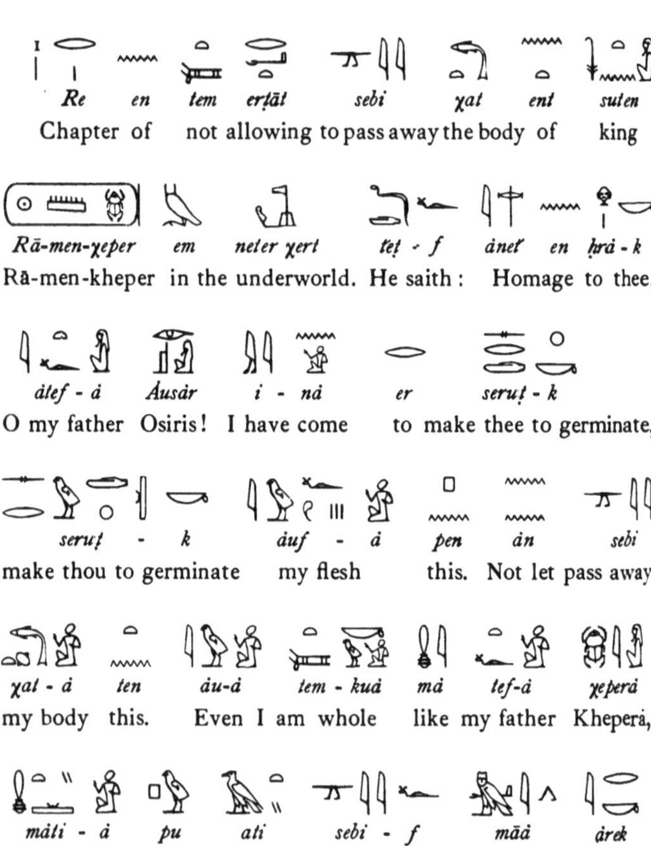

Re en tem erṭāt sebi χat ent suten
Chapter of not allowing to pass away the body of king

Rā-men-χeper em neter χert ṭeṭ - f ȧnet' en ḥrȧ - k
Rā-men-kheper in the underworld. He saith: Homage to thee,

ȧtef - ȧ Ȧusȧr i - nȧ er seruṭ - k
O my father Osiris! I have come to make thee to germinate,

seruṭ - k ȧuf - ȧ pen ȧn sebi
make thou to germinate my flesh this. Not let pass away

χat - ȧ ten ȧu-ȧ tem - kuȧ mȧ tef-ȧ χeperȧ
my body this. Even I am whole like my father Kheperȧ,

mȧti - ȧ pu ati sebi - f māȧ ȧrek
a type to me in that without decay is he. Come, therefore,

seχem *nefu - à* *erek* *neb* *nefu* *θ'n*

provide breath for me then, O lord of breath; {O [thou who art] greater}

er *màta-f* *ṭeṭṭeṭ* *erek* *nub* - *kuà*

than those like unto him. Stablish [me] therefore, [and] mould me

em *neb* *qerest* *ṭā* - *k* *ha* - *à* *er*

like the Lord of the tomb. Grant thou that I may walk for

neḥeḥ *mà* *ennu* *àri* - *nek* *ḥenā*

ever and ever according to that which thou didst do unto

tef - *k* *Tem* *àn* *sebi* *χat* - *f* *pa*

thy father Temu; not did pass away his body [for] he it is

pu *ati* *sek* - *f* *àn* *àri* - *à* *mesṭeṭet* - *k*

who is without diminution. Not have I done {what is hateful to thee,}

ḥaui *meru* - *à* *ka* - *k* *àn* *uàn* - *f*-

nay verily I have loved thyself; not may he reject

uà *seśeṭ* - *kuà* *em-χet-k* *tem* - *à*

me. Perfect me after thy likeness, and let not be to me

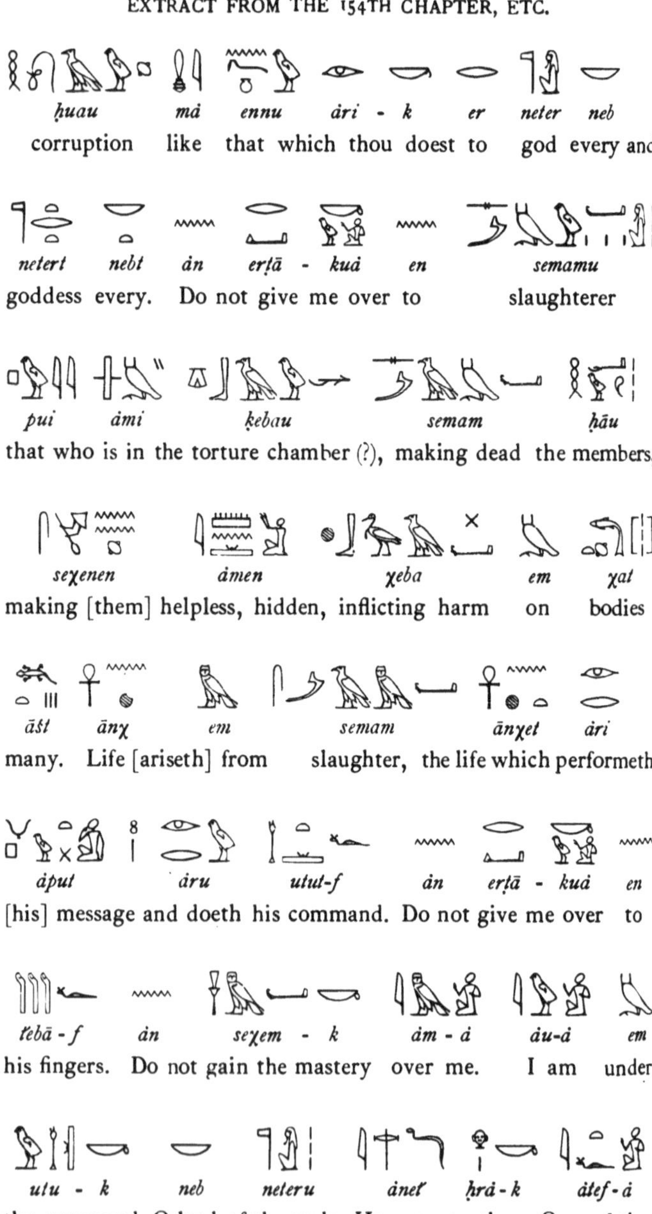

ḥuau *mȧ* *ennu* *ȧri* - *k* *er* *neter* *neb*
corruption like that which thou doest to god every and

netert *nebt* *ȧn* *erṭā* - *kuȧ* *en* *semamu*
goddess every. Do not give me over to slaughterer

pui *ȧmi* *ḳebau* *semam* *ḥāu*
that who is in the torture chamber (?), making dead the members,

seχenen *ȧmen* *χeba* *em* *χat*
making [them] helpless, hidden, inflicting harm on bodies

āšt *ānχ* *em* *semam* *ānχet* *ȧri*
many. Life [ariseth] from slaughter, the life which performeth

ȧput *ȧru* *utut-f* *ȧn* *erṭā* - *kuȧ* *en*
[his] message and doeth his command. Do not give me over to

ṭebā - *f* *ȧn* *seχem* - *k* *ȧm* - *ȧ* *ȧu-ȧ* *em*
his fingers. Do not gain the mastery over me. I am under

utu - *k* *neb* *neteru* *ȧnet'* *ḥrȧ* - *k* *ȧtef* - *ȧ*
thy command, O lord of the gods. Homage to thee, O my father

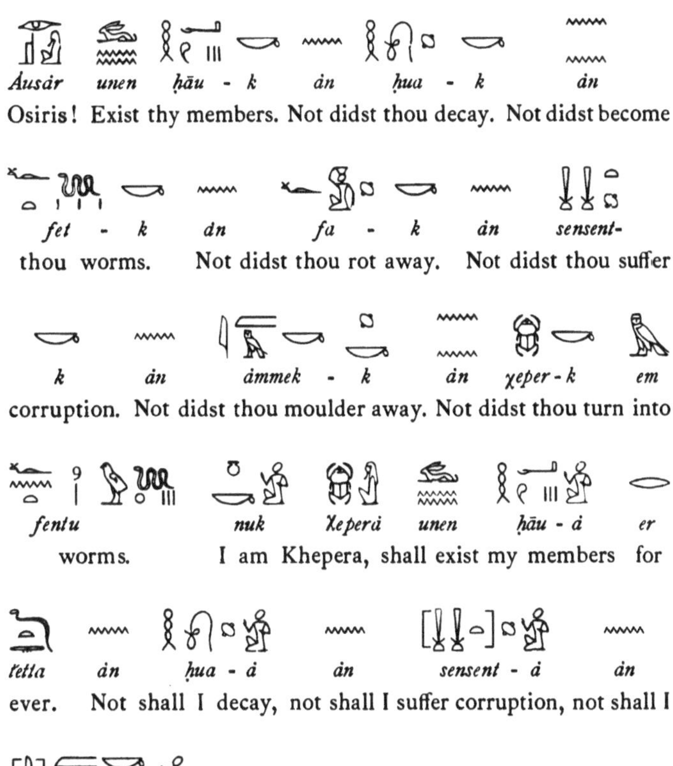

Ausȧr unen ḥāu - k ȧn ḥua - k ȧn
Osiris! Exist thy members. Not didst thou decay. Not didst become

fet - k ȧn fa - k ȧn sensent-
thou worms. Not didst thou rot away. Not didst thou suffer

k ȧn ȧmmek - k ȧn χeper - k em
corruption. Not didst thou moulder away. Not didst thou turn into

fentu nuk Χeperȧ unen ḥāu - ȧ er
worms. I am Khepera, shall exist my members for

ṭetta ȧn ḥua - ȧ ȧn sensent - ȧ ȧn
ever. Not shall I decay, not shall I suffer corruption, not shall I

ȧmmek - ȧ
moulder away.

SPECIMENS OF THE MAXIMS OF ANI.

[XVIIIth dynasty.]

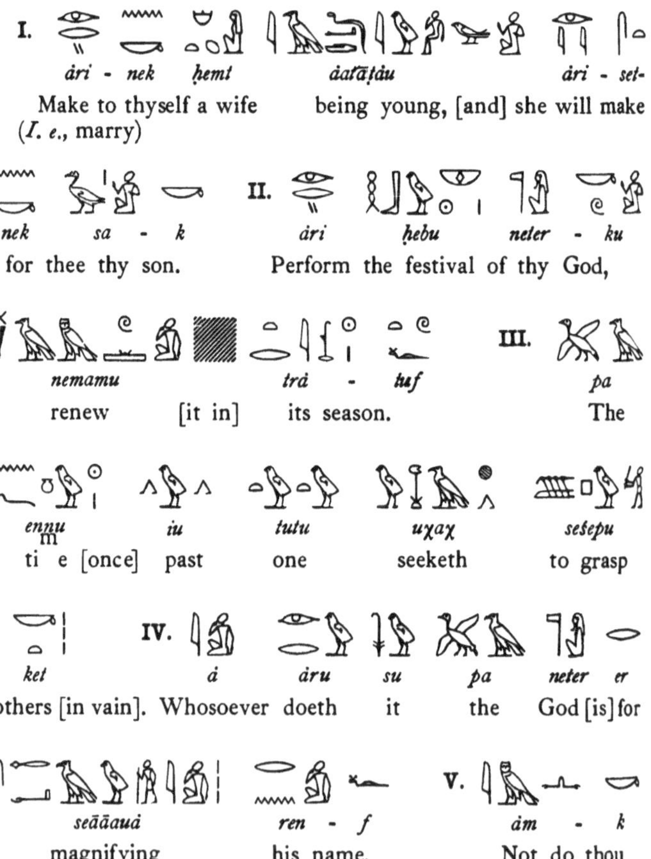

I.
ȧri - nek ḥemt ȧaṭāṭȧu ȧri - set-
Make to thyself a wife being young, [and] she will make
(*I. e.*, marry)
nek sa - k
for thee thy son.
II.
ȧri ḥebu neter - ku
Perform the festival of thy God,
nemamu trȧ - tuf
renew [it in] its season.
III.
pa
The
ennu iu tutu uχaχ sešepu
time [once] past one seeketh to grasp
ket
others [in vain].
IV.
ȧ ȧru su pa neter er
Whosoever doeth it the God [is] for
seāāauȧ ren - f
magnifying his name.
V.
ȧm - k
Not do thou

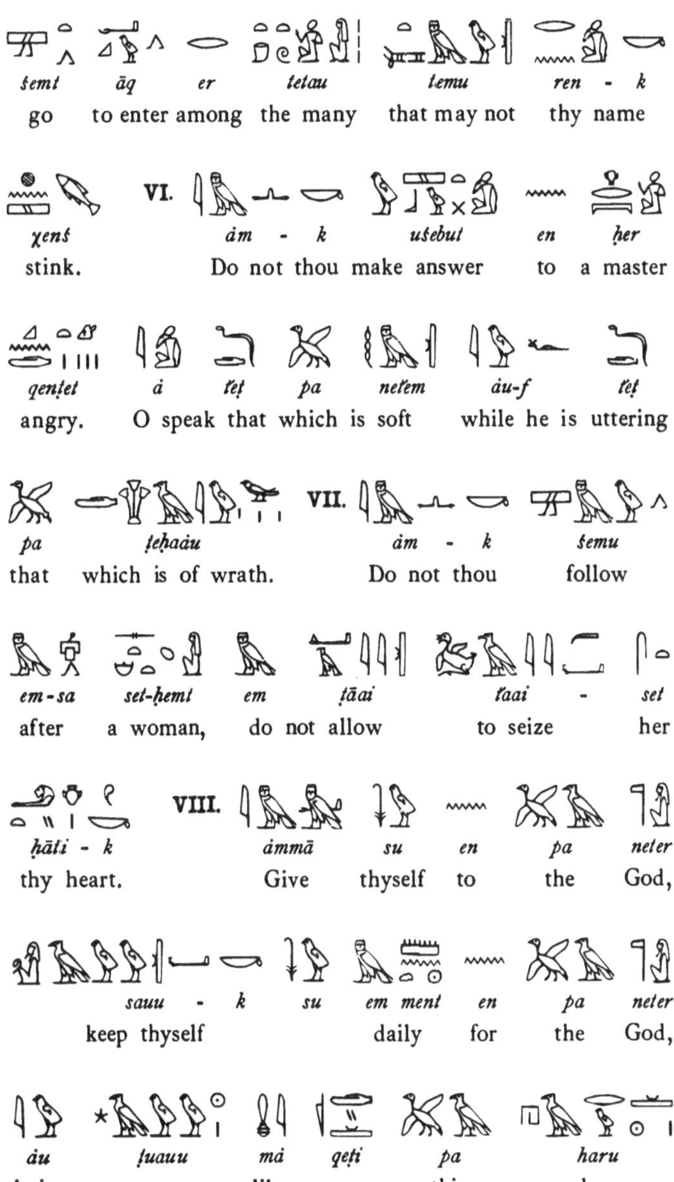

šemt āq er tetau temu ren - k

go to enter among the many that may not thy name

χenš VI. *àm - k ušebut en ḥer*

stink. Do not thou make answer to a master

qenṭet à ṭeṭ pa neṭem àu-f ṭeṭ

angry. O speak that which is soft while he is uttering

pa ṭeḥaàu VII. *àm - k šemu*

that which is of wrath. Do not thou follow

em-sa set-ḥemt em ṭāai ṭaai - set

after a woman, do not allow to seize her

ḥāti - k VIII. *àmmā su en pa neter*

thy heart. Give thyself to the God,

sauu - k su em ment en pa neter

keep thyself daily for the God,

àu ṭuauu mà qeṭi pa haru

being to-morrow like as this day.

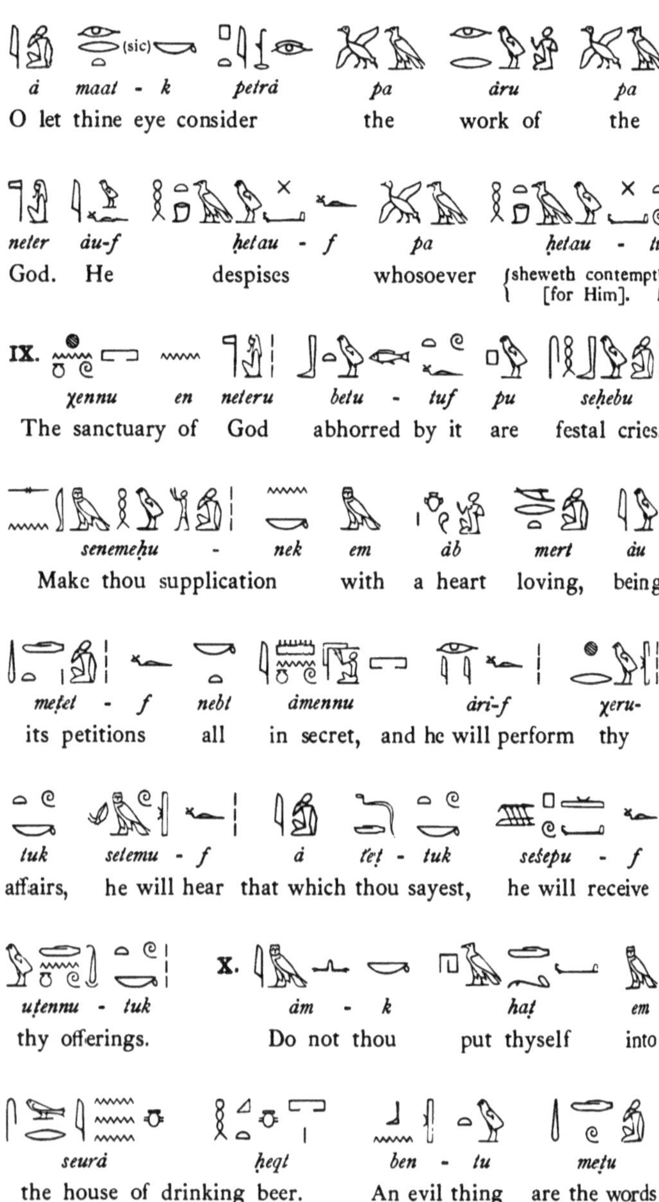

à maat - k petrà pa àru pa
O let thine eye consider the work of the

neter àu-f ḥetau - f pa ḥetau - tu
God. He despises whosoever {sheweth contempt [for Him].}

IX. *χennu en neteru betu - tuf pu seḥebu*
The sanctuary of God abhorred by it are festal cries.

senemeḥu - nek em àb mert àu
Make thou supplication with a heart loving, being

meṭet - f nebt àmennu àri-f χeru-
its petitions all in secret, and he will perform thy

tuk setemu - f à ṭeṭ - tuk sešepu - f
affairs, he will hear that which thou sayest, he will receive

uṭennu - tuk
thy offerings.

X. *àm - k haṭ em*
Do not thou put thyself into

seurà ḥeqt ben - tu meṭu
the house of drinking beer. An evil thing are the words

semäi sen per em re-k ȧn reχ-

reported second-hand coming forth from thy mouth, not knowing

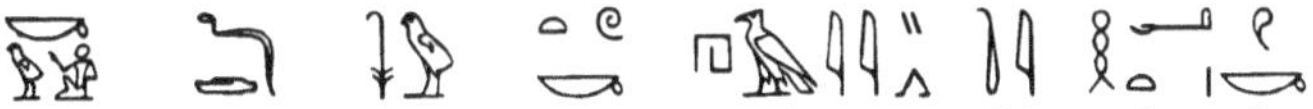

ku ṭeṭ su tuk hai - θȧ ḥāt - k

thou have been said they by thee. Having fallen thy members

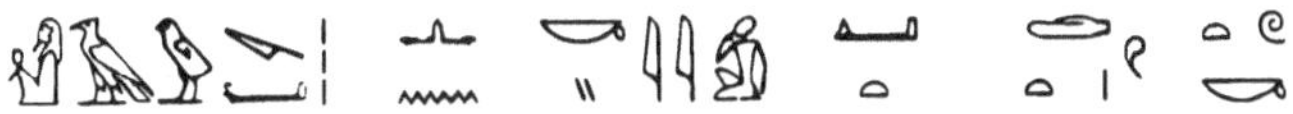

sau ȧn ki ṭāt ṭet - tuk

are broken, not another giveth the hand to thee.

nai - k ȧri seurȧ set āḥā

Thy companions [in] drink they stand up

 XI.

ṭeṭu ḥerȧu pai seurȧ ȧm-

saying, "Away with this drunkard". Do not

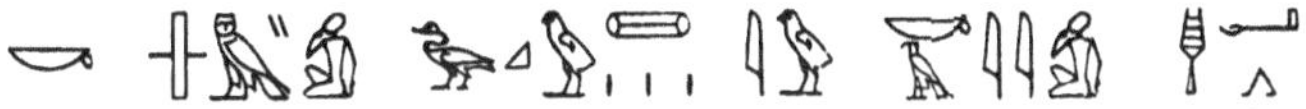

k ȧmi āqu ȧu kai āḥā

thou eat bread being another standing,

em-tuk temu ȧāut - nef ṭet - tuk

thou not stretching out to him thy hand

 XII.

er pa āqu ïui pa met

with the bread. Cometh death

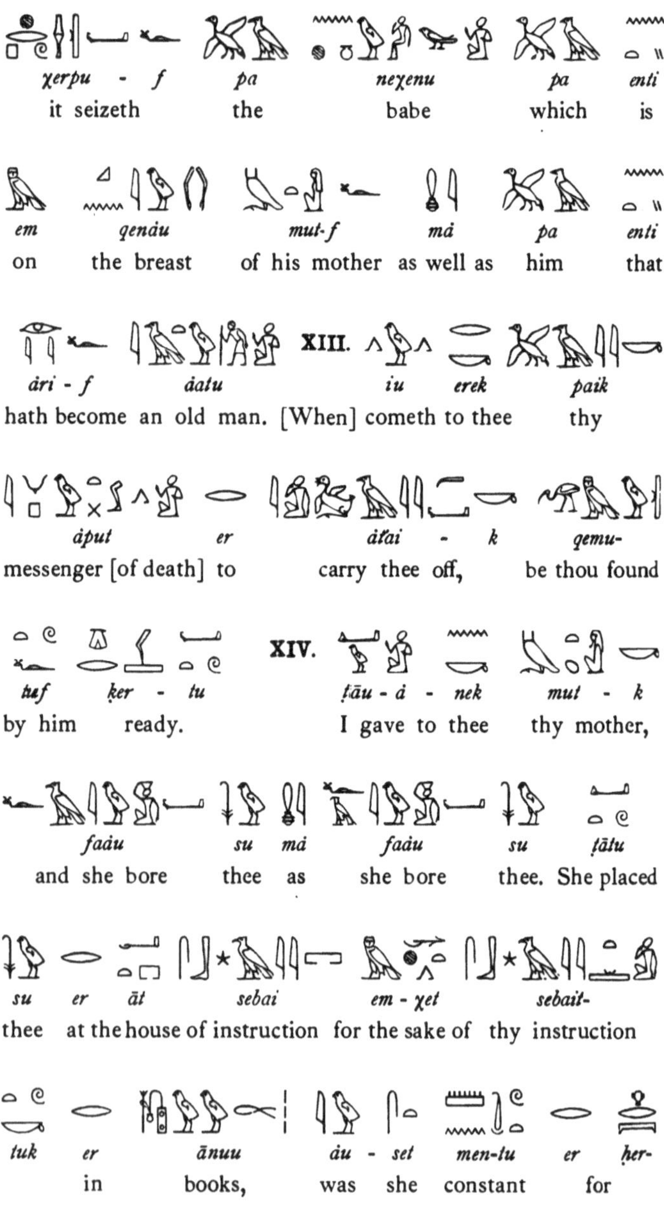
χerpu - f pa neχenu pa enti
it seizeth the babe which is
em qenȧu mut-f mȧ pa enti
on the breast of his mother as well as him that
ȧri - f ȧatu XIII. iu erek paik
hath become an old man. [When] cometh to thee thy
ȧput er ȧťai - k qemu-
messenger [of death] to carry thee off, be thou found
tuf ḳer - tu XIV. ťāu - ȧ - nek mut - k
by him ready. I gave to thee thy mother,
faȧu su mȧ faȧu su ťātu
and she bore thee as she bore thee. She placed
su er āt sebai em - χet sebait-
thee at the house of instruction for the sake of thy instruction
tuk er ānuu ȧu - set men-tu er ḥer-
in books, was she constant for

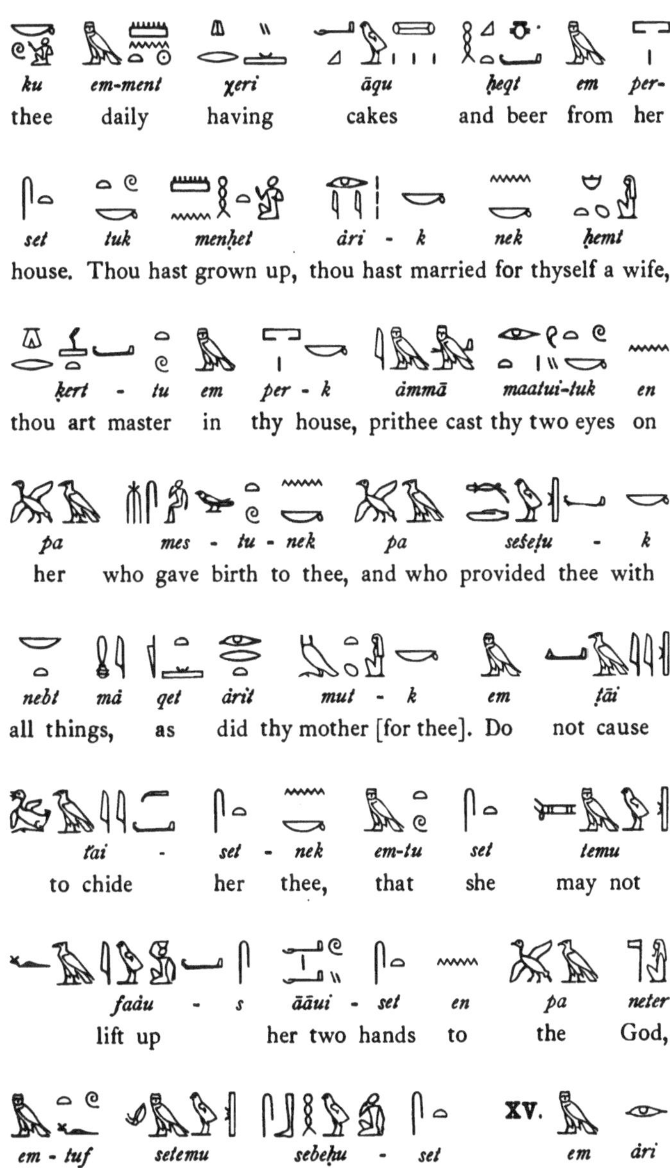

ku em-ment χeri āqu ḥeqt em per-
thee daily having cakes and beer from her

set tuk menḥet ȧri - k nek ḥemt
house. Thou hast grown up, thou hast married for thyself a wife,

ḳert - tu em per - k ȧmmā maatui-tuk en
thou art master in thy house, prithee cast thy two eyes on

pa mes - tu - nek pa seśeṭu - k
her who gave birth to thee, and who provided thee with

nebt mȧ qet ȧrit mut - k em ṭāi
all things, as did thy mother [for thee]. Do not cause

ṭai - set - nek em-tu set temu
to chide her thee, that she may not

faȧu - s āāui - set en pa neter
lift up her two hands to the God,

em - tuf setemu sebeḥu - set **XV.** *em ȧri*
and he hear her petition [and punish thee]. Do not make

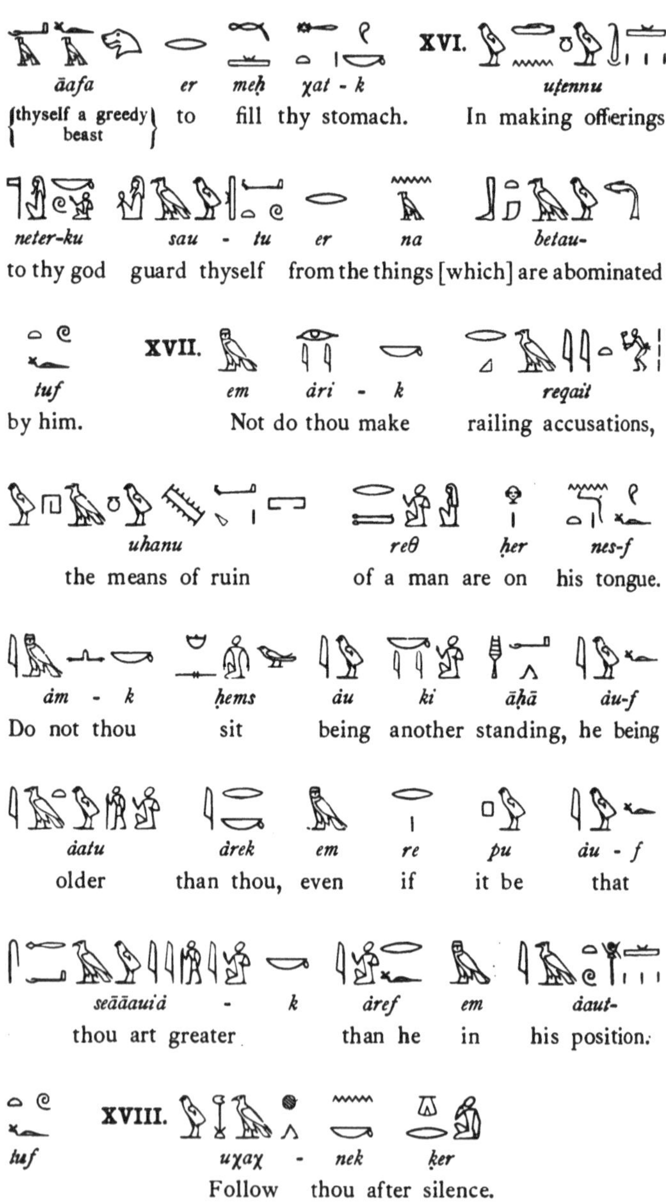

āafa *er* *meḥ* *χat - k* XVI. *uṭennu*

{thyself a greedy beast} to fill thy stomach. In making offerings

neter-ku *sau - tu* *er* *na* *betau-*

to thy god guard thyself from the things [which] are abominated

tuf XVII. *em* *àri - k* *reqait*

by him. Not do thou make railing accusations,

uhanu *reθ* *ḥer* *nes-f*

the means of ruin of a man are on his tongue.

àm - k *ḥems* *àu* *ki* *āḥā* *àu-f*

Do not thou sit being another standing, he being

àatu *àrek* *em* *re* *pu* *àu - f*

older than thou, even if it be that

seāāauià - k *àref* *em* *àaut-*

thou art greater than he in his position.

tuf XVIII. *uχaχ - nek* *ḳer*

Follow thou after silence.

HYMN TO OSIRIS.

[XVIIIth dynasty.]

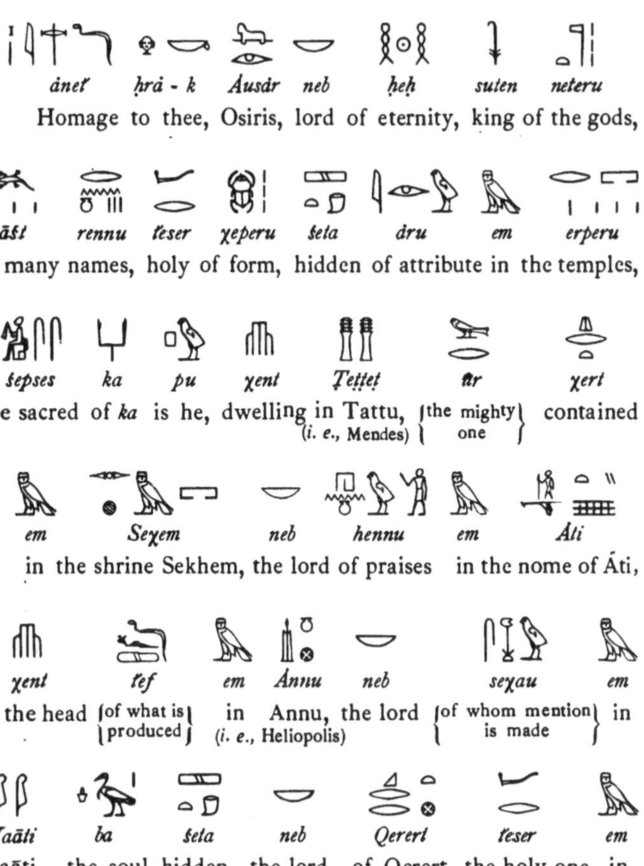

1 *ȧneṭ ḥrȧ - k Ȧusȧr neb ḥeḥ suten neteru*
Homage to thee, Osiris, lord of eternity, king of the gods,

āšt rennu ṭeser χeperu šeta ȧru em erperu
of many names, holy of form, hidden of attribute in the temples,

šepses ka pu χent Ṭeṭṭeṭ ur χert
the sacred of *ka* is he, dwelling in Tattu (*i. e.*, Mendes), {the mighty one} contained

2 *em Seχem neb hennu em Ȧti*
in the shrine Sekhem, the lord of praises in the nome of Ȧti,

χent ṭef em Annu neb seχau em
at the head {of what is produced} in Annu (*i. e.*, Heliopolis), the lord {of whom mention is made} in

Maāti ba šeta neb Qerert ṭeser em
Maāti, the soul hidden, the lord of Qerert, the holy one in

Åneb ḥet' ba Rā t'et - f t'esef ḥetep em

{[the city of the] White Wall,} the soul of Rā, his body his very own, resting in

Ḥenen-su menχ hennu em nārt χeper seθet

Ḥenen-su, beneficent one, praised in Nārt, making to ascend

ba - f neb ḥet-āa em χemennu āa nerȧu

his soul, the lord {of the Great Temple} in Khemennu, (*i. e.*, Hermopolis) {the mighty one} of terror

em Śas-ḥetep neb ḥeḥ χent Åbṭu ḥer

in Shas-ḥetep, the lord of eternity, the dweller in Abtu. (*i. e.*, Abydos) The path of

ȧuset - f em Ta-t'esert ṭeṭṭeṭ ren em re en

his seat is in Ta-tchesert, stablished of name in the mouth of

reθ paut en taui tem t'ef

mankind, {the matter (*or* substance)} of the two lands, the god Tmu [who] feedeth

kau χent paut neteru χu menχ emmā

ka's {in the presence of the} companies of the gods, a *khu* beneficent among

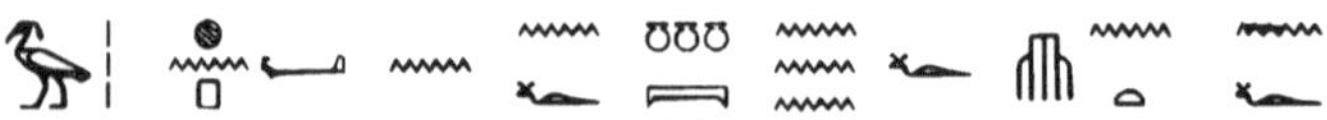

χu χenp en nef Nu mu - f χent - nef

khu's. Draweth from him Nu his waters, he bringeth forth

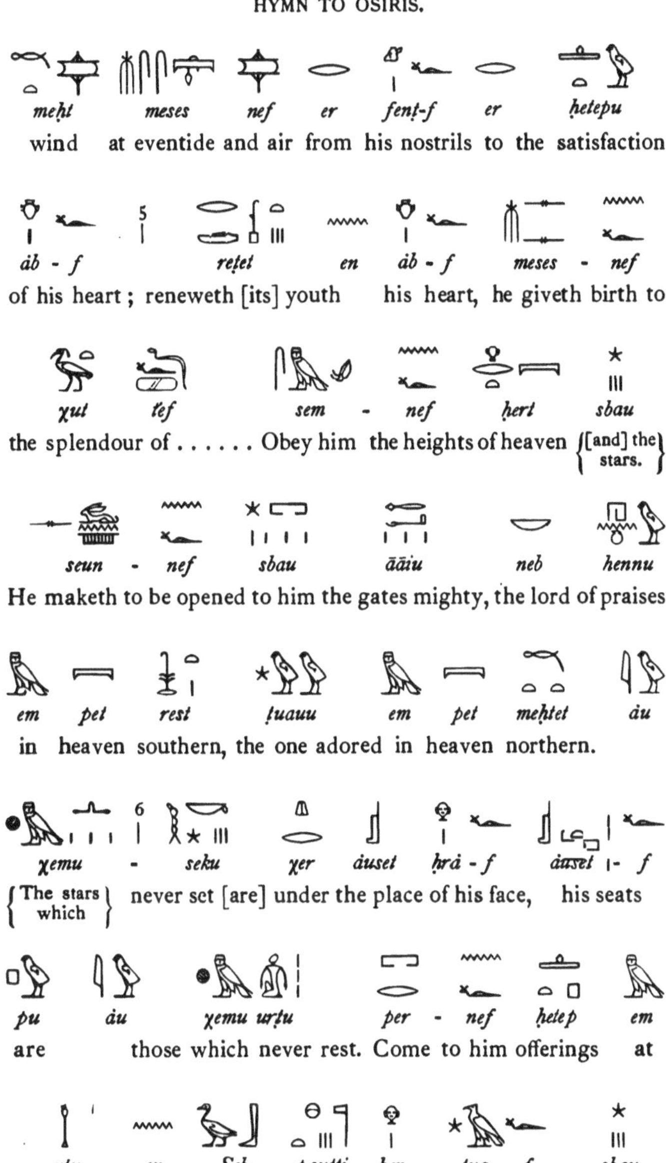

meḥt meses nef er fenṭ-f er ḥetepu
wind at eventide and air from his nostrils to the satisfaction

ȧb - f reṭeṭ en ȧb - f meses - nef
of his heart; reneweth [its] youth his heart, he giveth birth to

χut ṭef sem - nef ḥert sbau
the splendour of . . . . . . Obey him the heights of heaven {[and] the stars.}

seun - nef sbau āāiu neb hennu
He maketh to be opened to him the gates mighty, the lord of praises

em pet rest ṭuauu em pet meḥtet ȧu
in heaven southern, the one adored in heaven northern.

χemu - seku χer ȧuset ḥrȧ - f ȧuset - f
{The stars which} never set [are] under the place of his face, his seats

pu ȧu χemu urṭu per - nef ḥetep em
are those which never rest. Come to him offerings at

utu en Seb pautti ḥer ṭua - f sbau
the command of Seb. {The divine companies are} for praising him, the stars

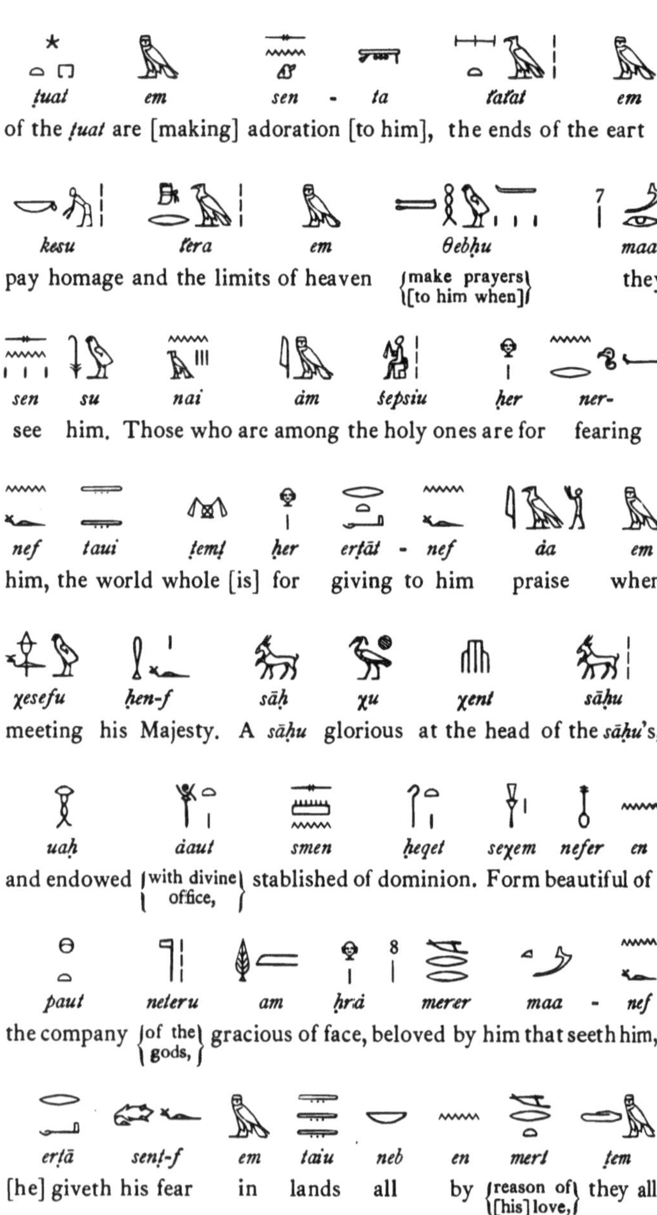

ṭuat em sen - ta ṭaṭat em

of the *ṭuat* are [making] adoration [to him], the ends of the eart

kesu ṭera em θebḥu maa-

pay homage and the limits of heaven {make prayers [to him when]} they

sen su nai ȧm šepsiu ḥer ner-

see him. Those who are among the holy ones are for fearing

nef taui ṭemṭ ḥer erṭāt - nef ȧa em

him, the world whole [is] for giving to him praise when

χesefu ḥen-f sāḥ χu χent sāḥu

meeting his Majesty. A *sāḥu* glorious at the head of the *sāḥu*'s,

uaḥ ȧaut smen ḥeqet seχem nefer en

and endowed {with divine office,} stablished of dominion. Form beautiful of

paut neteru am ḥrȧ merer maa - nef

the company {of the gods,} gracious of face, beloved by him that seeth him,

erṭā sent-f em taiu neb en mert ṭem

[he] giveth his fear in lands all by {reason of [his] love,} they all

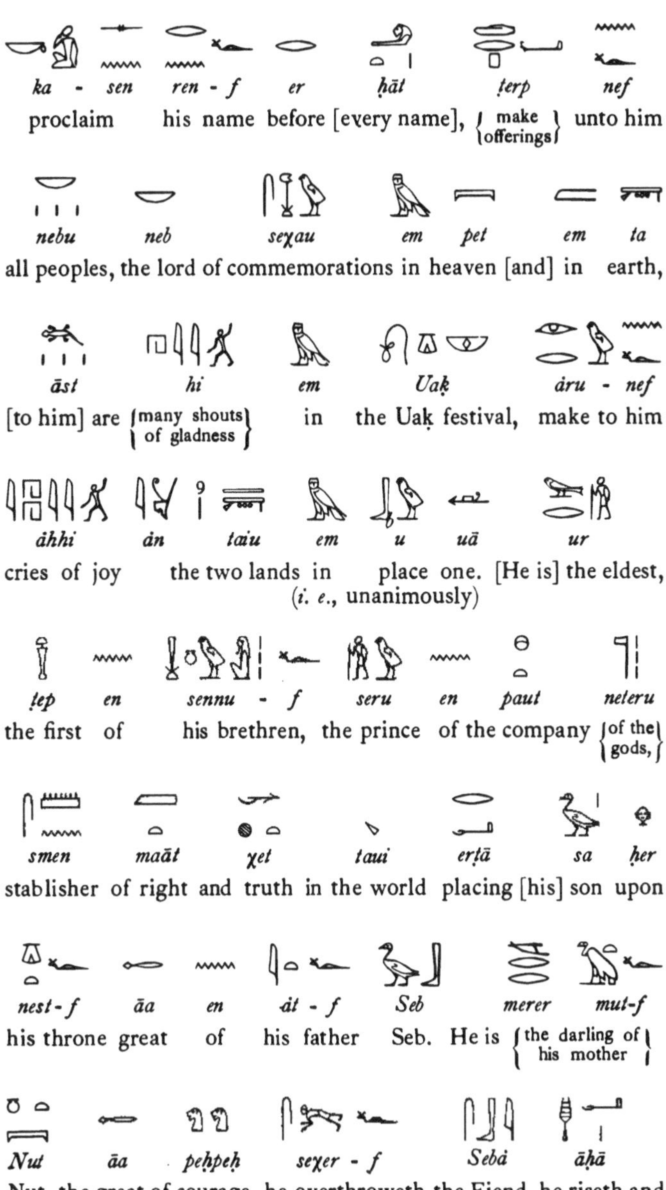

ka - sen ren - f er ḥāt ṭerp nef

proclaim his name before [every name], {make offerings} unto him

nebu neb seχau em pet em ta

all peoples, the lord of commemorations in heaven [and] in earth,

āst hi em Uaḳ āru - nef

[to him] are {many shouts of gladness} in the Uaḳ festival, make to him

āhhi ān taïu em u uā ur

cries of joy the two lands in place one. [He is] the eldest, (*i. e.*, unanimously)

ṭep en sennu - f seru en paut neteru

the first of his brethren, the prince of the company {of the gods,}

smen maāt χet taui erṭā sa ḥer

stablisher of right and truth in the world placing [his] son upon

nest - f āa en āt - f Seb merer mut-f

his throne great of his father Seb. He is {the darling of his mother}

Nut āa peḥpeḥ seχer - f Sebȧ āḥā

Nut, the great of courage, he overthroweth the Fiend, he riseth and

10

sma - f χeft - f erṭā senṭ - f em χeru - f

slaughtereth his enemy, he placeth his fear in his adversary,

ȧn ṭeru . . . . men ȧb reṭ-

[he] carrieth off the boundaries . . . . . ., [he is] fixed of heart, his legs

f seθet (?) āuāu Seb sutenit taui

are raised up; [he is] the heir of Seb {and of the kingdom} of the world.

maa - f χu - f seutu - nef nef sem

He hath seen his powers, he hath given command to him to direct

11

taiu en em ā er uaḥ en sep

the lands by [his] hand as long as the abiding of {times and seasons.}

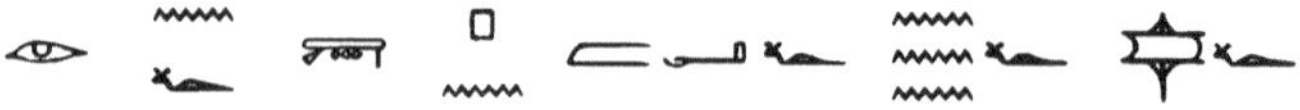

ȧri - nef ta pen em ā - f mu - f nef - f

He hath made earth this with his hand, its waters, its air,

sem - f menment - f nebt pait nebt

its vegetation, its cattle all, [its] birds all,

χepanen nebt ṭetfet - f āut - f

[its] fishes all, its creeping things [all], its four-footed beasts [all].

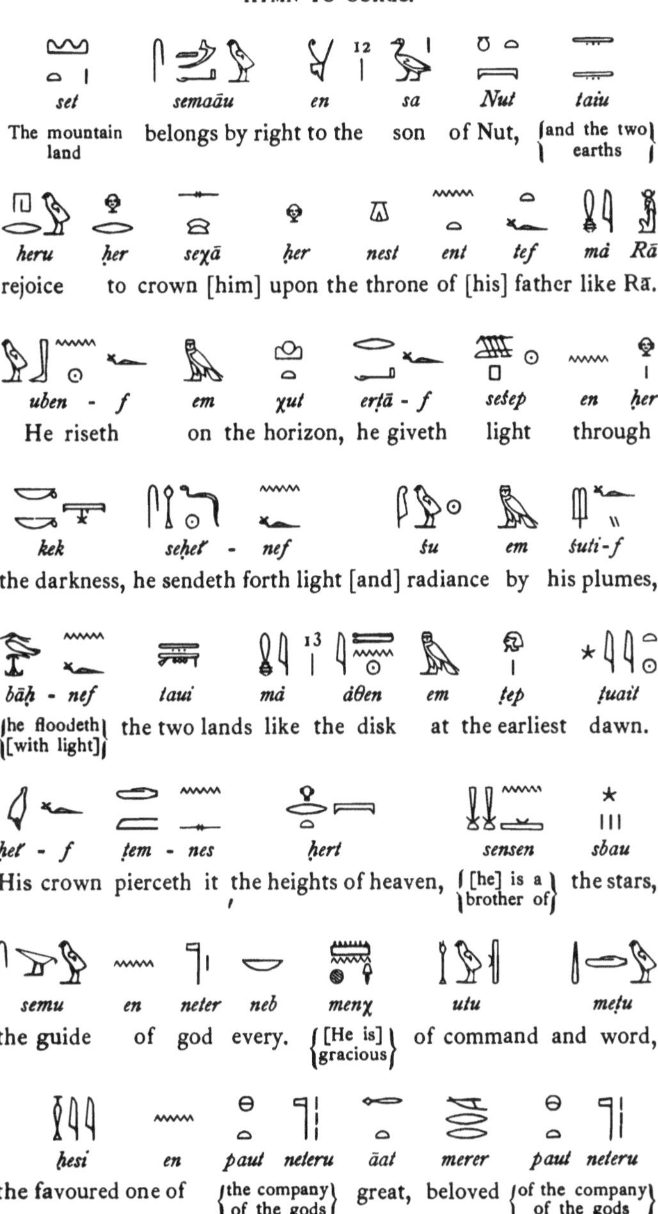

set *semaāu* *en* *sa* *Nut* *taiu*
The mountain land belongs by right to the son of Nut, {and the two earths}

heru *ḥer* *seχā* *ḥer* *nest* *ent* *tef* *mȧ* *Rā*
rejoice to crown [him] upon the throne of [his] father like Rā.

uben - f *em* *χut* *erṭā - f* *sešep* *en* *ḥer*
He riseth on the horizon, he giveth light through

kek *seḥet' - nef* *šu* *em* *šuti-f*
the darkness, he sendeth forth light [and] radiance by his plumes,

bāḥ - nef *taui* *mȧ* *ȧθen* *em* *ṭep* *ṭuaït*
{he floodeth [with light]} the two lands like the disk at the earliest dawn.

ḥet' - f *ṭem - nes* *ḥert* *sensen* *sbau*
His crown pierceth it the heights of heaven, {[he] is a brother of} the stars,

semu *en* *neter* *neb* *menχ* *utu* *meṭu*
the guide of god every. {[He is] gracious} of command and word,

ḥesi *en* *paut* *neteru* *āat* *merer* *paut* *neteru*
the favoured one of {the company of the gods} great, beloved {of the company of the gods}

neṫeset àri en sent - f māket - f seḥerit

little. Hath made his sister protection for him, driving away

14 *χeru seḥemet sepu seśeṭ χeru em*

[his] enemies, turning back evil hap, pronouncing the word with

χu re - s àqert nes àn uh en

the strength of her mouth, strong of tongue, not fallible in

meṭu semenχet utu meṭu Àuset

speech. Acting beneficently by command and word [is] Isis,

χut neṫet sen - s ḥeḥet su àtet

the mighty one, the avenger of her brother. Seeking him without

bekeḳ 15 *reret ta pen em ḥai àn*

rest, going round earth this with cries of grief, not

χen - nes àn qemtu - s su àrit śut

alighted she not had she found him. Making light

(*i. e.*, until she had found)

em śut - s χepert nefu em ṭenḥ àrit hennu

with her hair, {making to become} air by [her] wings, making cries

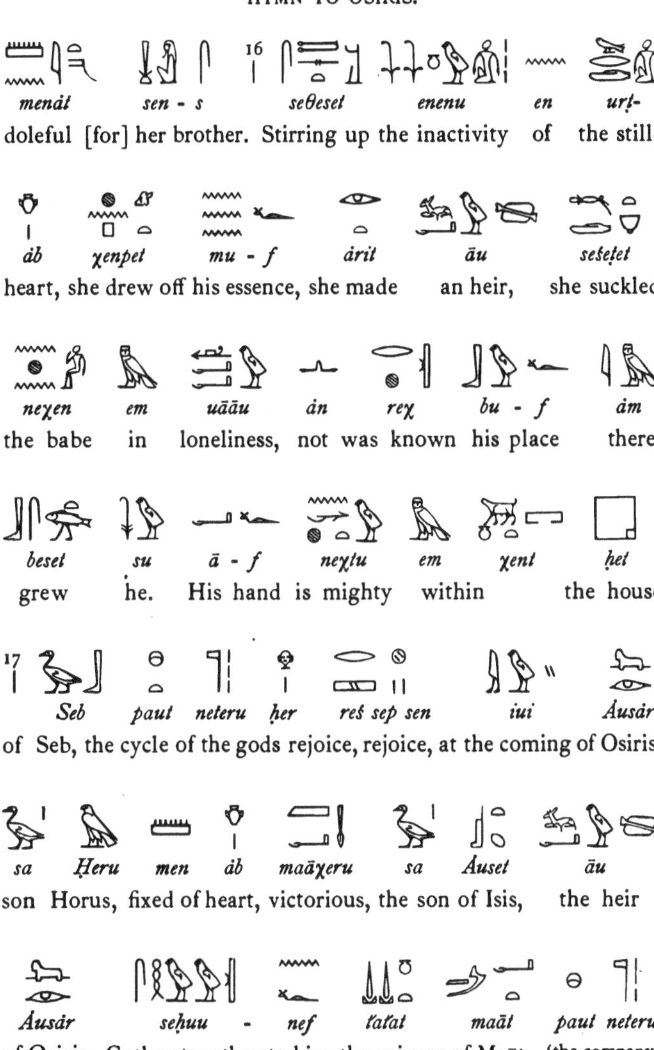

menåt *sen - s* 16 *seθeset* *enenu* *en* *urṭ-*
doleful [for] her brother. Stirring up the inactivity of the still-

åb *χenpet* *mu - f* *årit* *āu* *sešeṭet*
heart, she drew off his essence, she made an heir, she suckled

neχen *em* *uāāu* *ån* *reχ* *bu - f* *åm*
the babe in loneliness, not was known his place there,

beset *su* *ā - f* *neχtu* *em* *χent* *ḥet*
grew he. His hand is mighty within the house

17 *Seb* *paut* *neteru* *ḥer* *reš sep sen* *iui* *Åusår*
of Seb, the cycle of the gods rejoice, rejoice, at the coming of Osiris'

sa *Ḥeru* *men* *åb* *maāχeru* *sa* *Åuset* *āu*
son Horus, fixed of heart, victorious, the son of Isis, the heir

Åusår *seḥuu - nef* *ťaťat* *maāt* *paut neteru*
of Osiris. Gather together to him the princes of Maāt, {the company of the gods,}

Neb - er - ťer *ťesef* *nebu* *Maāt* *sami* *åm - s*
and Neb-er-tcher himself, and the lords of Maāt, assemble therein,

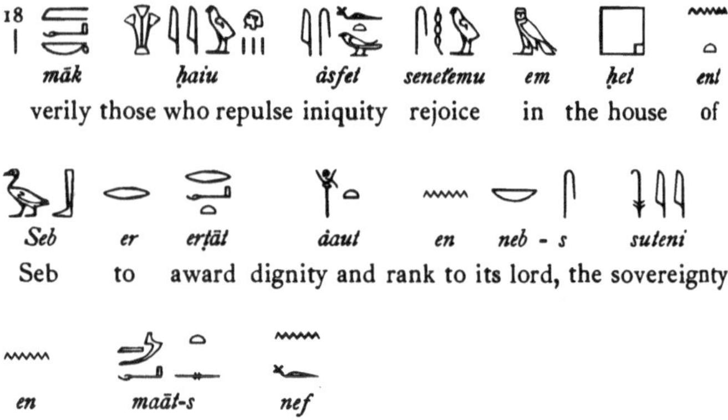

18 *māk* *ḥaiu* *àsfet* *seneṭemu* *em* *ḥet* *ent*

verily those who repulse iniquity rejoice in the house of

Seb *er* *erṭāt* *àaut* *en* *neb - s* *suteni*

Seb to award dignity and rank to its lord, the sovereignty

en *maāt-s* *nef*

of its right and truth is to him.

FROM THE STELE OF TEḤUTI-NEFER.

[XVIIIth dynasty.]

I. 

suten ḥetep ṭā Ȧmen-Rā neb nest

May a royal oblation give Amen-Rā, the lord of the thrones

taiu pautti en sep ṭep χent Ȧptet

of the world, the matter of time primeval, dweller in the Apts,

seχem šeps χeper ṭesef Neb-er-ṭer em ȧuset-f

form sacred, creator of himself and Neb-er-tcher in seat his

nebt ṭā - f ānχ en mer - nef ȧaut en

every. May he give life to him that loveth him, and old age to him

ṭāṭā su em ȧb - f nef en re - f em

that hath set him in his heart, and the breath of his mouth in

ḥesut - f ȧn feχ - nef χer ṭetta maa - f neter

his favoured one, not may he decay for ever. May he see the god,

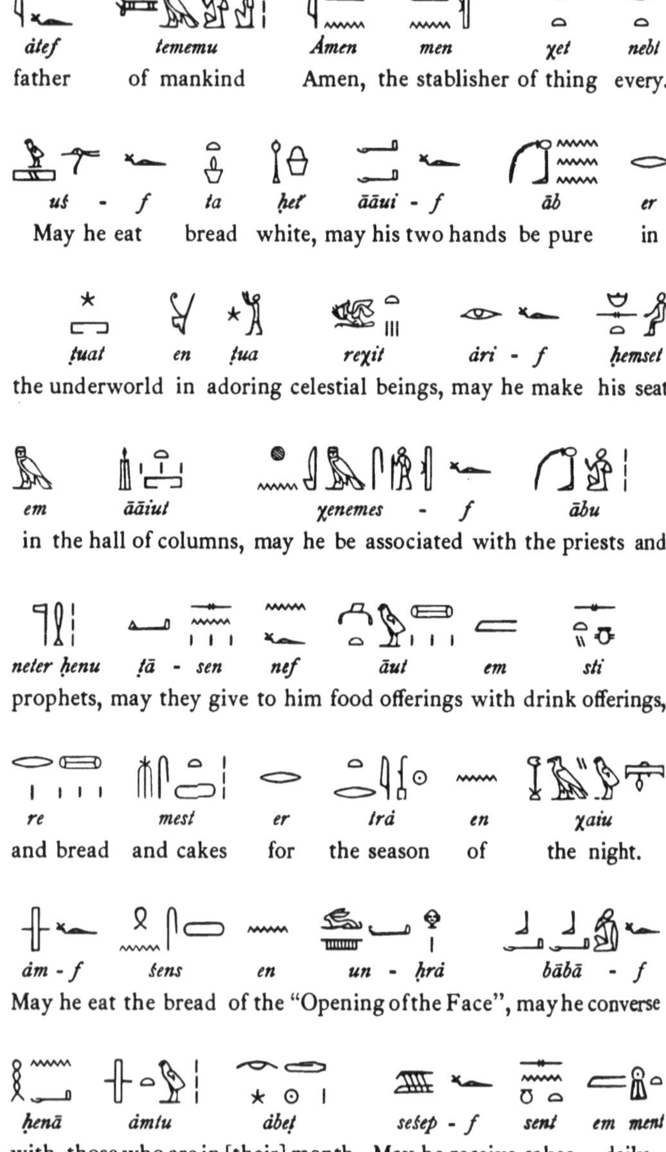

àtef tememu Àmen men χet nebt
father of mankind Amen, the stablisher of thing every.

uś - f ta ḥet' āāui - f āb er
May he eat bread white, may his two hands be pure in

ṭuat en ṭua reχit àri - f ḥemset
the underworld in adoring celestial beings, may he make his seat

em āāiut χenemes - f ābu
in the hall of columns, may he be associated with the priests and

neter ḥenu ṭā - sen nef āut em sti
prophets, may they give to him food offerings with drink offerings,

re mest er trà en χaiu
and bread and cakes for the season of the night.

àm - f śens en un - ḥrà bābā - f
May he eat the bread of the "Opening of the Face", may he converse

ḥenā àmtu àbeṭ seśep - f sent em ment
with those who are in [their] month. May he receive cakes daily

FROM THE STELE OF TEHUTI-NEFER.

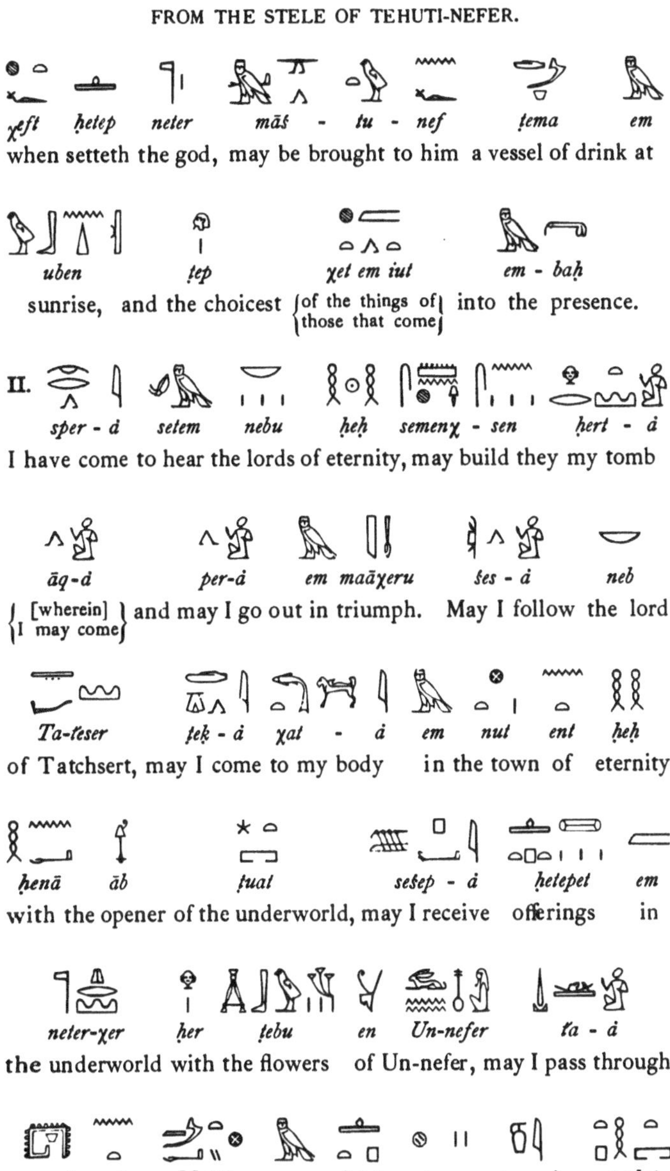

χeft ḥetep neter māš - tu - nef ṭema em
when setteth the god, may be brought to him a vessel of drink at

uben ṭep χet em iut em - baḥ
sunrise, and the choicest {of the things of those that come} into the presence.

II. *sper - à setem nebu ḥeḥ semenχ - sen ḥert - à*
I have come to hear the lords of eternity, may build they my tomb

āq - à per-à em maāχeru šes - à neb
{[wherein] I may come} and may I go out in triumph. May I follow the lord

Ta-ṭeser ṭek - à χat - à em nut ent ḥeḥ
of Tatchsert, may I come to my body in the town of eternity

ḥenā āb ṭuat sešep - à ḥetepet em
with the opener of the underworld, may I receive offerings in

neter-χer ḥer ṭebu en Un-nefer ṭa - à
the underworld with the flowers of Un-nefer, may I pass through

useχt ent Maāti em ḥetep sep sen χnem-à tepḥet
the hall of two-fold Maāt in peace; twice. May I attain {to the shrine}

FROM THE STELE OF TEḤUTI-NEFER.

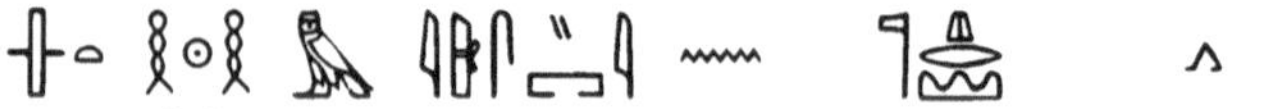

ȧmt ḥeḥ em ȧsi - ȧ en Neter-χer āq

in eternity in my tomb of the underworld, may I go in

per emm tera per sāḥ

{and come out} among [my] ancestors, may come forth [my] glorified body,

šes - f Ḥennu ṭerp - tuf em

may it follow Hennu, may be offered to it from

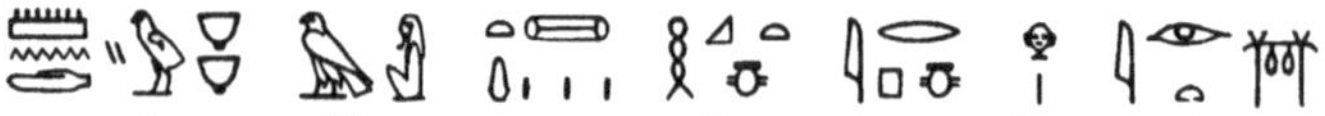

menṭiu Ḥeru ta ḥeqt ȧrp ḥer ȧrt

the breasts of Horus cakes, ale, wine and milk

em ment ent hru neb

daily day every.

III. 

ȧ neteru ȧmu Neter-χert ḥemsiu er ḳes Neb-er-

Hail gods in the underworld, who sit near Neb-er-

ṭer setemiu ṭepet - re - f seχa - θen ān

tcher, who hear his orders, remember ye the scribe

Teḥuti-nefer maāχeru em Uaḳ em Teḥutit

Thoth-nefer, triumphant at the Uaḳ festival, at the Thoth festival,

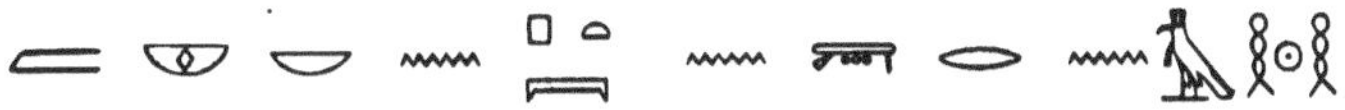

em ḥeb neb en pet en ta er neḥeḥ

at festival every of heaven [and] of earth for ever

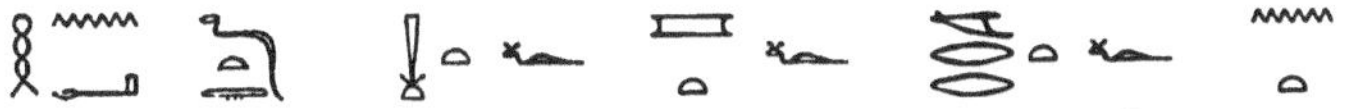

ḥenā tetta sent - f mert - f merert - f ent

and ever, [and] his sister, his darling, who loved him, of

àuset àb - f nebt per Ḥent-àri maāχeru

the seat of his heart, the lady of the house, Ḥent-àri, triumphant.

FROM THE STELE OF TCHANNI, A SCRIBE.

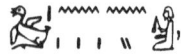

[XVIIIth dynasty.]

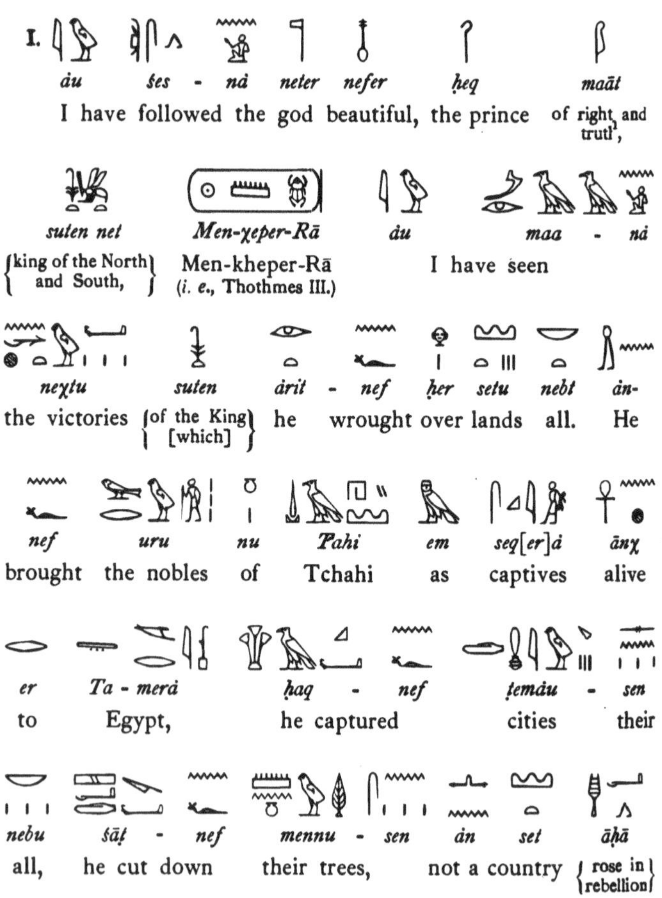

I. *àu šes - nà neter nefer ḥeq maāt*
I have followed the god beautiful, the prince of right and truth,

suten net Men-χeper-Rā àu maa - nà
king of the North and South, Men-kheper-Rā (*i. e.*, Thothmes III.) I have seen

neχtu suten àrit - nef ḥer setu nebt àn-
the victories of the King [which] he wrought over lands all. He

nef uru nu Ṭahi em seq[er]à ānχ
brought the nobles of Tchahi as captives alive

er Ta - merà ḥaq - nef ṭemàu - sen
to Egypt, he captured cities their

nebu šāṭ - nef mennu - sen àn set āḥā
all, he cut down their trees, not a country rose in rebellion

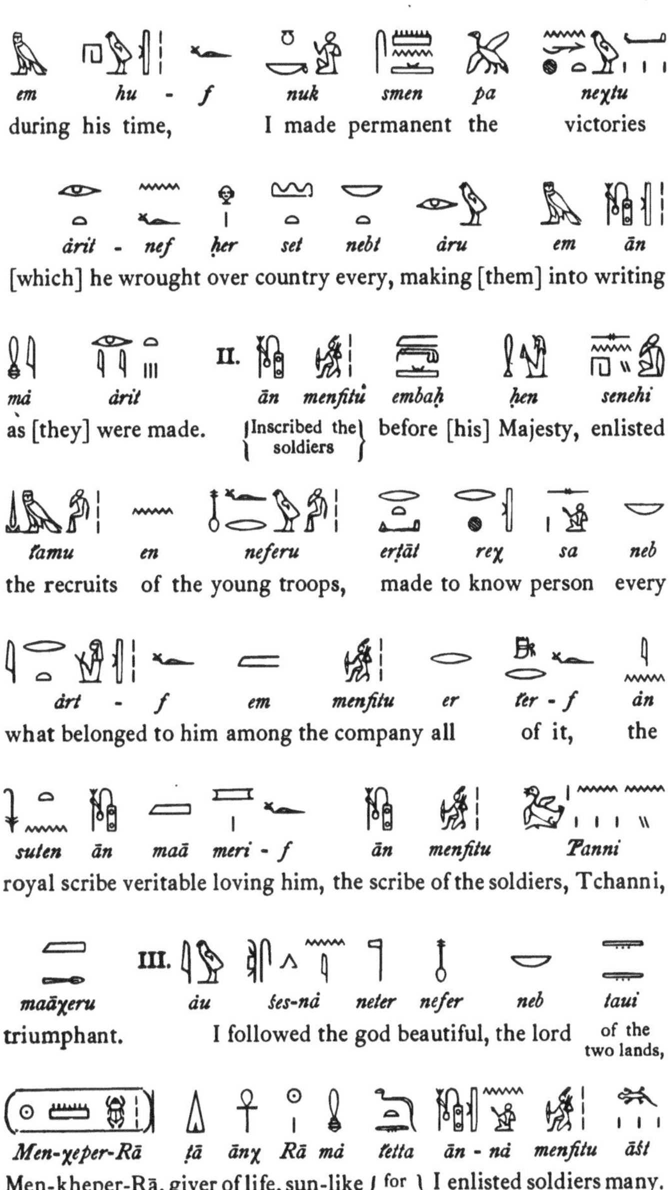

em hu - f nuk smen pa neχtu
during his time, I made permanent the victories

àrit - nef ḥer set nebt àru em ān
[which] he wrought over country every, making [them] into writing

mà àrit II. *ān menfitu embaḥ ḥen senehi*
as [they] were made. {Inscribed the soldiers} before [his] Majesty, enlisted

t̲amu en neferu ertāt reχ sa neb
the recruits of the young troops, made to know person every

àrt - f em menfitu er t̲er - f àn
what belonged to him among the company all of it, the

suten ān maā meri - f ān menfitu T̲anni
royal scribe veritable loving him, the scribe of the soldiers, Tchanni,

maāχeru III. *àu šes-nà neter nefer neb taui*
triumphant. I followed the god beautiful, the lord of the two lands,

Men-χeper-Rā t̲ā ānχ Rā mà t̲etta ān - nà menfitu āšt
Men-kheper-Rā, giver of life, sun-like {for ever,} I enlisted soldiers many.
(*i. e.,* Thothmes III.)

FROM THE STELE OF SESH, A SCRIBE.

[XVIIIth dynasty.]

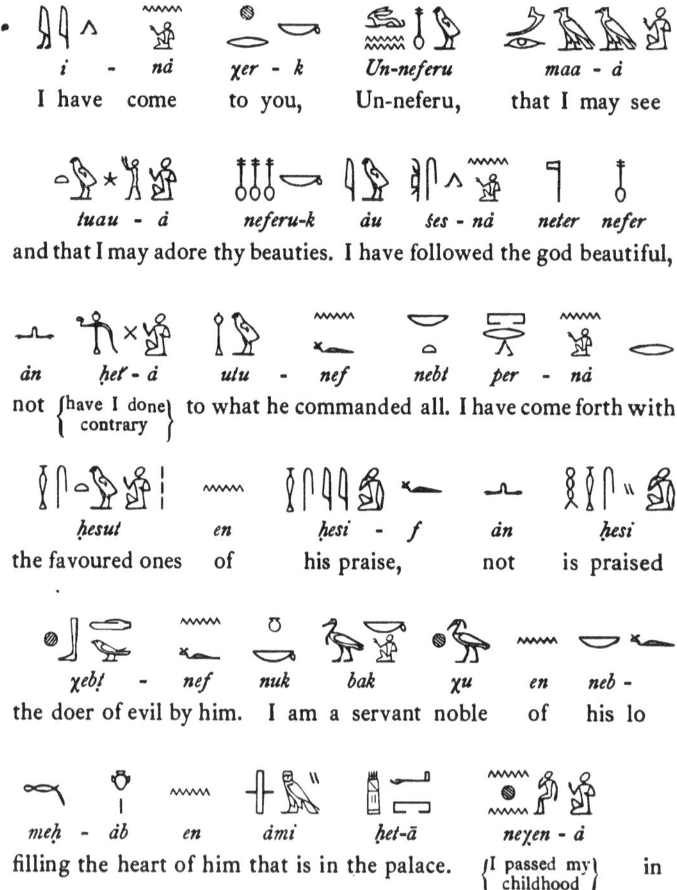
i - nȧ χer - k Un-neferu maa - ȧ
I have come to you, Un-neferu, that I may see
tuau - ȧ neferu-k ȧu śes - nȧ neter nefer
and that I may adore thy beauties. I have followed the god beautiful,
ȧn ḥet' - ȧ ulu - nef nebt per - nȧ
not {have I done contrary} to what he commanded all. I have come forth with
ḥesut en ḥesi - f ȧn ḥesi
the favoured ones of his praise, not is praised
χebṭ - nef nuk bak χu en neb -
the doer of evil by him. I am a servant noble of his lo
meḥ - ȧb en ȧmi ḥet-ā neχen - ȧ
filling the heart of him that is in the palace. {I passed my childhood} in

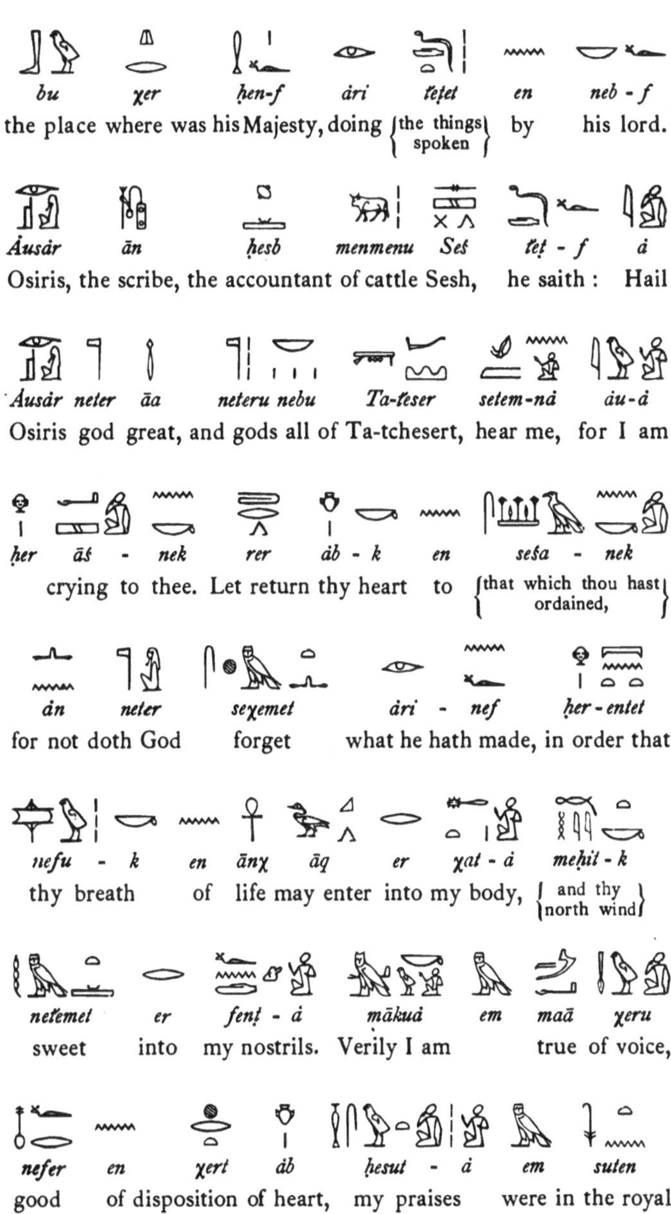

bu χer ḥen-f ȧri t̲'et̲et en neb-f

the place where was his Majesty, doing {the things spoken} by his lord.

Ȧusȧr ān ḥesb menmenu Seś t̲'et̲-f ȧ

Osiris, the scribe, the accountant of cattle Sesh, he saith: Hail

Ȧusȧr neter āa neteru nebu Ta-t̲'eser setem-nȧ ȧu-ȧ

Osiris god great, and gods all of Ta-tchesert, hear me, for I am

ḥer āś-nek rer ȧb-k en seśa-nek

crying to thee. Let return thy heart to {that which thou hast ordained,}

ȧn neter seχemet ȧri-nef ḥer-entet

for not doth God forget what he hath made, in order that

nefu-k en ānχ āq er χat-ȧ meḥit-k

thy breath of life may enter into my body, {and thy north wind}

net̲'emet er fent̲-ȧ mākuȧ em maā χeru

sweet into my nostrils. Verily I am true of voice,

nefer en χert ȧb ḥesut-ȧ em suten

good of disposition of heart, my praises were in the royal

per em ment åu šes - nå ḥeq er nemmat-f

house daily. I have followed [my] prince in his goings,

ån åri - å sep χasi em seχeru - f

not have I caused a case of failure in his plans

neb ån ṭeṭ reθ er - å petrå - nef ån

all, never said men concerning me, "Behold him". Not

uni - å ån beta - å ån χeper seχeṭ - å

did I wrong, not did I evil, not caused I injury,

ån āqu χer ḥaχ - å ṭer mesti - å

not hath entered wickedness into me since my childhood,

åpu ḥer årit maāt en neb taui nuk

but only the doing of {the right and truth} of the lord {of the two lands.} I

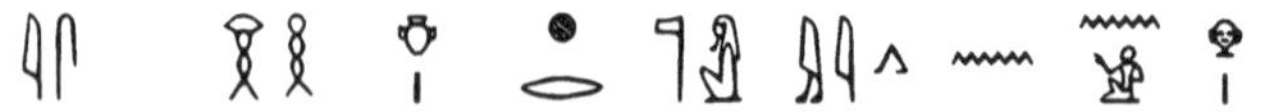

ås uaḥ åb χer neter i en nå ḥer

behold, was constant in heart unto God. I have come over

māten nefer en āq åb en mert seṭamāt

the path fair of straightness of heart, and of the love of virtues (?) (*i. e.*, justice)

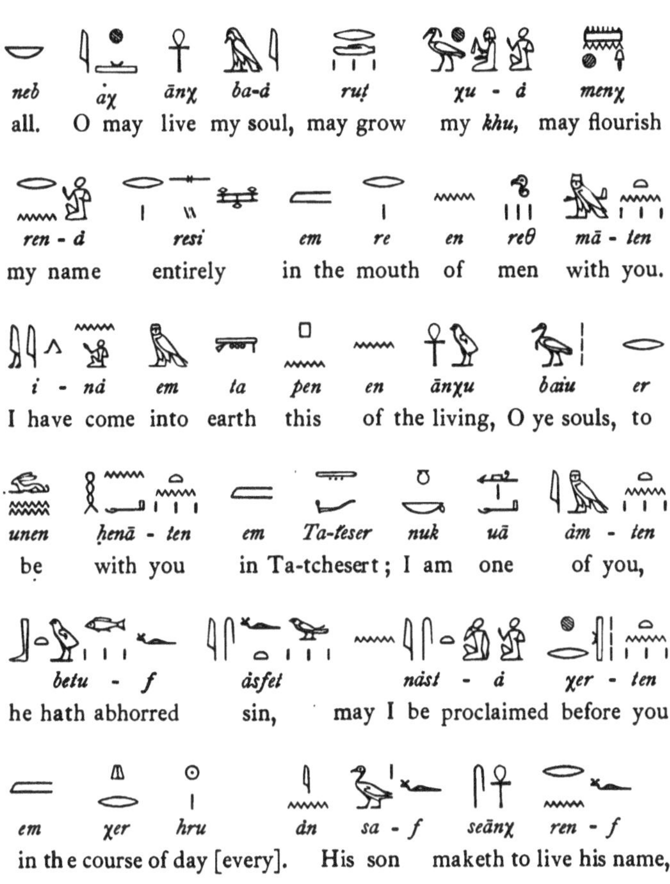

neb *ȧχ* *ānχ* *ba-ȧ* *ruṭ* *χu - ȧ* *menχ*
all. O may live my soul, may grow my *khu,* may flourish

ren - ȧ *resi* *em* *re* *en* *reθ* *mā - ten*
my name entirely in the mouth of men with you.

i - nȧ *em* *ta* *pen* *en* *ānχu* *baiu* *er*
I have come into earth this of the living, O ye souls, to

unen *ḥenā - ten* *em* *Ta-ṫeser* *nuk* *uā* *ȧm - ten*
be with you in Ta-tchesert; I am one of you,

betu - f *ȧsfet* *nȧst - ȧ* *χer - ten*
he hath abhorred sin, may I be proclaimed before you

em *χer* *hru* *ȧn* *sa - f* *seānχ* *ren - f*
in the course of day [every]. His son maketh to live his name,

ān *Meḥu*
the scribe Mehu.

FROM A SEPULCHRAL STELE.

[XVIIIth dynasty (?).]

suten ṭā ḥetep Ȧusȧr ḥeq t̀etta neter āa neb

Royal may give oblation Osiris, prince of eternity, god great, lord

Ȧbṭu Ȧp-uat qemā Ȧp-uat meḥt Ȧnpu ȧm

of Abydos, Ap-uat of the south, Ap-uat of the north, Anubis dweller

ut Ptaḥ-Seker neb śeta - θȧ ȧt ṭā - sen

{in the town of embalmment,} Ptaḥ-Seker, lord of the hidden place, may they give

χu em pet us[r] em ta maāχeru em Neter-χert

glory in heaven, strength upon earth, triumph in Neter-khert,

(sic)

pert āq er ȧsi - ȧ qebḥ - ȧ śuit - f (sic)

{and a coming forth from and} a going in to my tomb. May I refresh my shadow,

surȧ - ȧ mu em mer - ȧ hru neb uat̀

may I drink water from my pool day every, may flourish

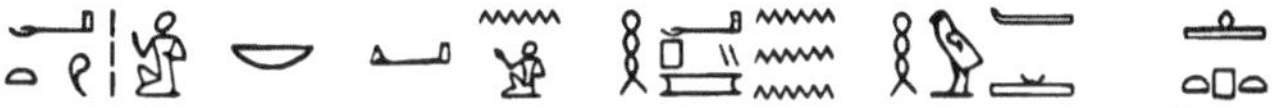

āt - ȧ neb ṭā - nȧ Ḥāpi ḥu ḥetepet
my limbs all, may give me the Nile food, and offerings,

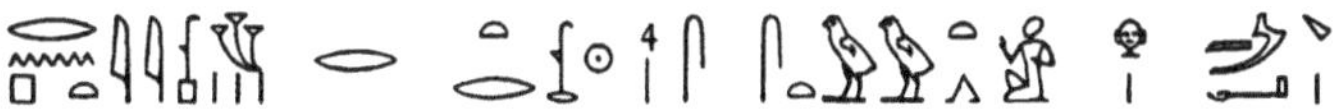

renpit er trȧ - s setuut - ȧ ḥer maā
and flowers at its season. May I walk by the side

nu še - ȧ hru neb ȧn ȧbu χeni ba - ȧ
of my lake day every without ceasing. May alight my soul

ḥer āχamu nu mennu ȧri - nȧ - s
upon the branches of the trees [which] I have made them,
(*i. e.*, planted)

seqebḥ - ȧ ḥer χeru neh - ȧ ȧm-ȧ tau
may I cool myself under my sycamores, may I eat the bread

en ṭāṭā - sen ȧu - nȧ re er meṭ - ȧ
of their giving, may be to me a mouth that I may speak

ȧm - f mȧ Ḥeru - šesu peru - ȧ χer ṭes
with it like the Horus followers, may I come forth bearing a vase

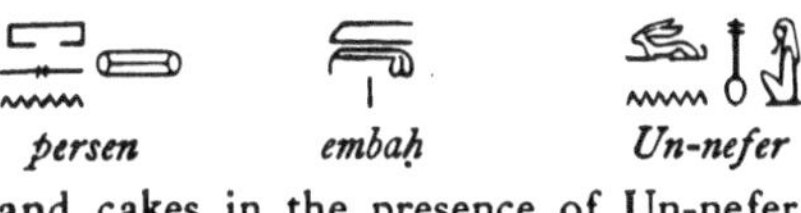

persen embaḥ Un-nefer
and cakes in the presence of Un-nefer.

THE STELE OF ÅMEN-ḤETEP, A ROYAL SCRIBE AT MEMPHIS.

[XVIIIth dynasty (?).]

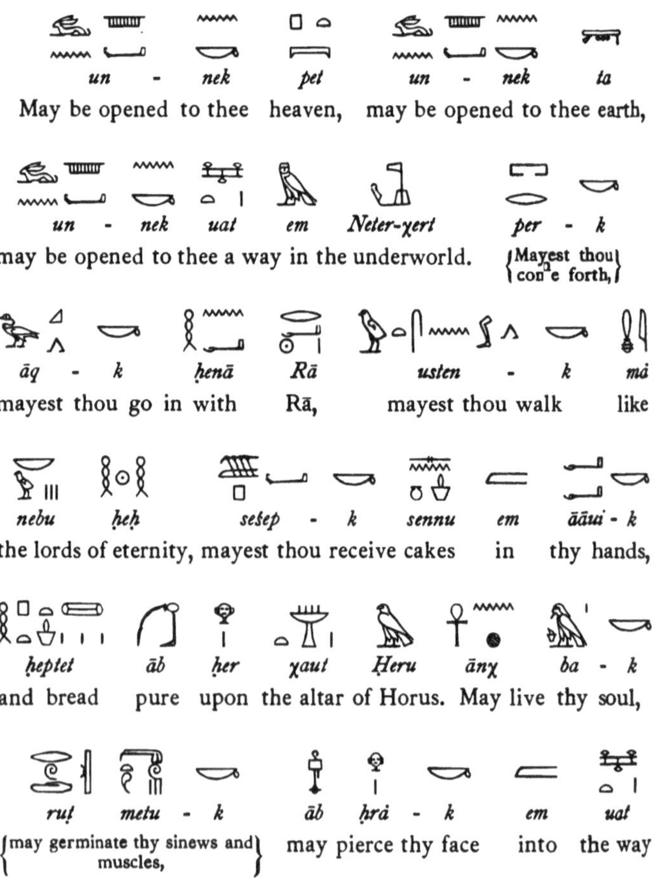

un - nek pet un - nek ta
May be opened to thee heaven, may be opened to thee earth,
un - nek uat em Neter-χert per - k
may be opened to thee a way in the underworld. {Mayest thou come forth,}
āq - k ḥenā Rā usten - k mȧ
mayest thou go in with Rā, mayest thou walk like
nebu ḥeḥ seśep - k sennu em āāui - k
the lords of eternity, mayest thou receive cakes in thy hands,
ḥeptet āb ḥer χaut Ḥeru ānχ ba - k
and bread pure upon the altar of Horus. May live thy soul,
ruṭ metu - k āb ḥrȧ - k em uat
{may germinate thy sinews and muscles,} may pierce thy face into the way

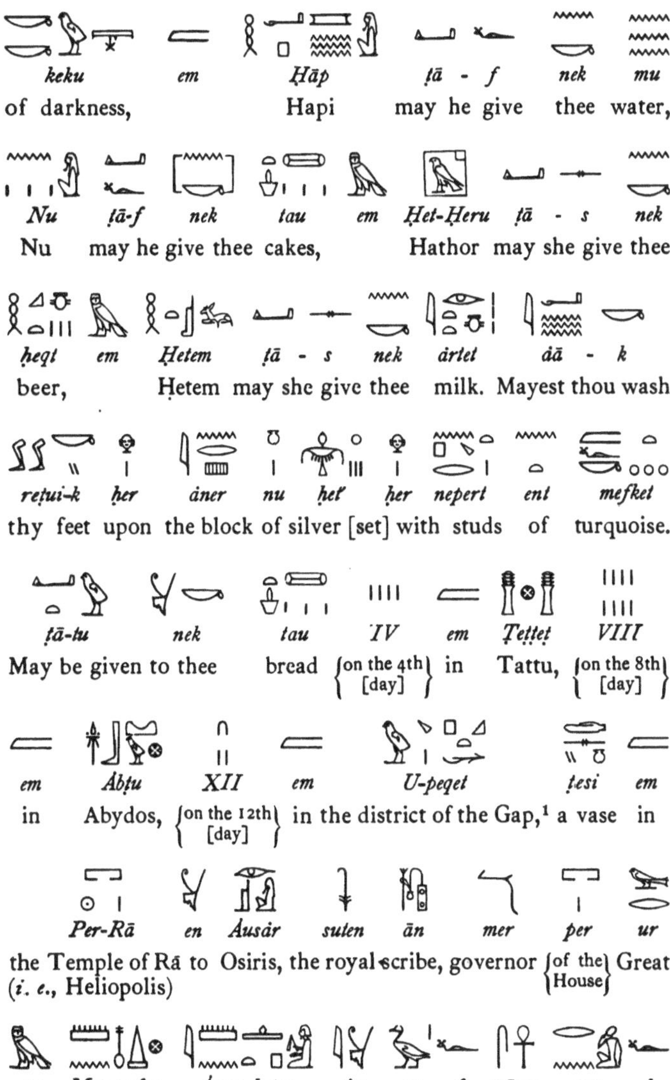

keku em Ḥāp ṭā - f nek mu

of darkness, Hapi may he give thee water,

Nu ṭā-f nek tau em Ḥet-Ḥeru ṭā - s nek

Nu may he give thee cakes, Hathor may she give thee

ḥeqt em Ḥetem ṭā - s nek årtet ȧā - k

beer, Ḥetem may she give thee milk. Mayest thou wash

reṭui-k her åner nu ḥet' her nepert ent mefket

thy feet upon the block of silver [set] with studs of turquoise.

ṭā-tu nek tau IV em Ṭeṭṭeṭ VIII

May be given to thee bread {on the 4th [day]} in Tattu, {on the 8th [day]}

em Åbṭu XII em U-peqet ṭesi em

in Abydos, {on the 12th [day]} in the district of the Gap,[1] a vase in

Per-Rā en Åusår suten ān mer per ur

the Temple of Rā (*i. e.*, Heliopolis) to Osiris, the royal scribe, governor {of the House} Great

em Men-nefer Åmen-ḥetep ån sa - f seānχ ren - f

in Memphis, Åmen-ḥetep. His son maketh to live his name.

[1] *I. e.*, the country round about Abydos near the opening in the mountains through which souls were supposed to pass into the next world.

FROM A HYMN TO ḤĀPI, THE GOD OF THE NILE.

[XVIIIth or XIXth dynasty.]

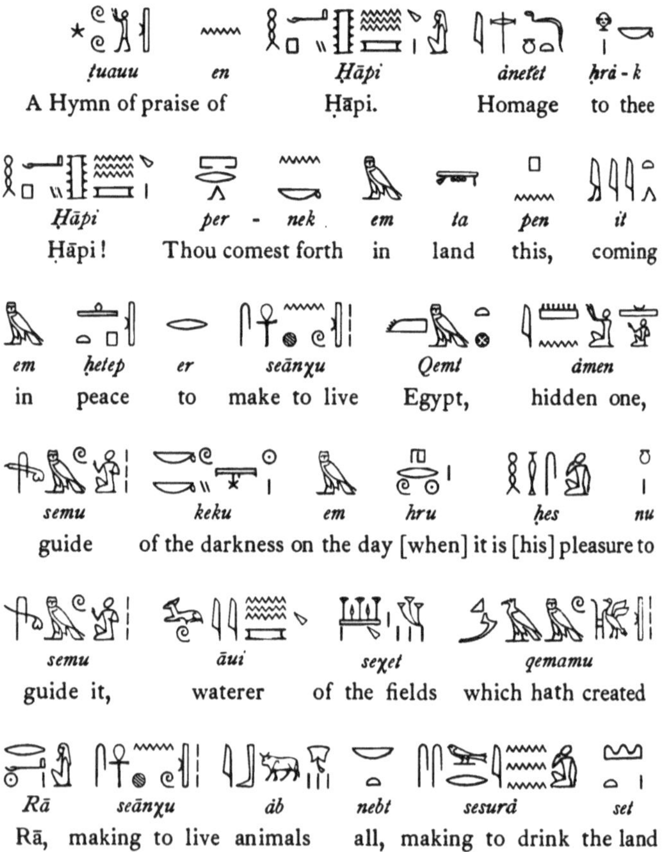

tuauu en Ḥāpi ȧnet'et ḥrȧ-k
A Hymn of praise of Ḥāpi. Homage to thee
Ḥāpi per - nek em ta pen it
Ḥāpi! Thou comest forth in land this, coming
em ḥetep er seānχu Qemt ȧmen
in peace to make to live Egypt, hidden one,
semu keku em hru ḥes nu
guide of the darkness on the day [when] it is [his] pleasure to
semu āui seχet qemamu
guide it, waterer of the fields which hath created
Rā seānχu ȧb nebt sesurȧ set
Rā, making to live animals all, making to drink the land

FROM A HYMN TO ḤĀPI, THE GOD OF THE NILE.

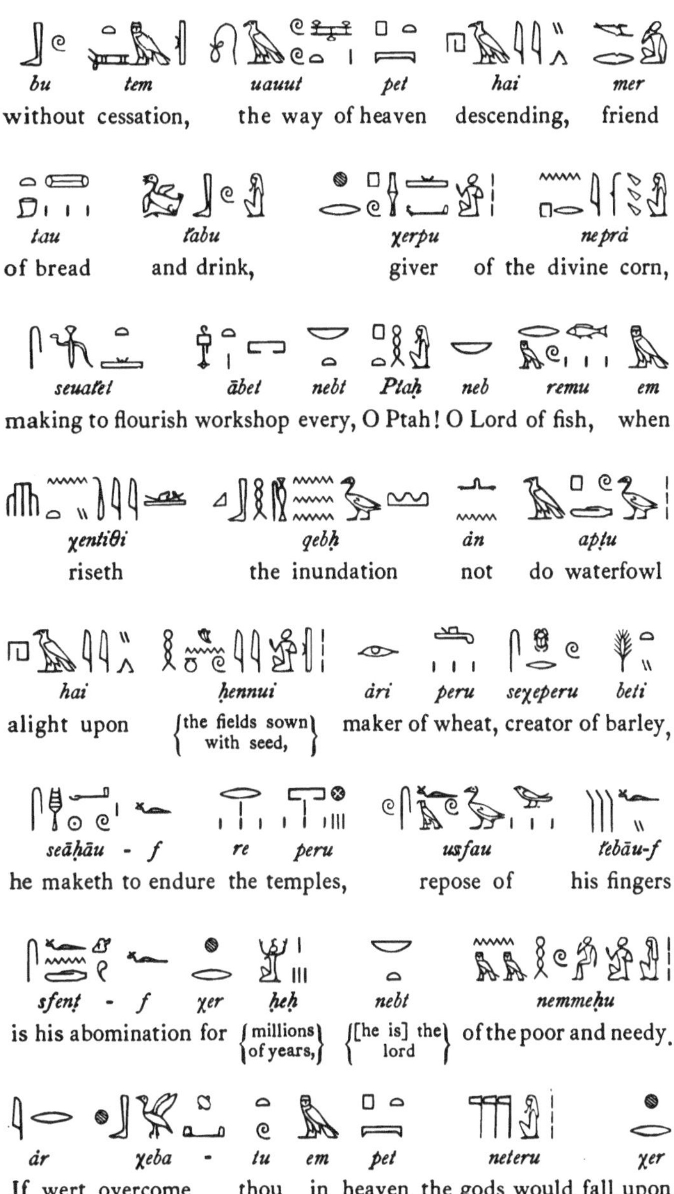

bu tem uauut pet hai mer
without cessation, the way of heaven descending, friend

tau t̔abu χerpu neprȧ
of bread and drink, giver of the divine corn,

seuat̔et ābet nebt Ptaḥ neb remu em
making to flourish workshop every, O Ptah! O Lord of fish, when

χentiθi qebḥ ȧn apṭu
riseth the inundation not do waterfowl

hai ḥennui ȧri peru seχeperu beti
alight upon {the fields sown with seed,} maker of wheat, creator of barley,

seāḥāu - f re peru usfau t̔ebāu-f
he maketh to endure the temples, repose of his fingers

sfenṭ - f χer ḥeḥ nebt nemmeḥu
is his abomination for {millions of years,} {[he is] the lord} of the poor and needy.

ȧr χeba - tu em pet neteru χer
If wert overcome thou in heaven the gods would fall upon

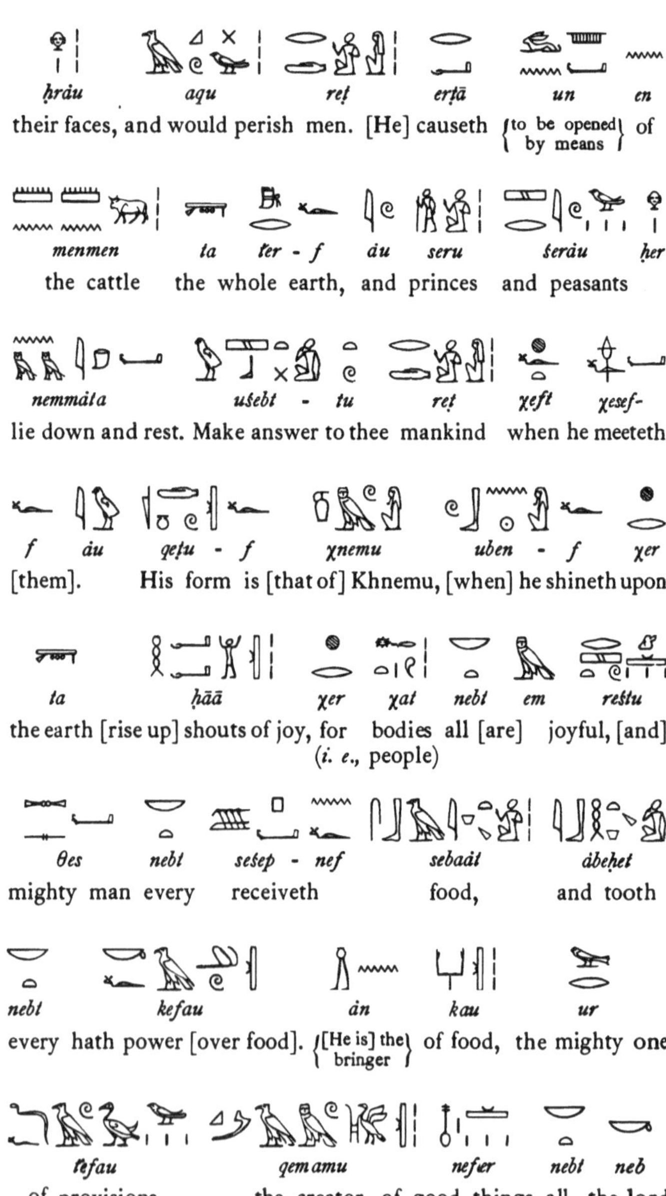

ḥrȧu aqu reṭ erṭā un en
their faces, and would perish men. [He] causeth {to be opened by means} of

menmen ta ṭer - f ȧu seru šerȧu ḥer
the cattle the whole earth, and princes and peasants

nemmȧta ušebt - tu reṭ χeft χesef-
lie down and rest. Make answer to thee mankind when he meeteth

f ȧu qeṭu - f χnemu uben - f χer
[them]. His form is [that of] Khnemu, [when] he shineth upon

ta ḥāā χer χat nebt em reštu
the earth [rise up] shouts of joy, for bodies (*i. e.,* people) all [are] joyful, [and]

θes nebt sešep - nef sebaȧt ȧbeḥet
mighty man every receiveth food, and tooth

nebt kefau ȧn kau ur
every hath power [over food]. {[He is] the bringer} of food, the mighty one

ṭefau qemamu nefer nebt neb
of provisions, the creator of good things all, the lord

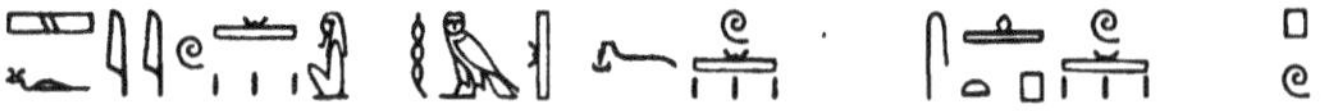

šefiu netem setepu seḥetepu pu

of meats (?) pleasant and choice, if one maketh offerings it is

àm - f seχeperu stimu en menmen

by him. He maketh to grow the herbs for the cattle,

erṭāu àb sfenṭ - tu en neter nebt

[he] giveth [his] heart to what is sacrificed unto god every.
(*i. e.*, he taketh heed)

neter senṭrà ṭepti pa enti er χet - f θetet

Incense the choicest is that which is in his train, he is lord

em ta sen meḥ uťat seb

of the lands two. [He] filleth storehouses, heaping high

šentut erṭāu àb aχet nemmeḥu

the granaries, and paying heed to the affairs of the poor and needy.

seruṭ er meḥ àbeb nebt àn

{He maketh plants to shoot} to satisfy those that desire all, not

ketket er-es set seχeperu àqemu peḥti

is [he] brought low thereby. He maketh to be a shield [his] strength,

ȧn mehu en ner tut ḥer uaḥ - set

Not can [he] be figured in stone, in the images on which are set

seχet ārat ȧn qemḥu entuf ȧn

{the double crown [with] uraei,} not to be seen is he, neither

bakȧ ȧn χerpu - tuf ȧn seset - tuf

works nor offerings can be made to him, not {can he be brought out}

em šettau ȧn reχ - tu bu entuf ȧn

from [his] secret places, not is known the place where he is, not

qem tepḥet ȧnu ȧn nāit enti

is [he] found [in] shrines inscribed, not is there a habitation which is

tennu - f ȧn semu em ȧb - k

sufficiently large for him, not can he be depicted in thy heart.

nehamu - nek t̔amu - k χaretu - k tu

Thou hast rejoiced thy peoples [and] thy children.

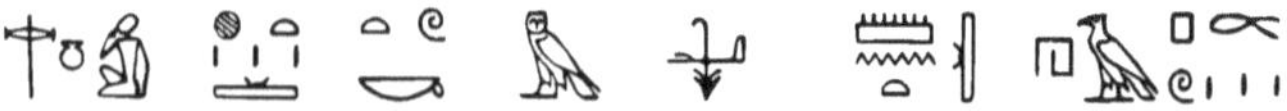

net̔ χet tuk em qemā ment hapu

Thou art a protector in the south, stablished are [thy] laws

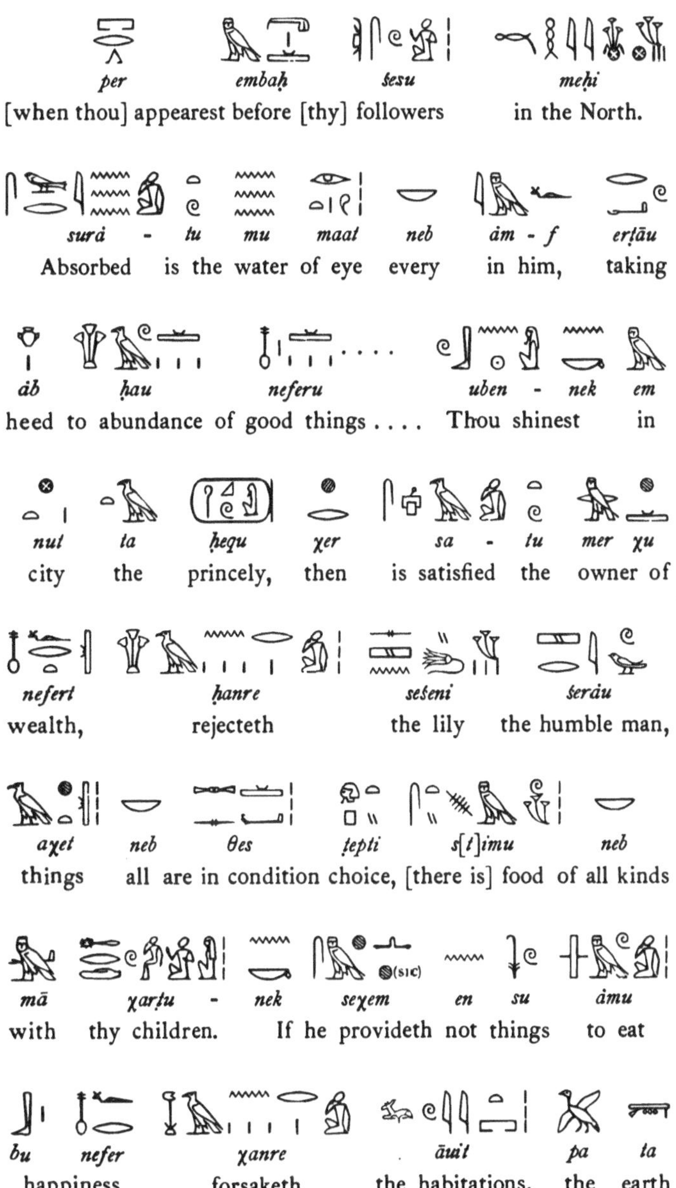
per embaḥ šesu meḥi
[when thou] appearest before [thy] followers in the North.
surȧ - tu mu maat neb ȧm - f erṭāu
Absorbed is the water of eye every in him, taking
ȧb ḥau neferu uben - nek em
heed to abundance of good things .... Thou shinest in
nut ta ḥequ χer sa - tu mer χu
city the princely, then is satisfied the owner of
nefert ḥanre sešeni šerȧu
wealth, rejecteth the lily the humble man,
aχet neb θes ṭepti s[t]imu neb
things all are in condition choice, [there is] food of all kinds
mā χarṭu - nek seχem (SIC) en su ȧmu
with thy children. If he provideth not things to eat
bu nefer χanre āuit pa ta
happiness forsaketh the habitations, the earth

FROM A HYMN TO ḤĀPI, THE GOD OF THE NILE.

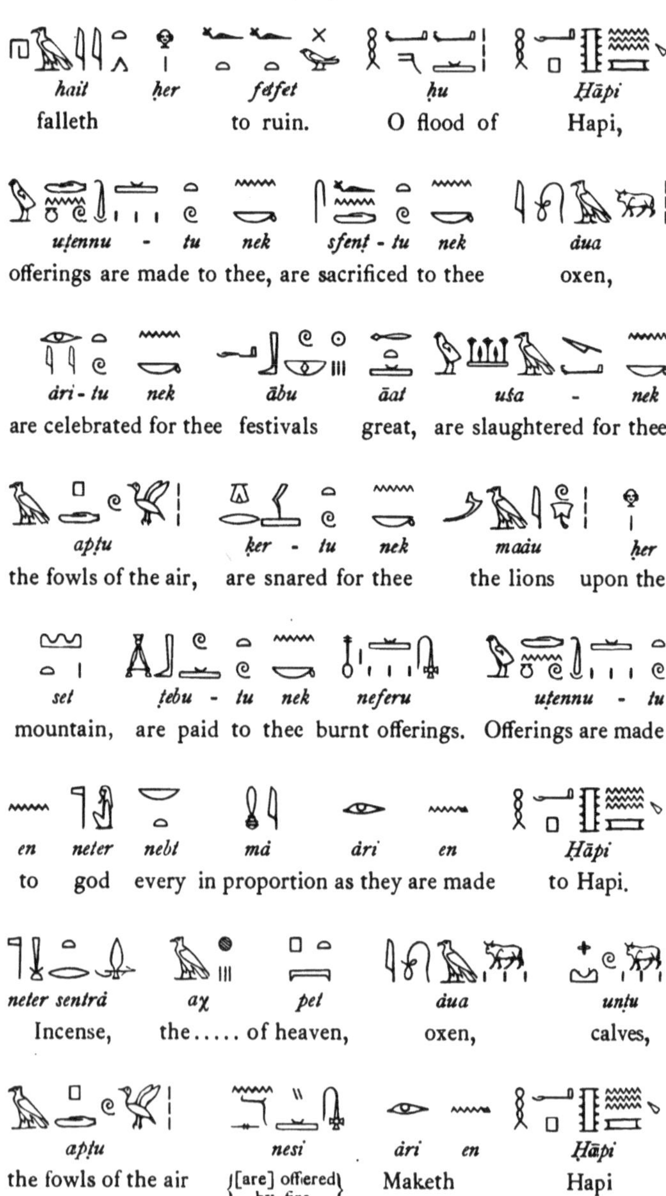

hait ḥer fetfet ḥu Ḥāpi
falleth to ruin. O flood of Hapi,

uṭennu - tu nek sfenṭ - tu nek àua
offerings are made to thee, are sacrificed to thee oxen,

àri - tu nek ābu āat uša - nek
are celebrated for thee festivals great, are slaughtered for thee

apṭu ḳer - tu nek maàu ḥer
the fowls of the air, are snared for thee the lions upon the

set ṭebu - tu nek neferu uṭennu - tu
mountain, are paid to thee burnt offerings. Offerings are made

en neter nebt mà àri en Ḥāpi
to god every in proportion as they are made to Hapi.

neter sentrà aχ pet àua unṭu
Incense, the..... of heaven, oxen, calves,

apṭu nesi àri en Ḥāpi
the fowls of the air {[are] offered by fire.} Maketh Hapi

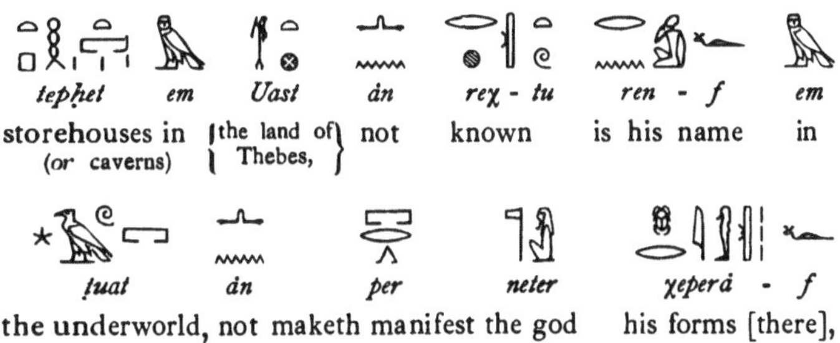

tepḥet em Uast ȧn reχ - tu ren - f em

storehouses in (or caverns) {the land of Thebes,} not known is his name in

ṭuat ȧn per neter χeperȧ - f

the underworld, not maketh manifest the god his forms [there],

usfa seχeru

idle [are] imaginings [concerning them].

THE PROVERBS OF ṬUAUU-F-SE-KHARTHȦI.

maa - nȧ ȧaut em mȧtet ȧu

I have seen (*or* considered) labour likewise, being

em t̆eṭet θes pen ȧm - set ṭā - ȧ

the words of proverb this concerning it. I will make

meri - k ānu mut - k ṭā - ȧ āq

thee to love literature thy mother, I will make to enter [its]

neferu em ḥrȧ - k urt su ḳert er ȧaut

beauties before thee, greater is it but than {dignities and honours}

nebt ȧn un em ta pen meṭet

of all kinds, not is it on earth this a [mere] word.

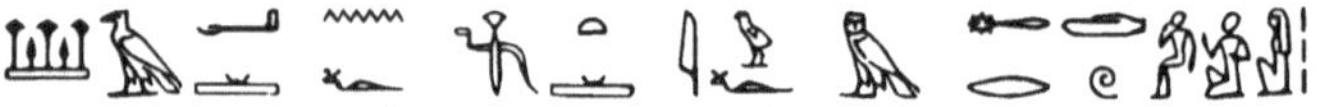

śaā - nef uat̆et ȧu-f em χarṭu-

He who began {to benefit [from it]} {while he was} among the children

tu net̆ χert - tuf tu hab - f er ȧrit

shall prosper his affairs. One sendeth him to carry out

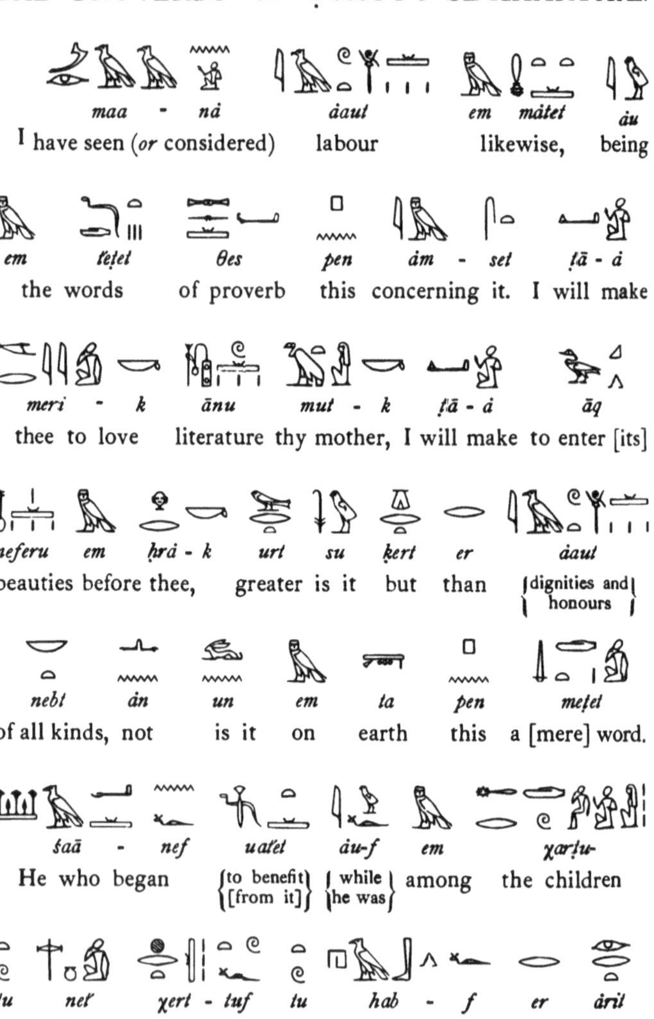

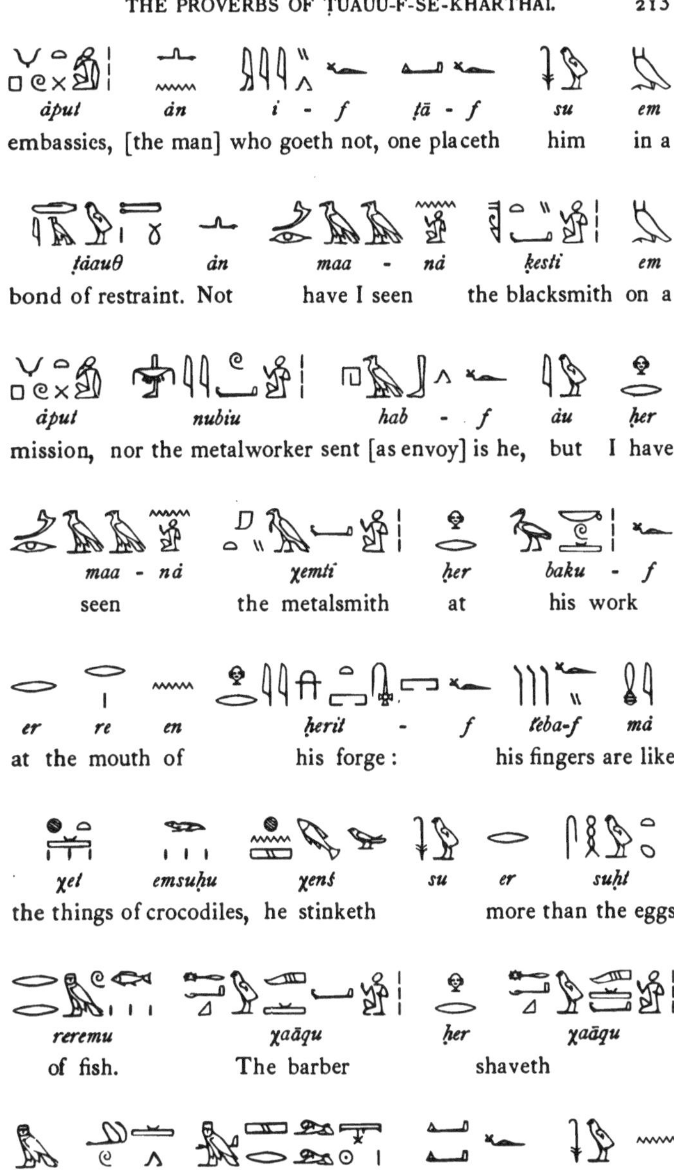

åput *ån* *i - f* *ṭā - f* *su* *em*
embassies, [the man] who goeth not, one placeth him in a

ṭåauθ *ån* *maa - nå* *ḳesti* *em*
bond of restraint. Not have I seen the blacksmith on a

åput *nubiu* *hab - f* *åu* *ḥer*
mission, nor the metalworker sent [as envoy] is he, but I have

maa - nå *χemti* *ḥer* *baku - f*
seen the metalsmith at his work

er *re* *en* *ḥerit - f* *ṭeba-f* *må*
at the mouth of his forge: his fingers are like

χet *emsuḥu* *χenš* *su* *er* *suḥt*
the things of crocodiles, he stinketh more than the eggs

reremu *χaāqu* *ḥer* *χaāqu*
of fish. The barber shaveth

em *peḥu* *māšer* *ṭāṭā - f* *su* *en*
far into the evening: [when] he setteth himself to

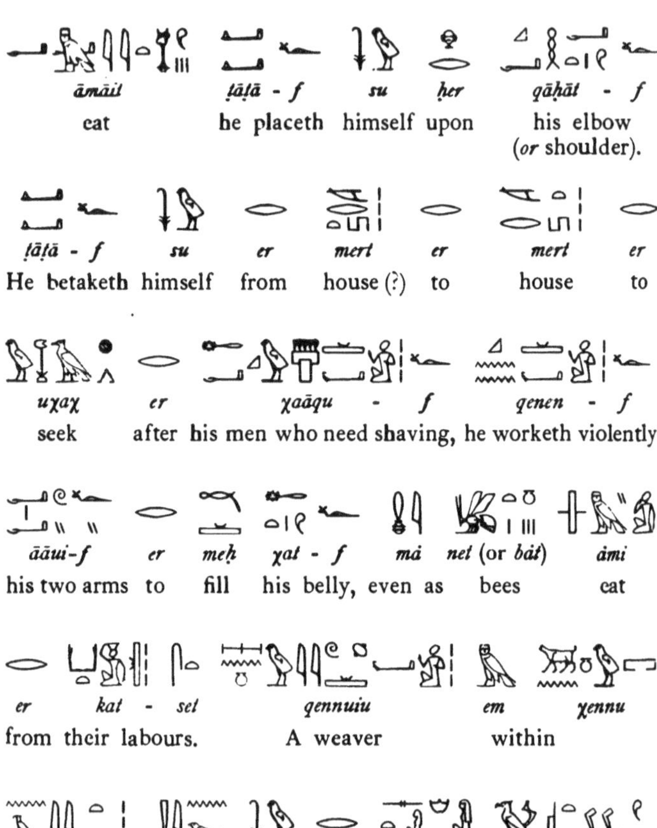

āmāit — *ṭāṭā - f* — *su* — *ḥer* — *qāḥāt - f*
eat — he placeth — himself — upon — his elbow (*or* shoulder).

ṭāṭā - f — *su* — *er* — *mert* — *er* — *mert* — *er*
He betaketh — himself — from — house (?) — to — house — to

uχaχ — *er* — *χaāqu - f* — *qenen - f*
seek — after — his men who need shaving, — he worketh violently

āāui-f — *er* — *meḥ* — *χat - f* — *mȧ* — *net* (or *bȧt*) — *ȧmi*
his two arms — to — fill — his belly, even as — bees — eat

er — *kat - set* — *qennuiu* — *em* — *χennu*
from — their labours. — A weaver — within

naït — *bȧn* — *su* — *er* — *set ḥemt* — *masti - f*
the factory, — wretched — is he — more than — a woman. — His legs

ȧm - f — *er* — *re* — *en* — *ȧb - f* — *ȧn* — *tepȧ - nef* — *nifu*
are under him — at the door — of — his heart, — not — breatheth he — the air.

ȧr — *χeba - nef* — *em* — *hru* — *em* — *seχet - tu*
If — he fail — for — a day — in — weaving,

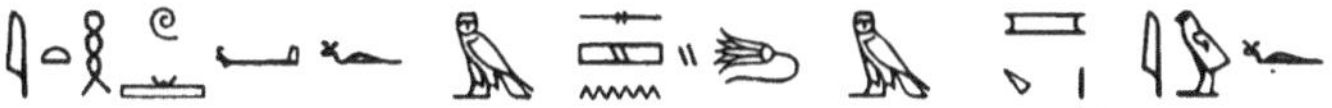

àtḥu - f em seśeni em mer (?) àu - f

he is dragged out like a lily from the pool. He,

ṭā - f āqu nu àri er ṭāt

he giveth the bread of the doorkeepers to let

petrà - f ta ḥet seχennuiu

him see the light. The dyer

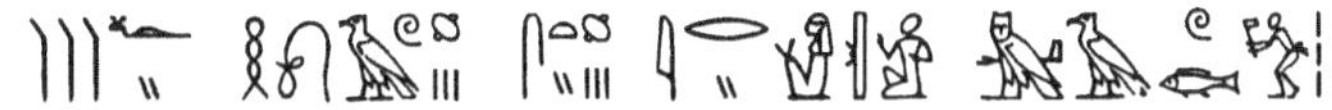

ṭebā-f ḥuau sti àri māau

his fingers stink [with] the smell of the keeper of dead bodies.

(sic)

maa-f uāu mā ḥuru - nà àn

His two eyes are destroyed by want of [rest], not

χesef - f ṭet - f urś - f em śāṭ

draweth back he his hand, he passeth his time in the cutting up

en àst betu - f pu ḥebsu ṭebuu

of garments, an abomination is he [in his] clothes. The shoemaker

bàn su er si χer ṭebḥet - f

unfortunate is he most of all, for he chattereth

em er neḥeḥ uṭa - f uṭa

everlastingly, his strength is the strength

māau peshet - f ȧmeskau

of dead bodies, he feeds upon leather.

ṭensmen ȧm - k ur šefit em

Being overburdened thyself by the Great of Terror do not

ṭeṭet meṭet en ḥapu ȧu ḥapu-

speak words of concealment, [for] he who acteth

f χat - f ȧri - nef ȧm - f em ṭeṭet

secretly his body worketh it against himself. Do not speak

meṭet en per-ā - ȧb ȧu ḥems - tu ḥenā - k

words of pride, even when thou art sitting with thyself,

ki ṭeṭ em uāu em ṭeṭet ḳer

{otherwise said,} alone by thyself. Let not [a man] speak calumny

er mutet - f er ȧbu ser pen ȧr

against his mother for the sake of Chief this.

emχet χeperu aχet āāui-f tu erṭāu

After hath come [to a man] wealth, let his hands be firm, {and let him give}

ȧb sfenṭ - f em erṭāt ḥer set ḥenā - k

his heart its desire; do not set [thyself] against it {[when thou art] with thyself,}

ki ṭeṭ em uāu ȧu χasi su χat

otherwise said, alone. By keeping in subjection the belly

setem - tu nek ȧr sa - tu χemt en tau

thou wilt be listened to. If thou hast eaten three loaves of bread,

sāau hanu sen en ḥeqt ȧn

and hast drunk vessels two of beer, not

ṭeruu χat ābau ḥer set ȧr

being filled [thy] belly, contend against it. If (*i. e.*, against greediness)

sa - tu en ki em āḥā mā

is satisfied another [therewith], do not stand up with those

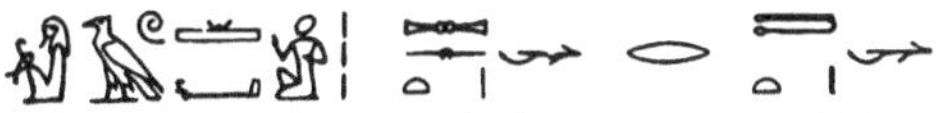

sau θest er θet

who break a board upon a stake.

THE DESTRUCTION OF MANKIND.

[XIXth dynasty.]

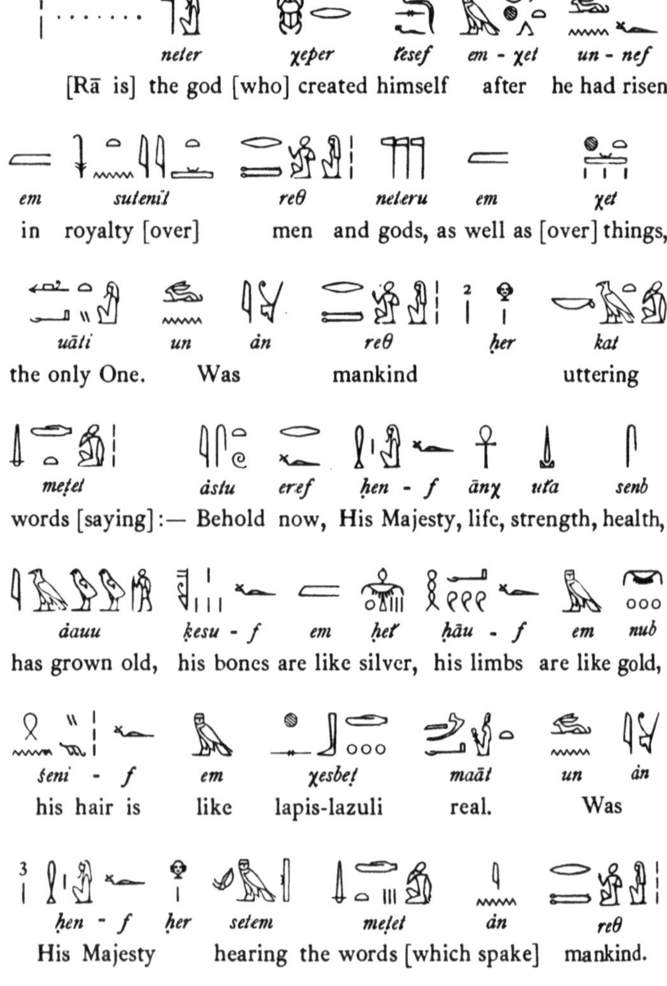

neter *χeper* *t̔esef* *em - χet* *un - nef*

[Rā is] the god [who] created himself after he had risen

em *sutenit* *reθ* *neteru* *em* *χet*

in royalty [over] men and gods, as well as [over] things,

uāti *un* *ȧn* *reθ* *ḥer* *kat*

the only One. Was mankind uttering

meṭet *ȧstu* *eref* *ḥen - f* *ānχ* *uṭa* *senb*

words [saying]:— Behold now, His Majesty, life, strength, health,

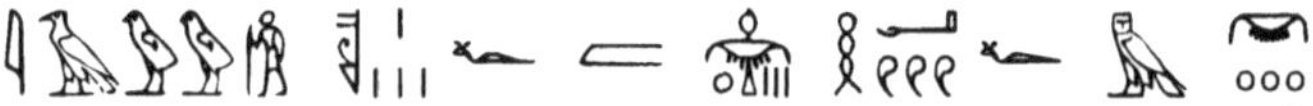

ȧauu *ḳesu - f* *em* *ḥet'* *ḥāu - f* *em* *nub*

has grown old, his bones are like silver, his limbs are like gold,

šeni - f *em* *χesbeṭ* *maāt* *un* *ȧn*

his hair is like lapis-lazuli real. Was

ḥen - f *ḥer* *setem* *meṭet* *ȧn* *reθ*

His Majesty hearing the words [which spake] mankind.

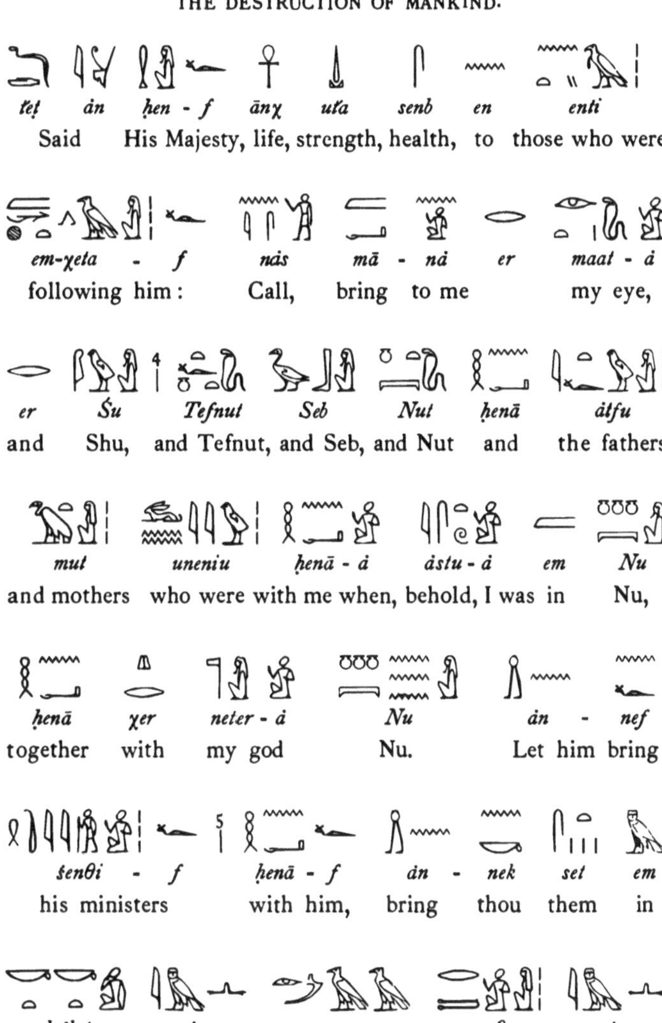

ṭeṭ ȧn ḥen - f ānχ uṭa senb en enti
Said His Majesty, life, strength, health, to those who were

em-χeta - f nȧs mā - nȧ er maat - ȧ
following him: Call, bring to me my eye,

er Šu Tefnut Seb Nut ḥenā ȧtfu
and Shu, and Tefnut, and Seb, and Nut and the fathers

mut uneniu ḥenā - ȧ ȧstu - ȧ em Nu
and mothers who were with me when, behold, I was in Nu,

ḥenā χer neter - ȧ Nu ȧn - nef
together with my god Nu. Let him bring

šenθi - f ḥenā - f ȧn - nek set em
his ministers with him, bring thou them in

ketket ȧm maa reθ ȧm
silence, that not may see mankind, not

uār ȧb - sen i - k ḥenā - sen er ḥet āat
may flee their hearts. Come thou with them into the temple,

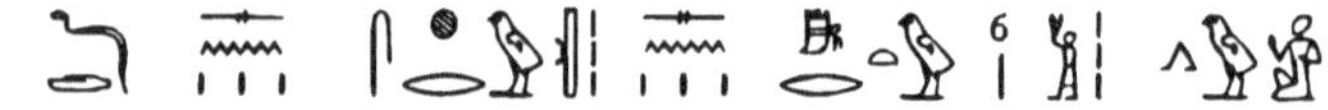

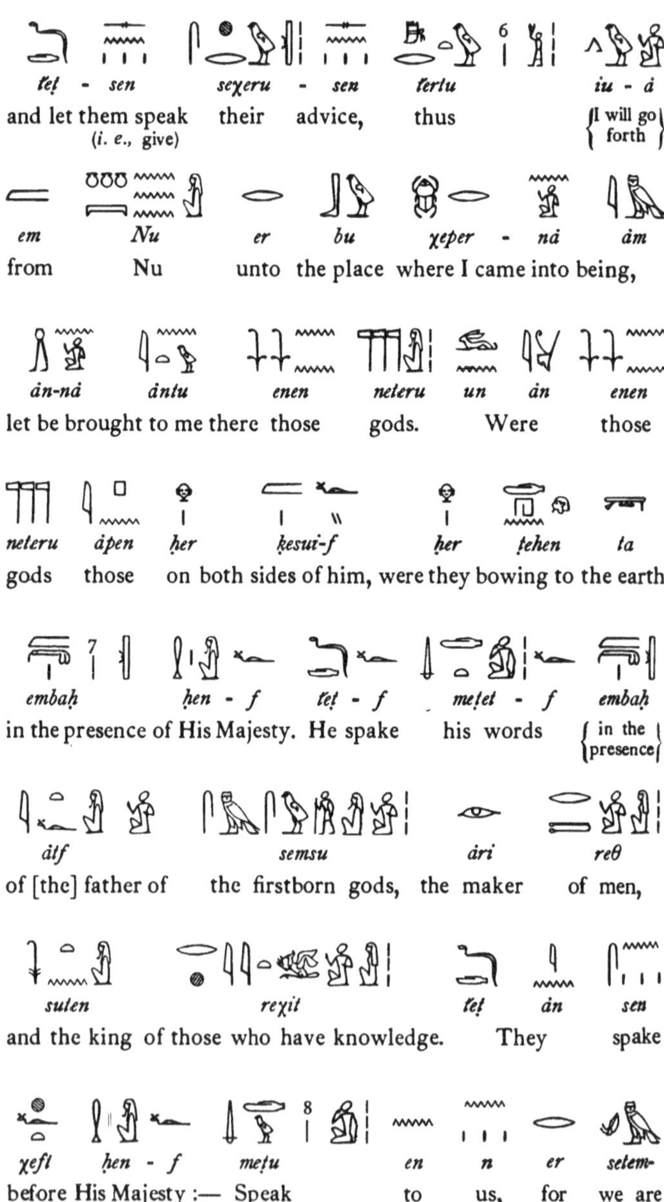

ṭeṭ - sen seχeru - sen ṭerṭu iu - ȧ

and let them speak (*i. e.*, give) their advice, thus {I will go forth}

em Nu er bu χeper - nȧ ȧm

from Nu unto the place where I came into being,

ȧn-nȧ ȧntu enen neteru un ȧn enen

let be brought to me there those gods. Were those

neteru ȧpen ḥer ḳesui-f ḥer ṭehen ta

gods those on both sides of him, were they bowing to the earth

embaḥ ḥen - f ṭeṭ - f meṭet - f embaḥ

in the presence of His Majesty. He spake his words {in the presence}

ȧtf semsu ȧri reθ

of [the] father of the firstborn gods, the maker of men,

suten reχit ṭeṭ ȧn sen

and the king of those who have knowledge. They spake

χeft ḥen - f meṭu en n er setem-

before His Majesty:— Speak to us, for we are

n *set* *ṭeṭ* *ȧn* *Rā* *en* *Nu* *neter*

listening to them. (*i. e.*, to thy words) Saith Rā to Nu:— O god

semsu *χeper* - *nȧ* *ȧm* - *f* *neteru* *ṭepāu*

firstborn, came I into being from whom, and ye gods ancestors,

mā - *ten* *reθ* *χeperu* *em* *maat* - *ȧ*

take ye heed to mankind, they have turned against my eye,

ka - *en* - *sen* *meṭet* *er* - *ȧ* *ṭeṭ* - *nȧ* *ȧrit* - *ten*

they speak words against me. Tell me [what] ye would do

er - *es* *mā* - *ten* - *uȧ* *ḥeḥi* - *ȧ* *ȧn* *sma-*

concerning it. Give ye me, {search out for me [a plan].} Not will I slay

nȧ *set* *er* *setem* - *uȧ* *ṭeṭθȧ* - *ten* *er* - *es*

them until I have heard what ye shall say concerning it.

ṭeṭ *ȧn* *ḥen* *en* *Nu* *sa* - *ȧ* *Rā* *neter* *āā*

Said the Majesty of Nu:— O my son Rā, god greater

er *ȧri* *su* *ur* *er* *qemaiu*

than [he] that made him, older than those divine beings who created

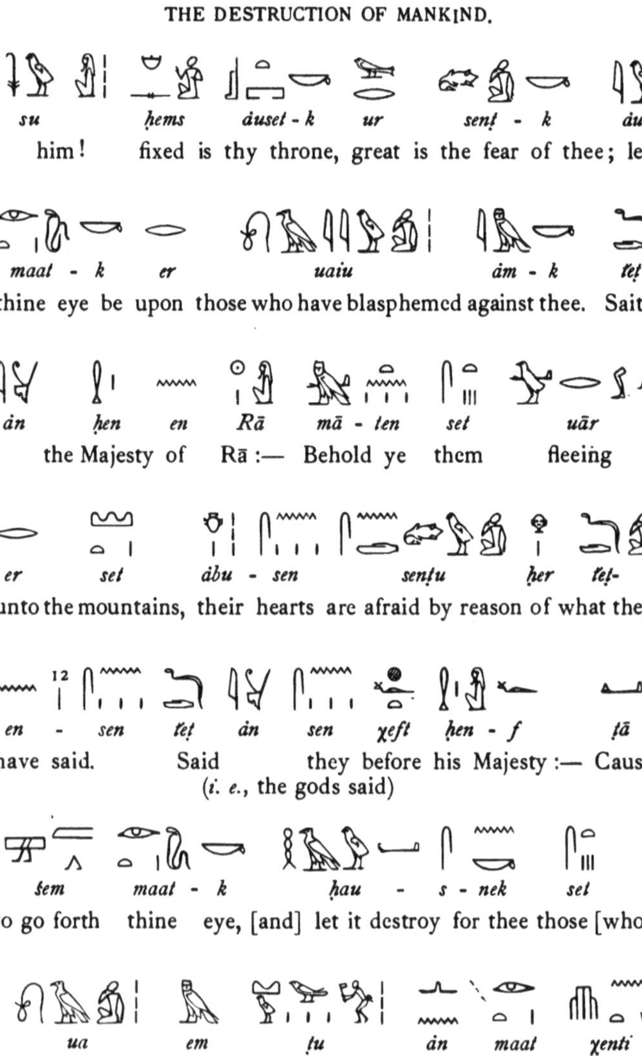

su *ḥems* *àuset - k* *ur* *senṭ - k* *àu*

him! fixed is thy throne, great is the fear of thee; let

maat - k *er* *uaiu* *àm - k* *ṭeṭ*

thine eye be upon those who have blasphemed against thee. Saith

àn *ḥen* *en* *Rā* *mā - ten* *set* *uār*

the Majesty of Rā :— Behold ye them fleeing

er *set* *àbu - sen* *sentu* *ḥer* *ṭeṭ-*

unto the mountains, their hearts are afraid by reason of what they

en - sen *ṭeṭ* *àn* *sen* *χeft* *ḥen - f* *ṭā*

have said. Said they before his Majesty :— Cause
(*i. e.*, the gods said)

ṭem *maat - k* *ḥau - s - nek* *set*

to go forth thine eye, [and] let it destroy for thee those [who]

ua *em* *ṭu* *àn* *maat* *χenti*

blaspheme [thee] with wickedness. Not an eye existeth

àm - s *er* *ḥu - k* *set* *ha - s* *em*

among them which can resist thee [when] it descendeth in

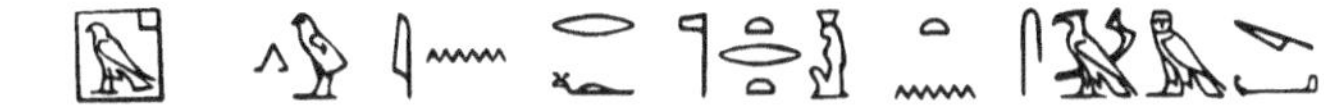

Ḥet-Ḥeru iu ȧn eref netert ten smam

{the form of Hathor.} Went forth then goddess this, it slew

nes reθ ḥer set ṭeṭ ȧn ḥen en

the people on the mountain. Said the Majesty of

neter pen iu em ḥetep Ḥet-Ḥeru ȧrit en ȧrit

this god :— Come, come in peace, Hathor, the deed is done (?)

ṭeṭ ȧn netert ten ānχ - k nȧ

. . . . . Said goddess this :— Thou livest for me.

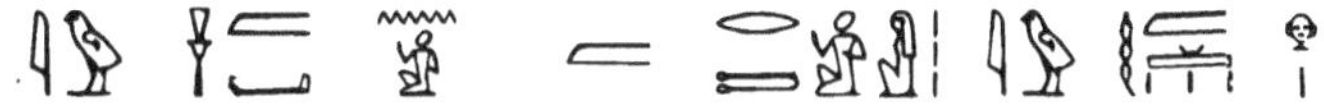

ȧu seχem - nȧ em reθ ȧu neṭem ḥer

[When] I had gotten power over men it was pleasing to

ȧb-ȧ ṭeṭ ȧn ḥen en Rā ȧu-ȧ er seχem

my heart. Said the Majesty of Rā :— I will gain the mastery

em sen em suten em se-ānṭu - set χeper

over them as king, destroying them. It came to pass that

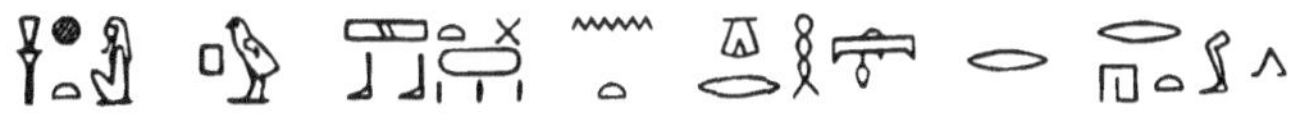

Seχet pu ṭebehet ent ḳerḥ er rehet

Sekhet of the offerings of the night waded about

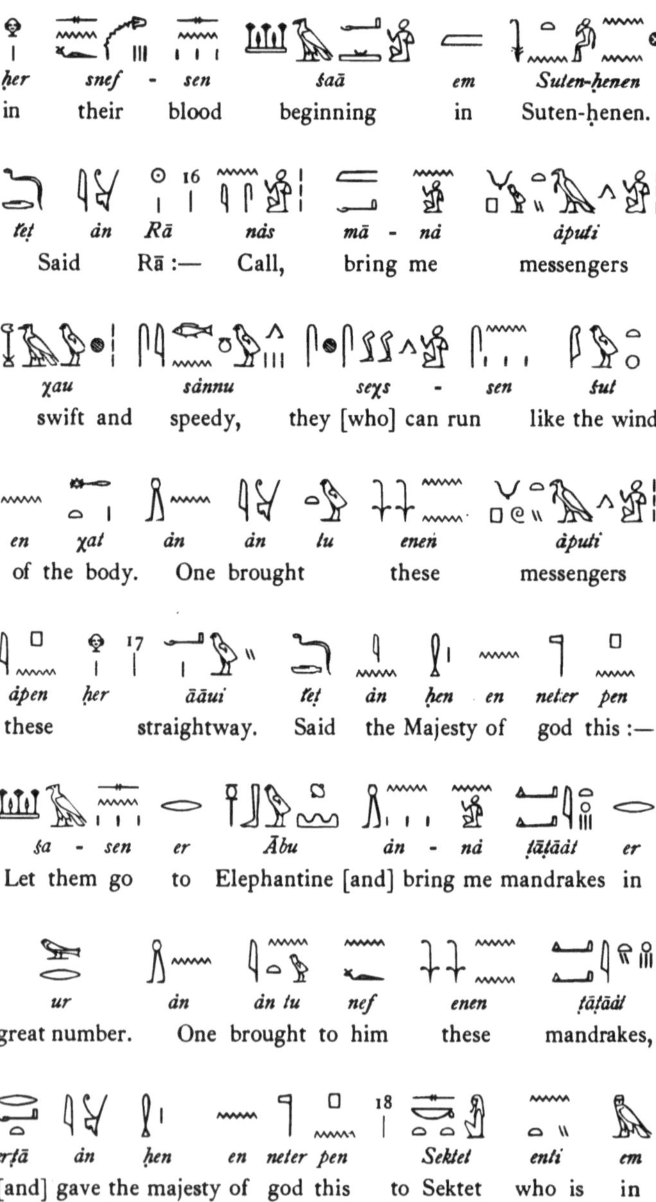

ḥer snef - sen šaā em Suten-ḥenen
in their blood beginning in Suten-ḥenen.

ṭeṭ àn Rā 16 *nàs mā - nà àputi*
Said Rā :— Call, bring me messengers

χau sànnu seχs - sen šut
swift and speedy, they [who] can run like the wind

en χat àn àn tu enen àputi
of the body. One brought these messengers

àpen ḥer 17 *āāui ṭeṭ àn ḥen en neter pen*
these straightway. Said the Majesty of god this :—

ša - sen er Ābu àn - nà ṭāṭāàt er
Let them go to Elephantine [and] bring me mandrakes in

ur àn àn tu nef enen ṭāṭāàt
great number. One brought to him these mandrakes,

erṭā àn ḥen en neter pen 18 *Sektet enti em*
[and] gave the majesty of god this to Sektet who is in

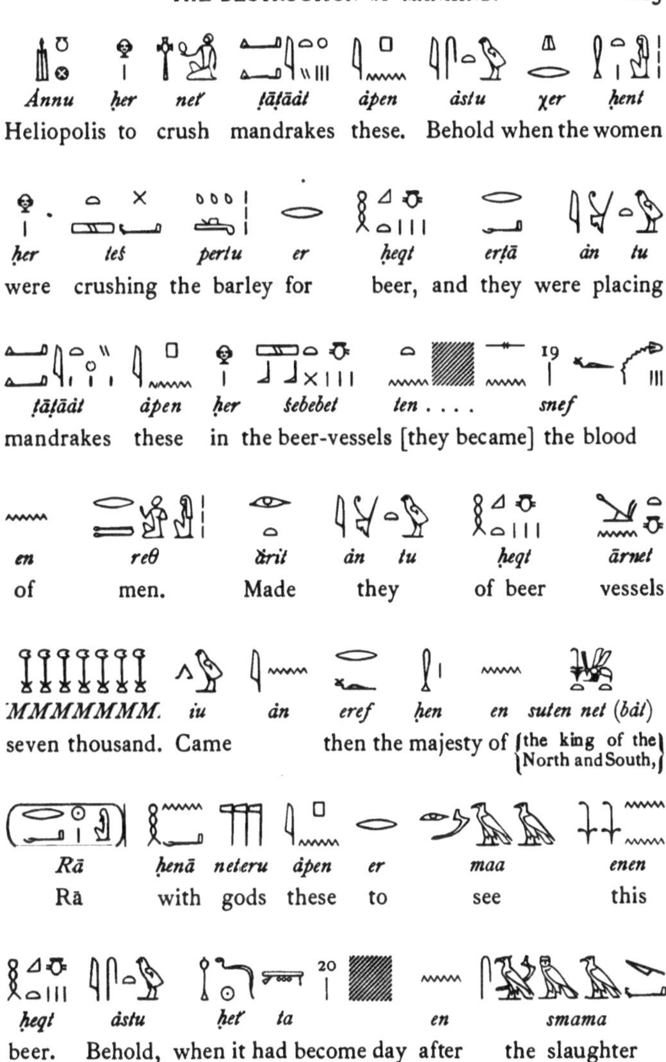

Ȧnnu ḥer neṭ ṭāṭāāt ȧpen ȧstu χer ḥent

Heliopolis to crush mandrakes these. Behold when the women

ḥer teš pertu er ḥeqt erṭā ȧn tu

were crushing the barley for beer, and they were placing

ṭāṭāāt ȧpen ḥer šebebet ten . . . . 19 *snef*

mandrakes these in the beer-vessels [they became] the blood

en reθ ȧrit ȧn tu ḥeqt ārnet

of men. Made they of beer vessels

MMMMMMM. iu ȧn eref ḥen en suten net (bȧt)

seven thousand. Came then the majesty of {the king of the North and South,}

Rā ḥenā neteru ȧpen er maa enen

Rā with gods these to see this

ḥeqt ȧstu ḥeṭ ta 20 *en smama*

beer. Behold, when it had become day after the slaughter

reθ ȧn netert em sesu - sen nu

of men by the goddess during their period (?) of

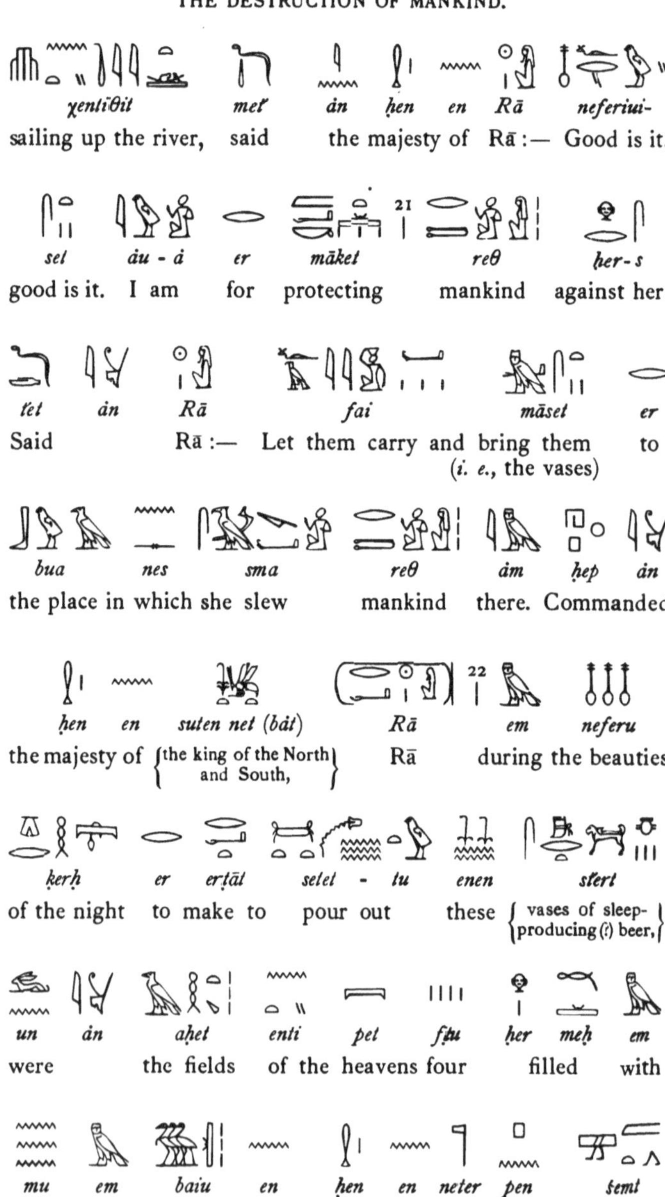

χentīθit *meť* *àn* *ḥen* *en* *Rā* *neferiui-*
sailing up the river, said the majesty of Rā :— Good is it,

set *àu - à* *er* *māket* 21 *reθ* *ḥer-s*
good is it. I am for protecting mankind against her.

ťet *àn* *Rā* *fai* *māset* *er*
Said Rā :— Let them carry and bring them (*i. e.*, the vases) to

bua *nes* *sma* *reθ* *àm* *ḥep* *àn*
the place in which she slew mankind there. Commanded

ḥen *en* *suten net (bàt)* *Rā* 22 *em* *neferu*
the majesty of {the king of the North and South,} Rā during the beauties

kerḥ *er* *erṭāt* *setet - tu* *enen* *sťert*
of the night to make to pour out these {vases of sleep-producing (?) beer,}

un *àn* *aḥet* *enti* *pet* *fṭu* *ḥer* *meḥ* *em*
were the fields of the heavens four filled with

mu *em* *baiu* *en* *ḥen* *en* *neter* *pen* *šemt*
liquid by the Will of the majesty of god this. Came

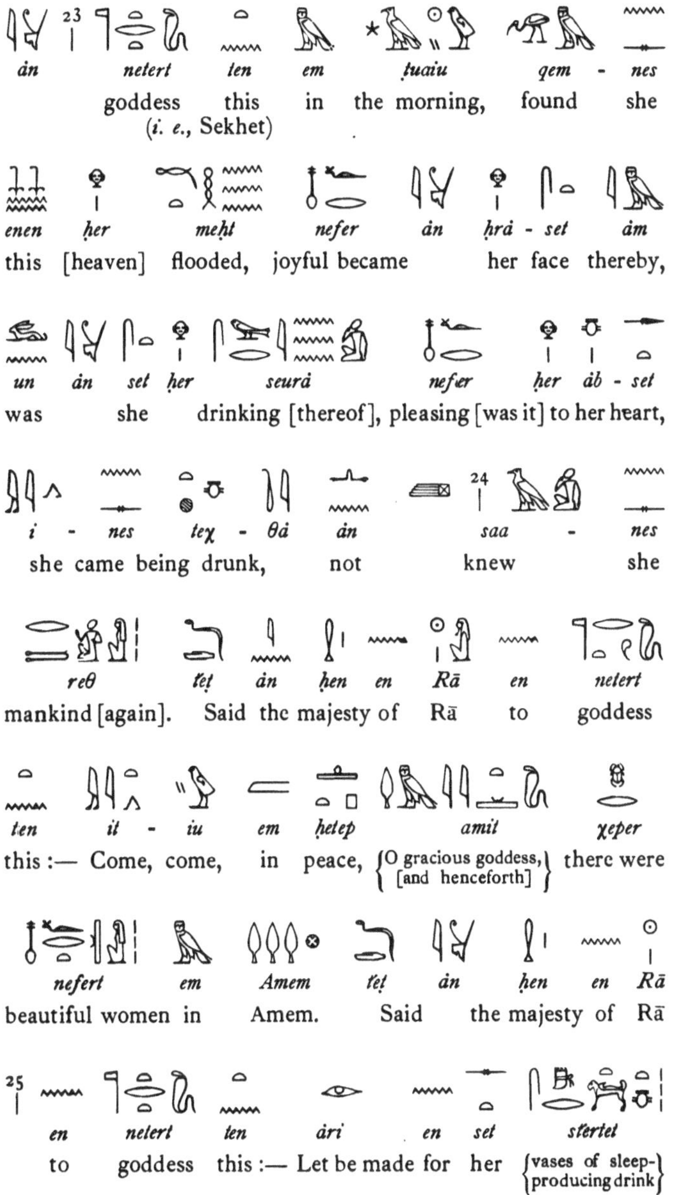

23 *àn* *netert* *ten* *em* *ṭuaiu* *qem* - *nes*
goddess (*i. e.*, Sekhet) this in the morning, found she

enen *ḥer* *meḥt* *nefer* *àn* *ḥrà* - *set* *àm*
this [heaven] flooded, joyful became her face thereby,

un *àn* *set* *ḥer* *seurà* *nefer* *ḥer* *àb* - *set*
was she drinking [thereof], pleasing [was it] to her heart,

i - *nes* *teχ* - *θà* *àn* 24 *saa* - *nes*
she came being drunk, not knew she

reθ *ṭeṭ* *àn* *ḥen* *en* *Rā* *en* *netert*
mankind [again]. Said the majesty of Rā to goddess

ten *it* - *iu* *em* *ḥetep* *amit* *χeper*
this :— Come, come, in peace, {O gracious goddess, [and henceforth]} there were

nefert *em* *Amem* *ṭeṭ* *àn* *ḥen* *en* *Rā*
beautiful women in Amem. Said the majesty of Rā

25 *en* *netert* *ten* *àri* *en* *set* *sṭertet*
to goddess this :— Let be made for her {vases of sleep-producing drink}

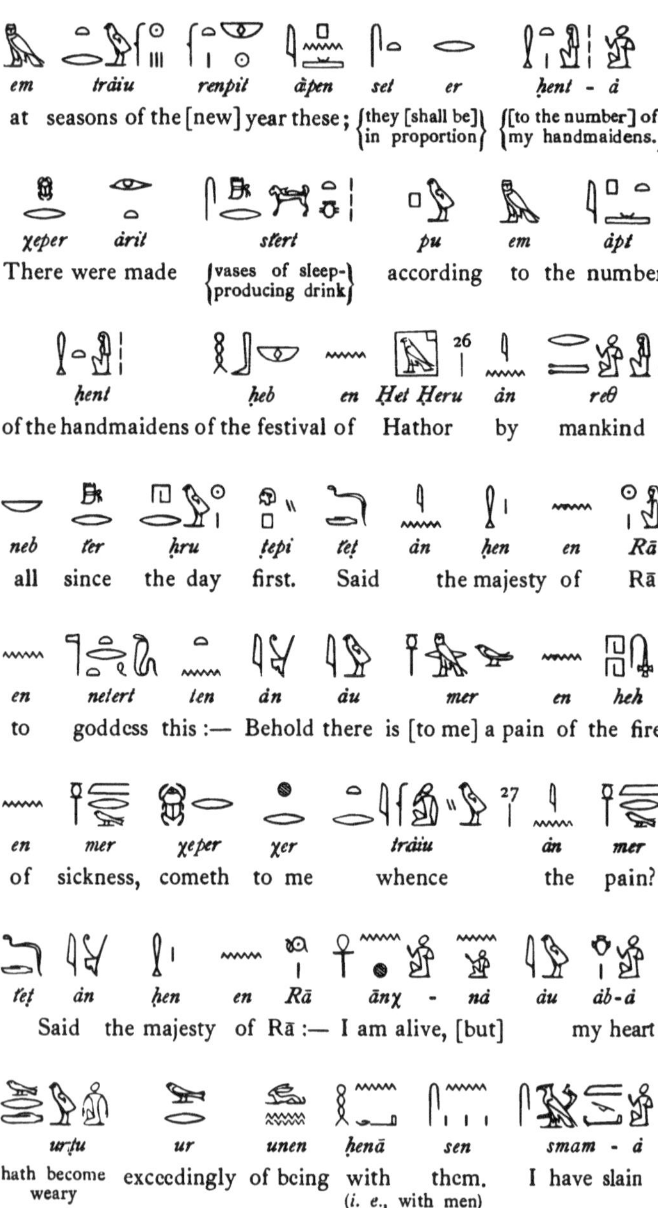

em trāiu renpit āpen set er ḥent - ā
at seasons of the [new] year these; {they [shall be] in proportion} {[to the number] of my handmaidens.}

χeper ārit sṫert pu em āpt
There were made {vases of sleep-producing drink} according to the number

ḥent ḥeb en Ḥet Ḥeru 26 *ān reθ*
of the handmaidens of the festival of Hathor by mankind

neb ṫer ḥru ṭepi ṭeṭ ān ḥen en Rā
all since the day first. Said the majesty of Rā

en netert ten ān āu mer en heh
to goddess this:— Behold there is [to me] a pain of the fire

en mer χeper χer trāiu 27 *ān mer*
of sickness, cometh to me whence the pain?

ṭeṭ ān ḥen en Rā ānχ - nā āu āb-ā
Said the majesty of Rā:— I am alive, [but] my heart

urṭu ur unen ḥenā sen smam - ā
hath become weary exceedingly of being with them. I have slain
(*i. e.*, with men)

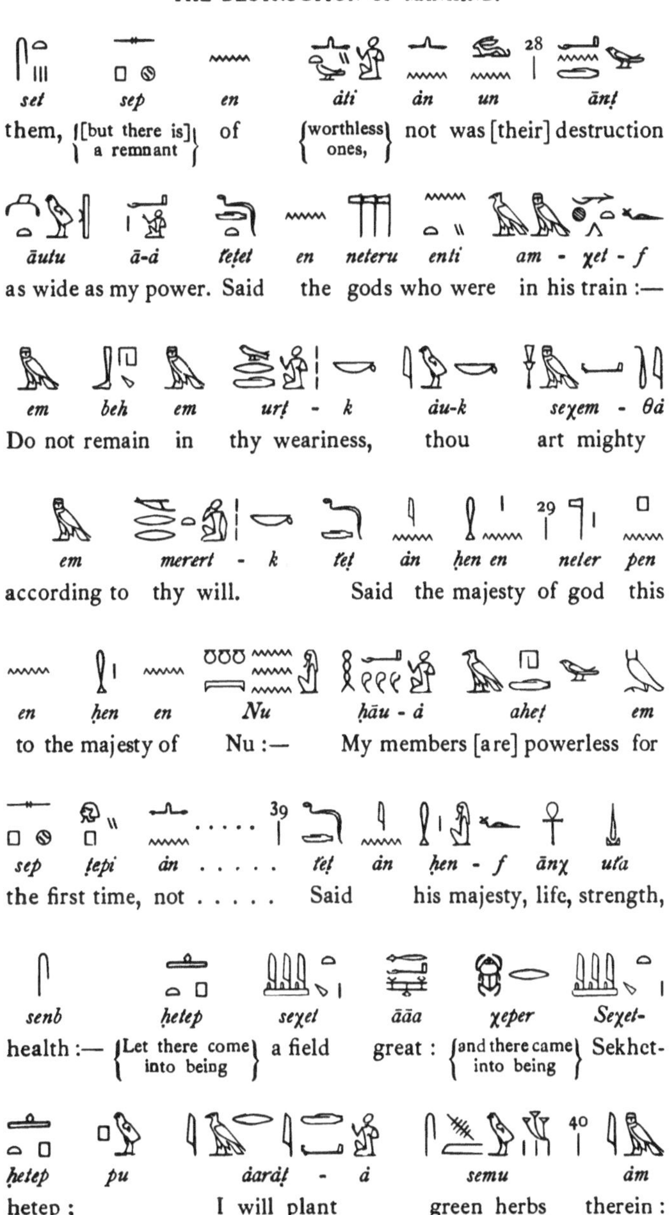

set sep en àti àn un ānṭ
them, [but there is] a remnant of worthless ones, not was [their] destruction

āutu ā-à ṭeṭet en neteru enti am - χet - f
as wide as my power. Said the gods who were in his train :—

em beh em urṭ - k àu-k seχem - θà
Do not remain in thy weariness, thou art mighty

em merert - k ṭeṭ àn ḥen en neter pen
according to thy will. Said the majesty of god this

en ḥen en Nu ḥāu - à aheṭ em
to the majesty of Nu :— My members [are] powerless for

sep ṭepi àn . . . . . ṭeṭ àn ḥen - f ānχ uṭa
the first time, not . . . . . Said his majesty, life, strength,

senb ḥetep seχet āāa χeper Seχet-
health :— Let there come into being a field great : and there came into being Sekhet-

ḥetep pu àaràṭ - à semu àm
ḥetep ; I will plant green herbs therein :

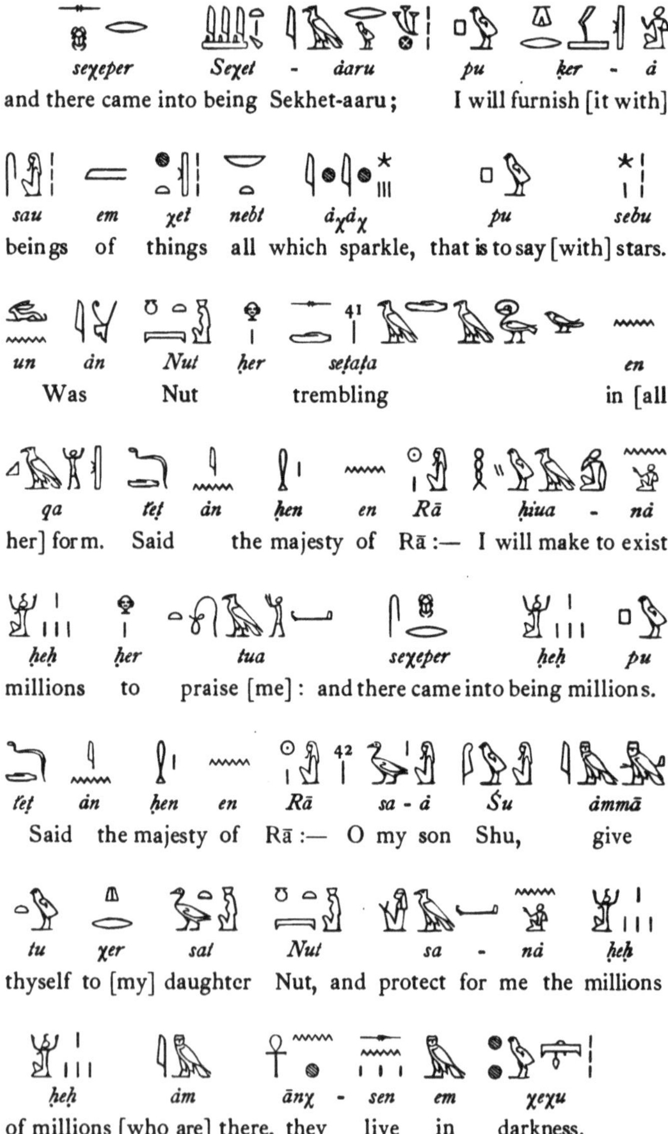

seχeper Seχet - àaru pu ḳer - à

and there came into being Sekhet-aaru; I will furnish [it with]

sau em χet nebt àχàχ pu sebu

beings of things all which sparkle, that is to say [with] stars.

un àn Nut ḥer 41 *seṭaṭa en*

Was Nut trembling in [all

qa ṭeṭ àn ḥen en Rā ḥiua - nà

her] form. Said the majesty of Rā :— I will make to exist

ḥeḥ ḥer tua seχeper ḥeḥ pu

millions to praise [me] : and there came into being millions.

ṭeṭ àn ḥen en Rā 42 *sa - à Śu àmmā*

Said the majesty of Rā :— O my son Shu, give

tu χer sat Nut sa - nà ḥeḥ

thyself to [my] daughter Nut, and protect for me the millions

ḥeḥ àm ānχ - sen em χeχu

of millions [who are] there, they live in darkness.

THE WAR OF RAMESES II AGAINST THE KHETA.

[XIXth dynasty.]

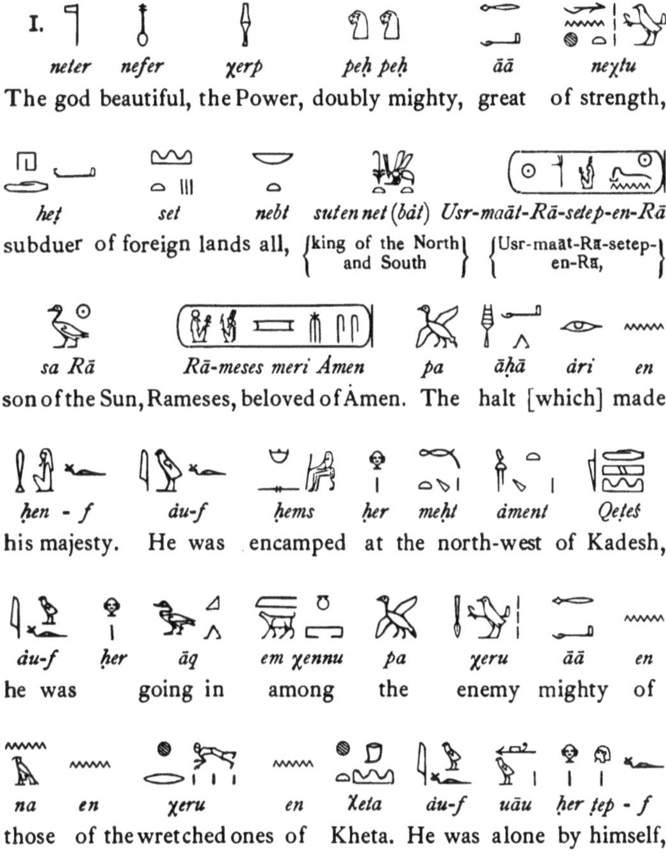

I. *neter nefer χerp peḥ peḥ āā neχtu*
The god beautiful, the Power, doubly mighty, great of strength,

heţ set nebt suten net (bȧt) Usr-maāt-Rā-setep-en-Rā
subduer of foreign lands all, {king of the North and South} {Usr-maāt-Rā-setep-en-Rā,}

sa Rā Rā-meses meri Ȧmen pa āḥā ȧri en
son of the Sun, Rameses, beloved of Ȧmen. The halt [which] made

ḥen - f ȧu-f ḥems ḥer meḥt ȧment Qeţeš
his majesty. He was encamped at the north-west of Kadesh,

ȧu-f ḥer āq em χennu pa χeru āā en
he was going in among the enemy mighty of

na en χeru en Χeta ȧu-f uāu ḥer ţep - f
those of the wretched ones of Kheta. He was alone by himself,

àn *ki* *ḥenā-f* *qem-nef* *ànḥu* *su*

not another [was] with him, he found surrounding him

MM + *D* *en ā* *en ḥetràu* *em* *fṭet* *χat*

two thousand five hundred horsemen in four companies

em *uat - f* *nebt* *àu-f* *ḥer* *āuāu - sen* *àr-u*

on his path every. Was he smiting them making them

em *àniu* *χer* *ḥāt* *sesemut - f* *àu-f* *ḥer*

into corpses before his horses. Was he

χaṭeb *uru* *neb* *en* *set* *neb* *na* *senu*

slaying the princes all of foreign lands all, the brethren

en *pa* *χer* *en* *χeta* *ḥenā* *naif* *seru*

of the wretched one of Kheta together with his nobles

āau *naif* *menfitu* *taif* *neθḥetr* *àu-f* *ḥer*

mighty, his soldiers, his cavalry. Was he

ḳebḳeb - set *χer* *ḥer* *ḥrà - sen* *àu-f* *ḥer*

casting down them throwing [them] upon their faces. Was he

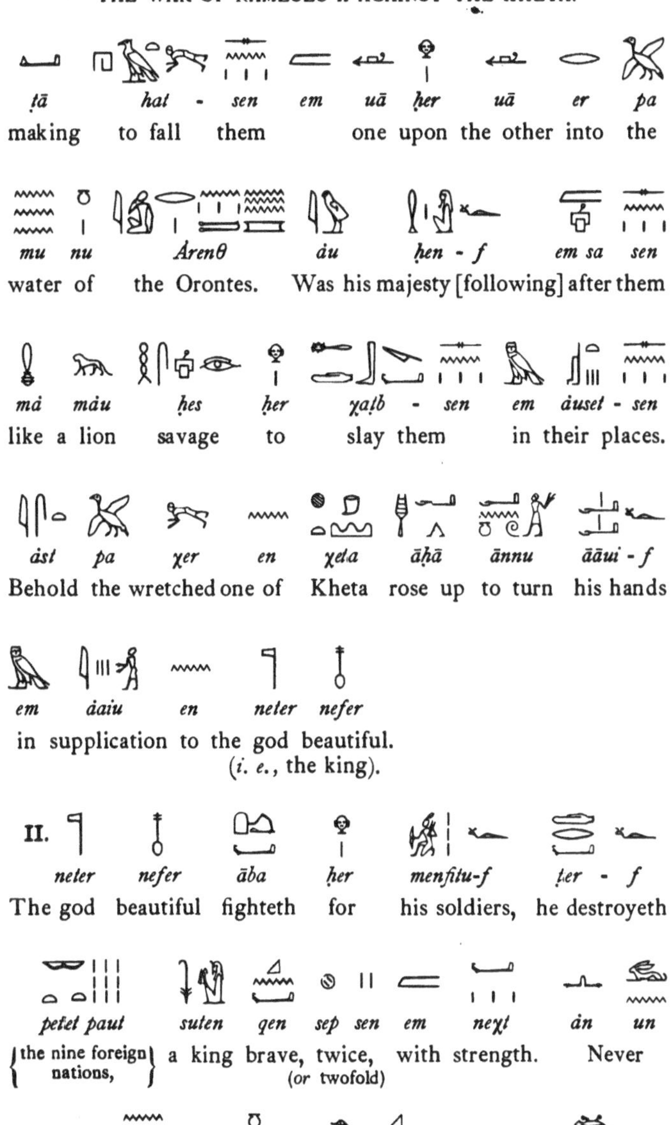

ṭā hat - sen em uā ḥer uā er pa
making to fall them one upon the other into the

mu nu Ȧrenθ ȧu ḥen - f em sa sen
water of the Orontes. Was his majesty [following] after them

mȧ mȧu ḥes ḥer χaṭb - sen em ȧuset - sen
like a lion savage to slay them in their places.

ȧst pa χer en χeṭa āḥā ānnu āāui - f
Behold the wretched one of Kheta rose up to turn his hands

em ȧaiu en neter nefer
in supplication to the god beautiful. (*i. e.*, the king).

II. *neter nefer āba ḥer menfitu-f ṭer - f*
The god beautiful fighteth for his soldiers, he destroyeth

peṭeṭ paut suten qen sep sen em neχt ȧn un
{the nine foreign nations,} a king brave, twice, (or twofold) with strength. Never

ȧri - nef sen āq em āšt
hath been made [his] second. Going in among the multitudes

menfitu *en* *set* *neb* *ȧrit* - *sen* *em*
of the soldiers of foreign lands all [he] was making them into

teblebet *ḥebs* *ȧrit* *ḥer* - *f* *em* *metet*
dead men. A reckoning was made for him of the *phalli*

ur *en* *Χeta* *ṭeṭ* *en* *Neherina*
of the chiefs of Kheta [and] the hands of Mesopotamia.

HYMN TO RĀ BY HUNEFER.

[British Museum papyrus No. 9901.]

[XIXth dynasty.]

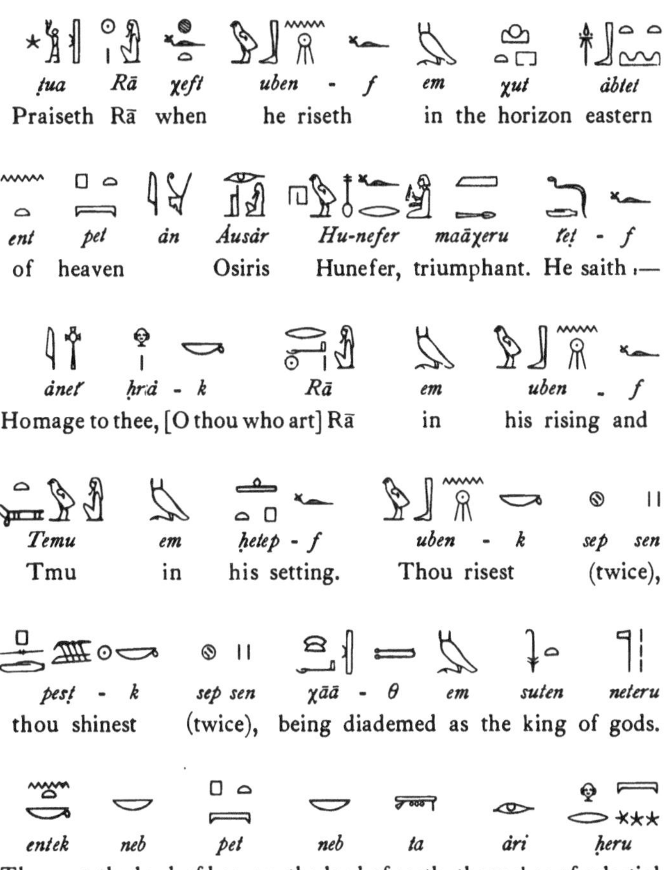

ṭua Rā χeft uben - f em χut ȧbtet

Praiseth Rā when he riseth in the horizon eastern

ent pet ȧn Ȧusȧr Hu-nefer maāχeru ṭeṭ - f

of heaven Osiris Hunefer, triumphant. He saith :—

ȧnet' ḥrȧ - k Rā em uben - f

Homage to thee, [O thou who art] Rā in his rising and

Temu em ḥetep - f uben - k sep sen

Tmu in his setting. Thou risest (twice),

pesṭ - k sep sen χāā - θ em suten neteru

thou shinest (twice), being diademed as the king of gods.

entek neb pet neb ta ȧri ḥeru

Thou art the lord of heaven, the lord of earth, the maker of celestial

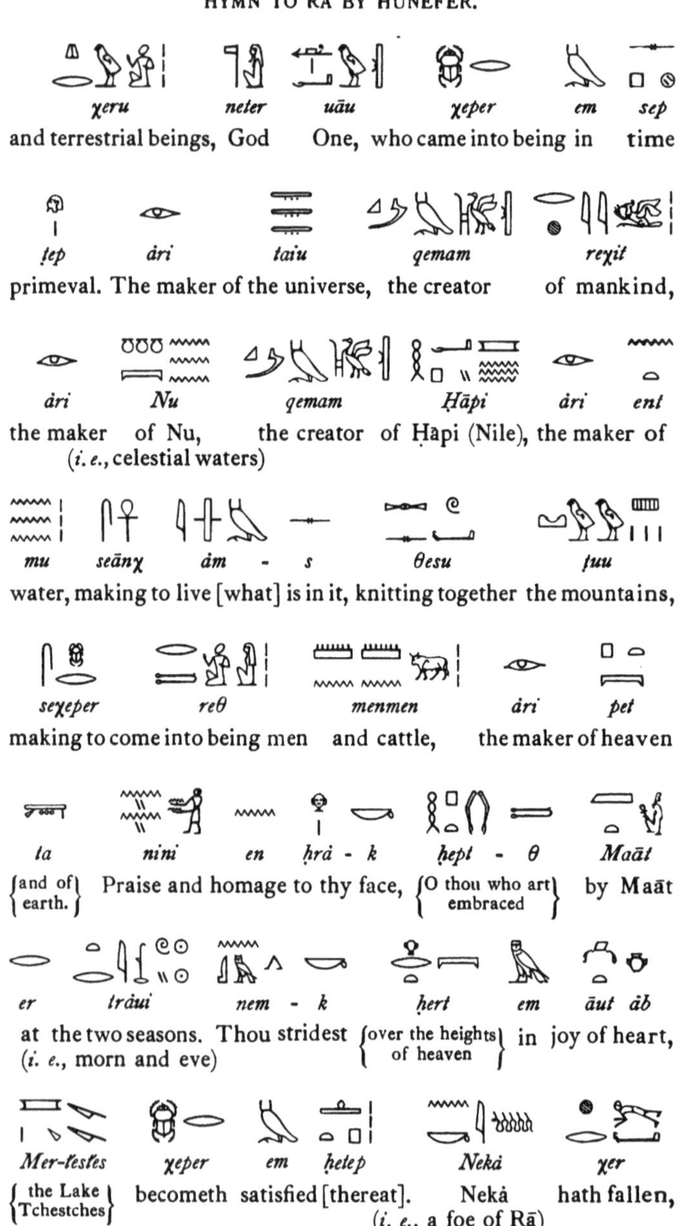

χeru *neter* *uāu* *χeper* *em* *sep*
and terrestrial beings, God One, who came into being in time

ṭep *ȧri* *taiu* *qemam* *reχit*
primeval. The maker of the universe, the creator of mankind,

ȧri *Nu* *qemam* *Ḥāpi* *ȧri* *ent*
the maker of Nu, (*i. e.*, celestial waters) the creator of Ḥāpi (Nile), the maker of

mu *seānχ* *ȧm* - *s* *θesu* *ṭuu*
water, making to live [what] is in it, knitting together the mountains,

seχeper *reθ* *menmen* *ȧri* *pet*
making to come into being men and cattle, the maker of heaven

ta *nini* *en* *ḥrȧ* - *k* *ḥept* - *θ* *Maāt*
{and of earth.} Praise and homage to thy face, {O thou who art embraced} by Maāt

er *trȧui* *nem* - *k* *ḥert* *em* *āut* *ȧb*
at the two seasons. (*i. e.*, morn and eve) Thou stridest {over the heights of heaven} in joy of heart,

Mer-ṭesṭes *χeper* *em* *ḥetep* *Nekȧ* *χer*
{the Lake Tchestches} becometh satisfied [thereat]. Nekȧ (*i. e.*, a foe of Rā) hath fallen,

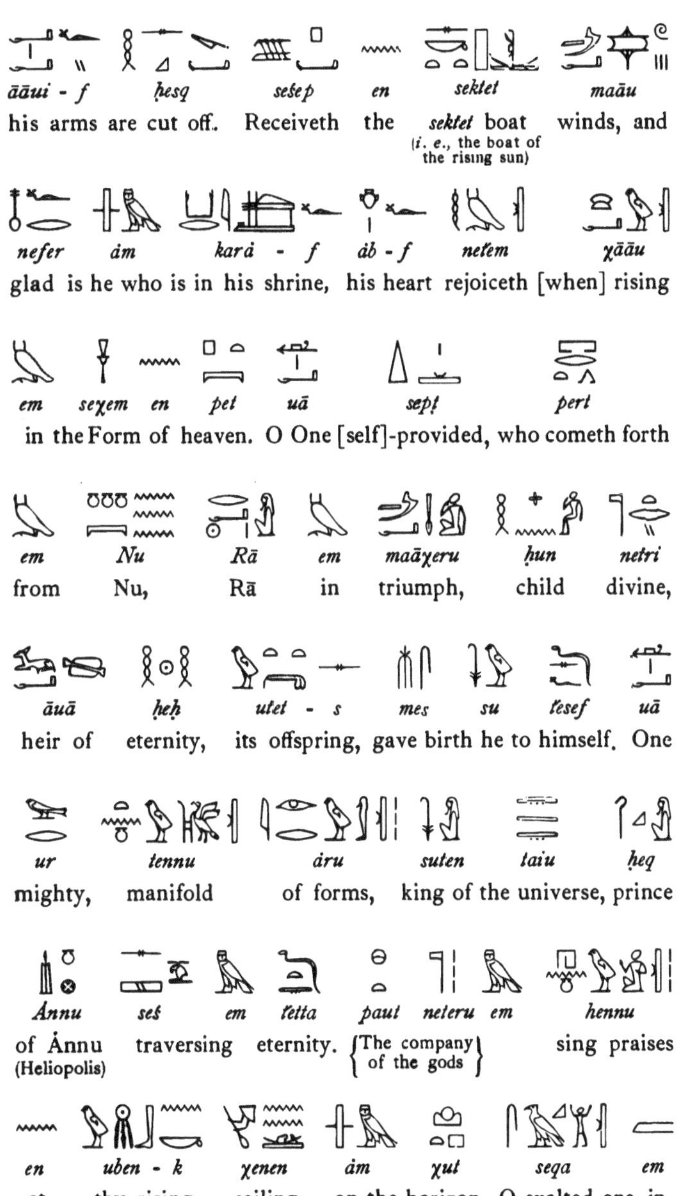

āāui - f *ḥesq* *sešep* *en* *sektet* *maāu*

his arms are cut off. Receiveth the *sektet* boat (*i. e.*, the boat of the rising sun) winds, and

nefer *àm* *karà - f* *àb - f* *neṭem* *χāāu*

glad is he who is in his shrine, his heart rejoiceth [when] rising

em *seχem* *en* *pet* *uā* *sepṭ* *pert*

in the Form of heaven. O One [self]-provided, who cometh forth

em *Nu* *Rā* *em* *maāχeru* *ḥun* *netri*

from Nu, Rā in triumph, child divine,

āuā *ḥeḥ* *utet - s* *mes* *su* *ṭesef* *uā*

heir of eternity, its offspring, gave birth he to himself. One

ur *tennu* *àru* *suten* *taiu* *ḥeq*

mighty, manifold of forms, king of the universe, prince

Ànnu *seś* *em* *ṭetta* *paut* *neteru* *em* *hennu*

of Ànnu (Heliopolis) traversing eternity. {The company of the gods} sing praises

en *uben - k* *χenen* *àm* *χut* *seqa* *em*

at thy rising sailing on the horizon, O exalted one in

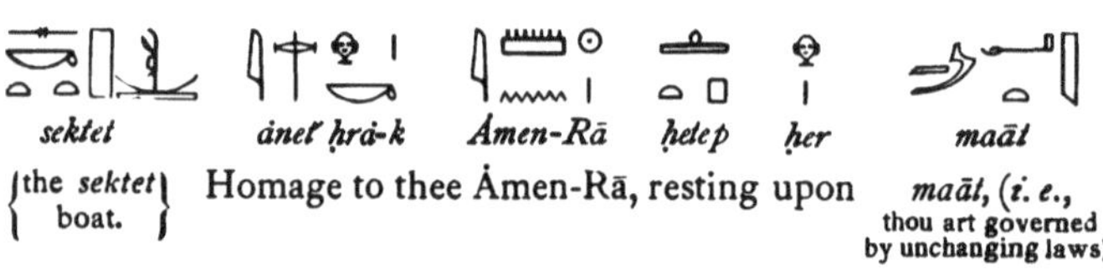

sektet *ȧnet' ḥrȧ-k* *Ȧmen-Rā* *ḥetep* *ḥer* *maāt*

{the *sektet* boat.} Homage to thee Ȧmen-Rā, resting upon *maāt*, (*i. e.*, thou art governed by unchanging laws).

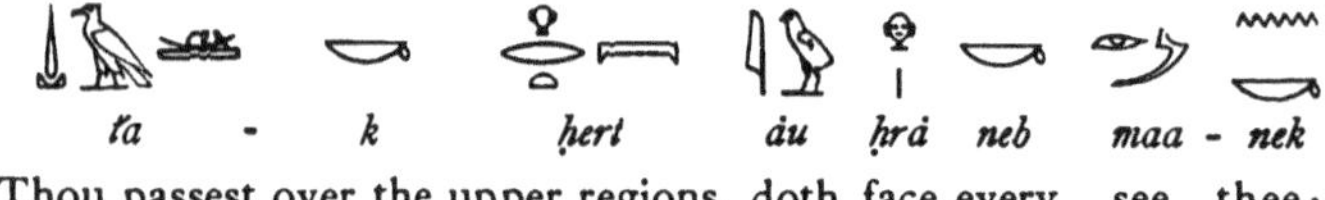

t'a - k *ḥert* *ȧu* *ḥrȧ* *neb* *maa - nek*

Thou passest over the upper regions, doth face every see thee;

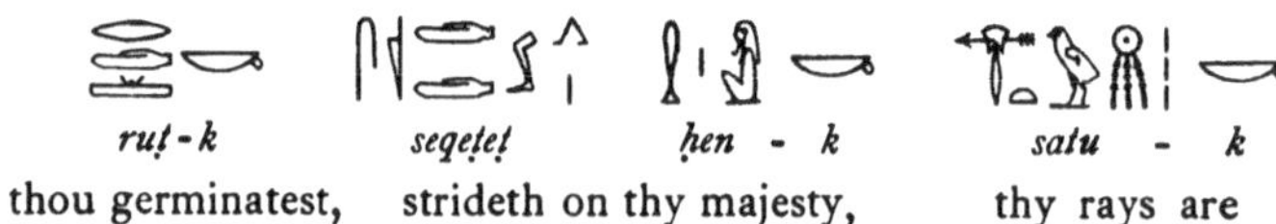

ruṭ - k *seqeṭeṭ* *ḥen - k* *satu - k*

thou germinatest, strideth on thy majesty, thy rays are

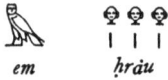

em *ḥrȧu*

upon [all] faces.

FROM THE PAPYRUS OF RAMESES III.

[XXth dynasty.]

nerāu *I* *ḥet'* *em* *qeḥqeḥ* *ānnu* *II*

Goat, one. Silver in beaten tablets, two.

nenibu *III* *χemti* *em* *qeḥqeḥ* *ānnu* *IV*

Trees, three. Bronze in beaten tablets, four.

qemā nefer *ṭu* *V* *θeḥennu* *hennu* *X* *χet*

Linen fine garments, five. Crystal, measures ten. Wood

en *ānti* *XV* *ānti* *hannu* *XX*

of *ānti* unguent, fifteen. *Ānti* unguent, measures twenty.

ḥetet *mesθȧ* *L* *reθ* *100* *māfek*

Plants, measures fifty. Men, one hundred. Turquoise,

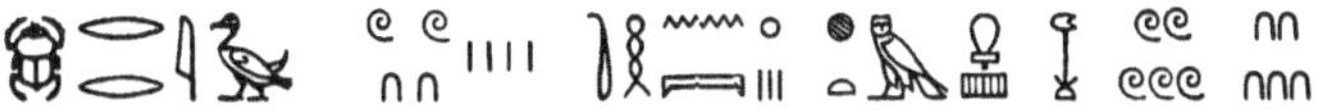

χeperȧ *200 + 20 + 4* *θeḥen* *χetem* *1000 + 500 + 50*

scarabs, 224. Crystal, rings, 1550.

tau nefer àuf šāi 9000 + 800 + 40 + 5
Nefer bread, flesh, cakes, 9845.

tau nefer tau berber 40,000 + 6000 + 500
Nefer bread, loaves of pyramid form, 46,500.

tau nefer tau ḥet' en uṭennu
Nefer bread, loaves white for offerings

100,000 × 5 + 70,000 + 2000 *ḥetep tau nefer āqu*
572,000. Total, *nefer* bread, cakes

šeben 100,000 × 28 + 40,000 + 4000 + 300 + 50 + 7
various 2,844,357.

THE LEGEND OF RĀ AND ISIS.

[XXth dynasty.]

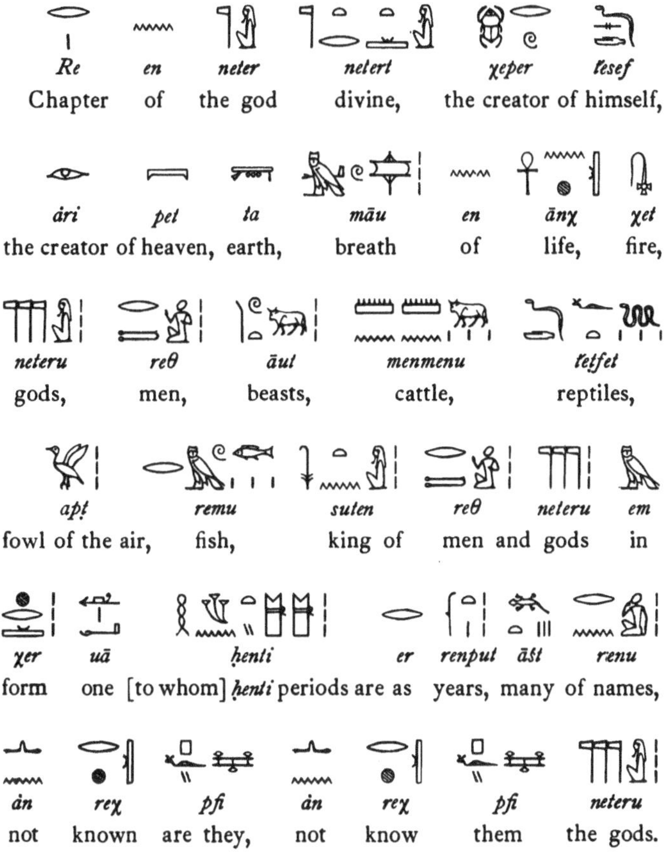

Re en neter netert χeper ṭesef
Chapter of the god divine, the creator of himself,

ȧri pet ta māu en ānχ χet
the creator of heaven, earth, breath of life, fire,

neteru reθ āut menmenu ṭetfet
gods, men, beasts, cattle, reptiles,

apṭ remu suten reθ neteru em
fowl of the air, fish, king of men and gods in

χer uā ḥenti er renput āšt renu
form one [to whom] *ḥenti* periods are as years, many of names,

ȧn reχ pfi ȧn reχ pfi neteru
not known are they, not know them the gods.

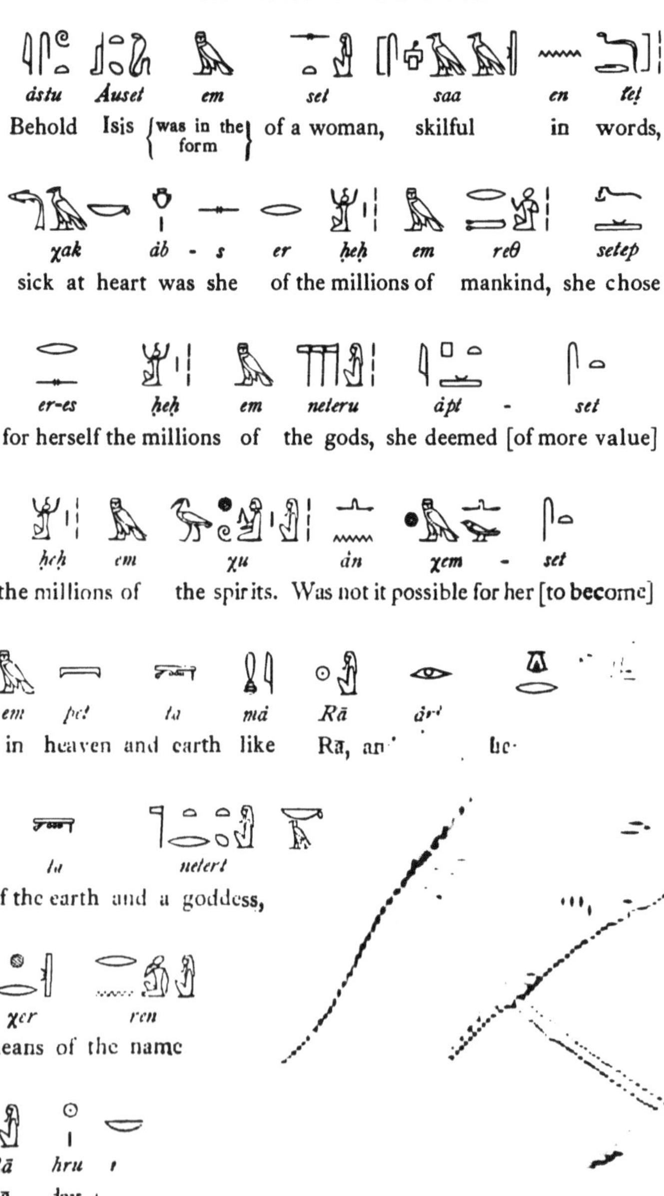

àstu Àuset em set saa en ṭeṭ
Behold Isis {was in the form} of a woman, skilful in words,

χak àb - s er ḥeḥ em reθ setep
sick at heart was she of the millions of mankind, she chose

er-es ḥeḥ em neteru àpt - set
for herself the millions of the gods, she deemed [of more value]

ḥeḥ em χu àn χem - set
the millions of the spirits. Was not it possible for her [to become]

em pet ta mà Rā àri
in heaven and earth like Rā, an ... he

ta netert
of the earth and a goddess,

χer ren
means of the name

Rā hru
Ra day

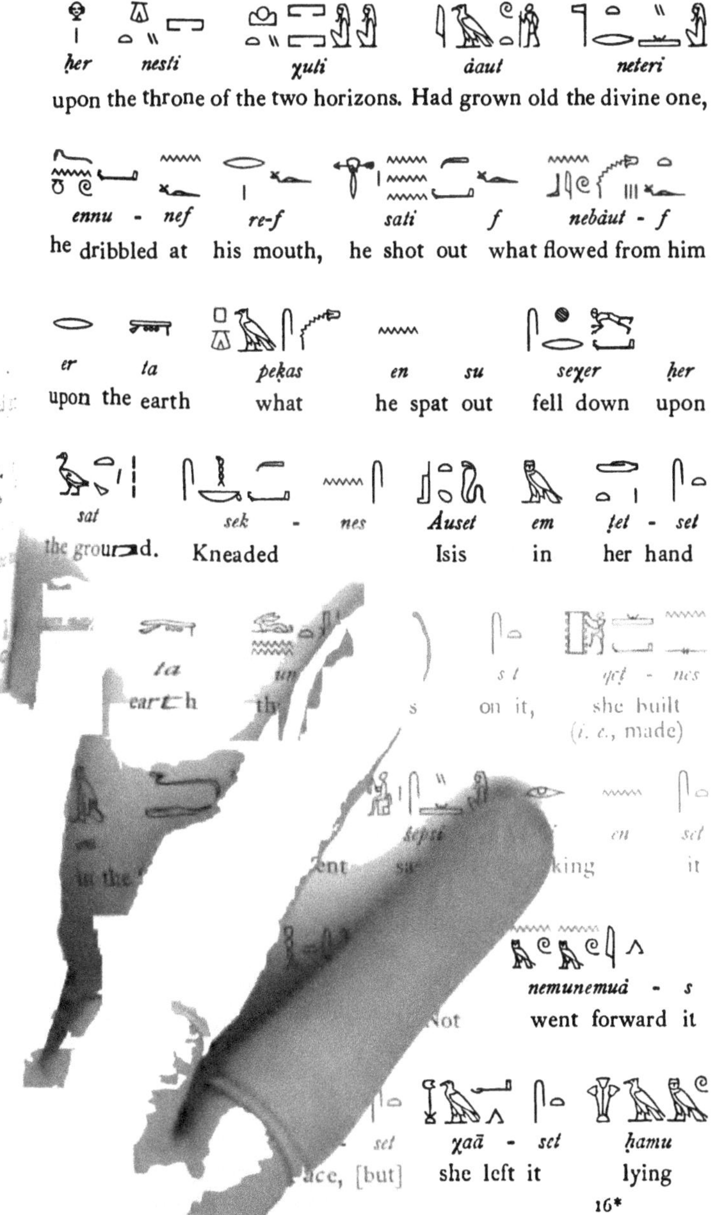

ḥer nesti χuti åaut neteri
upon the throne of the two horizons. Had grown old the divine one,

ennu - nef re-f sati f nebåut - f
he dribbled at his mouth, he shot out what flowed from him

er ta pekas en su seχer ḥer
upon the earth what he spat out fell down upon

sat sek - nes Åuset em ṭet - set
the ground. Kneaded Isis in her hand

ta
earth

on it, she built (*i. e.*, made)

en set
it

nemunemuå - s
went forward it

set χaā - set ḥamu
ace, [but] she left it lying

ḥer uat āpep neter āa ḥer set er àba - f

on the path went the god great along it according to his wish

emχet taui-f neter šepsi χāā - f er

in his two lands. The god sacred rose [and came]

ḥa neteru em Āa-perti ānχ uṭa

forth, the gods of the great double house, life, strength,

senb emχet - f sefetsefet - f mà hru neb

health, following him; he strode on as [he did] day every.

unχu - set em ṭetfet šepsi χet

Shot out its fang the serpent sacred, and the fire

ānχet per - θà àm - f ṭesef ṭer - nes

of life was going out from his own body, it destroyed

àmi na āšu neter neteri - f

the dweller among the cedars, the god divine he opened

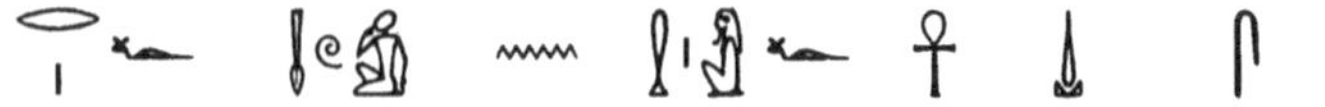

re - f χeru en ḥen - f ānχ uṭa senb

his mouth, the cry of his Majesty, life, strength, health,

peḥ - nef er pet paut neteru tuf ḥer

reached up to heaven. The company of the gods it was for [saying],

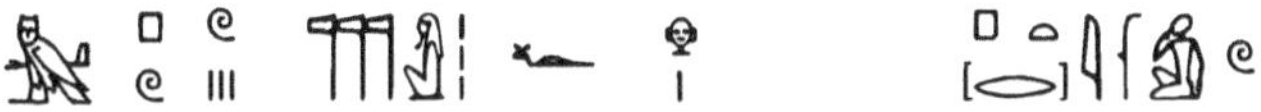

mā pu - u neteru - f ḥer petrà-u

What is it? and its gods [were] for [saying], What is the matter?

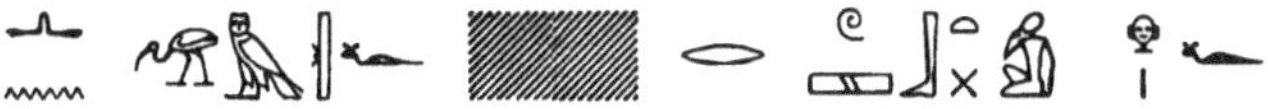

àn qem - f er ušebt ḥer - f

Not found he [the power] to answer concerning it.

àrti - f ḥer χetχet āt - f neb

His two jawbones rattled, his limbs all

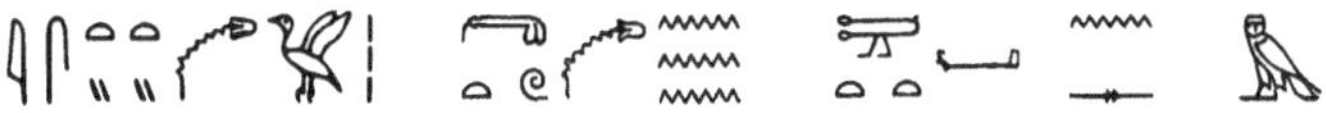

àstiti metu θetet - nef em

trembled, the poison gained the mastery in

àuf - f mà θetet Ḥāpi em χet - f

his members as gains the mastery Ḥāpi in his course.

neter āa smen - nef àb - f - f er

The god mighty stablished his heart, he cried out to

àmi χet - f māi - ten nà χepert em

those in his train :— Come to me, {you [who] are produced} from

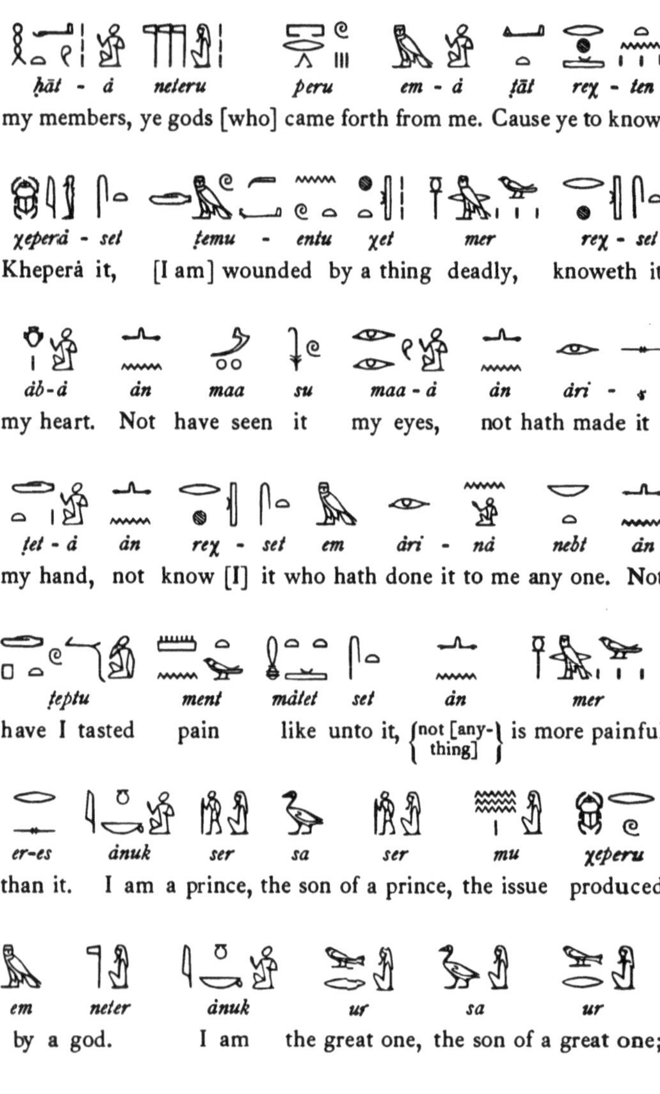

ḥāt - à neteru peru em - à ṭāt rex - ten

my members, ye gods [who] came forth from me. Cause ye to know

xeperà - set ṭemu - entu xet mer rex - set

Kheperà it, [I am] wounded by a thing deadly, knoweth it

àb - à àn maa su maa - à àn àri - s

my heart. Not have seen it my eyes, not hath made it

ṭet - à àn rex - set em àri - nà nebt àn

my hand, not know [I] it who hath done it to me any one. Not

ṭeptu ment màtet set àn mer

have I tasted pain like unto it, {not [anything]} is more painful

er-es ànuk ser sa ser mu xeperu

than it. I am a prince, the son of a prince, the issue produced

em neter ànuk ur sa ur

by a god. I am the great one, the son of a great one;

maut en àtf - à ren - à ànuk āšt

hath thought out my father my name. I am of many

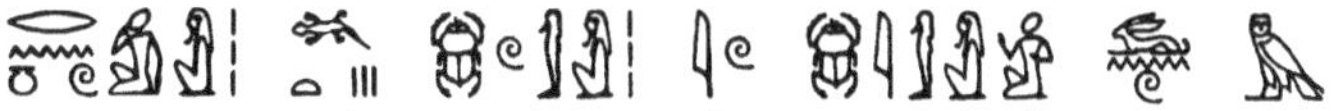

rennu āšt χeperu àu χeperà - à unu em

names, of many forms, my being existeth in

neter neb nàs - à - tu Temu Ḥeru

god every. I have been proclaimed by Tmu and Horus,

ḥekennu à ṭeṭ àtf - à mut - à ren - à

{the gods who give names.} Have uttered my father and my mother my name,

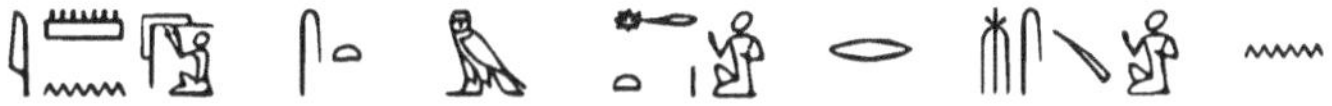

àmen - set em χat-à er mes - à en

hidden was it in my body by my begetter so

meri tem erṭāt χeperu peḥti

that not might be allowed to gain power

ḥekau - à en ḥekai er - à peru-

he who would enchant me by [his] enchantments over me. I had

k[uà] er ḥa er maa àri - nà

come from within to see what I had made,

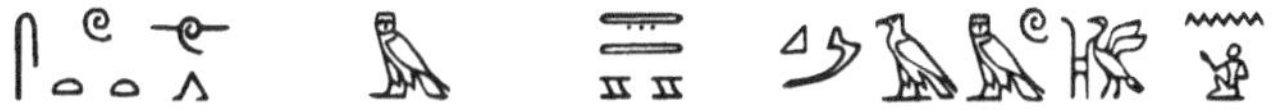

stutet em taui qemamu - nà

[and] was passing through the universe [which] I had created,

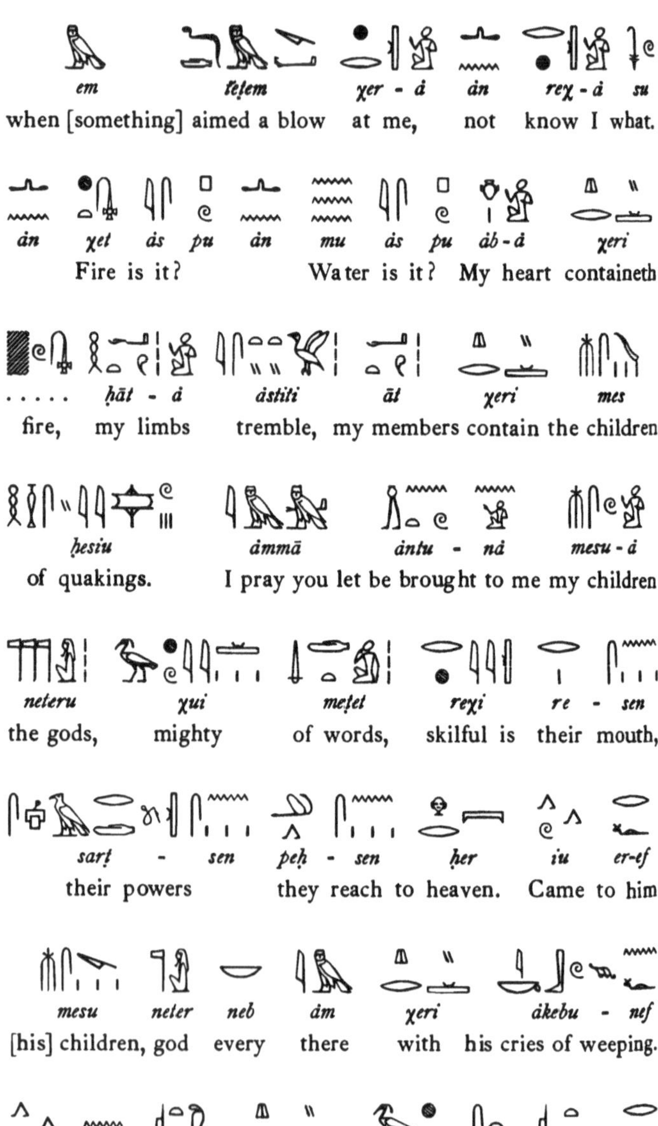

em *ṭeṭem* *χer - à* *àn* *reχ - à* *su*

when [something] aimed a blow at me, not know I what.

àn *χet* *às* *pu* *àn* *mu* *às* *pu* *àb - à* *χeri*

Fire is it? Water is it? My heart containeth

. . . . . *ḥāt* - *à* *àstiti* *āt* *χeri* *mes*

fire, my limbs tremble, my members contain the children

ḥesiu *àmmā* *àntu* - *nà* *mesu* - *à*

of quakings. I pray you let be brought to me my children

neteru *χui* *meṭet* *reχi* *re* - *sen*

the gods, mighty of words, skilful is their mouth,

sarṭ - *sen* *peḥ* - *sen* *ḥer* *iu* *er-ef*

their powers they reach to heaven. Came to him

mesu *neter* *neb* *àm* *χeri* *àkebu* - *nef*

[his] children, god every there with his cries of weeping.

iu *en* *Àuset* *χeri* *χut* - *set* *àuset* *re-*

Came Isis with her powerful words, the place of

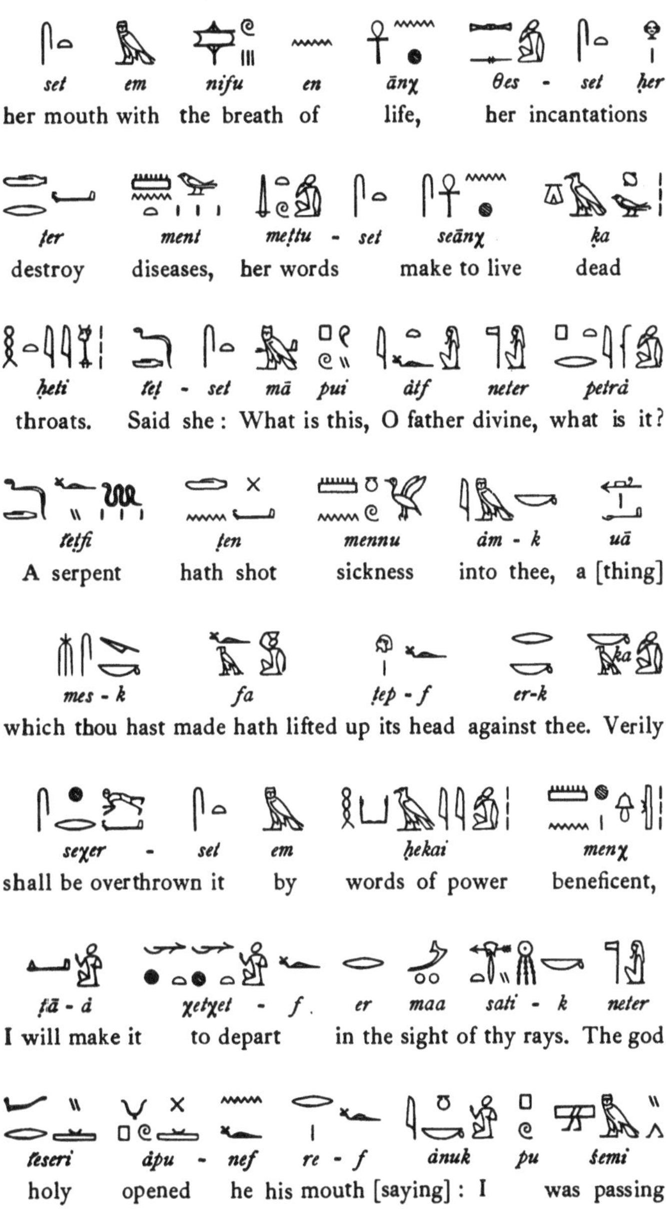

set em nifu en ānχ θes - set ḥer
her mouth with the breath of life, her incantations

ṭer ment meṭtu - set seānχ ḳa
destroy diseases, her words make to live dead

ḥeti ṭeṭ - set mā pui àtf neter petrà
throats. Said she: What is this, O father divine, what is it?

ṭeṭfi ṭen mennu àm - k uā
A serpent hath shot sickness into thee, a [thing]

mes - k fa ṭep - f er-k
which thou hast made hath lifted up its head against thee. Verily

seχer - set em ḥekai menχ
shall be overthrown it by words of power beneficent,

ṭā - à χetχet - f er maa sati - k neter
I will make it to depart in the sight of thy rays. The god

ṭeseri àpu - nef re - f ànuk pu šemi
holy opened he his mouth [saying]: I was passing

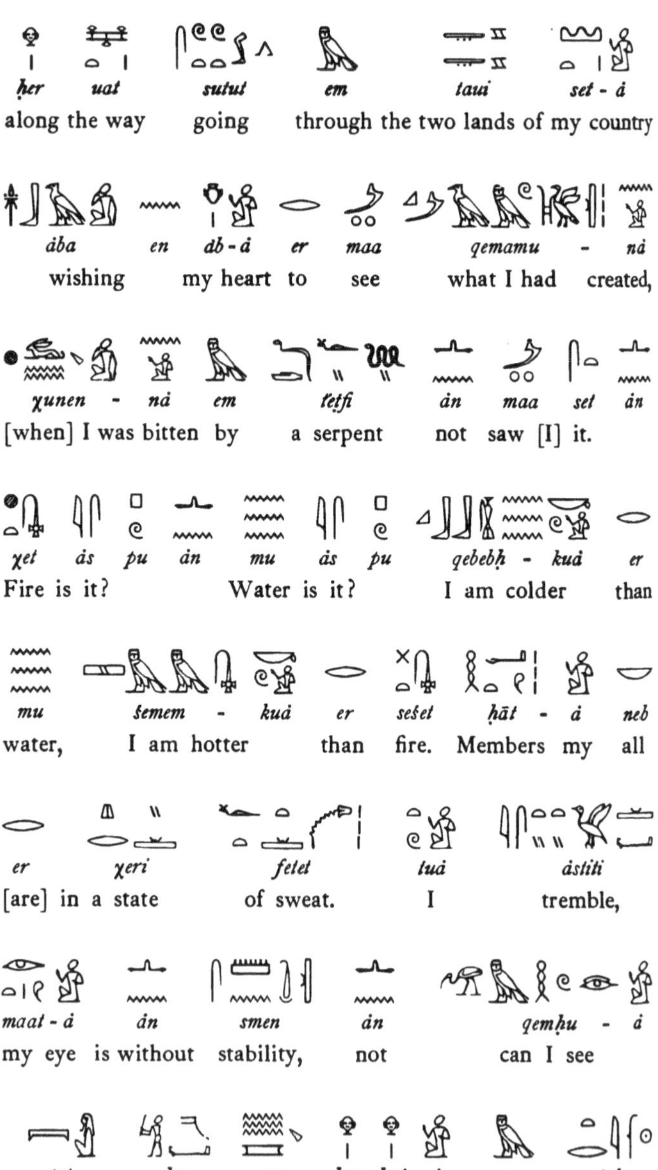

ḥer uat sutut em taui set - ȧ

along the way going through the two lands of my country

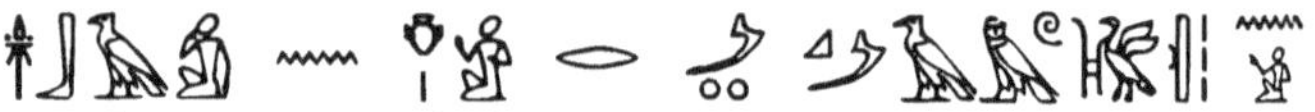

ȧba en ȧb - ȧ er maa qemamu - nȧ

wishing my heart to see what I had created,

χunen - nȧ em ťetfi ȧn maa set ȧn

[when] I was bitten by a serpent not saw [I] it.

χet ȧs pu ȧn mu ȧs pu qebebḥ - kuȧ er

Fire is it? Water is it? I am colder than

mu šemem - kuȧ er sešet ḥāt - ȧ neb

water, I am hotter than fire. Members my all

er χeri fetet tuȧ ȧstiti

[are] in a state of sweat. I tremble,

maat - ȧ ȧn smen ȧn qemḥu - ȧ

my eye is without stability, not can I see

pet ḥu mu ḥer ḥrȧ - ȧ em trȧ

the heavens. Riseth water on my face [as] in the time

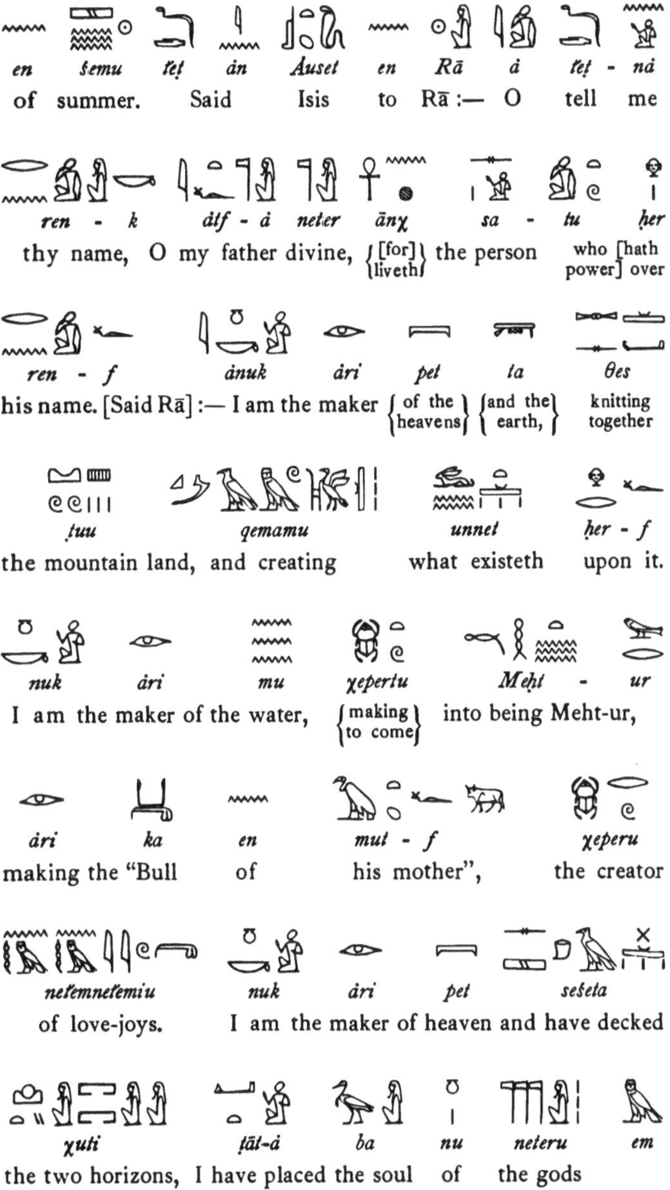

en šemu ṭeṭ ȧn Ȧuset en Rā ȧ ṭeṭ - nȧ

of summer. Said Isis to Rā :— O tell me

ren - k ȧtf - ȧ neter ānχ sa - tu ḥer

thy name, O my father divine, {[for] liveth} the person who [hath power] over

ren - f ȧnuk ȧri pet ta θes

his name. [Said Rā] :— I am the maker {of the heavens} {and the earth,} knitting together

ṭuu qemamu unnet ḥer - f

the mountain land, and creating what existeth upon it.

nuk ȧri mu χepertu Meḥt - ur

I am the maker of the water, {making to come} into being Meht-ur,

ȧri ka en mut - f χeperu

making the "Bull of his mother", the creator

neṭemneṭemiu nuk ȧri pet sešeta

of love-joys. I am the maker of heaven and have decked

χuti ṭāt-ȧ ba nu neteru em

the two horizons, I have placed the soul of the gods

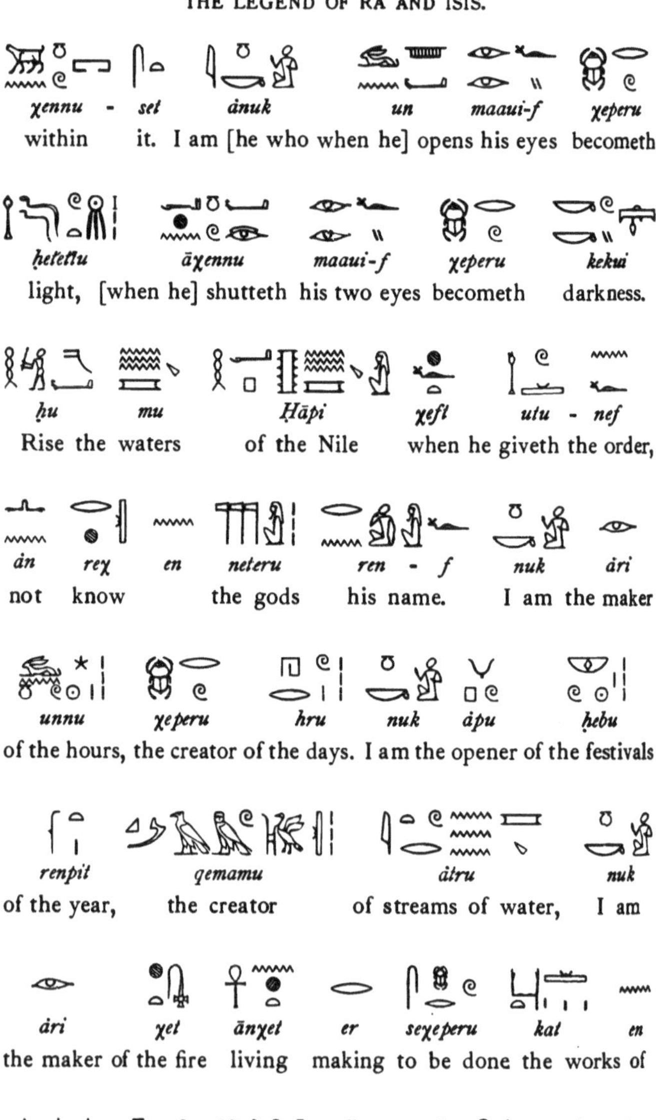

χennu - set ȧnuk un maaui-f χeperu
within it. I am [he who when he] opens his eyes becometh

ḥeṭeṭu āχennu maaui-f χeperu kekui
light, [when he] shutteth his two eyes becometh darkness.

ḥu mu Ḥāpi χeft utu - nef
Rise the waters of the Nile when he giveth the order,

ȧn reχ en neteru ren - f nuk ȧri
not know the gods his name. I am the maker

unnu χeperu hru nuk ȧpu ḥebu
of the hours, the creator of the days. I am the opener of the festivals

renpit qemamu ȧtru nuk
of the year, the creator of streams of water, I am

ȧri χet ānχet er seχeperu kat en
the maker of the fire living making to be done the works of

am nuk χeperȧ em ṭuauu Rā em
the houses, I am Khepera in the morning, Rā in

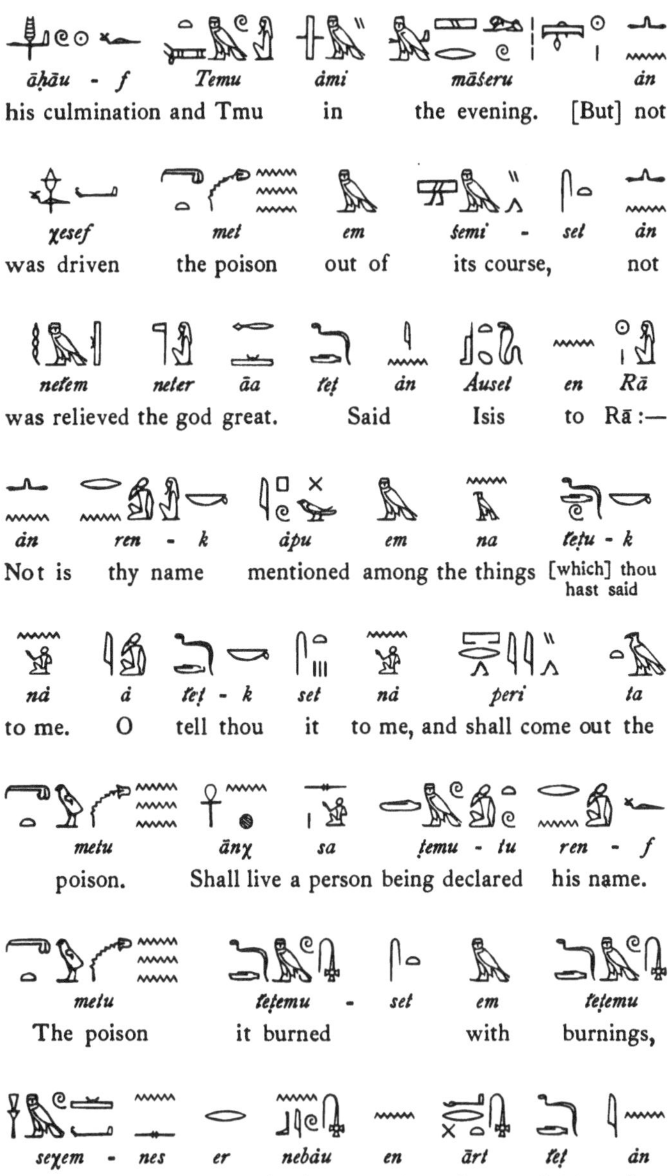

āḥāu - f Temu ȧmi māśeru ȧn

his culmination and Tmu in the evening. [But] not

χesef met em śemi - set ȧn

was driven the poison out of its course, not

neťem neter āa ṭeṭ ȧn Ȧuset en Rā

was relieved the god great. Said Isis to Rā:—

ȧn ren - k ȧpu em na ṭeṭu - k

Not is thy name mentioned among the things [which] thou hast said

nȧ ȧ ṭeṭ - k set nȧ peri ta

to me. O tell thou it to me, and shall come out the

metu ānχ sa ṭemu - tu ren - f

poison. Shall live a person being declared his name.

metu ṭeṭemu - set em ṭeṭemu

The poison it burned with burnings,

seχem - nes er nebȧu en ārt ṭeṭ ȧn

it was stronger than the flames of fire. Said the

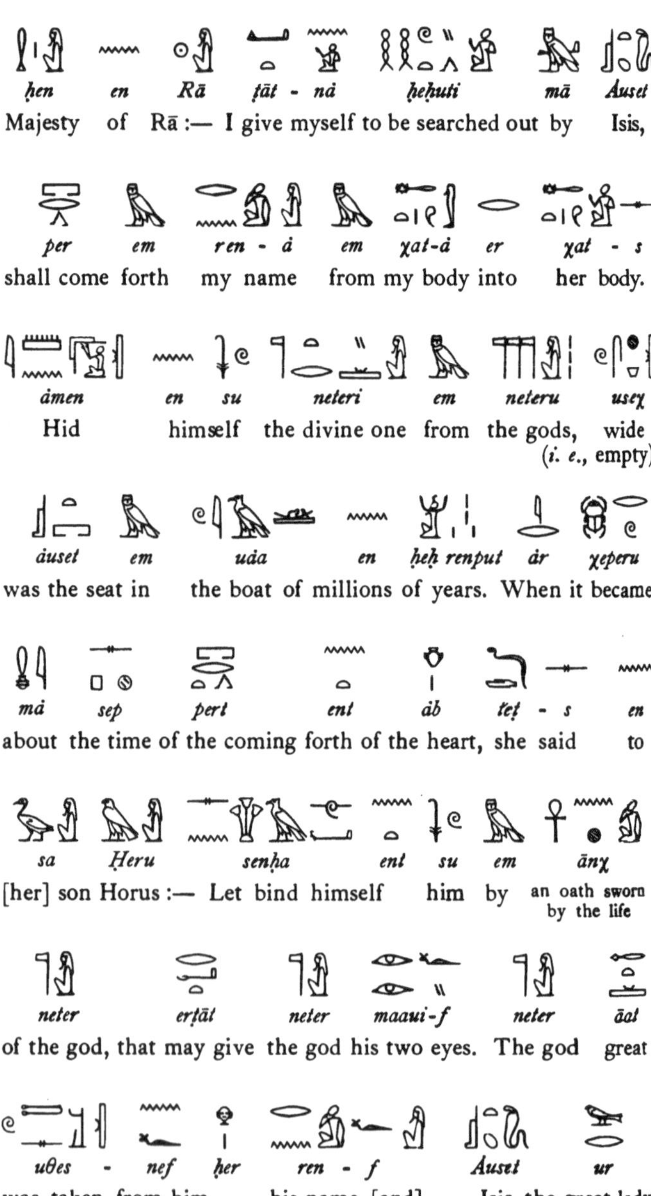
ḥen en Rā ṭāt - nȧ ḥeḥuti mā Ȧuset
Majesty of Rā :— I give myself to be searched out by Isis,
per em ren - ȧ em χat-ȧ er χat - s
shall come forth my name from my body into her body.
ȧmen en su neteri em neteru useχ
Hid himself the divine one from the gods, wide (i. e., empty)
ȧuset em uȧa en ḥeḥ renput ȧr χeperu
was the seat in the boat of millions of years. When it became
mȧ sep pert ent ȧb ṭeṭ - s en
about the time of the coming forth of the heart, she said to
sa Ḥeru senḥa ent su em ānχ
[her] son Horus :— Let bind himself him by an oath sworn by the life
neter erṭāt neter maaui-f neter āat
of the god, that may give the god his two eyes. The god great
uθes - nef ḥer ren - f Ȧuset ur
was taken from him his name, [and] Isis the great lady

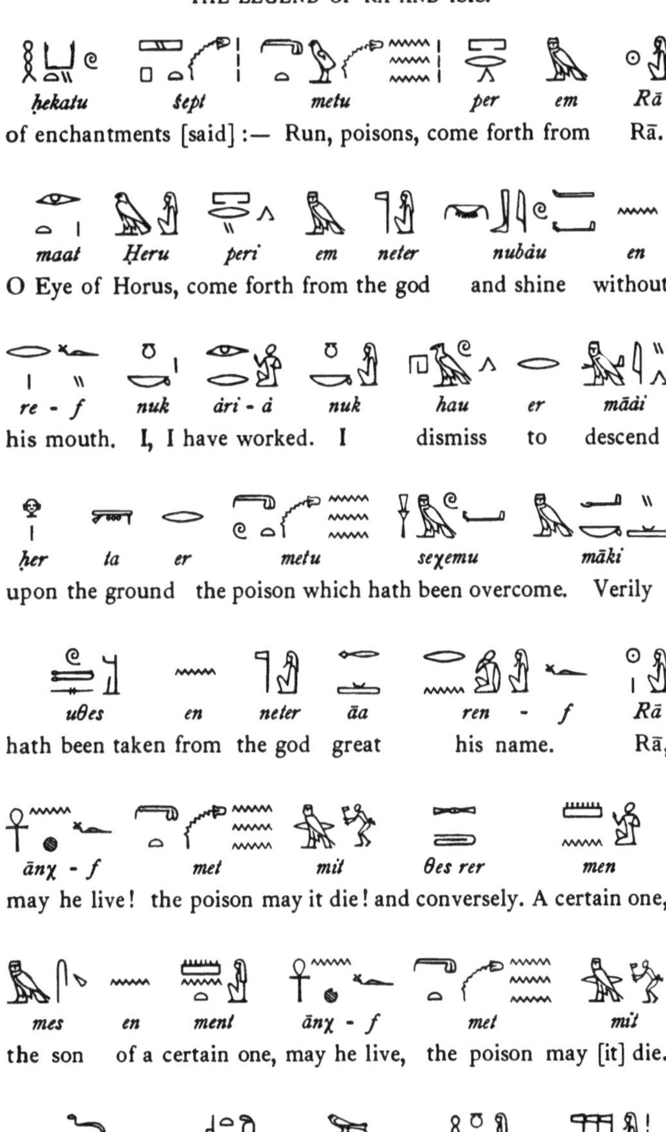

ḥekatu šept metu per em Rā
of enchantments [said] :— Run, poisons, come forth from Rā.

maat Ḥeru peri em neter nubȧu en
O Eye of Horus, come forth from the god and shine without

re - f nuk ȧri - ȧ nuk hau er māȧi
his mouth. I, I have worked. I dismiss to descend

ḥer ta er metu seχemu māki
upon the ground the poison which hath been overcome. Verily

uθes en neter āa ren - f Rā
hath been taken from the god great his name. Rā,

ānχ - f met mit θes rer men
may he live! the poison may it die! and conversely. A certain one,

mes en ment ānχ - f met mit
the son of a certain one, may he live, the poison may [it] die.

ṭeṭ en Ȧuset ur ḥent neteru
[This] said Isis, the mighty lady, the mistress of the gods,

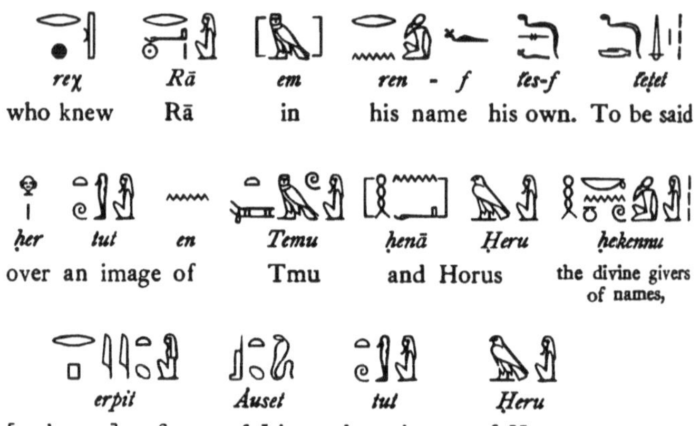

reχ Rā em ren - f ṭes-f ṭeṭet

who knew Rā in his name his own. To be said

ḥer tut en Temu ḥenā Ḥeru ḥekennu

over an image of Tmu and Horus the divine givers of names,

erpit Ȧuset tut Ḥeru

[and over] a figure of Isis, and an image of Horus.

FROM THE MONUMENT OF UAḤ-ÀB-RĀ EM KHU.

[XXVIth dynasty.]

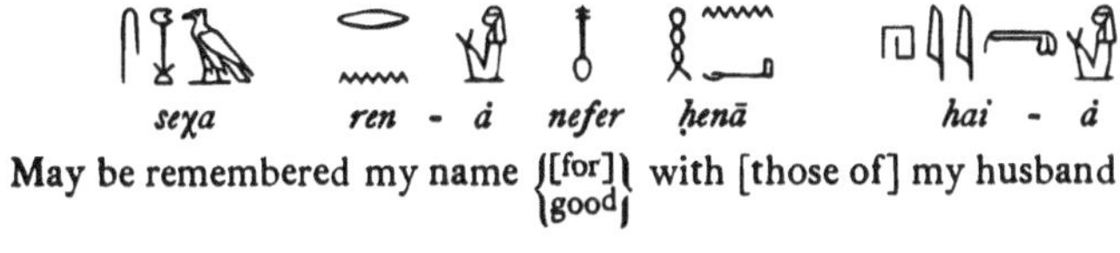

seχa *ren - à* *nefer* *ḥenā* *hai - à*

May be remembered my name {[for] good} with [those of] my husband

mesu - à *er-ḳes* *neteru* *àmu* *χa*

and my children by the gods dwelling in the nome of Mendes.

TEXTS FROM THE SARCOPHAGUS OF PAṬEPEP.

[XXVIth dynasty.]

1. 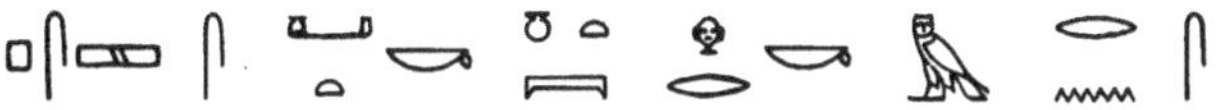

peseš - s *māt - k* *Nut* *ḥer - k* *em* *ren - s*

Spreadeth she thy mother Nut over thee in her name

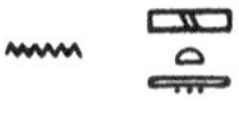

en *šeta*

of "Hidden".

TEXTS FROM THE SARCOPHAGUS OF PAṬEPEP.

2. 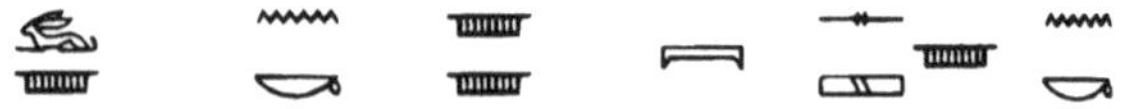 *un - nek āā pet seś - nek*

Shall be opened to thee the doors of heaven, shall be unbolted for thee

āā seḥeṭ seśep - θ mut-k nut

the doors of the stars of light, shall receive thee thy mother Nut.

3.  *meṭ ȧn Ṭep - ṭu - f χent neter ḥet ȧm*

Saith he who is on his hill, the chief {of the divine house,} who is

Ut neb Ta-teser neter āa neb qeres

in Ut, the lord {of Ta-tcheser,} the god great, the lord of the sarcophagus,

erṭā - nȧ em - sa - s em sa neb

"I work behind her with protection every".

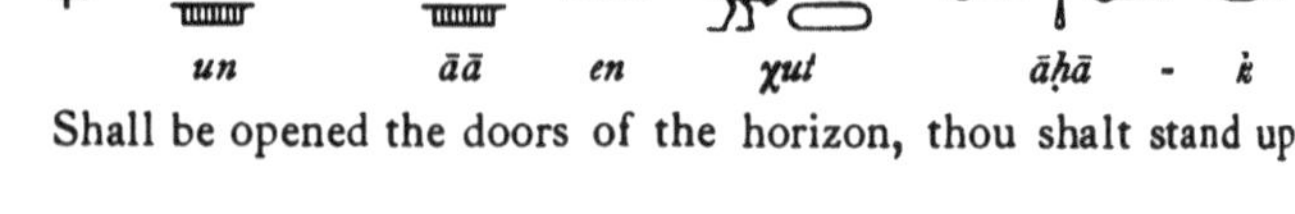

4.  *un āā en χut āḥā - k*

Shall be opened the doors of the horizon, thou shalt stand up

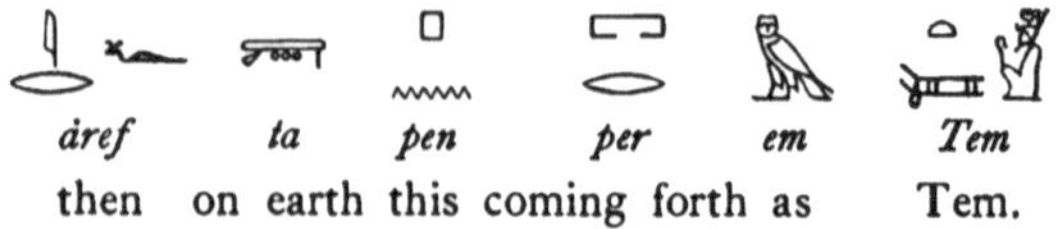

ȧref ta pen per em Tem

then on earth this coming forth as Tem.

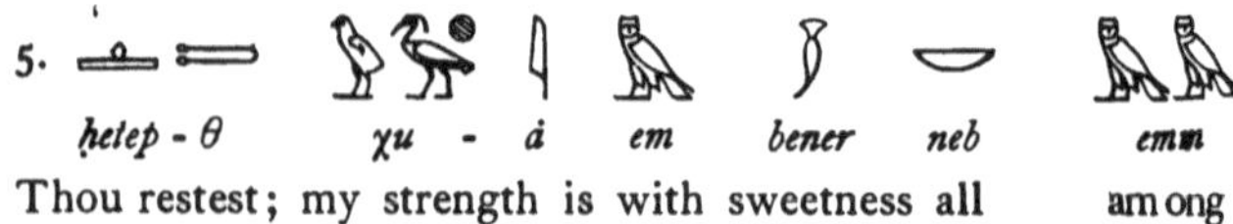

5. *ḥetep - θ χu - ȧ em bener neb emm*

Thou restest; my strength is with sweetness all among

ṡesu Ȧusȧr erṭā - nȧ uat em χabesu ȧn
the servants of Osiris. I give a way among the stars. Not

mit - k ṭetta
shalt thou die for ever.

6. *ha Ȧusȧr erṭāt en Ḥeru ṭemṭ - θu*
Hail Osiris! Granteth Horus [that] thou shalt be gathered together.

neteru sen - sen er-k em ren - sen pu en
The gods they join with thee in name their of

sen ent ȧteruȧt
"Brethren of the shrines of the North and South".

7. *ha Ȧusȧr ȧḥ - nek neteru āt - k*
Hail Osiris! Unite for thee the gods thy members,

ṭemṭ ḳesu - k seruṭ en Ȧnpu masṭ - k
collecting thy bones. Maketh strong Anubis thy legs

χent mennu - f seṡeṭ - f tu er pet
in his building; he leadeth thee into heaven.

8. *ha Ȧusȧr ȧn - nek Ḥeru ȧbu neteru nebu em*

Hail Osiris! {Bringeth to thee} Horus {the hearts} of gods all at

sep ȧn bȧn ȧm - sen mā - f nem ānχ

once, not is there evil in them {in respect of him,} {[O thou who] again} livest!

9.  *renp - k mȧ qet - k Ȧusetet uben - s em*

Thou becomest young as thou wast. Isis she shineth in

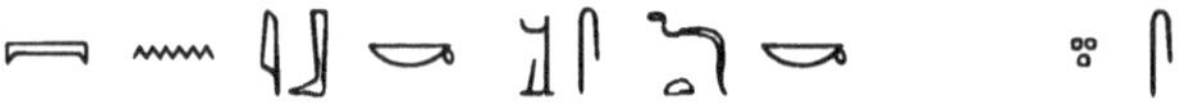

pet en ȧb - k θes-s ṫet - k χu - s

heaven at thy wish, she raiseth up thy body, she strengtheneth

ḥāu - k ṫetta

thy members for eternity.

10.  *erṭā - nȧ uben - k em χu ȧḥā - k*

I have granted that shalt shine thou, in splendour shall be thy limbs;

ȧm - k āś seḥetep - nek ka - k

not shalt thou lament; thou art at peace with thy Ka,

seḥetep - f - θu ṫetta

it shall be at peace with thee for ever.

THE LEGEND OF THE SEVEN YEARS' FAMINE IN THE REIGN OF TCHESER.

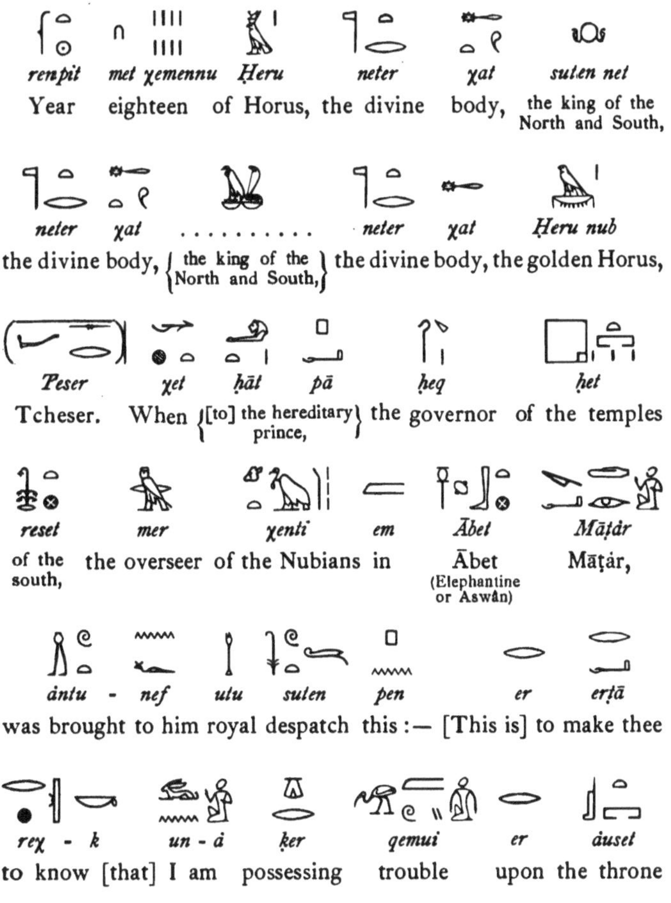

renpit met χemennu Ḥeru neter χat suten net
Year eighteen of Horus, the divine body, the king of the North and South,
neter χat . . . . neter χat Ḥeru nub
the divine body, {the king of the North and South,} the divine body, the golden Horus,
Ṭeser χet ḥāt pā ḥeq ḥet
Tcheser. When {[to] the hereditary prince,} the governor of the temples
reset mer χenti em Ābet Māṭār
of the south, the overseer of the Nubians in Ābet (Elephantine or Aswân) Māṭār,
ȧntu - nef utu suten pen er ertā
was brought to him royal despatch this :— [This is] to make thee
reχ - k un - ȧ ḳer qemui er ȧuset
to know [that] I am possessing trouble upon the throne

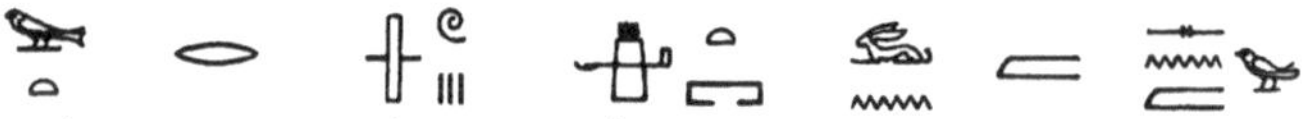

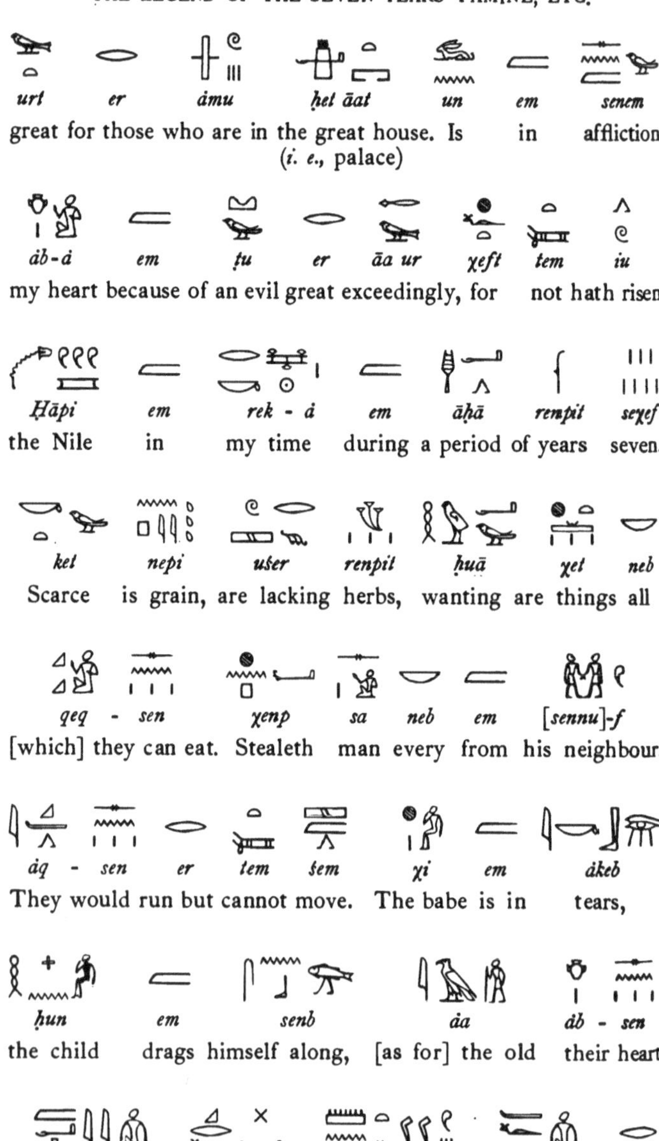

urt er ȧmu ḥet āat un em senem

great for those who are in the great house. (*i. e.*, palace) Is in affliction

ȧb-ȧ em ṭu er āa ur χeft tem iu

my heart because of an evil great exceedingly, for not hath risen

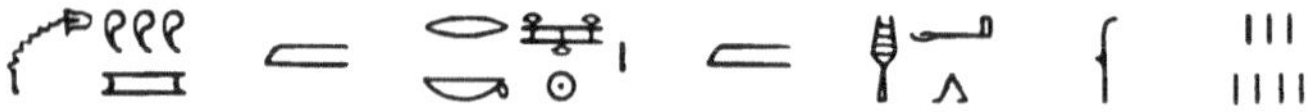

Ḥāpi em rek - ȧ em āḥā renpit seχef

the Nile in my time during a period of years seven.

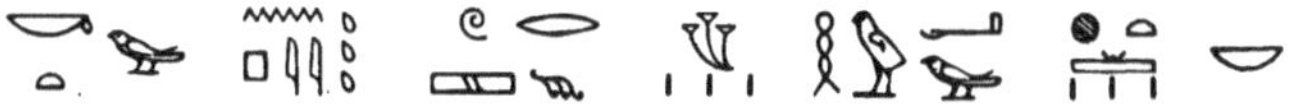

ket nepi ušer renpit ḥuā χet neb

Scarce is grain, are lacking herbs, wanting are things all

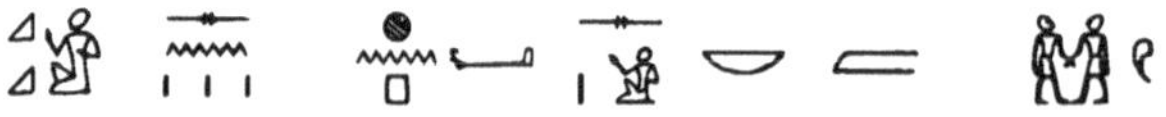

qeq - sen χenp sa neb em [sennu]-f

[which] they can eat. Stealeth man every from his neighbour.

ȧq - sen er tem šem χi em ȧkeb

They would run but cannot move. The babe is in tears,

ḥun em senb ȧa ȧb - sen

the child drags himself along, [as for] the old their heart

māḳi qeref menseti - u ḥufeṭ er

is stricken down; totter their legs [and they] sprawl upon

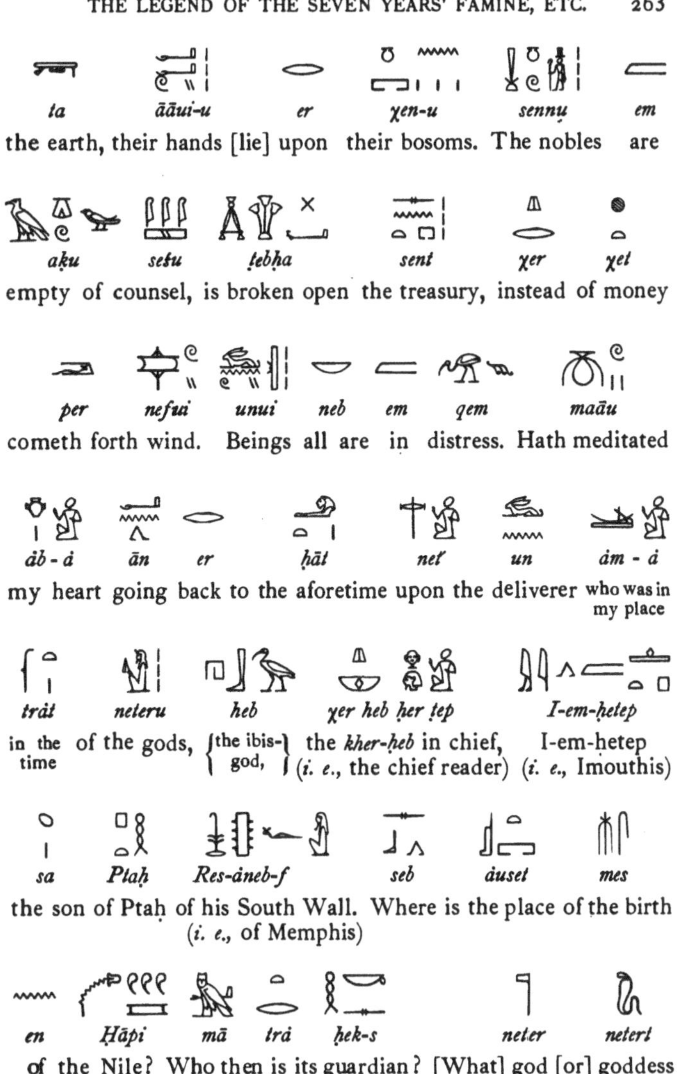

ta āāui-u er χen-u sennụ em
the earth, their hands [lie] upon their bosoms. The nobles are

aḳu setu ṭebḥa sent χer χet
empty of counsel, is broken open the treasury, instead of money

per nefui unui neb em qem maāu
cometh forth wind. Beings all are in distress. Hath meditated

ȧb-ȧ ān er ḥāt neṭ un ȧm-ȧ
my heart going back to the aforetime upon the deliverer who was in my place

trȧt neteru heb χer heb ḥer ṭep I-em-ḥetep
in the time of the gods, {the ibis-god,} the *kher-ḥeb* in chief, (*i. e.*, the chief reader) I-em-ḥetep (*i. e.*, Imouthis)

sa Ptaḥ Res-ȧneb-f seb ȧuset mes
the son of Ptaḥ of his South Wall. (*i. e.*, of Memphis) Where is the place of the birth

en Ḥāpi mā trȧ ḥek-s neter netert
of the Nile? Who then is its guardian? [What] god [or] goddess

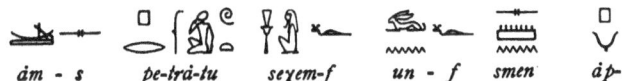

ȧm-s pe-trȧ-tu seχem-f un-f smen ȧp-
is in it? What then is his form? Is it he who hath announced

nȧ āḥā renenet sem - ȧ en χent Ḥet-seχet

to me the provisions {of the harvest?} I will go to the dweller in Ḥet-sekhet

su ermen ȧb - f en sa neb er ȧri - sen

who weareth out his patience on person every in [what] they do.

bes-ȧ er ḥet ānχet peṭ-ȧ barā (?)

I will enter into the house of life, I will unroll the written scrolls,

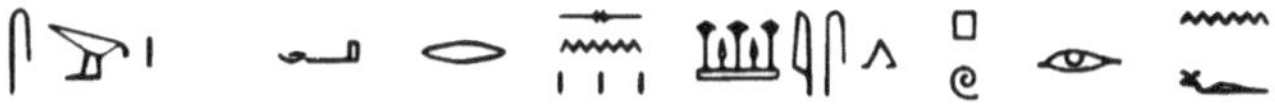

sem-ȧ ā er - sen šȧs pu ȧri - nef

I will bring [my] hand upon them. A going forth he made, (*i. e.*, Māṭȧr)

ānnu - f s er - ȧ ḥer-ā saut - f - ȧ em

he came back to me immediately, he informed me concerning

ḥait Ḥāpi χet neb ān-

the source of the Nile [and concerning] things all [which] written

sen ȧm qefa - f - nȧ reu ȧmen

are they therein. He revealed to me the chapters hidden

ȧu ṭepāu θet metet er sen ȧn

[my] ancestors took [their] way to them; not [existed]

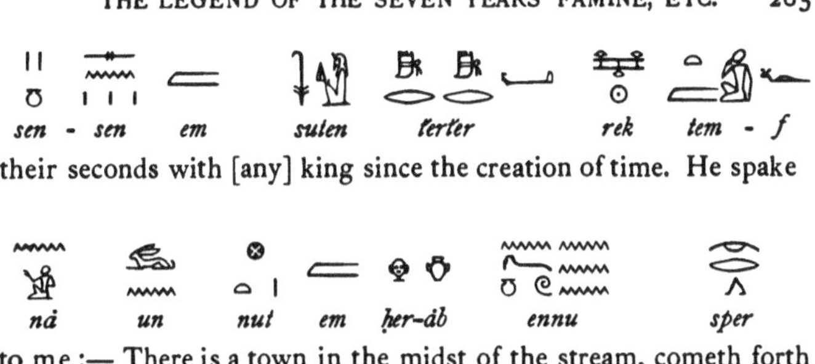

sen - sen em suten ṭerṭer rek tem - f

their seconds with [any] king since the creation of time. He spake

nȧ un nut em ḥer-ȧb ennu sper

to me:— There is a town in the midst of the stream, cometh forth

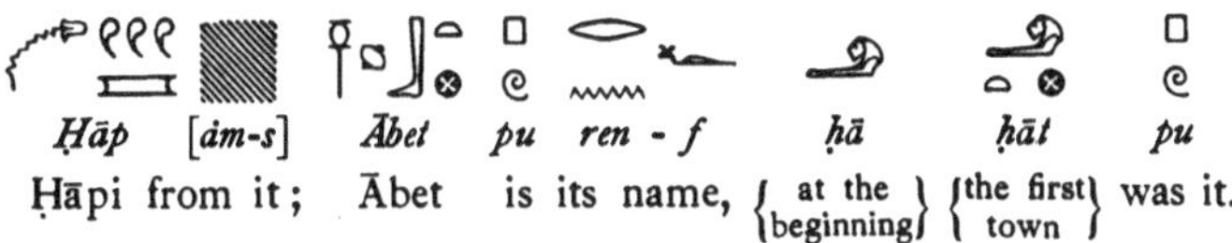

Ḥāp [ȧm-s] Ābet pu ren - f ḥā ḥāt pu

Ḥāpi from it; Ābet is its name, {at the beginning} {the first town} was it.

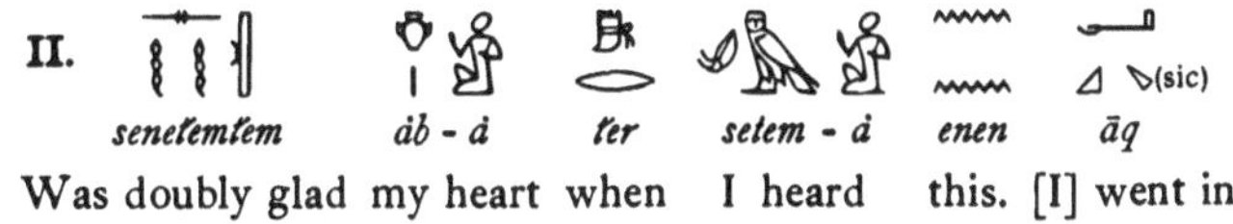

II. *seneṭemṭem ȧb - ȧ ṭer seṭem - ȧ enen āq*

Was doubly glad my heart when I heard this. [I] went in,

seš meru unχ ȧri

revealed [to me] the superintendents what was sealed. Was made

āb ȧri sem šeta ȧri

the libation, was made the celebration of the mysteries, was made

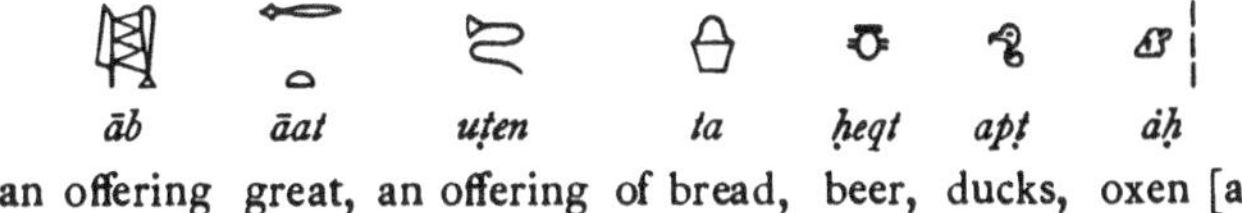

āb āat uṭen ta ḥeqt apṭ ȧḥ

an offering great, an offering of bread, beer, ducks, oxen [and]

χet neb nefer en neteru neteret ȧmu

things all good to the gods [and] goddesses who are in

Ābet tem - tu ren - sen em ḳes

Elephantine, are proclaimed their names in the place [called]

sṫer ȧb em ānχ usr qem - ȧ neter āḥā

"Resteth the heart in life and strength". I found the god standing

em senk-ȧ seḥetep - nef em ṭua semeḥ-

before my sight, he was gratified at [my] adoration, and I made

s embaḥ - f ābi maat - f ser ȧb - f

supplication before him. Opening his eyes, was moved his heart,

uaṫet χeru - f nuk χnemu nub - k āāui-ȧ

spake his voice, {[saying]: I am} Khnemu thy creator. My two hands

ḥaui - k er seqa ṫet - k er snib

were upon thee to knit together thy body, to make healthy

āḥāu - k ut-ȧ ȧb - nek āat χer āat

thy members; I gave a heart to thee. Stones [lie] upon stones

. . . . ṫer baḥ ȧn ȧri kat ȧm - sen

. . . from times of old, {[but] no one hath} done work with them

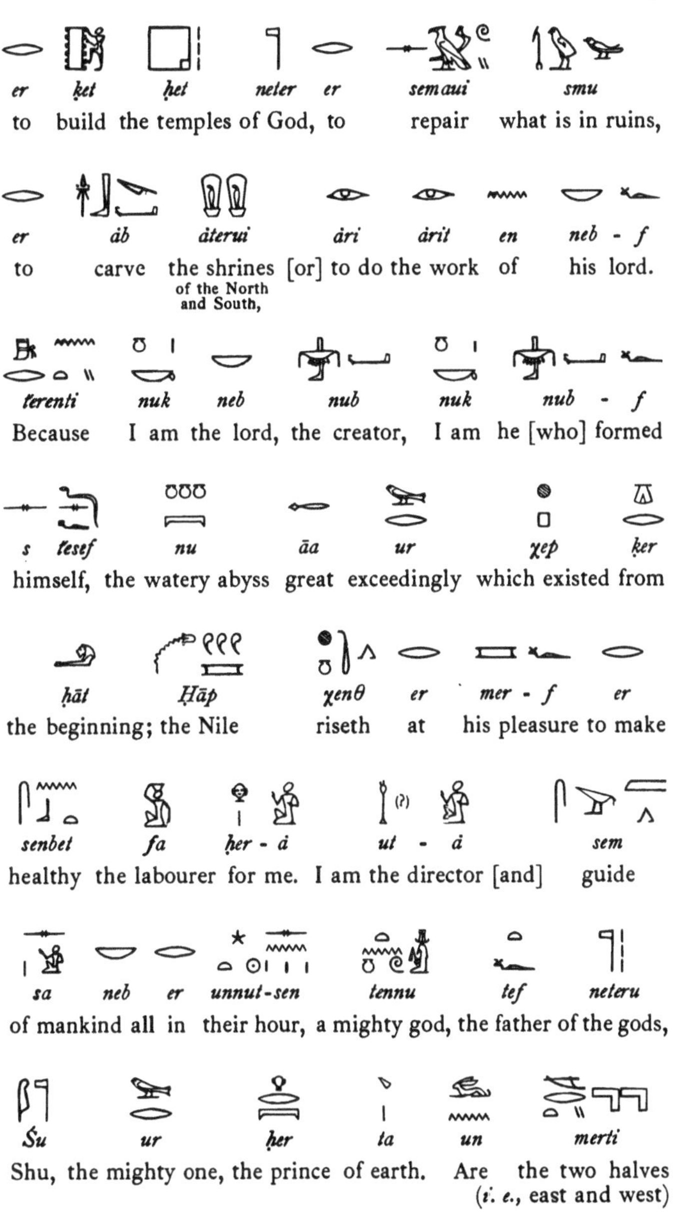

er ḳet ḥet neter er semaui smu
to build the temples of God, to repair what is in ruins,

er ȧb ȧterui ȧri ȧrit en neb - f
to carve the shrines of the North and South, [or] to do the work of his lord.

ṫerenti nuk neb nub nuk nub - f
Because I am the lord, the creator, I am he [who] formed

s ṫesef nu āa ur χep ḳer
himself, the watery abyss great exceedingly which existed from

ḥāt Ḥāp χenθ er mer - f er
the beginning; the Nile riseth at his pleasure to make

senbet fa ḥer - ȧ ut - ȧ sem
healthy the labourer for me. I am the director [and] guide

sa neb er unnut-sen tennu tef neteru
of mankind all in their hour, a mighty god, the father of the gods,

Šu ur ḥer ta un merti
Shu, the mighty one, the prince of earth. Are the two halves (*i. e.*, east and west)

em ṭebt ḳer - à χnemut - nà sefeχ
of heaven {the abode [which]} I possess. A fountain is to me, to open (?) it

reχ - à Ḥāp seχen-tef er seχet seχen-tef
I know, Hapi (Nile) he embraceth the fields, his embrace

seχ ānχ fent neb mà seχen-ut
maketh abundant {[the means] of life} for nose every, (*i. e.*, all people) according to [his] embrace

er seχet er neχeχ seχer bes - à nek
of the fields. . . . . I will make to flow for thee

Ḥāp àn renpit àb enen er ta
Ḥāp (Nile), without a year of need, , subsiding upon land

neb reṭ semu neb en χertu χer neṫ
the whole. {Shall shoot up} vegetation all, {shall bend [the plants]} [which] bear grain,

ārāt (?) *χent χet neb sepa χet*
the goddess shall be over things all, shall increase things

neb em ḥeḥ er meḥ renpit
all by millions according to the cubit of the year.

INSCRIPTION OF THE REIGN OF PTOLEMY V.

[Gizeh Museum, No. 5576.]

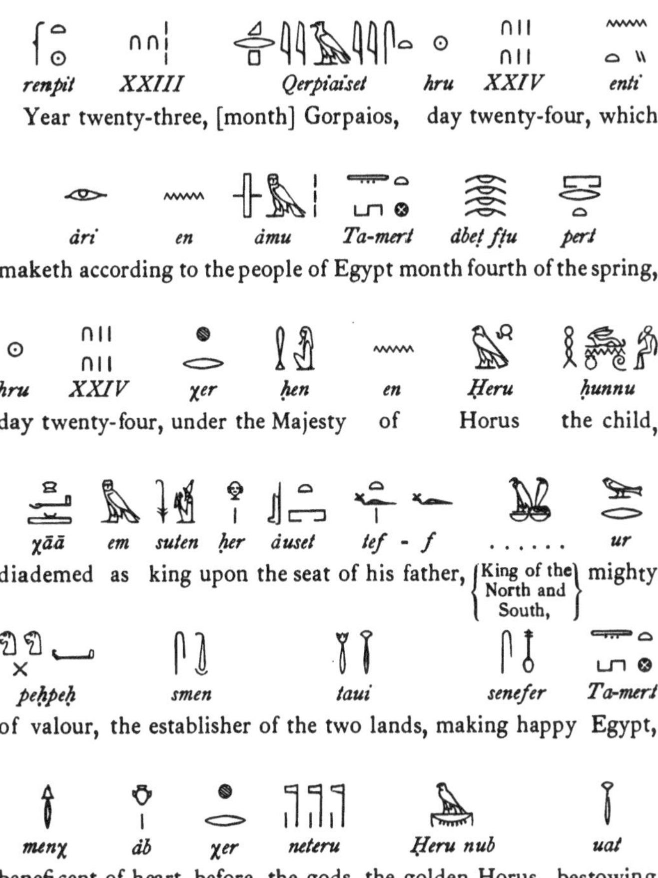

renpit XXIII Qerpiaïset hru XXIV enti
Year twenty-three, [month] Gorpaios, day twenty-four, which

ȧri en ȧmu Ta-mert ȧbeṭ fṭu pert
maketh according to the people of Egypt month fourth of the spring,

hru XXIV χer ḥen en Ḥeru ḥunnu
day twenty-four, under the Majesty of Horus the child,

χāā em suten ḥer ȧuset tef - f . . . . . . ur
diademed as king upon the seat of his father, {King of the North and South,} mighty

peḥpeḥ smen taui senefer Ta-mert
of valour, the establisher of the two lands, making happy Egypt,

menχ ȧb χer neteru Ḥeru nub uat
beneficent of heart before the gods, the golden Horus, bestowing

ānχ en hamemu neb ḥeb Ptaḥ mȧ ȧθi

life upon mankind, the lord of festivals Ptah like, prince

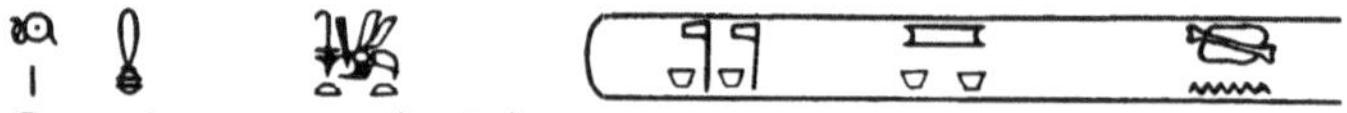

Rā mȧ suten net (or *bȧt*) *neterui ȧtf meri āu en*

Rā like, {king of the North and South,} of the gods the father-lovers the heir,

Ptaḥ setep usr ka Ȧmen Rā seχem meri

of Ptaḥ the chosen one, mighty one of the *ka* the Form of Rā beloved, of Amen,

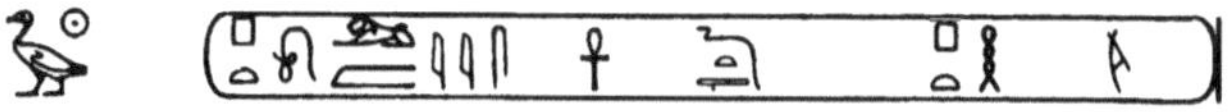

sa Rā Ptualmis ānχ tetta Ptaḥ meri

son of the Sun, Ptolemy, may he live for ever, beloved of Ptah,

neterui per sa en Ptualmis ḥenā

the gods made manifest, son of Ptolemy and

Ȧrsenat neteru ȧtf meri āb en

Arsinoë, the gods the father-lovers, [being] priest of

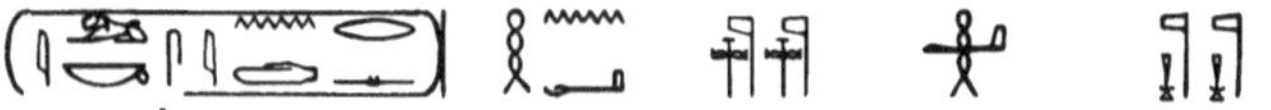

Ȧlksȧnṭers ḥenā neterui net' ḥā neterui sen

Alexander and of the gods Saviours, and the gods brothers,

ḥā neterui menχ ḥenā neterui ȧtf meri ḥā

and the gods beneficent, and the gods father-lovers,

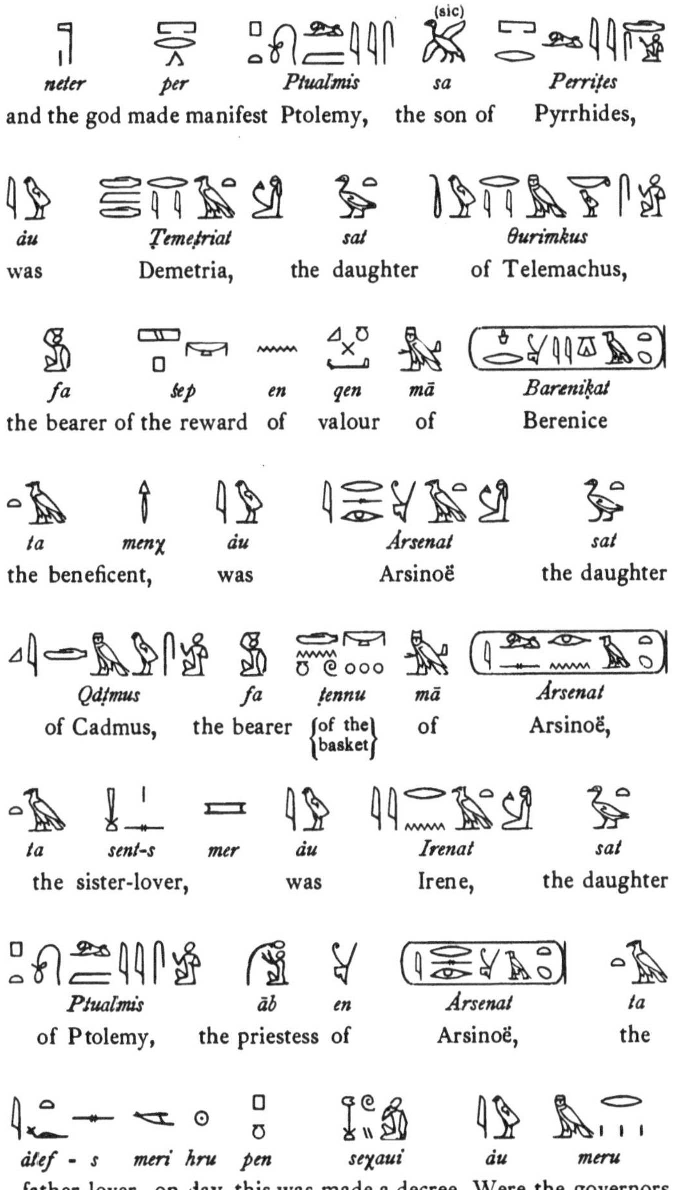

(sic)

neter per Ptualmis sa Perriṭes

and the god made manifest Ptolemy, the son of Pyrrhides,

àu Ṭemeṭriat sat θurimkus

was Demetria, the daughter of Telemachus,

fa ṡep en qen mā Bareniḳat

the bearer of the reward of valour of Berenice

ta menχ àu Àrsenat sat

the beneficent, was Arsinoë the daughter

Qdṭmus fa ṭennu mā Àrsenat

of Cadmus, the bearer {of the basket} of Arsinoë,

ta sent-s mer àu Irenat sat

the sister-lover, was Irene, the daughter

Ptualmis āb en Àrsenat ta

of Ptolemy, the priestess of Arsinoë, the

àtef - s meri hru pen seχaui àu meru

father-lover, on day this was made a decree. Were the governors

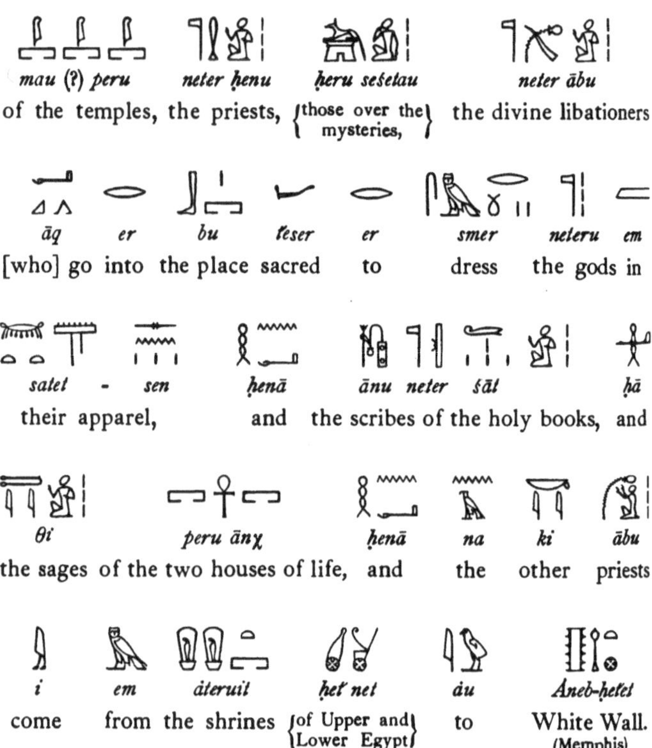

mau (?) *peru* *neter ḥenu* *ḥeru sešetau* *neter ābu*

of the temples, the priests, {those over the mysteries,} the divine libationers

āq *er* *bu* *t̆eser* *er* *smer* *neteru* *em*

[who] go into the place sacred to dress the gods in

satet - *sen* *ḥenā* *ānu* *neter* *šāt* *ḥā*

their apparel, and the scribes of the holy books, and

θi *peru* *ānχ* *ḥenā* *na* *ki* *ābu*

the sages of the two houses of life, and the other priests

i *em* *àteruit* *ḥet̆ net* *àu* *Àneb-ḥet̆et*

come from the shrines {of Upper and Lower Egypt} to White Wall. (Memphis)

TEXTS

TO BE TRANSLITERATED AND TRANSLATED

Titles of Usertsen III., King of Egypt.

Address to the gods of Judgment.

[From the Papyrus of Nebseni.]

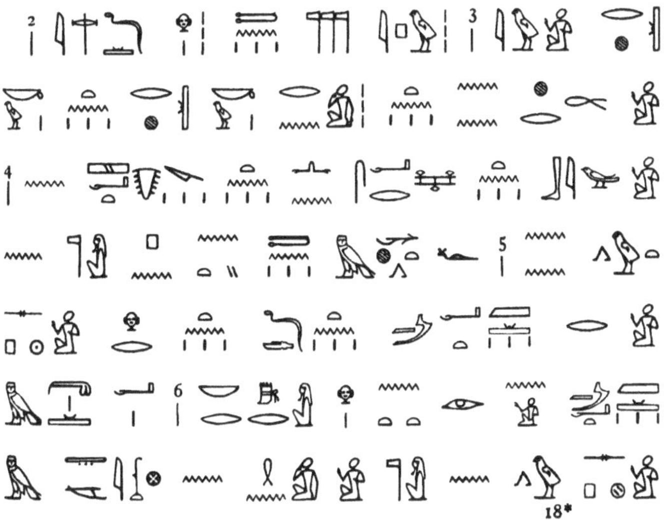

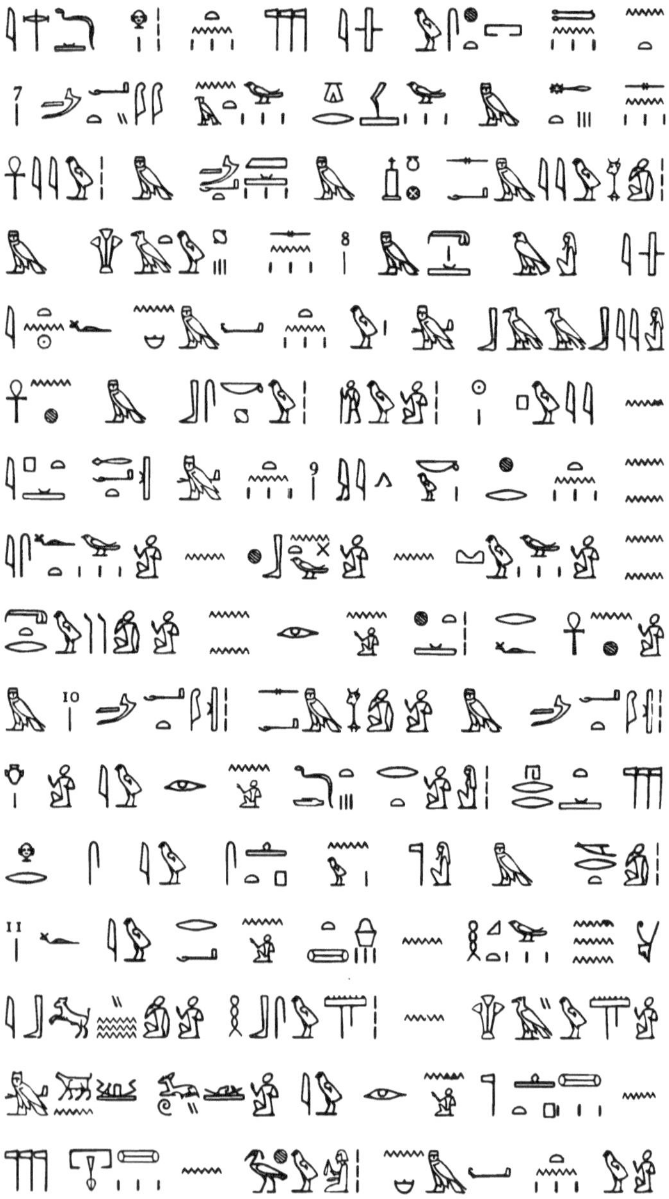

A prayer to the gods of the Underworld.

[From the Papyrus of Ani.]

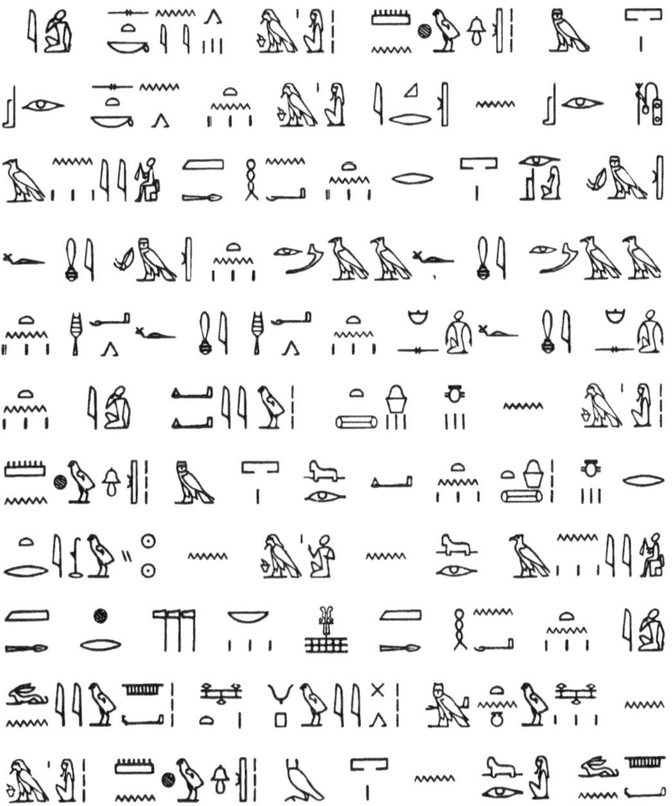

Hymn to Rā.

[From the Papyrus of Ani.]

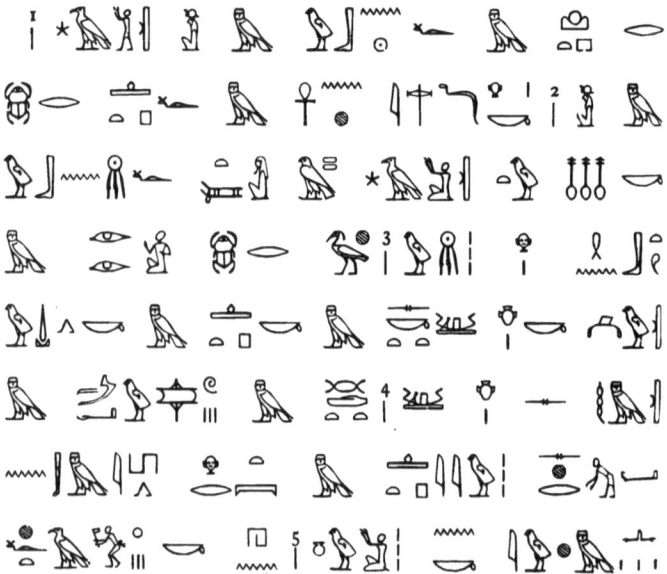

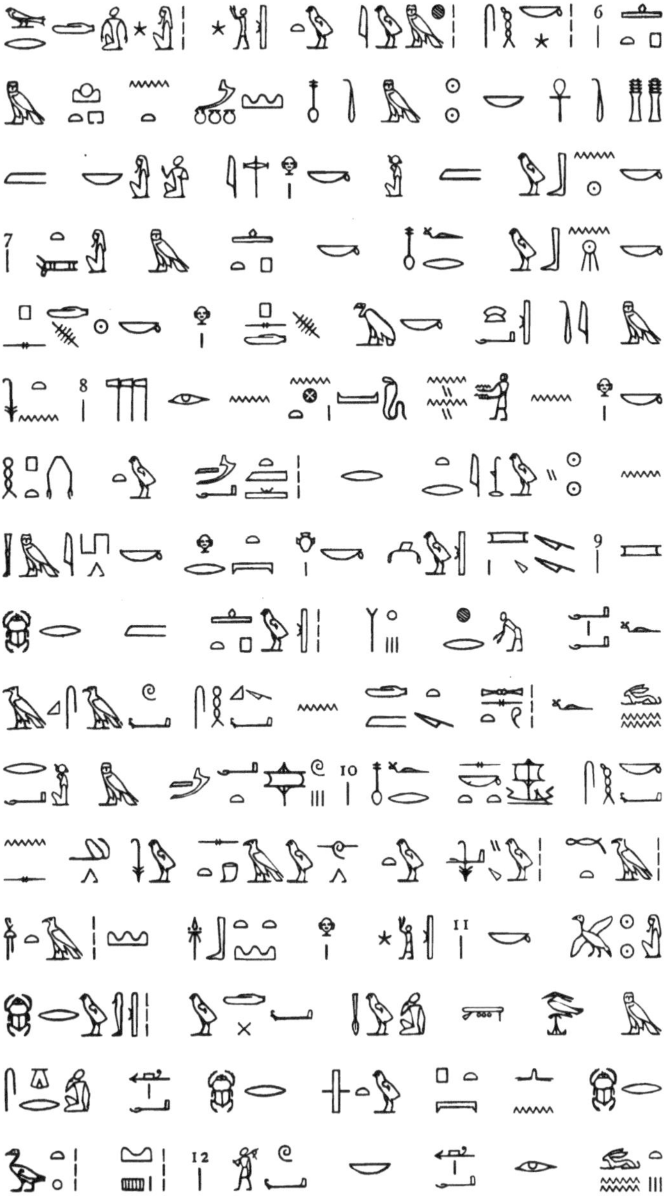

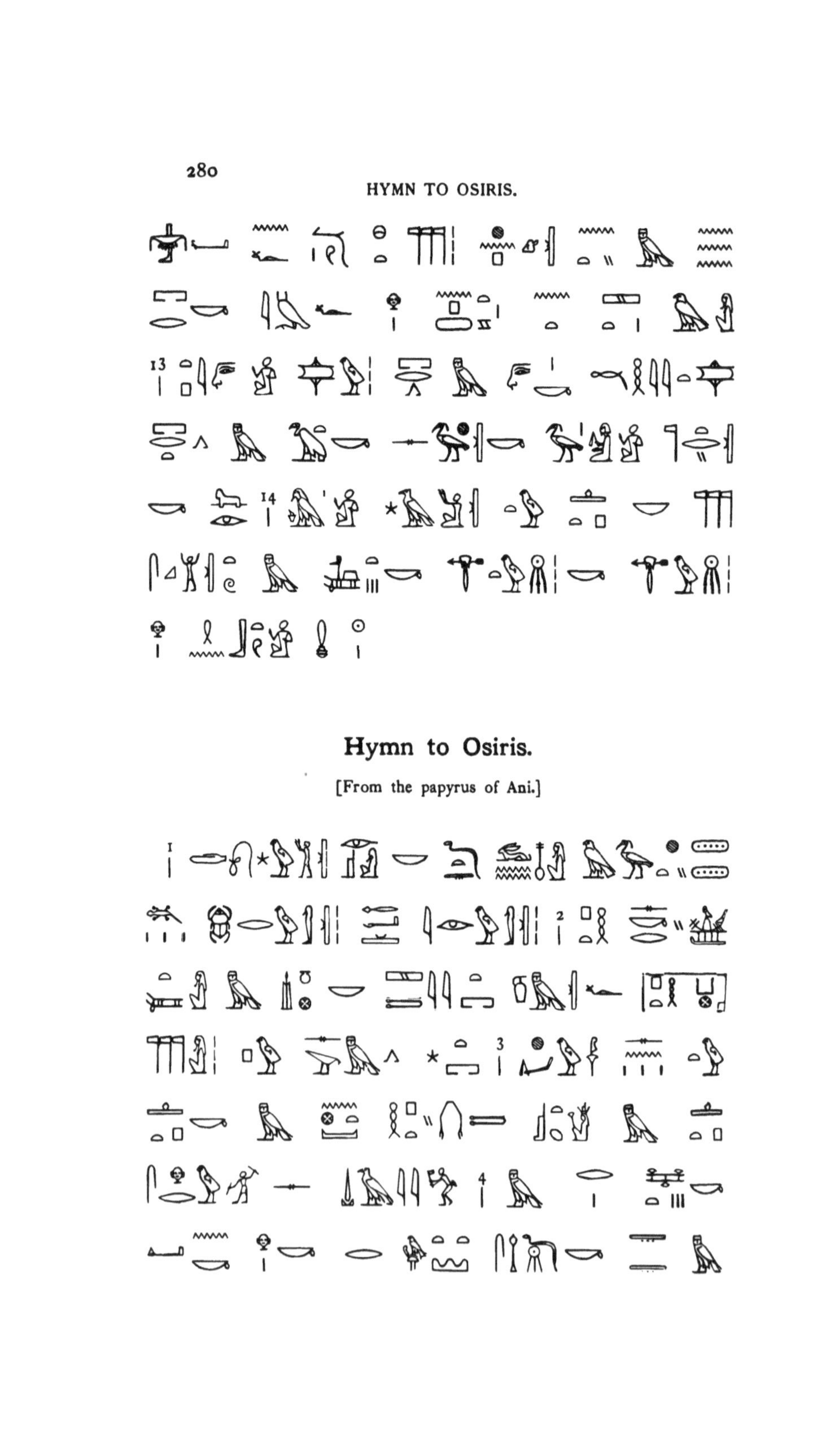

Hymn to Osiris.

[From the papyrus of Ani.]

A Litany.

[From the Papyrus of Ani.]

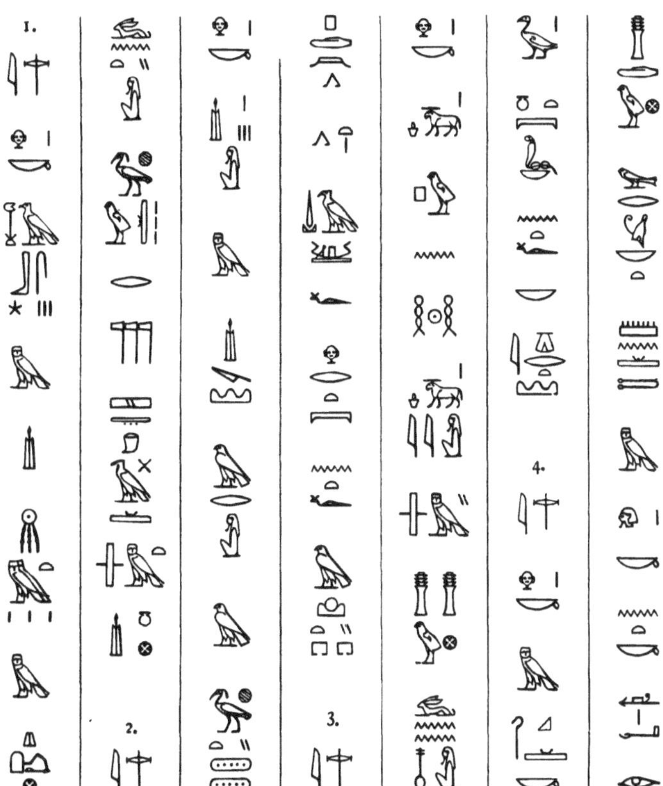

LITANY FROM THE BOOK OF THE DEAD.

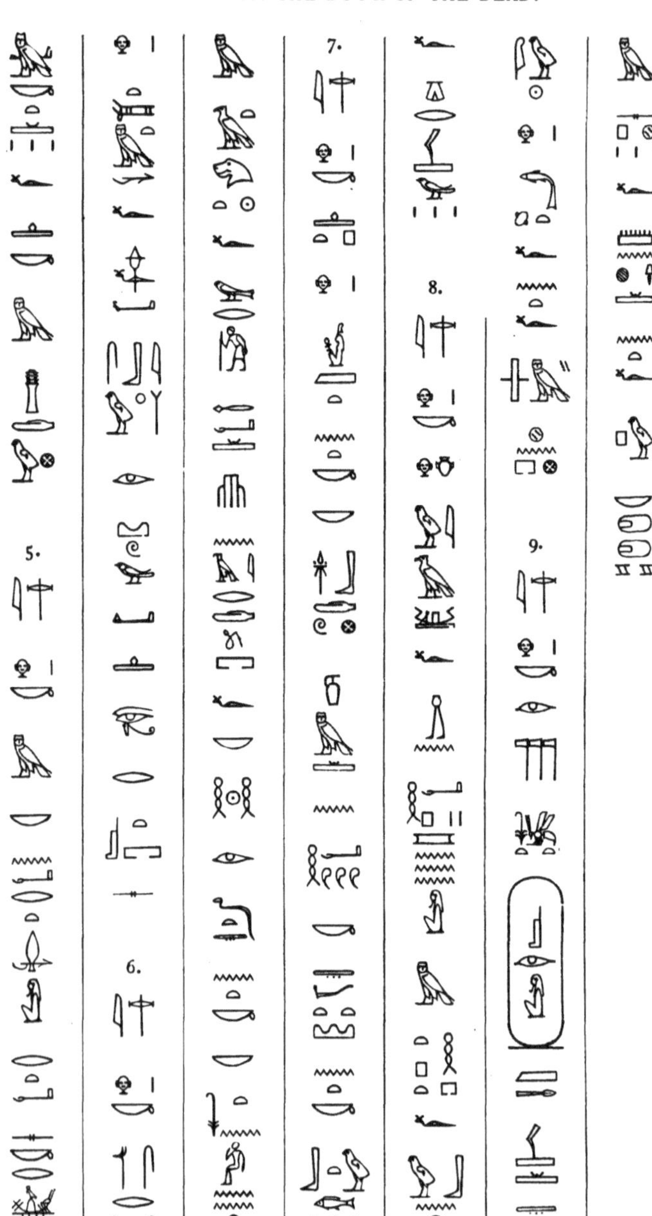

A Prayer of Ani.

[From the Papyrus of Ani.]

Inscription of Seti I. King of Egypt.

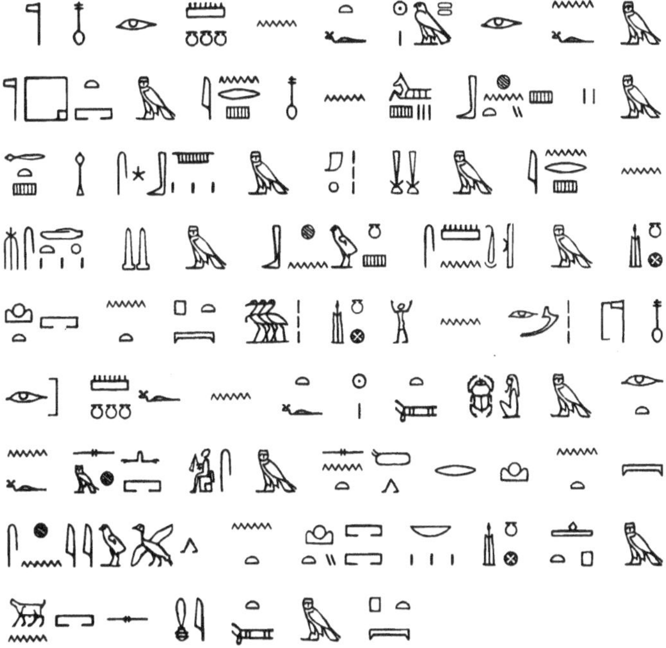

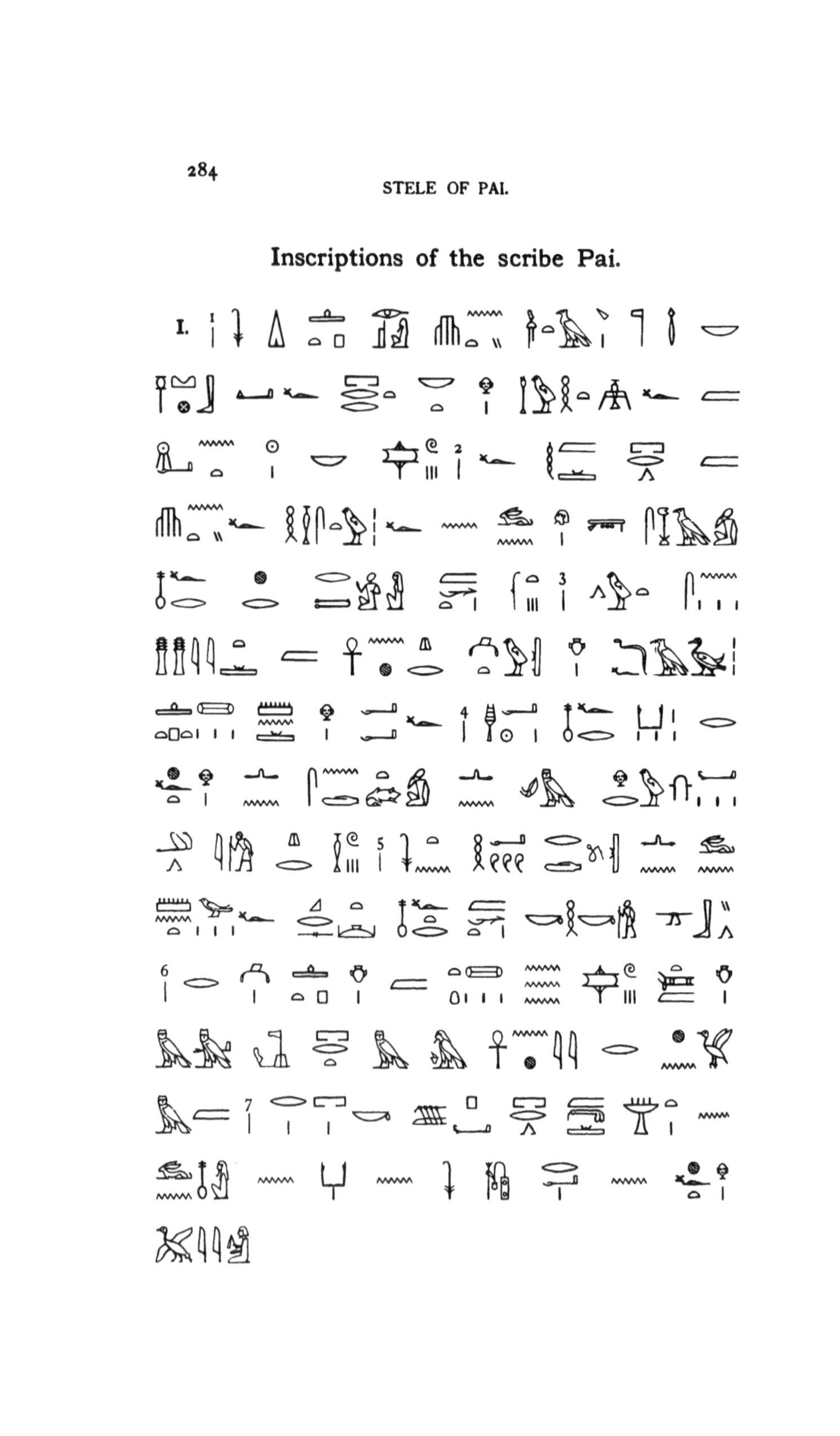

Inscriptions of the scribe Pai.

I.

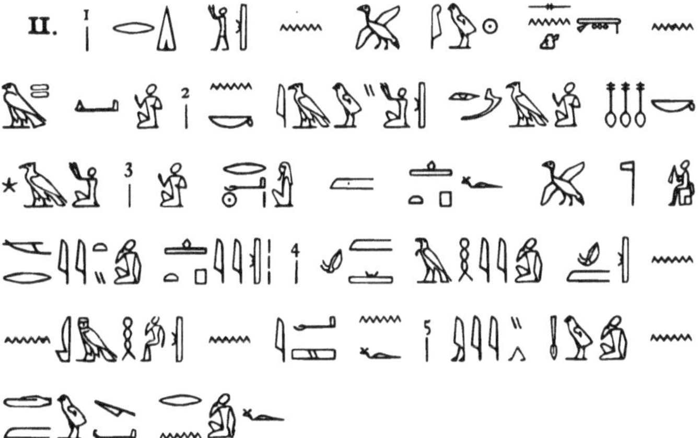

Hymn to Ȧmen-Rā.

§ X.

§ XI.

§ XII.

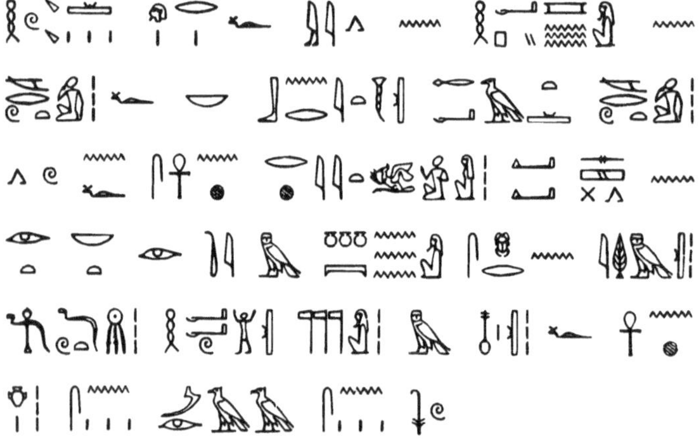

Address to the lady Ta-χerṭ-p-uru-åbṭu.

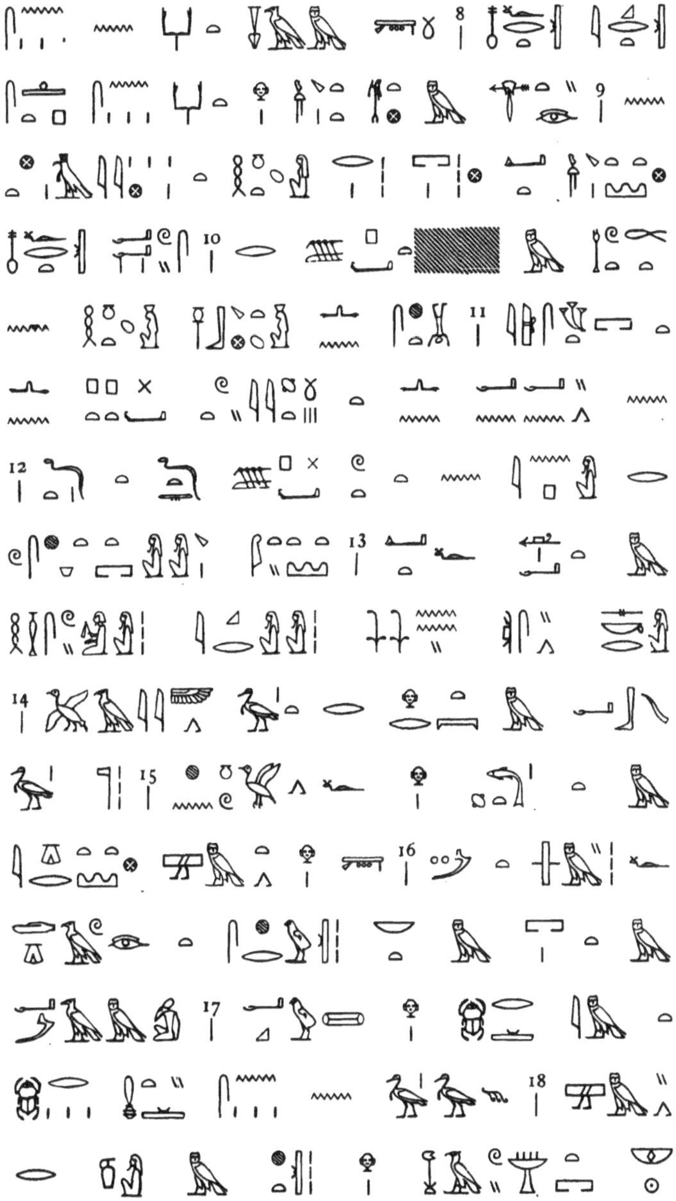

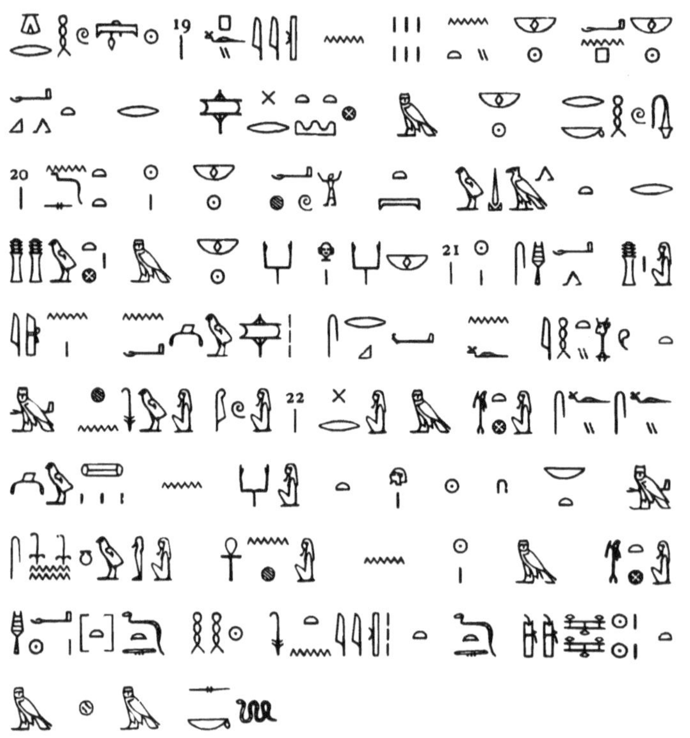

Stele of Ṭāṭāu.

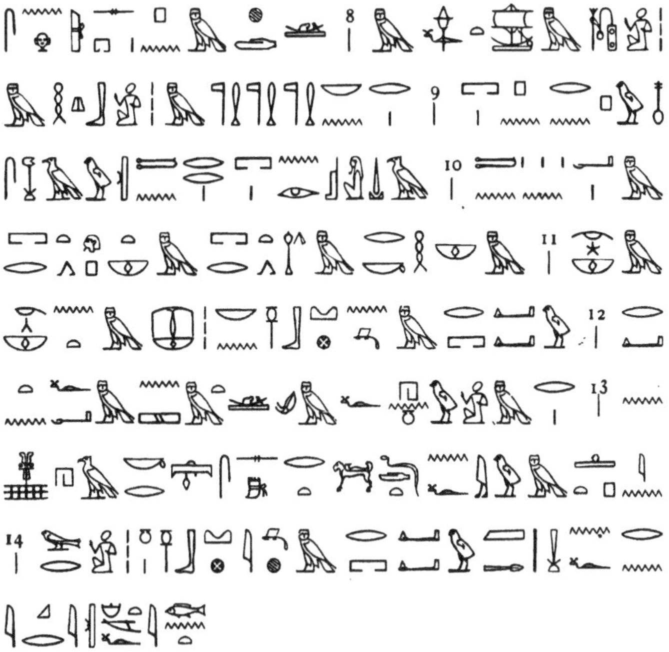

GLOSSARY.

A

Ani	a proper name
aqesau	to cut off
atet	moment

Ȧ

ȧ	I, me
ȧ	I, me
ȧ	O
ȧ	O
ȧau	old age
ȧaui	praise, adoration
ȧāś	to cry out
ȧu	to be
ȧuχemu	those who do not
Ȧusȧr	Osiris
Ȧuset	Isis

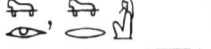

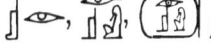

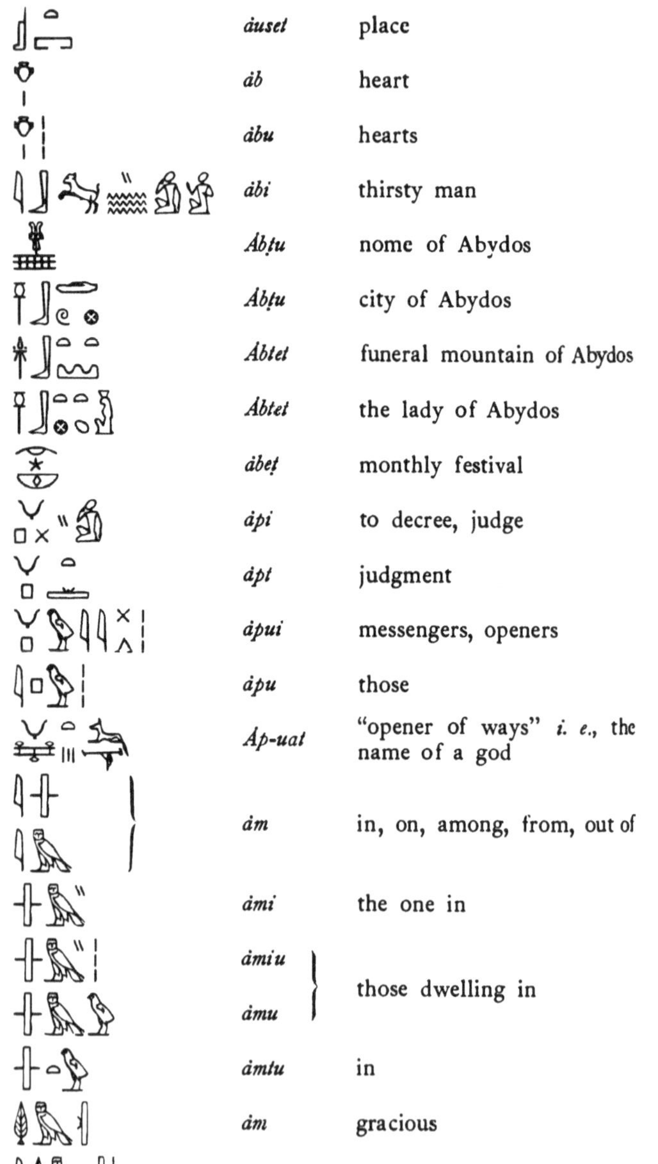

	ȧuset	place
	ȧb	heart
	ȧbu	hearts
	ȧbi	thirsty man
	Ȧbṭu	nome of Abydos
	Ȧbṭu	city of Abydos
	Ȧbtet	funeral mountain of Abydos
	Ȧbtet	the lady of Abydos
	ȧbeṭ	monthly festival
	ȧpi	to decree, judge
	ȧpt	judgment
	ȧpui	messengers, openers
	ȧpu	those
	Ȧp-uat	"opener of ways" *i. e.*, the name of a god
	ȧm	in, on, among, from, out of
	ȧmi	the one in
	ȧmiu / *ȧmu*	those dwelling in
	ȧmtu	in
	ȧm	gracious
	ȧm	delights

ȧmemmem	to weep
ȧmen	hidden
Ȧmenta	the hidden place, the West
Ȧmentaiu	those in the West
Ȧmentet	the funeral mountain or city on the west bank of the Nile
ȧmaχ	venerated
Ȧmsu	name of a god or star
ȧn	not, without, destitute of
ȧn	by
ȧn	to bring, carry
Ȧn	name of a god
Ȧnnu	Heliopolis
Ȧnpu	Anubis
ȧnnu	skin, colour
ȧner	stone
Ȧnt	name of a female
Ȧn-ṭes	a mythological place
ȧnet' ḥrȧ	homage to thee!
ȧr	then
ȧri	to make, maker, to do

àrit	work
àritu	made
àru	forms
àref	therefore
àḫti	throat
às	tomb
àst	tomb
àsiu	those who are rewarded with something
àsfet	sins, faults
àsn	breath of air
àten	disk
àtebui	the two banks of the celestial Nile
àqer	to be perfect
àqert	a perfect thing
àqeru	perfected divine beings
Åkertet / *Åkert*	a name of the underworld

Ā

ā	hand, power
āāui	the two hands
āa	great

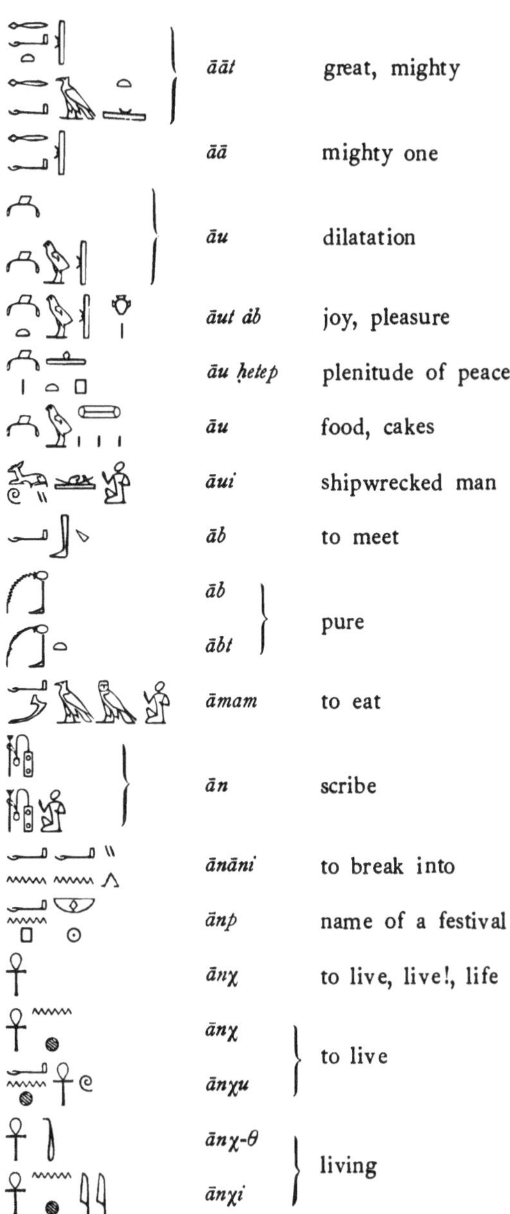

āāt	great, mighty
āā	mighty one
āu	dilatation
āut ȧb	joy, pleasure
āu ḥetep	plenitude of peace
āu	food, cakes
āui	shipwrecked man
āb	to meet
āb, *ābt*	pure
āmam	to eat
ān	scribe
ānāni	to break into
ānp	name of a festival
ānχ	to live, live!, life
ānχ, *ānχu*	to live
ānχ-θ, *ānχi*	living

ānχu *ānχiu*	living beings
ānχ	land of life
āḥā	to stand
āḥā	period of existence
āχu	to lift up, to support
āš	many
āat	a kind of stone
āṭtet	name of a boat of the sun
āq	just, true, equal
āq	to enter, to go in
āqu	food

I

i	to come
iu	to come

U

u	they, them
uat	way, road, path
uat	roads

uaḥi	to be permanent
Uast	Thebes
Uaṭet	name of a goddess
uȧ	I, me
uȧa	boat
uā	one
uāt	one
uben	to rise (of the sun)
un	to be, to exist
unen	to be, is
unenet	things which are
un	to open
uniu	openers
Un-nefer	a name of Osiris
Unti	a name of a god
ur	great, great one
uru	chiefs
Ur	name of a god
urt	name of a crown
urṭ	those who rest

	usu	weak, feeble
	usm	electrum (?)
	user	to be strong
	user	power
	Usertsen	a king's name
	useχt	a hall
	useχtet maātet	hall of double right and truth
	utit	mummy bandages
	utu	to decree
	utut	decree
	utḥet	altar of offerings
	ut'a	to go forth, set out
	ut'at	the eye of the Sun
	uṭ	to shoot out
	uṭeṭet	commands

B

	ba	soul
	ba	divine soul
	baiu	souls

	baiu	divine souls
	ba	ram
	Bai	the divine Ram
	Baba	proper name
	Baabi	name of a god
	bāḥ	to overflow, inundate to flood
	bȧt	wonders, marvels
	bȧt	a kind of stone
	bȧn	evil, wicked
	benerȧt	graciousness
	beχenti	pylons
	beχennu	a kind of stone
	beseku	intestines
	betu	to abominate
	betennu	oppression

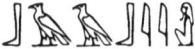

P

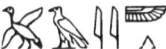

	p	the
	pa	the
	Pai	proper name
	pai	to fly
	paut	company, cycle
	pautti	the double company of the gods

pu	is
pui	this
pfi	that
pen	this
per	house
per / *peru*	to come forth
perert	thing which is brought forth
pert	appearance, manifestation
perχeru	sepulchral meals of bread, beer, oxen, fowl, linen bandages, etc.
peḥ	to arrive at, attain to
peḥreru	runner
pesṭ	back
pesṭ	to shine
pet	heaven
petpet	to break open
Ptaḥ	name of a god
Ptaḥ-Sekeri-Tem	the triad of Ptaḥ, Socharis, and Tmu
peṭ	to stretch out, extend

F

f	he, his
fenṭ	nose

M

em	in, among, upon, when, as, with
emm	in
embaḥ	in the presence of, before
emmā	with, from
em reχ	knowingly
em χenti	among
em χet	following
emχetu	followers
em sent	round about, following
em sati	in front of
maa	to see
maati	the two eyes
manu	the mountain of the setting sun
maär	to be strong, mighty

maāt	to be right and true, right and truth
Maāt	the goddess of right and truth
Maāti	twofold right and truth
maā-χeru	one whose word is right and true
maāu	winds
mȧ	like, as
mȧti	like, as
mȧn	daily
māχen	boat
māket	strength, protection
mātennu	ways, paths
mu	water
mut	mother
men	to stablish
men	monuments
menχu	beneficent, perfect
ment	pain, sickness
ment	daily
mer	to love, be loved

	meri	loving
	meriti	beloved
	meru / *mert*	will, wish
	mer	superintendent
	Mer-ṭesṭes	a mythological locality
	meḥit	north wind
	meḥta	dwellers in the north
	mestu	what is born
	mestu	children
	mestet	a kind of stone
	met	ten
	meteru	to bear [false] witness
	meṭu / *meṭet*	words, speech

N

,	*n*	of, to, before, by, with
n =	*àn*	not, without
enen =	*àn*	not, without
	nat	without
= ; *i. e.*, "nothing grows in it"	*Naà-ruṭ* / *Àn-ruṭ-f*	a mythological locality,

	nȧ	I, me
	nȧs	to call, invoke, proclaim
	nini	to do homage
	nāāu	winds
	Nārt	name of a god
	nuȧ	I, me
	nuk	
	Nu	name of a god
	Nut	name of a goddess
	nut	city
	nuti	citizens
	neb	every, all
	neb	lord
	nebu	lords, all
	nebt	all, every, lord, lady
	nub	to form, to mould
	Neb-er-ṭer	name of a god
	nept	inundated land
	nef	him, to him
	nefu	winds
	Nef-urtet	a mythological locality

nefer	to be good, or beautiful, a good thing
nefer-θ	good
nefert	a good thing
neferu	beauties
nemȧ	to stride
nemmȧt	step
nemeḥ	feeble, weak
eneniu	things which, those which
neḥi	suppliant
neḥem	to deliver
Neχen	name of a city
nes	her, it
nes	tongue
neš	to enter
nešemet	boat
nek	thee
ent	of, which
net	thou
neter	god, divine
neteru	gods

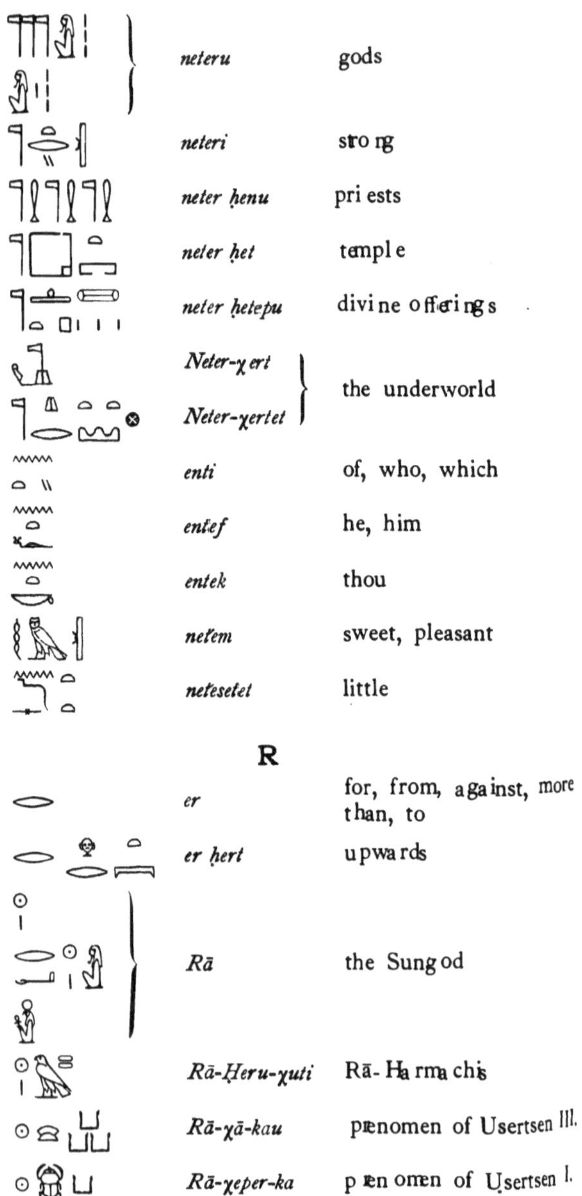

	neteru	gods
	neteri	strong
	neter ḥenu	priests
	neter ḥet	temple
	neter ḥetepu	divine offerings
	Neter-χert / *Neter-χertet*	the underworld
	enti	of, who, which
	enṭef	he, him
	entek	thou
	neṭem	sweet, pleasant
	neṭesetet	little

R

	er	for, from, against, more than, to
	er ḥert	upwards
	Rā	the Sungod
	Rā-Ḥeru-χuti	Rā-Harmachis
	Rā-χā-kau	prenomen of Usertsen III.
	Rā-χeper-ka	prenomen of Usertsen I.

Rā-Tem-χeperȧ	a triad of gods
re	mouth
re-per	temple
re-peru	temples
eref	therefore
ren	name
Ren-ȧqer	a proper name
renpit	year
renput	years
reχ	to know
reχit	intelligent beings
rekḥ	name of a festival
rekḥu	heat
ret / *reθ*	men and women
ruṭ	to grow
erṭāt / *erṭā*	to give

H

hai	O
haker	name of a festival
hamemet	human beings

	hennu	to praise
	hennu	praises
	hru	day
	hereret	what is pleasing

Ḥ

	ḥaiu	naked man
	ḥatu	foul, filth
	ḥu	food
	ḥāāu	to rejoice
	ḥā	limbs, members
	Ḥāpi	the Nile
	ḥeb	festival
	ḥebu	festivals
	ḥebsu	clothing
	ḥept	to embrace
	ḥems	to sit
	ḥemt	wife
	ḥen	Majesty, pri
	ḥenā	and, with
	ḥenti	two periods of 60 years each

ḥent	mistress, lady
ḥer	to, for, on, upon, by
ḥer-ȧb / *ḥeri-ȧb*	within
ḥer entet	because
ḥer-s	thereat
Ḥeru	Horus
Ḥeru nub	golden Horus
Ḥeru-χuti	Harpocrates
ḥrȧ	face
ḥrȧu	faces
ḥeru	terrors
ḥert	celestial regions
ḥeḥ	eternity
ḥesu	to be pleased
ḥesu / *ḥestu*	favours
ḥesui	favoured ones

ḥetep	to rest, to repose, to be at peace, to set down, peace, to set (of the sun)
ḥetep	offering
ḥetepiu	those who give peace
ḥetepu	offerings
ḥetepet	offerings
ḥetrȧ	to pay something due
Ḥet-ḥert	Hathor
Ḥet-Ptaḥ-ka	Memphis
ḥet'	white
ḥett'ut	light
ḥeq	to rule
ḥeq	beer, ale
ḥeqert	hungry
Ḥeqt	name of a goddess

χ

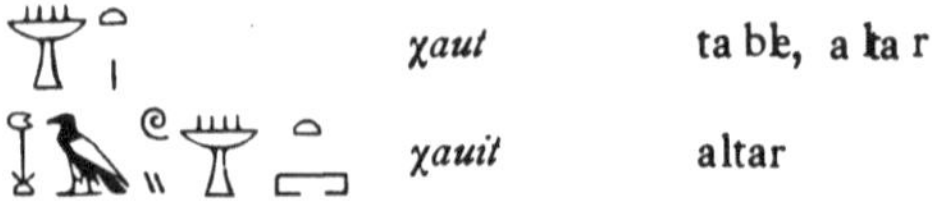

χaut	table, altar
χauit	altar

χabesu	stars
χat	dead body
χat	body, bodies
χā	to be crowned
χā-θȧ	crowned
χā	crown
χu	a spiritual part of a man
χu	to glorify, be glorified, to protect
χu	rays of light
χu	shining, spiritual beings
χut	horizon
χebent	sin, wickedness
χeper	to come into being
χeperu	product, what exists
χeperu	transformations, forms of existence
Χeperȧ	a god of creation

χeft	towards, opposite, in face of
χefta	enemies
χemt	three
χemt	copper, bronze
χnem	to join, to unite
Χnemu	a god of creation
χen	interior of
χen	to alight, to hover over
χennu	to alight, to hover over
χenp	to draw out
χenti	before, dwelling at
Χensu	name of a god
χer	under, to, with
χer	to cast down, be overthrown
Χer-āba	a city near Memphis
χeru	voice, word

χer ḥebu	chief readers
χesef	to meet, to repulse
χeseft	to sail up the river
χet	things
χeṭ	to float down the river

S

	she, it, her, sign of the causative
sa	son, child
sa Rā	son of the Sun
Sa	the god of intelligence
sam ta	burial
sat	earth
satu	to shine, rays
sȧs	six
sām	to eat
sāmiu	devourers
sānχ	to vivify
sār	to bring forward
sāḥā	to make to stand up
sāḥu	the spiritual body

su	he, him
suat	to make to travel
Seb	the god of the earth
sebu	doors
sebȧu	fiends
sebi	to pass on
sep	case, moment, time
sep sen	twice, duplicity
sepu	times
sefisefi	abundance
smauti (?)	uniter of North and South
sem	to guide, leader
smȧ	to accuse
smȧt (?)	half monthly festival
smen	to establish
sen	they, them
sen	two
sent	twice
sen	brother
sensen	bases of statues
senb	good health

sennu	image
sen ṭa	adoration
senṭet	to fear, fear
senṭet	timid man
seru	nobles, chiefs
serq	to make to breathe
seχa	to remember, remembrance
seχu	to glorify
seχeper	to make to come into being
seχem	shrine
seχem	strong
seχeniu	those who make to alight
seχer	to overthrow
seχeru	things which go on, affairs, plans, schemes
seχet	to be overthrown
seḥeru	to drive away
seḥet'	to illuminate
seḥeq	to cut, to sever
seḥetep	to lay to rest, to appease
seś	to pass, motion
seśep	to receive

sek	infinity
sek	to draw on
seku	those who set
Seker	name of a god
seker	name of sacred boat
sektet	a boat of the sun
seqa	to exalt
seḳer	silence
sta	to be towed along
setem	to hear
suten	king, royal
suteni	sovereignty
suten ān	royal scribe
suten net (or *bȧt*)	King of the North and South
Suten-ḥenen	Heracleopolis
suten ḥetep ṭā	give a royal offering!
setekeni	those who make to enter
s'ert	a lying down
s'eri	to lie down

SH

šāt	slaughter
Šu	name of a god
šu	light
šeps	sacred, holy
šem	to go
šen	to curse
šenār	to repulse, be repulsed
šenbet	body
šesi	to follow
šet Ḥeru	"Lake of Horus", a mythological locality
šeta	hidden
šeθit	hidden place

T

	thee, thou
ta	bread, cakes
ta	land, the earth
taui	the lands of the North and South, the world
Ta-merà	a name of Egypt
Ta-ṭesertet	the underworld
tu	thee, mark of the passive

tepȧ	to smell
tepḥet	storehouse
tef	father
Tem / *Temu*	a god of Heliopolis
tem ȧb	strong of heart
temt	sledge
ten	ye, you
ten	how many
trȧui	morning and evening
teχenui	a pair of obelisks

Ṭ

ṭā	to give, giver
ṭāṭāiu	givers
Ṭāṭāu	name of a man
ṭu	mountains
ṭu / *ṭu*	evil, sin
ṭua	a hymn of praise
ṭuau	to praise, adoration

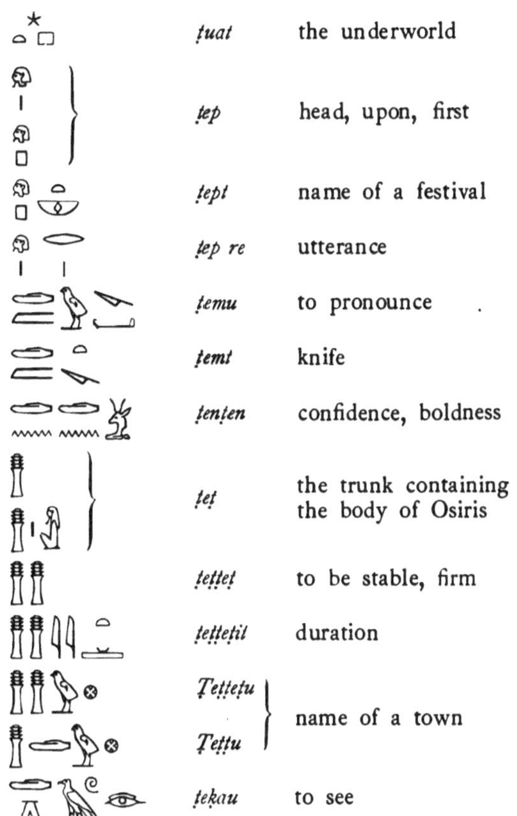

	ṭuat	the underworld
	ṭep	head, upon, first
	ṭept	name of a festival
	ṭep re	utterance
	ṭemu	to pronounce
	ṭemt	knife
	ṭenṭen	confidence, boldness
	ṭeṭ	the trunk containing the body of Osiris
	ṭeṭṭeṭ	to be stable, firm
	ṭeṭṭeṭit	duration
	Ṭeṭṭeṭu / *Ṭeṭṭu*	name of a town
	ṭeḳau	to see

TH

	θ	thou, thee
	θen	ye, you
	θent-nubt	name of a woman
	θest	vertebrae

TCH

ťa	to go forth
ťa	husband
ťai	fiend
ťefau	funeral food or meals
ťet	body
ťetta	eternity, for ever
ťeṭ	to speak, to declare
ťeṭet	words, things said

K

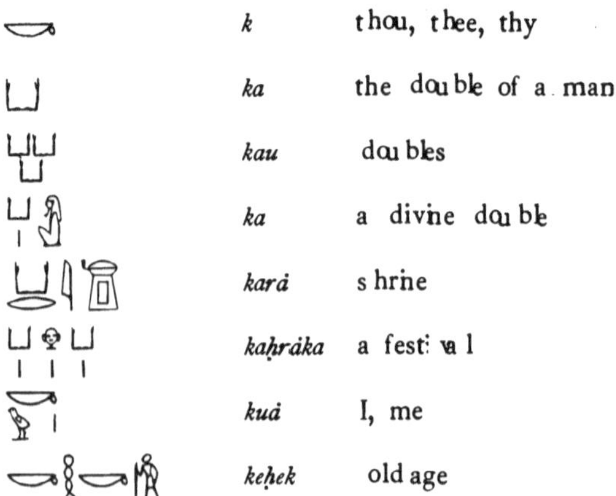

k	thou, thee, thy
ka	the double of a man
kau	doubles
ka	a divine double
karȧ	shrine
kaḥrȧka	a festival
kuȧ	I, me
keḥek	old age

Q

qemāiu	those in the south
qereset	burial
qeṭ	dispositions, natures

Ḳ

ḳer	silence
ḳer	wicked, evil
ḳer	to possess
ḳer-tu	furnished
ḳerḥu	night

www.ingramcontent.com/pod-product-compliance
Lightning Source LLC
Chambersburg PA
CBHW040153270326
41929CB00040B/3364
9781639236237

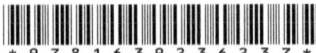